Law of the European Community

Christopher Vincenzi

MA, PhD, Solicitor of the Supreme Court
Senior Research Fellow
Manchester Metropolitan University

PITMAN
PUBLISHING

London · Hong Kong · Johannesburg · Melbourne · Singapore · Washington DC

PITMAN PUBLISHING
128 Long Acre, London WC2E 9AN
Tel: +44 (0)171 447 2000
Fax: +44 (0)171 240 5771

A Division of Pearson Professional Limited

First published in Great Britain in 1996

ISBN 0 273 61471 1

British Library Cataloguing in Publication Data
A CIP catalogue record for this book can be obtained from the British Library

10 9 8 7 6 5 4 3 2 1

Typeset by Land & Unwin (Data Sciences) Ltd
Printed and bound in Great Britain by Clays Ltd, St Ives plc

The Publishers' policy is to use paper manufactured from sustainable forests.

Contents

PART I: THE INSTITUTIONS AND THE PRINCIPLES OF EUROPEAN COMMUNITY LAW

Preface

Over the last few years the number of books on European Community law has proliferated, and it might seem that there could not be any need for yet another. The breadth and depth of Community law has, however, meant that all those books, especially those primarily written for students, have had to be selective, emphasising either the institutional and administrative aspects of Community law, or selecting a limited range of substantive topics, such as social and employment policy, free movement of persons, competition or agriculture. The tendency, until recently, has been to treat the working of the Community and the application of Community law as essentially matters for the Community institutions. Community law tended to seem a somewhat exotic subject for common law students, located somewhere between international law, constitutional law and jurisprudence. Decisions of the European Court of Justice on the need for effective judicial protection in the national courts, and the growing realisation in those courts that much of what appeared to be national legislation had, in fact, originated in Community measures, has brought the importance of Community law home to practising lawyers in the United Kingdom.

This has resulted in Community law becoming a 'core' subject for those hoping to qualify as a solicitor. The widening legislative competence of the Community, so that Community law now reaches into almost every aspect of law, both public and private, has meant that an understanding of the fundamentals of Community law is essential for every working lawyer. In making a selection of topics for this book I have, therefore, had three principal aims. The first is to provide an account of the institutions of the Community and the selected topics in a way which I hope is accessible to those who have not already studied others areas of law in depth. The second is to provide a selection of topics of substantive Community law in the areas of free movement of persons, goods and services. Competition law and policy which, though far from exhaustive, provide illustrations of much wider principles of Community law, how these relate to the national legal systems, and how they can be applied in areas of Community law which have not been examined. The third, and most important, distinctive aim of the book is to illustrate the links between Community institutions and the government, legislature and judiciary of the United Kingdom, including the effect of Community law on the law within the United Kingdom.

I have endeavoured to look at how Community principles of the supremacy of Community law and the direct effect of directives have been applied by our courts. Specific sections, and in some cases, whole chapters, have been devoted to show how the United Kingdom has met, and in some cases failed to meet, its obligations under Community law in the areas of substantive law which have been examined. This will, I hope, help the reader to see how Community law is integrated into our own and how far it has developed so as to give effect to Community rights. Even though only a necessarily limited range of topics has been covered, it is hoped that these will provide the reader with a good grounding in those areas. There is, however, a further reading section at the end of each chapter providing titles of books and articles in which the issues covered can be explored in more depth. I have endeavoured to state the law as at 1 November 1995.

I acknowledge, with thanks, permission by the Incorporated Council of Law Reporting for England and Wales to publish extracts from the *Law Reports Appeal Cases* and the *Weekly Law Reports*; by Blackstone Press Ltd in relation to an extract from *Textbook on Constitutional and Administrative Law* (2nd Edition) (1995) by Brian Thompson; by Butterworths for consent to publish an extract from *An Introduction to Intellectual Property Law* (1995) by Jeremy Phillips and Alison Firth, and extracts from the *All England Law Reports* and the *New Law Journal*; and for leave from Kluwer Academic Publishers to publish an extract from an article by Judge Federico Mancini published in the *Common Market Law Review*. I am also grateful to Advocate-General Francis Jacobs and the *European Advocate* for permission to publish extracts from an article in the Winter 1994 edition of that journal, and to Professor Terence Daintith, Professor Noreen Burrows, Hilary Hiram and John Wiley & Sons for consent to publish extracts from *Implementing EC Law in the United Kingdom: Structures for Indirect Rule (1995)*. Extracts from judgments of the European Court of Justice and the Court of First Instance are taken with leave of the publishers either from the summaries of the judgments published by the Court or from the official reports.

I am also most grateful to my publishers, and especially to Patrick Bond and Julianne Mulholland for all their help and advice. Finally, the greatest debt I owe is to my wife Ruth, without whose support and continuing encouragement this book would never have been completed.

Christopher Vincenzi
June 1996

Table of cases before the European Court of Justice and the Court of First Instance (numerical)

Table of cases before European Court of Justice and the Court of First Instance (alphabetical)

Table of cases before the European Court of Human Rights

Table of cases before national courts

French

Minister for the Interior *v* Cohn-Bendit (Conseil d'Etat) [1980] 1 CMLR *297*
The State *v* Vitaret and Chambron [1995] 1 CMLR 185 (Cour de Cassation) *210*

Irish

Attorney-General *v* X and Others [1992] 2 CMLR 277 *154, 169*

United Kingdom

Blackburn *v* Attorney-General [1971] 1 WLR 1037 *66, 81, 332*
Buyukyilmaz *v* Secretary of State for the Home Department (IAT) 19 January 1995 *118*
Derbyshire County Council *v* Times Newspapers [1991] 4 All ER 795 *66*
De Falco *v* Crawley Borough Council [1980] QB 460, [1980] 1 All ER 913 *120*
Doughty *v* Rolls Royce plc [1992] 1 CMLR 1045, [1992] IRLR 126 *75*
Equal Opportunities Commission *v* Secretary of State for Employment [1994] 1 All ER 910 *67, 83*
Finnegan *v* Clowney Youth Training Programme Ltd [1990] 1 AC 407, [1990] 2 All ER 546 *84*
Gould & Cullen *v* Commissioners for Customs and Excise (VAT Tribunal) [1994] 1 CMLR 347 *84, 330*
Griffen *v* South West Water Services [1995] Current Law Week Vol 3, 20 January *76*
Johnson *v* Chief Adjudication Officer [1994] 1 CMLR 819 *330*
Kwong (IAT) (10661) 11 February 1994 (unreported) *119, 171*
Litster *v* Forth Dry Dock & Engineering Co Ltd [1990] 1 AC 546, [1989] 2 WLR 634 *83, 227*
Lubbersen *v* Secretary of State for the Home Office [1994] 3 CMLR 77 *109*
Re M [1994] 1 AC 377 *66, 337*
Pasha *v* Home Office [1993] 3 CMLR 350 *102, 170*
Proll, Astrid (No 2) [1988] 2 CMLR 387 *158*
Puttick *v* Attorney-General [1979] 3 WLR 542 *171*
R *v* Coventry City Council, ex parte Phoenix Aviation [1995] 3 All ER 37 *214, 333*
R *v* Home Secretary, ex parte Gallagher [1994] 3 CMLR 295 *163, 166, 177, 179*
R *v* Hillingdon London Borough Council, ex parte Islam [1981] 3 WLR 942 *120*
R *v* Kraus (1982) 4 Cr App R (s) 113 *176*
R *v* Ministry of Agriculture, Fisheries and Food, ex parte Hamble (Offshore) Fisheries Ltd [1995] 2 All ER 714 *63*

United States of America

Table of European Commission decisions

Table of European Community treaties

Table of other treaties

Table of European Community regulations

Table of European Community directives

Rules of Procedure of the European Court of Justice

Table of United Kingdom Statutes

Table of United Kingdom Statutory Instruments

List of abbreviations

AC	Appeal Cases
ACP	African Caribbean Pacific states
AJCL	American Journal of Comparative Law
AJIL	American Journal of International Law
All ER	All England Law Reports
Anglo-Am LRev	Anglo-American Law Review
BDMA	British Direct Mailing Association
Bull EC	Bulletin of the European Communities
BYIL	British Yearbook of International Law
CAP	Common Agricultural Policy
CFI	Court of First Instance
CFSP	Common Foreign and Security Policy
CJHA	Co-operation in Justice and Home Affairs
CLJ	Cambridge Law Journal
CLP	Current Legal Problems
COM	Common Organisation of the Market or Commission Document
COREPER	Committee of Permanent Representatives (*Comité des Représentants Permanents*)
CMLR	Common Market Law Reports
CMLRev	Common Market Law Review
DG	Directorate General
EAGGF	European Agricultural Guidance and Guarantee Fund (often referred to as FEOGA - *Fonds européen d'orientation et de garantie agricole*)
EC	European Community
ECB	European Central Bank
ECSC	European Coal and Steel Community
ECU	European Currency Unit
ECJ	European Court of Justice
ECLR	European Competition Law Review
ECR	European Court Reports
EEA	European Economic Area
EEC	European Economic Community
EELR	European Environmental Law Review
EFTA	European Free Trade Association
EHRR	European Human Rights Reports Review
EIPL	European Intellectual Property Law
ELRev	European Law Review
EP	Euopean Parliament
EPC	European Political Co-operation

ESCB	European System of Central Banks
EU	European Union
Euratom	European Atomic Energy Community
FamLaw	Family Law
FSR	Fleet Street Reports
GATT	General Agreement on Tariffs and Trade
HarvLR or Harvard LR	Harvard Law Review
HRLJ	Human Rights Law Journal
IAT	Immigration Appeals Tribunal
IBL	International Business Lawyer
ICLQ	International and Comparative Law Quarterly
Ind LJ	Industrial Law Journal
Int Lawyer	International Lawyer
IRLR	Industrial Relations Law Reports
JBL	Journal of Business Law
JCMS	Journal of Common Market Studies
JESP	Journal of European Social Policy
JLIS	Journal of Law and Information Science
JLS	Journal of Law and Society
JPL	Journal of Planning and Environmental Law
JSWL	Journal of Social Welfare Law (now JSWFL – Journal of Social Welfare and Family Law)
LIEI	Legal Issues of European Integration
LQR	Law Quarterly Review
OJ	Official Journal of the European Communities
MCA	Monetary Compensatory Amount
MGQ	Maximum Guaranteed Quantities
MLR	Modern Law Review
NILQ	Northern Ireland Legal Quarterly
NLJ	New Law Journal
OJLS	Oxford Journal of Legal Studies
PA	Public Administration
PL	Public Law
PPLR	Public Procurement Law Review
SCA	Special Committee on Agriculture
SEA	Single European Act
SJ	Solicitors' Journal
TEU	Treaty on European Union
WLR	Weekly Law Reports
Yale LJ	Yale Law Journal
YEL	Yearbook of European Law

Part I
THE INSTITUTIONS AND THE PRINCIPLES OF EUROPEAN COMMUNITY LAW

1 The origins of the European Community

The European Community came into existence in the aftermath of the Second World War, but the impetus for its creation, to a large extent, came from a desire not to repeat the mistakes made by the victorious powers in the inter-war years. The Treaty of Versailles of 1919 recognised the new nation-states of Central and Eastern Europe that had emerged following the collapse of the Austro-Hungarian and Ottoman empires. It also imposed heavy reparations on Germany, which the new Weimar Republic was unable to pay. The hyper-inflation that followed, and the crash of 1929, wiped out the savings of the large German middle class and pushed unemployment in Germany to more than 40 per cent of the labour force, (Hobsbawm, 1994). The instability that this created led directly to the rise of the Nazi Party and the outbreak of the Second World War. It also gravely affected the economies of the other Western European powers: Britain, France and Italy, the victors who were the architects of Versailles, suffered almost as much as the vanquished from its consequences. Attempts at protecting national economies by tariff barriers were largely unsuccessful and did little more than maintain the economies of Western Europe in a state of stagnation until they were lifted by preparations for another World War. The experience of the inter-war years made clear beyond doubt that it was no longer possible for the states of Western Europe, including states like Britain and France which still had large colonial markets, to operate their national economies without regard to the effect on their immediate neighbours.

Another important lesson of the First World War and its aftermath was learned from the failure of linked defence treaties and the new League of Nations to avert war. The French, above all, grasped the importance of binding Germany's coal and steel industry, the sinews of her war machine, into a new political and economic alliance. At the same time, fear of the apparently expansionist Soviet Union that now occupied the whole of Eastern and Central Europe, including East Germany, impelled the democratic states of Western Europe and North America to come together in 1949 into the North Atlantic Treaty Organisation. West Germany did not join NATO until October 1954 (The Paris Agreements, NATO Facts and Figures. Brussels 1971). The USA, instead of withdrawing from Europe as it had in 1919, was a founder member of the new defence organisation and took a major part in European rehabilitation and reconstruction. Millions of dollars were poured into West Germany in grants and loans under the Marshall Plan, and it started on a rapid economic recovery. Other European States were also assisted under the Plan.

The recognition of the reality and, indeed, the need for mutual interdependence by Western European States, created a receptive atmosphere for resurgent ideas about European political unity. These were expressed with force and vision by Winston Churchill at Zurich in September 1946. He proposed the construction of a 'kind of United States of Europe', based on a partnership between France and Germany. This would require an imaginative leap by the French, who were only just beginning to recover from German occupation and who had been the victims of three wars of aggression by Germany. The idea of European federation, based on a Franco-German partnership, was, however, taken up with enthusiasm by two French politicians, Jean Monnet and Robert Schumann, the former with responsibility for French economic planning and the latter as foreign minister. The first step in the construction of a new European order was the creation of the European Coal and Steel Community in 1950.

THE EUROPEAN COAL AND STEEL COMMUNITY

The Treaty creating the European Coal and Steel Community (ECSC) was signed in April 1951 by Germany, Belgium, France, Italy, the Netherlands and Luxembourg. The preamble to the Treaty made it quite clear that the long-term aims of the participants went a great deal further than the control of the production of coal and steel. The Treaty recognised that 'Europe can be built only through practical achievements which will first of all create solidarity, and through the establishment of common bases for economic solidarity.' The participants were 'resolved to substitute for age-old rivalries the merging of their essential interests; to create, by establishing an economic community, the basis for a deeper and broader community among peoples long divided by bloody conflicts': (Preamble). Although there was some support from the United Kingdom for the objective of creating a common market in coal and steel, there was now little UK enthusiasm for the idea of European Union, and the UK governments (including the new Conservative administration headed by Winston Churchill) was prepared to support only the loosest association with their Continental neighbours. These fell far short of the aspirations of the six founding states and, for two decades, the UK remained on the sidelines of Community developments.

The ECSC Treaty created five institutions :

1   an executive, called the High Authority;
2   a Consultative Committee attached to the High Authority;

3   a Special Council of Ministers;
4   an Assembly; and
5   a Court of Justice.

The most striking thing about the new Community was the fact that it had legal personality and a High Authority that was to be responsible for policy relating to the coal and steel industries in the member states and which had the power to make decisions directly affecting the economic agents in each country without regard to the wishes of the governments of those states. Investment in the coal and steel industries was to be influenced by the High Authority, though not subject to much control. Powers were reserved to regulate prices and production, but only if there were crises of shortage or over-production. There was also a social dimension to the new community: policies were to be framed for training, housing and redeployment. Competition was, at the same time, to be stimulated by rules on price transparency, as well as anti-trust laws on US lines. These decisions could be enforced against the member states in the new Court of Justice.

THE EUROPEAN ECONOMIC COMMUNITY AND THE EUROPEAN ATOMIC ENERGY COMMUNITY

Three of the founding states of the ECSE (Belgium, the Netherlands and Luxembourg) had already formed themselves into the Benelux customs union. From 1 January 1948, customs barriers were removed between Belgium, the Netherlands and Luxembourg and a common customs tariff was agreed between them in relation to the outside world. In 1954 they authorised a free flow of capital, which meant a freedom of investment and unrestricted transfer of currency within the three countries, and in 1956 they accepted free movement of labour. The internal trade of these countries between 1948–1956 increased by 50 per cent. This mini-common market proved to be profitable to all the three countries involved and its success whetted the appetites of neighbouring states and led to pressure to project this experiment on a European scale.

That pressure created the political climate for a much more ambitious project. In March 1957 the Treaty of Rome (the EEC Treaty) was signed to set up a new European Economic Community (EEC) in goods, labour, capital and services among the six member states of the ECSC. The Common Market established by the Treaty was, at the time, the biggest free trade area in the world. At the same time, a treaty establishing the European Atomic Energy Community for the co-operation in the use of atomic energy (Euratom) was signed. The United Kingdom participated in the initial negotiations for both treaties but withdrew because of fears of loss of national sovereignty and damage to favourable trading links with the Commonwealth.

The preamble to the Treaty of Rome sets out the objective of the contracting parties:

> to lay the foundations of an ever close union among the peoples of Europe ... to ensure the economic and social progress of their countries by common action to eliminate the barriers which divide Europe ... [to secure] the constant improvement of the living and working conditions of their peoples ... [and] to strengthen the unity of their economies and to ensure their harmonious development by reducing differences existing between various regions ... [and] by means of a common commercial policy, to [secure] the progressive abolition of restrictions on international trade.

The common market to be created by the Treaty of Rome covered the whole economic field except those areas falling within the scope of the ECSC or Euratom. The Treaty of Rome was intended to create, on a community scale, economic conditions similar to those in the market of a single state. It involved the creation of a customs union, by the abolition of all customs duties and quantitative restrictions in trade between the member states, a common external tariff, and provisions for the free movement of labour, business and capital. These objectives reflected what had already largely been achieved in the Benelux states. The main institutions of the EEC – the Commission, the Council of Ministers, the Assembly and the Court of Justice – were modelled on those of the ECSC, and the Community had a similar legal structure.

The object of Euratom was to develop nuclear energy, distribute it within the Community and sell the surplus to the outside world. For political reasons originally associated with France's nuclear weapons programme and, subsequently, as a result of widespread doubts about the safety and viability of nuclear power, Euratom never developed as originally envisaged. Euratom has however, remained an important focus for research and the promotion of nuclear safety.

THE MERGER OF THE INSTITUTIONS

One of the consequences of the new Treaties was that there were now three Communities, with three sets of Councils and Commissions, roughly corresponding to each other in function. It became clear that this made little sense. Immediately following the signing of the Treaties, agreement was reached so that there would be only one Parliamentary Assembly and one Court of Justice for the ECSC, EEC and Euratom. For some time after the new Treaties came into effect, however, there remained separate Councils of Ministers and separate executive bodies – a High Authority in the case of the ECSC and a Commission each for the EEC and Euratom.

On 8 April 1965, the simplification of the institutional structure of the Communities was completed by the signature of a Merger Treaty, the result of which was that there was thereafter one Council, one European Commission, one European Court of Justice and one Assembly for all three Communities.

ENLARGEMENT

The UK's response to the creation of the EEC in 1957 was to propose a much looser 'free trade area'. This proposal was not welcomed by the Community, but in 1959 it resulted in the creation of a rival organisation, the European Free Trade Area (EFTA), comprising Austria, Denmark, Norway, Portugal, Sweden, Switzerland and the UK. Although trade increased between these states, it lacked the structure and coherence of the EEC, and its members' economies grew only modestly by comparison. By 1961, the British Government had realised that its failure to join the Communities had been a mistake and, in that year, the Macmillan Government applied for membership of the EEC. After prolonged negotiations, the application, which needed the unanimous agreement of the member states, was vetoed by the French President, General de Gaulle. The French were reluctant to accept the UK's membership because it was feared that the UK would attempt to retain preferences for Commonwealth trade and that the UK government was, politically, too close to the USA. They were afraid that the special relationship between the UK and the USA would obstruct French efforts to create a European defence community free from US dominance. A further attempt was made by the Government of Harold Wilson in 1967, but this was again vetoed by the French. In 1970 a third application was made by the Heath Government and this was successful. The Treaty of Accession was signed on 22 January 1972 and the UK, together with Denmark and Ireland, became members of the EEC on 1 January 1973. Norway, which had participated in the accession negotiations, did not join, as a result of a hostile national referendum.

The Treaty of Accession bound the new member states to accept the three Treaties and to accept the existing rules of the Communities. The UK Parliament, after a debate that split both the Conservative and Labour parties, passed the European Communities Act 1972, which was intended to give effect to both present and future Community law in the UK. Divisions within the Labour Party about Community membership led the newly-elected Labour government to promise a referendum. This was held in 1975 and resulted in endorsement of continuing membership by a majority of almost 2:1.

Danish, Irish and UK membership was followed by Greece in 1981 and Spain and Portugal in 1986. Three of the remaining EFTA members, Finland, Austria and Sweden, joined the Communities on 1 January 1995. Norway, having once more successfully negotiated terms for entry, again failed to join after another adverse national referendum.

THE SINGLE EUROPEAN ACT

The Single European Act (SEA) was a response to both development and lack of it in the three Communities and was the first major amendment to the founding Treaties. It was signed in February 1986 and came into force on 1 July 1987. Until 1979 members of the European Assembly were nominated by their national parliaments. The first direct elections to the newly-named European Parliament took place in June 1979 (*see* Chapter 2), and their effect was that the Parliament became the only directly elected European institution. It had, at the same time, only a consultative status in the legislative process and this situation generated pressure on the member states to address the 'democratic deficit' in the Communities' decision making. The SEA added a new 'co-operation procedure' to the Treaties, giving the Parliament a much more important role in the legislative process.

Since the signing of the Treaties in 1957, concerns about war in Western Europe and mass unemployment tended, by the mid-1970s and early 1980s, to have given way to pressure for greater consumer protection and protection at work. There were also growing anxieties about the degradation of the natural environment. The response to these new concerns was, initially, on a national level, resulting in a whole range of different national standards for both goods and industrial production that seriously threatened the growth in a genuinely common market in goods and services. The development of a multiplicity of national standards was accompanied by a slowing down of the economies of all the member states, following the explosion in oil prices in 1973. Implementing the recommendations of the Commission's White Paper, *Completing the Internal Market* (1985), the SEA attempted to tackle this problem on two fronts. It extended the competence of the EEC to enable it to legislate for the whole area of the Community on environmental matters, economic and social cohesion, and in the fields of health, safety, consumer protection, academic, professional and vocational qualifications, public procurement (competition for public contracts), VAT, excise duties and frontier controls, research and technological development. It also aimed to give the completion of the Common Market a new boost by setting a target for creating a new Single Market by removing all the remaining legal, technical and physical obstacles to the free movement of goods, persons, capital and services by the 1 January 1993 (Art 8A EC Treaty (added by the SEA)).

THE TREATY ON EUROPEAN UNION

The next step in the constitutional development of the Communities was the Treaty on European Union (TEU), which was negotiated at Maastricht and signed on 7 February 1992: it came into force on 1 November 1993. The Treaty was intended to extend further the competences of the Communities and to create two new 'pillars' outside the legally binding, formal decision making processes of the three 'old' Communities, which will continue to exist. The two new 'pillars' of the European Union are common foreign and security policy and co-operation in the fields of justice and home affairs. These two pillars of the Union are really only inter-governmental in character, and, like the foreign policy provisions of the SEA, create a broad framework for co-operation rather than a process for the making of binding rules. The whole structure, including the old Communities and the two new pillars are, together, called 'the European Union' (EU).

Of more constitutional and legal significance are the amendments to the Treaty of Rome. The EEC became simply 'the European Community' (EC), marking the legal recognition of the reality that the activities and competences of the former economic Community ranged far beyond its original economic goals. The European Parliament's co-operative powers were enlarged further by the conciliation procedure with, for the first time, a veto on legislation in certain circumstances. The re-unification of Germany in 1990 is reflected by increased representation in the Parliament, so that Germany now has the largest group of MEPs. It did not, however, gain any more votes in the qualified majority voting procedure (*see* Chapter 3). A further institution was also created, the Committee of the Regions, which has a role analagous to the Economic and Social Committee (*see* Chapter 2).

The central economic feature of TEU is the section designed to lead to economic and monetary union by three stages. The UK and Denmark opted out of compulsory participation in the third stage. The UK also refused to participate in the social chapter, which incorporated the principles previously agreed by the heads of government in the Community Charter of Fundamental Social Rights of Workers in Strasbourg in December 1989 on behalf of all the member states, except the UK.

THE EUROPEAN ECONOMIC AREA

The remaining EFTA states continued to work together as a free-trade area after the departure of Ireland, Denmark and the UK in 1973. In 1992 they signed an agreement with the EC which secured access for their goods, services, workers and capital to the markets of the Community. Equally, the same facilities are granted by

EFTA states in their territories to member states of the Community: only Switzerland refused to participate in the European Economic Area (EEA), after a hostile national referendum. In this new trading area, all the rules of the EC apply, although the member states of EFTA are not represented in any of the EC institutions and do not participate in the EC's decision making process. There are, however, four new bodies to co-ordinate the functioning of this new trading area:

1 the EEA Council;
2 Joint Committee;
3 Joint Parliamentary Committee; and
4 Consultative Committee.

The EEA came into effect on the 1 January 1994. On 1 January 1995, three of the remaining EFTA members became full members of the EC, so that the EEA states now comprise the existing 15 EC member states, together with Iceland and Norway.

'TWO-SPEED' EUROPE?

The unwillingness of the UK to accept Community social legislation and some loss of economic sovereignty in the interest of the creation of a single currency for the EU has led to proposals from politicians in France and Germany for a 'two-speed' Europe, in which the more integration-orientated member states at the centre of Europe, for example, France, Germany, the Netherlands and Italy, would press on with political and economic integration. An outer group of member states, consisting, for example, of Denmark, Finland, Ireland, Sweden and the UK would hold back from such political and economic developments and remain, essentially, no more than participants in a free-trade area.

Although such an arrangement holds considerable attractions for the more nationalistic politicians in those member states where Community membership seems less attractive – in a period of prolonged recession and high unemployment – such a development is not very likely. There are two principal reasons for this. First, a Community in which there are different rules between the 'outer' and 'inner' areas would be extremely difficult to operate in practice. It would, in effect, create two Communities. Second, it would tend to accentuate the already serious drift of industry and commerce towards the geographical centre of Western Europe. If Germany, with the most powerful economy and the largest market of all the member states, is in the 'inner circle' businesses will tend to re-establish themselves nearer to the heart of Europe. Businesses from outside the Community seeking to jump over the Community's external tariff wall, such as the many Japanese companies which have already established manufacturing plants in the UK, will look to the centre rather than the periphery for new locations. The UK and the outer states will tend to become marginalised, both economically and politically.

It is probable that the notion of a 'two-speed' Europe has been suggested, not so much because it is seriously contemplated as an alternative to closer political and economic integration and the strengthening of Community institutions, but because the proposal is an attempt to bring home to the more reluctant member states that all member states must move in the same direction together if the whole enterprise is not to fall apart. The speed of that movement, and the depth of the integration contemplated, remains much disputed but it is widely hoped that some progress will be made at the Intergovernmental Conference in 1996.

THE INTERGOVERNMENTAL CONFERENCE 1996

Provisions were made in the TEU for a major conference of the member states in 1996 to discuss the future shape of the Community (Art N(2)). It will provide an opportunity for them to decide whether the EC should make enlargement its principal goal – especially in relation to the states currently benefiting from association agreements with the EC, such as Poland, the Czech Republic, Slovakia and Hungary – or whether its priority should be meeting the goal of monetary union (set by TEU for 1999), the strengthening of the powers of the Parliament and the streamlining of the decision making process in the Council of Ministers. The alternatives are often described in terms of either 'widening' or 'deepening' the EC.

Germany, Italy, the Netherlands and Spain, and to a lesser extent, France, support the idea of greater powers for the Parliament. The same member states are also supporters of monetary union and closer economic integration, although Germany has recently expressed doubts as to whether monetary union can be achieved by 1999. The UK has, so far, been opposed to both policies and to greater qualified majority voting in the Council of Ministers, which would increase the pace of decision making (*see* Chapter 3). Some member states have been hoping for a change in government in the UK, in the expectation that a Labour government might adopt a more integrationist approach and be more sympathetic to structural reform. Whatever the political developments in the UK, there is no doubt that a further increase in Community membership to, say, 18 or 19 states, will inevitably make demands for structural reform more pressing: the increased size of the Commission, the Council of Ministers and the Court of Justice will make them even more cumbersome and bureaucratic than they are at present.

THE EUROPEAN CONVENTION ON HUMAN RIGHTS, THE COUNCIL OF EUROPE AND THE COURT OF HUMAN RIGHTS: A STRUCTURE OUTSIDE THE COMMUNITIES AND THE UNION

It is important to distinguish the international structure created by the European Convention on Human Rights from the quite separate supra-national institutions of the EC. Newspapers talk loosely about taking a case 'to Europe', without identifying whether or not the case is a human rights matter involving the Convention on Human Rights and to be dealt with by the Court of Human Rights in Strasbourg, or a matter of EC law to be referred to the European Court of Justice in Luxembourg. Decisions made by the Human Rights Court are not legally binding on national courts, although they may be taken into account by these courts. Decisions by the European Court of Justice are legally binding on all national courts.

The European Convention on Human Rights was drafted in 1950 under the auspices of the Council of Europe, an international organisation composed of 21 Western European states. It is intended to uphold common political traditions of individual civil liberties and the rule of law. All the member states of the EC are members together with the emerging democracies of Eastern Europe. The Convention is not part of the law of the United Kingdom, whereas, as we shall see (in Chapter 4), Community obligations *are* part of national law and prevail over it in the event of conflict.

Decisions of the Court of Human Rights may result in compensation being paid by the UK government to victims of human rights abuses, but such decisions are not binding on the government, and may simply be ignored. The European Court of Justice (ECJ), like national courts, takes account of the Convention when interpreting Community law. Unlike national courts, however, the ECJ treats the Convention as a source of basic Community law principles (*see* Chapter 16). The European Convention on Human Rights has been formally accepted in TEU as part of the Community's fundamental principles, but it has no application under Community law to matters outside the Community's legal competence, and thus the recognition of the provisions of the Convention as a source of law falls far short of full incorporation into Community law.

Further reading

Charlesworth, A. and Cullen, H. (1994) *European Community Law*, Pitman Publishing. Chapter 1.

Hartley, T. C. (1994) *The Foundations of European Community Law*, (3rd Edn.), Clarendon Press. Introduction.

Hobsbawm, E., (1994) *Age of Extremes: The Short Twentieth Century*, Michael Joseph. Chapters 2, 3 and 8.

Lasok, D. and Bridge, J. W. (1989) *Law and Institutions of the European Communities*, Butterworths. Chapter 1.

Noel, E., (1988) *Working Together; the Institutions of the European Community*.

Nugent, N. *The Government and Politics of the European Union*, (3rd Edn.), Macmillan Press. Chapter 1.

Pinder, J. (1991) *European Community: The Building of a Union*, Oxford University Press. Chapters 1–4.

Weatherill, S. (1994) *Cases and Materials on EC Law* (2nd Edn.) Blackstone Press. Chapters 1 and 12.

Weatherill, S. and Beaumont, P. (1993) *EC Law*, Penguin Books. Chapter 1.

Weigall, D. and Stirk, A. (Eds.), (1992) *The Origins and Development of the European Community*, Leicester University Press.

Wyatt, D. and Dashwood, A. (1993) *European Community Law*, (3rd Edn.) Sweet & Maxwell. Chapters 1 and 23.

2 Community institutions and related bodies

The Treaty of Rome 1957 created four institutions to enable 'the tasks entrusted to the Community … [to be] … carried out.' (Art 4 EC Treaty). Those institutions are:

1   the European Commission;
2   the Council of Ministers;
3   the European Parliament; and
4   the Court of Justice.

A fifth institution, the Court of Auditors, was added by the Treaty on European Union.

Each institution is obliged to act within the limits of the powers conferred on it by the Treaty. It can, in other words, only do those things which it has been expressly authorised by the Treaty to do. The Court has, by and large, been strict in limiting the activities of the other institutions to their specified functions, although it has been more liberal when interpreting the powers of the European Parliament *Les Verts* (Case 294/83); *Parliament* v *Council* (Case C-388/92).

There are two other bodies which have only an advisory function in the decision making process: the Economic and Social Committee and the Committee of the Regions.

The work of each of the above institutions will be considered in turn. The institutions that are to be examined are considered in the context of their role in the European Community (which, until the Treaty on European Union (TEU), was called the *European Economic Community* (Art GA(1) TEU)), unless otherwise stated. In this chapter, and throughout the book, the focus will be on the European Community and not the *European Union*. This is because the European Union created by the TEU, includes not only the European Community, but also the European Coal and Steel Community, Euratom and the new, non-legally binding, co-operative decision making processes of the member states on defence, foreign policy and home affairs that are outside the competence of the institutions altogether. The focus of this book is on the institutions as the constituent parts of those Community acts which have legal effect. Each institution has a defined role in the decision and law making process, or in relation to adjudication or the audit of the Community's accounts. There is one body, however, which is outside the Community's formal structure, but plays an increasingly important political role in the Community. That body is the European Council.

THE EUROPEAN COUNCIL

The European Council did not exist when the Community was set up in 1957. It came into being following a meeting of heads of government in Paris in 1974 and received formal recognition in the Single European Act 1986.

The role of the European Council (not to be confused with the Council of Ministers, *see* below) is described, in Art D EC Treaty (as amended by TEU), as being to 'provide the Union with the necessary impetus for its development ... [and to] ... define the general political guidelines.' It is, essentially, a political forum in which the heads of government, meeting every six months, accompanied by their foreign ministers, thrash out the political agenda for the Community in the ensuing months and years. General programmes worked at in outline at these meetings are taken up and fleshed out by the European Commission and may, in some cases, form the background to a whole raft of legislation or more detailed policy making in such areas as monetary policy and the measures necessary to complete the Single Market.
The subject matter of European Council meetings depends on a number of different factors but the following are relevant in determining what is discussed.

The work of the European Council will depend, to some extent, on the political issues which currently preoccupy a majority of the heads of the government. These might involve, for example, a foreign policy crisis in the Balkans, a run on the national currencies in the financial markets, or a major environmental disaster. Other items will appear regularly on the Council's agenda, such as the general economic situation, the extent of unemployment, the progress being made by the Community towards European monetary union and a review of the development of the single market. The Commission will quite often be involved in bringing forward new policy initiatives, usually with some support from the head of government of the state which holds the presidency of the Council. Major initiatives have started in this way, such as those leading to the adoption of the Social Charter at the Strasbourg Summit in 1989, and the programme that led up to TEU, which was approved at the Dublin Summit in 1990.

As we shall see, it is the task of the European Commission to carry forward the Community towards its goals as set out in the Treaty, but the European Council has proved a valuable means for ensuring that measures proposed by the Commission are actually approved. They are much more likely to be accepted by the Council of Ministers since they will, in principle at least, have been accepted by the heads of the governments of which the ministers are part.

THE EUROPEAN COMMISSION

The role of the Commission is laid down in Art 155 EC Treaty. It has four primary duties :

1   to ensure that the provisions of the Treaty and the measures taken by the institutions under the Treaty are applied;
2   to formulate recommendations or deliver opinions on matters dealt with in the Treaty if the Treaty either expressly requires it or if the Commission considers it necessary;
3   to take part in the decision-making and legislative processes of the Community with the Council of Ministers and the European Parliament;
4   to exercise the powers conferred on it by the Council of Ministers for the implementation of rules laid down by the latter.

Essentially, the Commission's function is, generally, to act as the executive of the Community and to see that Community policy is carried out, to formulate new policy and to draft legislation to give it effect, to police observance of Community rules (whether primary, in the shape of Treaty provisions, or secondary, in the form of Community legislation) and, to a lesser extent, to act as a legislative body in its own right. This fourth function is largely related to the making and enforcement of detailed rules for the implementation of the Common Agricultural Policy.

Composition

Since the entry of Austria, Finland and Sweden, the Commission has consisted of 20 Commissioners (Art 156(1) Act of Accession, Art 30 Decision 95/1/EC OJ L1 1.1.95 pp 1–7). Under Art 157 EC Treaty, the numbers can, however, be increased by a unanimous vote of the Council of Ministers and it is likely that there will be a further increase if, and when, any new states join the Community. Further enlargement is, however, likely to make the Commission unwieldy and less effective, and the size of the Commission and the work of Commissioners will be an important item when the functions of the Community institutions are considered at the Intergovernmental Conference in 1996. There are currently 23 portfolios. A Commissioner may, like Martin Bangemann of Germany, have one major one, industrial policy, or, in the case of Neil Kinnock of the United Kingdom, transport, or two less substantial portfolios, as in the case of Emma Bonnino of Italy, who has fish (originally intended for the anticipated Norwegian Commissioner) and consumer affairs. The Commission offices are in Brussels and employs a staff of some 18 000 people.

The Commissioners, including the President, and the two vice-presidents, each serve a term of five years. It is the President who is primarily responsible for handing out the portfolios to each Commissioner, although their allocation will take into account both the wishes of the governments which appointed them and the views of the European Parliament. The Parliament must now approve the new Commissioners and has commenced a process of 'vetting' hearings before the new Commissioners are approved (Art 158 (2) EC Treaty).

Within the Commission structure, there are 23 departments, called *Directorates-General*. Each Commissioner will be responsible, according to his portfolio, for one or more of these Directorates and he or she, will be assisted by a personal staff, a *cabinet*, headed by a *Chef de Cabinet* who will, usually be the same nationality as the Commissioner. The remainder of the staff may comprise of any of the Community nationalities: the majority of them are involved in the interpretation of documents, although the working language of the Community is French.

The Commission acts as a collegiate body and decisions are made by a simple majority. Once taken, they bind the Commissioners (*see* Chapter 3). Although each Commissioner is nominated by the governments of the member states, two from the larger states and one from the smaller ones, he or she does not represent those states at the Commission: each Commissioner is required to be completely independent in the performance of his duties and should not 'seek nor take instructions from any government or any other body'. (Art 157 (2)) The President, although he or she has few special powers, is a powerful figure and represents the Community where other countries are represented by their head of state. The effectiveness of the Commission depends very much on the ability and the dynamism of the President. Under Jacques Delors, it has been said that 'the office became a key focus of power, not just in the Commission, but in Europe as a whole. He gave the Commission a purpose and taught it to respond to his will.' (Grant, 1994). Under a weak President, it becomes a fragmented bureaucracy.

Although the Commissioners are bound to act as a collegiate body on behalf of the Community rather than for the states from which they originate, it would be unrealistic to expect them to divest themselves of all political contacts with their national governments. Indeed, it would not be helpful for the Community for them to do so. They frequently use such contacts within the governments and civil services of member states to promote Community policies, and to sound out the extent of support which new legislation might secure in the Parliament and the Council of Ministers. Tensions do, however, arise when they appear to be too assiduous in promoting the policies of their own states. Equally, they may also experience difficulties if their approach is seen by their home government as too *Communautaire*. After a period of five years, Commissioners need to be re-appointed by their national state. The UK Commissioner largely responsible for creating and promoting the development of the Single Market in 1986, Lord Cockfield, is widely believed to have failed to achieve re-appointment because he was seen by the then British Prime Minister, Margaret Thatcher, as having 'gone native' in Brussels and lost sight of UK interests.

Despite this, most Commissioners see themselves as having a much freer hand in devising and promoting new policies. Unlike national politicians, they have no political platform to which they must adhere. They simply need to follow the very broad objectives established by the Treaties and, increasingly, by the European Council (*see* p 15). Although they need to promote a good working relationship with the European Parliament, there are few issues which will unite the Parliament sufficiently to secure their removal *en bloc* (*see* the European Parliament, pp 22–27).

The Commission as initiator of changes in policy and legislation

In recent years the Commission has annually adopted a *work programme*. The work programme for 1995 was presented for approval to the Commissioners in February of that year, and it gives a useful indication of current priorities for the Commission:

> The annual work programme, which has to be seen in the context of the five-year term of the Commission and the Parliament, is a comprehensive, target-orientated tool, ensuring the transparency of the Commission's priorities in its task of meeting the policy imperatives of the European Union. It has been designed to enable maximum co-operation between the Union institutions, notably with Parliament, and to make it easier for European citizens to grasp the purpose of Union action. The main thrust of the 1995 programme is clear: building a strong economy to create new jobs; establishing economic and monetary union on sound economic foundations; strengthening economic, social and regional solidarity; improving security within the Union by increasing co-operation in the fields of home affairs and justice; establishing the Union as a strong and reliable partner in the international arena; managing the Union better; and preparing for the intergovernmental conference of 1996.

On the legislative side, the Commission outlined a programme in which increasing emphasis is placed on subsidiarity (*see* Chapter 3) and co-operation with national governments:

> Addressing the imperatives of subsidiarity, transparency and effective Community decision making the Commission makes a clear distinction between four complementary aspects of the action it plans to undertake:
>
> - making proposals for new legislation: the aim here will be 'less action but better action' in compliance with the principle of subsidiarity and proportionality, focused on advanced technology and the information society, with a horizontal approach being used to draft the new proposals (*see* Chapter 14).
> - adopting the proposals which are still outstanding, with priority going to the internal market in electricity and natural gas, international agreements in the nuclear field, the environment and major networks, and the establishment of economic and monetary union;
> - launching wide-ranging discussions before legislation is introduced with a view to increasing openness, efficiency and joint consultation in numerous areas, including industrial competitiveness, security for citizens and the pre-accession strategy for the countries of Central and Eastern Europe;
> - managing and implementing policies in a spirit of rigour and with emphasis on accessibility, focusing on the enforcement of Community law, the fight against fraud and the simplification and streamlining of legislation. (COM (95) 26, Bull. EU 1/2 1995 pp. 128, 129)

Although the Commission is often described as the Community's executive, that description does less than justice to its major policy-making role. Although the Treaty does not expressly stipulate, in general terms, that law and policy changes must be initiated by the Commission, it contains a large number of references to 'The Council … acting on a proposal from the Commission' may draw up a programme, adopt appropriate regulations, and so forth. The work programme described above is part of that process. The references in the Treaty to the role of the Commission have been interpreted as providing a more or less exclusive role for the Commission in policy initiation, so much so that the position has often been summarised by the maxim that 'the Commission proposes and the Council disposes'. As we shall see, in Chapter 3, when considering the decision-making process, this no longer accurately reflects the position, partly because of the increasingly important role of the European Council and partly because of the much enhanced role of the European Parliament. These aspects are considered in more detail in relation to the decision-making process (*see* Chapter 3). Directorates-General, assisted by a large number of specialist advisory committees drawn from the appropriate industrial, commercial and other sectors in the member states, take an active part in drafting new provisions. This process has been particularly visible in the measures proposed to harmonise product standards, consumer safety measures and health and safety at work measures in the single market under Art 100A EC Treaty.

Policy initiation takes place at many levels within the Commission. Senior Commission officials who have moved from civil service posts within their member states are often surprised by the extent to which they are enabled to bring forward their own policy initiatives. Since there is no equivalent of a Cabinet with a political programme, either at Council of Ministers or at Commission level, there is much greater scope for even middle-ranking officials to bring forward proposals to implement the work programme.

As the Work Programme for 1995 indicates, the Commission also has an important external role, representing the Community in negotiations with other groups of states and trading organisations, such as the last GATT round on the development of world trade in 1993. It is also the holder of Community funds and administers four special funds:

1   the European Social Fund;
2   the Cohesion Fund;
3   the European Agricultural Guidance and Guarantee Fund; and
4   the European Regional Development Fund.

The European Social Fund seeks mainly to expand vocational training for workers in order to promote employment and occupational mobility (Arts 123,124 EC Treaty). Its rules were revised in 1983 to gear its activities more to current unemployment.

The Cohesion Fund was established in 1993 to provide financial support for projects in the environment and in relation to trans-European networks in the area of transport infrastructure (Art 130d EC Treaty). It was created as part of a process of transferring resources from some of the Community's wealthier states to those with less-developed economies. The four countries initially to benefit from the Cohesion Fund – those with Gross National Products (GNP) per capita at 90 per cent or less of the Community average – are Spain, Portugal, Greece and Ireland (*see* O'Keefe, D. and Twomey, P. (eds), 1994).

The European Agricultural Guidance and Guarantee Fund was set up to assist in the re-structuring of national agricultural economies (Art 43 EC Treaty).

The European Regional Development Fund is intended to help to redress the main regional imbalances in the Community through participation in the development of regions which are lagging behind economically. It is also used to assist declining industrial regions typically, old coal, steel and textile areas of the Community (Art 130 C).

The Commission as 'Guardian of the Treaties'

This expression is used to describe the Commission's role both as the keeper of the 'soul' of the Community, maintaining its course towards it declared aims of political and economic unity, and the more mundane, but equally important, role of ensuring that the member states honour their obligation to give effect to the Treaty and the implementing legislation (Art 5 EC Treaty). This role is discharged both through political contact and, if need be, by the initiation of proceedings against member states under Art 169 (*see* Chapter 22).

The Commission has another important policing and regulating function in relation to Art 85 and 86. As we shall see in Chapters 18 and 19, the preservation of a genuine common market within the Community of goods, services and capital is dependent not just on the collaboration of governments in removing both visible and invisible barriers, it also depends on the exercise, by the Community, of substantial powers to prevent large private and state undertakings using restrictive agreements, and other abuses of their dominant market position, from excluding Community produced goods and services from domestic markets. These powers of intervention, including the power to demand information, to enter and search premises, and to impose fines and other penalties, are given to the Commission (Art 87 EC Treaty and Regulation 17/62). They are examined in detail in Chapter 20.

THE COUNCIL OF MINISTERS

The Council consists of members of the governments of the member states 'authorised to commit the government of that member state' (Art 146 EC Treaty). The membership will vary according to the matter under discussion and specialised

Council meetings may have special titles. The General Affairs Council, in which the foreign ministers participate, deals with institutional and policy issues. The Council of Economic and Finance Ministers (ECOFIN) meets monthly, and covers the abolition of fiscal barriers and the co-ordination of the economic policies of the member states. Agriculture ministers, transport ministers, and so forth, meet to consider policy and legislation in their areas of responsiblity. The President of the European Commission, although not a member of the Council and not entitled to vote, will in practice, attend these meetings, or another Commissioner may attend on his behalf.

Although member states are normally represented by the senior minister in each department, this may not always be possible and there are occasions when Council meetings comprise ministers of different levels of seniority. The Council is presided over by a President drawn from each of the member states in rotation, with each state holding the presidency for six months. For the first six months of 1995 the Presidency was held by France, followed, in the second half-year, by Spain and then by Italy, Ireland, Netherlands, Luxembourg, UK, Austria, Germany, Finland, Portugal, France, Sweden, Spain, Denmark and Greece (Art 1 Decision 95/2/EC, OJ L1 1.1.95 p 220). The President is responsible for preparing the agenda for Council meetings, so that holding the presidency provides an opportunity for member states to ensure that issues that are of importance to them are placed at the top of the agenda. There is also an element of competition between member states, so that success or failure of a presidency will, to some extent, be judged by the volume of legislation passed during that six month period.

Council of Ministers meetings are normally convened by the country holding the presidency. In some cases, however, the Commission, or another member state, may take the initiative in convening a meeting.

The government of the member state holding the presidency is primarily responsible for arranging and chairing ministerial meetings of the Council and of its sub-committees. It also has to attempt to gain support among the other member states for new initiatives, for maintaining their momentum once they are launched and for representing the Council's views to the other institutions. The presidency's control of the agenda allows it considerable scope to change and affect the pace of policy changes in the Community. Achievement of the policy goals set by the presidency will depend to a large extent on its ability to persuade the other member states to go along with new initiatives, often by a process of trade-offs and mutual concessions in other, sometimes quite unrelated, policy areas. Continuity between successive presidencies is maintained by a close process of co-operation between the outgoing and incoming member states.

The function of the Council is set out in Art 145 EC Treaty in very broad terms:

> To ensure that the objectives set out in the Treaty are attained the Council shall ensure co-ordination of the general economic policies of the member states, and have the power to take decisions.

The power to co-ordinate economic policy has assumed a greater importance since TEU. Under the amended Treaty, the Council now has the duty of conducting assessments of national economies to determine how far they have 'converged'. This is preliminary to the taking of important steps to securing economic and monetary union. If member states run deficits that are too large, the Council has the power to take action against them, and even impose fines (Art 104c, and see Dunnett, D.R., *Legal and Institutional Issues affecting Economic and Monetary Union in Legal Issues of the Maastricht Treaty* p 146.) These provisons are, however, not binding on the UK, which opted out of certain aspects of the convergance policy (para 11 UK Protocol OJ C224 1992 p 123).

Decision making remains the central role of the Council and the different methods of decision making are considered in detail in Chapter 3. Despite the increasingly important role of the Parliament, the Council is the place where final decisions will be made, in the overwhelming majority of cases. Decisions are made after preliminary discussions between officers of the Council Secretariat, the Commission and the Council's own subordinate body, COREPER.

COREPER

COREPER, which is the French acronym for the Committee of Permanent Representatives, plays an important role in providing continuity during the inevitable absences of relevant ministers from the Council. The Committee consists of senior national officials who are permanently located in Brussels. The Committee was originally established by Art 4 of the Merger Treaty in 1965, but it has now been formally integrated into the Community's decision-making structure by Art 151. The Committee 'shall be responsible for preparing the work of the Council and for carrying out the tasks assigned to it by the Council.' The Committee operates on two levels, COREPER I, which consists of the ambassadors from the member states who are accredited to the Community in Brussels, and COREPER II, which is comprised of their deputies. The primary task of COREPER is to prepare items for discussion at Council meetings and will be assisted in this by a whole range of specialist advisory committees. If the text of a policy statement, or legislation can be agreed before the meeting, it will be tabled in Part A of the Council agenda, where it will normally be adopted without further discussion. More difficult, controversial items, on which agreement has not been possible, will appear on Part B of the agenda. In these cases, the issue may, ultimately, have to be decided by a majority vote (*see* Chapter 3).

THE EUROPEAN PARLIAMENT

The Treaty, as it was originally drawn in 1957, included provision for 'an Assembly' whose task was to 'exercise the advisory and supervisory powers' conferred upon it

(Art 137 EC Treaty). The Assembly is now called 'The European Parliament' and the words 'advisory and supervisory' have disappeared. The Parliament which in 1979 became a directly elected body, now simply exercises the powers conferred on it by the Treaty (Art 137 (as amended by TEU)). Prior to that date, its members were drawn from nominees from the national parliaments. It is currently the only directly elected institution in the Community but, the name 'Parliament' is misleading: it shares a number of important features with national parliaments and has considerable influence but it falls far short of being a real, sovereign parliament as would be understood in the United Kingdom. The principal difference is that it lacks both the power to initiate legislation and to impose taxes. Its powers have increased, however, and are likely to continue to do so following the Intergovernmental Conference in 1996.

Composition

The Parliament consists of 626 members (MEPs) elected on different variants of proportional representation, except in the UK, where the 'first past the post' system applies, although a concession to proportional representation has been made in Northern Ireland. The number of MEPs was increased in 1993 from 518 to 567. The smaller member states, such as Luxembourg and Denmark, did not see any increase, while Spain's MEPs increased by four, France, Italy and the UK by six and Germany achieved the largest increase – 18 – to reflect her much enlarged population following re-unification in 1990 (OJ L33/15 1.2.93). Following the accession of Austria, Finland and Sweden on 1 January 1995, the number of MEPs was further increased by 21 for Austria, 16 for Finland and 22 for Sweden (Art 11 Act of Accession; Art 5 Decision 95/1/EC, OJ L1 1995 p 1).

Political groups

MEPs are elected for a term of five years. They stand as members of national political parties, but sit within broad political, rather than national, groupings in the Parliament. Following the elections in 1994, the largest groups were the Socialists with 221 members, the European People's Party with 173 members, the Liberal, Democratic and Reformist Group with 52, the European United Left with 31, Forza Europa with 29, European Democratic Alliance with 26, EP Green Group with 25, European Radical Alliance with 19 and Europe of Nations 19. Thirty one members are not attached to any group. Under the Treaty (as amended by TEU), political parties at European level are now recognised as 'a factor for integration within the Union' and 'contribute to forming a European awareness and to expressing the political will of the citizens of the Union'. (Art 138 a).

Political activity in the European Parliament largely takes place through the groups. Under the current Rules of Procedure (9th edition, 1993) the minimum number of MEPs required to form a political group is 26 if they come from one member state, 21 if they come from two member states, 16 if they come from three member states, and 13 if they come from four or more member states. There are a number of reasons why groups have developed. Primarily they are formed to provide mutual ideological support and identification. In addition, there are organisational benefits, including funds for administrative and research purposes which are better deployed in support of groups than for individuals. There are also advantages in the conduct of Parliamentary business that stem from group status, since the Parliament arranges much of its business around the groups. Although non-attached members are not formally excluded and, indeed, are guaranteed many rights under the Rules of Procedure, they can, in practice, be disadvantaged in the distribution of committee chairmanships or in the preparation of the agendas for plenary sessions.

Parliamentary meetings

The Parliament holds plenary sessions in Strasbourg, committee meetings in Brussels and is serviced by staff located in Luxembourg. A new building has been erected in Brussels for full Parliamentary sessions but the European Council meeting in Brussels in October 1993 confirmed that the Parliamant would remain based in Strasbourg. MEPs and officials will continue to live a highly peripatetic existence, largely because the Parliament is a major employer and the member states cannot agree on a single, permanent site for it.

Except in August, the Parliament sits for one week in each month – usually in Strasbourg – as well as, on occasion, for shorter periods in between, to discuss special items, such as the budget. Between the monthly part-sessions, two weeks are set aside for meetings of the 18 Parliamentary Committees, and the third week for meetings of the political groups. The Committees follow legislative and policy matters in detail and, as they usually meet in camera, are given confidential information, both by Commission officials and by the independent experts and representatives of pressure groups who appear before them.

Powers of the Parliament

There are three main powers exercised by the Parliament:

1   participation in the legislative processes of the Community;
2   acting as the budgetary authority; and
3   the supervision of the Commission.

Besides these formal processes, the Parliament takes an active part in the political life of Europe, commissioning reports, passing resolutions on social and political issues, human rights, defence and foreign policy, and on many other matters. It can, however, do little more than express a view on the issues about which the majority of MEPs are concerned.

The Maastricht Treaty (TEU) has strengthened the position of the Parliament by the addition of Art 138b to the Treaty, which provides that it may:

... request the Commission to submit any appropriate proposal on matters on which it considers that a Community act is required for the purposes of implementing this Treaty.

The Parliament also gained the important power under the Single European Act 1986 (Art 237 EC Treaty, now Art 228 (3)) of approval of new member states. This may possibly prove an important bargaining counter in relation to the acquisition by the Parliament of further powers when the further enlargement of the Community is discussed in 1996. The TEU also gave the Parliament the power to set up *Committees of Inquiry* to 'investigate alleged contraventions or maladministration in the implementation of Community law (Art 138c), and to appoint a *Parliamentary Ombudsman* to investigate complaints about any of the other institutions, except the Court of Justice and the Court of First Instance acting judicially (Art 138e)'. More than 18 months after the TEU came into effect no Ombudsman had been appointed, largely because the political groups could not agree on the qualities which would be required by the holder of the post.

The Budget

The role of Parliament in the law-making process is covered in Chapter 3. In relation to the budget, the Parliament has an important function, which it shares with the Council of Ministers: the Community's budget is drafted by the Commission and placed before the Council of Ministers and Parliament before 1 September each year. This is necessary because the Community's financial year runs from 1 January to 31 December. The budget is divided into two parts, compulsory expenditure (CE) and non-compulsory (NCE). Compulsory Expenditure relates to those items where the expenditure is required by the Treaty, chiefly the Common Agricultural Policy, which usually absorbs between 60–70 per cent of the total budget, whereas NCE covers such items as social and regional policy, research and aid to non-European Union countries in Central and Eastern Europe.

The Treaty gives the Parliament wide powers to amend NCE items, but its powers to modify CE items is more limited under Art 203 EC. The Parliament can, however, by a two-thirds majority, reject the whole of the draft budget and ask for a new draft to be submitted to it (Art 203 (8)). If that happens, the Community institutions have to continue on a month–by–month basis, spending no more than one-twelfth per month of the last year's budget until a new budget is approved (Art 204 EC Treaty).

Supervision of the Commission

There is close and continuous contact between the Commissioners and the Parliament. Although Commissioners are not members of the Parliament, they frequently take part in debates where legislation is under discussion, and they will often attend the specialist committees of the Parliament to deal with detailed points arising from Commission proposals. Under the Treaty, they have the right to attend and to be heard (Art 140 EC Treaty).

Commissioners have a duty to respond, orally or in writing, to questions put to them by MEPs (Art 140 EC Treaty). Since 1974, this has become formalised into a Westminster-type Question Time during every week when the Parliament is in full session (Art 47 Rules of Procedure). Outside plenary sessions, there are regular exchanges between Commission, the various Parliamentary Committees and individual MEPs.

The Parliament has the right to dismiss the Commission *en bloc* under the Treaty (Art 144). It has never done so, and tends, if anything, to regard it as an ally against the Council of Ministers. 'The Commission pays a great deal of attention to the views of the Parliament' (Pinder, 1991). Since the TEU, this position has, if anything, been reinforced by the new requirement for the new Commission, at the start of its term of office, to be approved by the Parliament (Art 158 (2) EC Treaty). Individual Commissioners were subjected to intensive questioning in American-style appointment committees of the Parliament in the run up to the taking of office in early 1995, and one, Padraig Flynn, the Commissioner for Social Affairs, gave up the chair of the Commission's women's rights committee to the President of the Commission, Jacques Santer, as a result (*The Guardian*, 31 October 1995).

As we have seen, the Commission's work programme is put together and implemented in close conjunction with the Parliament, and there is a considerable coincidence of interest to both the Commission and the Parliament in developing Community-wide policies. Where these fail to materialise, it is often as a result of the more nationally-orientated policies of the member states, reflected in the Council of Ministers. One of the most striking examples of this is the failure of the Community to develop a common transport policy, as required by Art 74 EC Treaty. The failure of the Council to make progress on the policy led to the initiation of proceedings in the Court of Justice (under Art 175 EC Treaty) by the Parliament with the support of the Commission. Regrettably, perhaps, the ECJ declared that the provisions of Art 74 where not sufficiently precise to create a legally enforceable obligation (*European Parliament* v *Council* (case 13/83)). The consequences of that case are, perhaps, evident in the fact that, ten years after the decision, there was still no Community transport policy.

Enlargement of the powers of the European Parliament

The most obvious difference between the European Parliament and national parliaments is its inability to initiate legislation. As we will see in Chapter 3, although the Parliament has, in most cases, the right to be consulted, such consultation may mean no more than the right to comment on a draft prepared by the Commission. Under some Treaty provisions there is no right of consultation at all, although Commission and Council practice is, in these cases, nonetheless, to seek the Parliament's views. Even where the Parliament's opinion must be sought, there remains considerable scope for rejection of its views by the Council of

Ministers, provided that the Parliament's opinion is properly considered by the Council. It is widely felt that these limitations are inappropriate for the only democratically elected institution in the Union, and that the Intergovernmental Conference 1996 should consider conferring on the Parliament the right to draft and initiate legislation, and to be involved at every level as a co-decision maker.

There is also felt to be a 'democratic deficit' in relation to the Parliament's inability to dismiss individual Commissioners and to make Ministers account to the Parliament for their decisions in the Council of Ministers. Discussion in the Council still takes place in more or less complete secrecy and there is considerable support, largely among MEPs, for a Minister from the Council to be required to attend the Parliamentary debate and to report back to the Parliament at the conclusion of the ministerial meeting, and for details of the discussions which have taken place in the Council to be published. Although there is some support for these proposals in Germany and the Netherlands, the UK government has remained firmly opposed to them, on the grounds that they would further undermine the powers of the Westminster Parliament to which national ministers are, in the last resort, solely accountable.

THE EUROPEAN COURT OF JUSTICE

The task of the Court of Justice (ECJ) is stated simply in all three Treaties. It '… shall ensure that in the interpretation and application of [the] Treaty the law is observed.' (Art 164 EC Treaty). The sources of the law to which the ECJ has to give effect are diverse, (and considered in detail in Chapter 4). Many of the Treaty provisions, and some of the implementing legislation, are expressed in the broadest terms, and the ECJ plays a crucial role in developing the law and the constitution of the Community. It recently emphasised the importance, and the breadth of that role in its submission to the Intergovernmental Conference of 1996:

> The Court … carries out tasks which, in the legal systems of the member states are those of the constitutional courts, the courts of general jurisdiction or the administrative courts or tribunals, as the case may be.
>
> In its constitutional role, the Court rules on the respective powers of the Communities and of the member states, and on those of the Communities in relation to other forms of co-operation within the framework of the Union and, generally, determines the scope of the provisions of the Treaties whose observance it is its duty to ensure. It ensures that the delimitation of powers between the institutions is safeguarded, thereby helping to maintain the institutional balance. It examines whether fundamental rights and general principles of law have been observed by the institutions, and by the member states when their actions fall within the scope of Community law. It rules on the relationship between Community law and national law and on the reciprocal obligations between the member states and the Community

institutions. Finally, it may be called upon to judge whether international commitments envisaged by the Communities are compatible with the Treaties. (*Report of the Court of Justice on Certain Aspects of the Application of the Treaty on European Union for the Purposes of the 1996 Intergovernmental Conference* (May 1995))

The ECJ has become accustomed to interpreting Community law 'teleologically', that is by reference to the broad policy objectives of the Treaty, rather than, as would an English court, by the meaning of the words before it and their immediate context. It has, for example, been accepted that the European Parliament has the right to bring an action for annulment against the Council or Commission, although only member states, the Council and affected individuals were specifically given such a right in Art 173 (1) EC Treaty. The ECJ held that not to imply such a right for the Parliament would deprive it of the legal means with which to protect its privileges against incursions by the other institutions (*Parliament* v *Council* (Case C-70/88)). Article 173 EC Treaty, indent 3 (as amended by TEU), now gives the Parliament the right to take such an action to protect its prerogatives. The ECJ has also extended the right of free movement of workers to those looking for work, even though the relevant Art 48 appears to confer the right only on those to whom an offer of work has actually been made. The ECJ felt that the object of the Treaty to secure the free movement of labour would not be achieved if only those already employed in another member state were enabled to move *Procureur du Roi* v *Royer* (Case 48/75). In these, and in many other matters, the ECJ has used its interpretative powers to put flesh on the bones of Treaty provisions, and to do so in such a way as to facilitate the effective development of the Community.

Underlying these decisions is what can only be described as the *policy* of the Court. All national courts have unstated policy objectives, such as the maintenance of the rule of law or the discouragement of what is seen as anti-social behaviour. The law will be interpreted as far as possible to achieve those ends. The Court's objectives are more clearly discernible. Broadly, the Court's policies could be said to comprise of strengthening the Union's structure, increasing the scope and effectiveness of Community law and enhancing the powers of the Community institutions. The series of cases in which the Parliament's ability to bring proceedings to protect its prerogatives have effectively been extended beyond those conferred by the EC Treaty, and the decisions under which its consultative role has been enhanced all reflect the concern of the Court to ensure that the Community's only democratically elected institution is given proper weight in the decision making process.

The Court's policy of securing greater effectiveness for Community law is achieved partly by interpreting the law in such a way that it achieves the broader objectives of the Treaty, even if this has to be done, in some cases, by ignoring the express words of the Community legislation. It can also be seen in the doctrine of the direct effect of directives (*see* Chapter 5) under which the measures originally only intended to bind the governments of member states have become the means by which individuals secure their rights in national courts. In pursuit of the same policy objective, remedies in national courts, which were originally seen as being of purely national concern and beyond the competence of the Court are now judged by the Court in terms of their effectiveness to secure the implementation of Community law. If they are not effective, they must be set aside and an effective remedy provided: *R* v *Secretary of State for Transport, ex parte Factortame* (Case C–213/89).

Members of the Court of Justice

The ECJ consists of 15 judges who are assisted by nine Advocates-General. The membership was increased following the accession of Austria, Finland and Sweden in January 1995 (Arts 17, 20, Act of Accession; Arts 10, 31, Decision 95/1/EC OJ L1 1.1.95 pp 1–4). The judges either sit as one Court in plenary sessions, or in chambers of three or five in each (Art 165). Member states that are parties to proceedings can insist that the Court sits in plenary. The judges and Advocates-General are appointed by the 'common accord' of the governments of the member states for a term of six years each. They are to be chosen from 'persons whose independence is beyond doubt and who possess the qualifications required for appointment to the highest judicial offices in their respective countries' (Art 167 EC). The requirements for these appointments are not intended to be confined to those who have made a career in the courts and are destined for, or already sit, on the bench in their member state. Appointments may also be made under Art 167 from the ranks of distinguished academic lawyers or 'jurisconsults of recognised competence'. Every three years there is a partial replacement of judges and Advocates-General; retiring judges and Advocates-General can be re-appointed. After these replacements, the newly constituted Court elects by secret ballot the President of the Court, who serves for three years.

Although the Treaty does not contain any provisions regarding the nomination and nationality of judges and Advocates-General, it has been the practice that each member state nominates one judge who is a national, and each of the four larger states (France, Germany, Italy and the UK) have done the same in relation to four of the Advocates-General. However, on the accession of Austria, Finland and Sweden, a Declaration was made by the member states in relation to the allocation of the posts of Advocates-General. Under the Declaration, France, Germany, Italy, Spain and the UK will be allocated a 'permanent' Advocate-General each. Spanish, Irish and Italian Advocate-Generals were appointed from 1 January 1995, and replacements will be filled for the non-permanent posts by the member states taking part in the rotation, in alphabetical order (Joint Declaration 1 January 1995, OJ L1 1.1.95 p 21). A new judge is required to take an oath to perform his duties impartially and conscientiously and to preserve the secrecy of the deliberations of the Court. He also signs a solemn declaration to behave with integrity and discretion in relation to the acceptance of benefits after he has left office Arts 2 and 4 Protocol on the Statute of the Court of Justice. Judges may not hold any political and administrative office and may not follow any other occupation, paid or unpaid, during their period of office (Art 4 Protocol).

Membership of the Court has been increased as a matter of course as the

Community has enlarged. The Court has expressed anxiety about the indefinite application of this policy in its submission to the Intergovernmental Conference of 1996. In relation to membership, two factors must be balanced:

> On the one hand, any significant increase in the number of judges might mean that the plenary session of the Court would cross the invisible boundary between a collegiate body and a deliberative assembly. Moreover, as the great majority of cases would be heard by Chambers, this increase would pose a threat to the consistency of the case law.
>
> On the other hand, the presence of members from all the national legal systems on the Court is undoubtedly conducive to harmonious development of Community case law, taking into account concepts regarded as fundamental in the various member states and thus enhancing the acceptability of the solutions arrived at. It may also be considered that the presence of a judge from each of the member states enhances the legitimacy of the Court.

Membership of the Court of First Instance

To cope with the great increase in the work of the European Court of Justice (ECJ), the SEA provided for the creation of a new Court of First Instance (CFI) to be attached to the ECJ (Art 168a EC Treaty). The work of the CFI is examined below. Although it is attached to the ECJ, it is staffed by judges who are separately appointed according to slightly different criteria. This partly relates to the type of work allocated to the CFI, and partly to the role of the CFI in hearing evidence and determining questions of fact.

Article 168a (3) of the Treaty provides that the 15 Members of the CFI shall be chosen from persons whose independence is beyond doubt and who 'possess the ability required for appointment to judicial office' (Art 21, Act of Accession; Art 12, Decision 95/1/EC). Like the members of the ECJ, members of the CFI are appointed by common accord of the governments of the member states for terms of six years, with partial renewal of membership every three years. The first members of the CFI were appointed on 1 September 1989 by a Decision of the governments (Decision 89/452/EEC, Euratom, ECSC, OJ 1989 L 220 p 76). To ensure partial renewal every three years, half of the new members had to be appointed for only three years. The allocation of the first terms was chosen by lot.

The Advocates-General

The main task of the Advocates-General is to deliver an oral and reasoned opinion in each case brought before the Court. The title Advocate is something of a misnomer, because the Advocate-General represents no-one and does not present a case on anyone's behalf. He is an independent adviser to the Court. Article 166 (second indent) provides:

> It shall be the duty of the Advocate-General, acting with complete impartiality and independence, to make, in open court, reasoned submissions on cases brought before the Court of Justice, in order to assist the Court in the performance of the task assigned to it in Art 164.

Although not a judge, the Advocate-General enjoys equal status with the judges. For that reason, the Report by the Court of Justice to the Intergovernmental Conference (IGC) has suggested that the Advocates-General should be able to take part in the election of the President of the Court (Report to IGC 1996).

At the start of each case, an Advocate-General is allocated to that case by the President of the Court and his/her function is to submit an Opinion before the Court. The Opinion normally deals with every aspect of the case, and will be generally be much longer and more wide-ranging than the judgment of the Court. It will usually attempt to set the case in a broader context than the issues which divide the parties. The Opinion will conclude with a recommendation for a solution which the Court may adopt.

The recommendation in the Opinion is not binding on the Court, or on the parties and the Court is free to follow it or not, as it chooses. However, in spite of their non-binding nature, the Opinions of Advocates-General carry considerable weight on account of the very high standard of the legal analysis which they contain and are frequently cited in the Court as well as in legal writing as persuasive sources of authority. On occasion, however, Advocates-General may take a more adventurous line than that which the Court is ready to follow. This has been particularly marked in relation to development of the law relating to the direct effect of directives (*see* Chapter 5).

The Jurisdiction of the European Court of Justice and the Court of First Instance

Besides the general function of ensuring that Community law is observed, ECJ and CFI (the Court) have a number of other tasks. Since the Court, like the other Community institutions, can only act within the limits of its powers, it has jurisdiction only where jurisdiction has been expressly conferred upon it (Arts 3 ECSC, 4 EC, 3 Euratom). This means that the Court has, unlike English courts, no 'residual' or 'inherent' powers and, consequently, cannot hear cases not expressly falling within its jurisdiction. It has, for example, been held that judicial protection cannot be afforded to private individuals who might otherwise be deprived of all legal redress at both national and Community level (Case 12/63 *Schlieker* v *HA* [1963] ECR 85), since there is no express provision authorising it to do so. More recently, however, the Court has shown more flexibility in ruling on cases which it might, hitherto, have refused to adjudicate *Imm Zwartveld* (Case 2/88); *Dzodzi* v *Belgium* (Case C-297/88).

The main heads of jurisdiction for the ECJ are as follows:

1 To establish whether or not a member state has failed to fulfil an obligation under the Treaty. Actions for this purpose can be brought by the Commission under Art 169, or a member state under Art 170. These actions are considered in detail in Chapter 22.
2 To exercise unlimited jurisdiction with regard to penalties in actions brought by the Commission under Arts 171(1) and 172.

3 To review the legality of an act or of a failure to act, of the Council, the Commission, the Parliament, at the request of member states, the Council and the Commission. Applications by the Parliament and the European Central Bank are limited to the protection of their prerogatives (Arts 173, 174 and 174 EC (as amended by TEU) and Art 9 of the Protocol on the Statute of the European System of Central Banks and of the European Central Bank) (*see* Chapter 23.)

4 To give preliminary rulings under Art 177 EC at the request of a national court or tribunal (*see* Chapter 24).

5 To grant compensation for damage caused by the institutions in actions brought by member states, and natural and legal persons under Arts 178 and 215 EC Treaty (*see* Chapter 24).

6 To act as a Court of Appeal from the CFI under Art 168a (1) EC (*see* below).

THE COURT OF FIRST INSTANCE

As we have seen, the CFI was established to take some of the pressure off the ECJ. The Decision establishing the CFI (Council Decision 88/591 ECSC, EC OJ 1988 L 319 p 1), laid down four categories of cases for the new Court:

1 Staff cases;

2 Actions by undertakings (but not by Community institutions or member states) against the Commission concerning individual acts relating to the ECSC Treaty provisions on levies, production controls, price regulation or competition;

3 Actions by natural or legal persons against a Community institution relating to the implementation of the EC competition rules applicable to undertakings;

4 Damages claims by natural or legal persons where the damage is alleged to arise from an act or failure to act which is the subject of an action under (1), (2), or (3) above or from breach of contract.
(Art 4 Decision 88/591).

Following amendments made to the EC Treaty by the TEU, one further important category has been added:

5 Claims brought by natural and legal persons under Arts 173 and 175 (including anti-dumping cases) for judicial review. The Court has no competence to hear applications by institutions or member states. There had been resistance by some member states to the transfer from the ECJ to CFI of the anti-dumping cases, but this change over was finally effected in March 1994 (Art 168a and Council Decision 93/350 OJ 1993 L 144 p 21).

In addition, Art 4 of the Decision provides for the CFI to have unlimited jurisdiction in relation to penalties, and gives it jurisdiction to suspend measures and to grant interim relief during the course of proceedings.

Staff cases have long been seen as more suitable for a first instance court, rather than the ECJ which is, essentially, a constitutional-type court. Employment lawyers have been appointed to sit on these cases, which largely concern the interpretation of individual employment contracts of staff employed by the institutions, Staff Regulations and related matters of fact (Art 179 EC).

Coal and steel cases relate to actions brought by coal and steel undertakings against the Commission. Most of these relate to restrictions on production imposed by the Commission to prevent over-production of steel during the recession in the early 1980s. The number of such cases has considerably diminished.

Most of the competition cases arise from challenges to decisions by the Commission relating to Arts 85 and 86 and, especially, the level of fines imposed for uncompetitive practices (*see* Chapters 18, 19 and 20).

Finally, challenges to Community institutions for failure to act or for unlawful action, can now be brought by individuals and undertakings in the CFI. These actions, which are similar to applications for judicial review in the English courts, can still only be brought by member states and by other institutions in the ECJ.

The organisation of the European Court of Justice and the Court of First Instance

The Court of Justice is permanently in session in Luxembourg and vacations are fixed according to the workload. During vacations, the functions of the President of the Court are exercised by the President or by the President of one of the Chambers, or by a judge selected by the President. The President's principal duties are to direct judicial business and the administration of the Court, and this includes the assignment of new cases to one of the Chambers and to designate the *Judge-Rapporteur* from that Chamber (*see* below) (Art 9 Protocol).

The volume of work and current balance of cases is shown by the statistics for 1994: there were 206 references under Art 177 EC Treaty from national courts, 13 appeals from the Court of First Instance and 128 'other' cases. There were 89 infraction proceedings brought against member states and, overall, the Court of Justice gave judgment in 215 cases. In the 30 infraction proceedings in which judgments were given, the European Court found against the member state in question in 29 cases. The Court of First Instance dealt with 450 cases in 1994, delivering 150 judgments. In terms of content, agriculture was at the top of the list, followed by competition, free movement of workers and social security, trade cases involving the free movement of goods, anti-dumping and customs duties. Fishing and the environment figured least frequently among cases coming to the Court.

The Procedure

The rules concerning the procedure of the Court are laid down in the Protocol on the Statute of the Court annexed to the Treaty and the Rules of Procedure (Rules of Procedure of the Court 1979–1991). It must be understood that the process is essentially inquisitorial. Unlike an English adversarial process, the procedure of the Court, after the initiation of the case by one or more of the parties, is Court-led: witnesses are heard at the instigation of the Court. Their evidence is part of the investigation by the Judge Rapporteur and not, as in an English case, part of the oral hearing. The procedure in a direct action (as opposed to a reference under Art 177, which is dealt with in Chapter 24), generally has four stages :

1   Written proceedings

Proceedings are begun by the filing of a *requête*, (an originating application), with the Registrar of the Court. There is no required form for this document, but it must set out the subject matter of the dispute and the grounds upon which the application is based. It is not the equivalent of either a writ or a statement of claim in the English High Court but it performs the function of both and more. It contains also a full statement of the law upon which the claim will be based.

2   Investigation or preparatory inquiry

Immediately after the lodging of the original application, the President will have assigned the case to one of the Chambers of the Court. He also nominates one of the judges of that Chamber to act as Rapporteur. At the same time, the senior Advocate-General will appoint the Advocate-General for the case. All the papers that have been lodged with the Court are distributed to the judges in the Chamber. Whatever the language of the case, documents will be translated into French, which is the working language of the Court.

It is at this stage that the Court takes over the direction of the proceedings. The first task of the Judge-Rapporteur is to study all the pleadings and evidence lodged and to prepare a preliminary report. Guided by this report and any views expressed by the Advocate-General, the Court will decide at an adminstrative meeting what issues of fact need to be proved, what additional evidence is needed (if any) and which witnesses are to be summoned to testify.

The investigation will then get under way. The investigation may include a range of activities conducted under the supervision of the Judge-Rapporteur, among which may be: the personal appearance by the parties, the production of documents or the supply of additional information by the parties or the commissioning of a report by an expert witness. Such an expert witness is a witness of the Court, not of the parties. The parties can ask for other witnesses to be called, but the decision on whether or not to call them is a matter for the Court. Witnesses will be examined before all the judges in the Chamber, but questioning is conducted by the presiding judge, and not by the advocates for the parties. Most investigations do not, however, go this far and the Court will normally content itself with obtaining additional written evidence from the parties.

3   Oral proceedings

Once the preparatory inquiry has been concluded, the President of the Court fixes the date for the public hearing. A few days before the hearing the Judge-Rapporteur issues his report for the hearing. This sets out the facts of the case and summarises the arguments of the parties. Copies of the report are given to all the judges in the Chamber, the parties, and are made available to members of the public before the hearing.

The oral proceedings are brief compared to those in an English court in a contested action. They consist of the addresses by counsel for the parties and the Opinion of the Advocate-General. There is usually a gap of some months between the conclusion of the addresses and the delivery of the Opinion to the reconvened Court. Addresses by counsel tend to be quite brief. They are expected to have lodged a copy of their submission before the hearing, and will normally use their address to emphasise their strongest arguments, and to attack the weakest points in those of their opponents.

The judges will quite frequently challenge points made, but the cut and thrust of forensic debate is somewhat blunted by the need for instant translation by interpreters as the argument proceeds. The purpose of the Opinion has already been discussed. It is delivered by the Advocate-General in open court. The Advocate-General sits on the same level as the judges, but apart from them. He takes no part in the discussions between the judges which precede the judgment, but his Opinion will have a significant influence on their decision.

4   Judgment

Judgments are adopted following secret deliberations in which only those judges who were present at the oral hearing may participate. The number of deliberating judges is always uneven, since the decision of the court is determined by a majority vote. Every participating judge must give his view and the reasons for it. The votes of the judges are taken in ascending order of seniority: this is to ensure that the younger judges do not merely follow their seniors. A single judgment is always given and no separate or dissenting opinions are ever made public (Arts 18,29 ECSC Statute; 15,32 EC Statute).

COURT OF AUDITORS

The Court was established by an amendment to the Treaties in 1975 (second Budgetary Treaty 1975). It is not, strictly speaking a court – more an audit commission – and is responsible for the external audit of the general budget of the European Communities and of the operating budget of the ECSC. The internal audit is the responsiblity of the Financial Controller of each institution.

The Court came into being, partly as a result of the desire of some of the newer member states to establish more effective audit arrangements and, partly as a result of the desire of the Parliament to have greater power in the financial affairs of the Communities. An independent audit body is seen by Parliament as an important part in establishing greater financial control. It had, initially, the status of a separate body but, since TEU came into effect in 1993, it has been classed by Art 4 EC Treaty as one of the institutions of the Community.

The Court consists of 15 full-time members who are chosen by the Council of Ministers (after consulting the European Parliament) from among persons who have had relevant auditing experience and whose independence is beyond doubt (Art 188 b (2), Art 22 Act of Accession, Art 13 Decision 95/1/EC). The 15 members include one from Austria, Finland and Sweden who were appointed in February 1995 (OJ L50 7.3.95).

THE ECONOMIC AND SOCIAL COMMITTEE ('ECOSOC')

This Committee was established by Art 193 EC Treaty and Art 165 Euratom to assist the Council and the Commission in an advisory capacity. The Committee consists of 'representatives of the various categories of economic and social activity, in particular, representatives of producers, farmers, carriers, workers, dealers, craftsmen, professional occupations and representatives of the general public'.

The 222 members of the Committee are appointed by the Council of Ministers, acting unanimously, for a period of four years (Art 194 EC, Art 23 Act of Accession, Art 14 Decision 95/1/EC) and they may be re-appointed. Membership is allocated according to the size of member states, as follows:

France, Germany, Italy and UK	24
Spain	21
Austria, Belgium, Greece, Netherlands, Portugal and Sweden	12
Denmark, Finland and Ireland	9
Luxembourg	6

Members of the Committee must be completely independent 'in the general interests of the Community'. The members serve on three interest groups of Employers, Workers and General Interest, although they are prohibited from being bound by any mandate from that group in their own state or any other (Art 194 as amended by TEU). The appointment of members is from a list of candidates provided by each member state, and is to take account of the need to ensure adequate representation of the various categories of economic and social activity. The ECJ has held that adequate representation must be ensured at Community level but that, because of the limited number of seats available, it is not possible to guarantee that all the elements from every category of economic and social activity are represented by nationals from each member state (*CIDA* v *Council* (Case 297/86)).

Function of the Committee

The Economic and Social Committee (ECOSOC) is not one of the institutions of the Community: a requirement in Art 24 of the Merger Treaty that the Council consult 'other institutions' when adopting or amending staff regulations, was held not to apply to ECOSOC (*Adam* v *Commission* (Case 828/79)). It must be consulted by the Council or the Commission where the Treaty provides for it and in other cases, consultation is at the discretion of those institutions. When the Committee is consulted, it responds by the submission of an opinion to the Commission and Council. These institutions can, if they wish, impose a deadline for the submission of the opinion, but this must not be less than one month (Art 198). Failure to deliver an opinion cannot prevent further action by the institutions. The Committee also has the right to submit opinions on its own initiative, when it considers such action appropriate (Art 198 EC). Opinions of ECOSOC are prepared by a Section designated by the Chairman and then discussed and adopted at plenary sessions of the full Committee which are held during the last seven days of the month (Title II ECOSOC's Rules of Procedure). Although the Committee's opinions are not legally binding, the expertise of the Committee's membership does mean that they carry considerable weight with the institutions. Where the Treaty requires consultation of ECOSOC, failure to do so could lead to the annulment of a measure by the Court, on the basis of failure to meet an essential procedural requirement.

THE COMMITTEE OF THE REGIONS

The Committee of the Regions was set up as an advisory body by TEU (Art 198a) and like ECOSOC, it is not a Community institution. It was intended to represent a move towards more region-orientated decision making, and to bring the Community and the European Union closer to the peoples of Europe, as required by Art 2 TEU. The Committee consists of 222 representatives of regional and representative bodies in the member states, with the same allocation of members to each state as ECOSOC. Its basic role is comparable to ECOSOC: the members of the Committee, whose principal role is to deliver opinions on legislation when consulted by the Council of Ministers and to issue own-initiative opinions in appropriate cases, are completely independent in the performance of their duties in the general interests of the Community.

The Committee must be consulted in relation to proposed legislation on culture (Art 128 EC), public health (Art 129 EC) and the revised provisions on economic and social cohesion (Art 130a–e EC). Somewhat anomolously, there is no provision for consultation with the Committee in relation to environmental policy, although it is likely that the Committee would wish to use its discretion to volunteer an opinion in relation to such legislation.

THE EUROPEAN CENTRAL BANK AND THE EUROPEAN INVESTMENT BANK

The European Central Bank (ECB) was established by Art 4a EC Treaty. It is an innovation of TEU and is linked to the establishment of a European System of Central Banks. The ECB was set up as part of the progression towards European monetary union. It is not a Community institution within the definition of Art 4 EC. It can, however, enact legislation, impose fines, submit opinions and be consulted within its field of operation (Title VI EC, Arts 105,105a,106 and 108a).

The European Investment Bank (EIB) was established by Art 4b EC (inserted by Art G (7) TEU) and is the Union's long term lending bank and the regional development bank for Europe. It makes grants and loans to projects affecting more than one member state, where they cannot be funded sufficiently from within those member states themselves.

Further reading

Arnull, A., (1990) 'Does the Court of Justice have an Inherent Jurisdiction?' (1990) 27 CML Rev 683.

Brown, N. and Jacobs F., (1994) *The Court of Justice of the European Communities* (4th edn.) Sweet & Maxwell.

Duff, A., Pinder, J. and Pryce, R., (1994) *Maastricht and Beyond*.

Dunnett, D. R. R., *Legal and Institutional Issues Affecting Economic and Monetary Union*, in O'Keefe, D. and Twomey, P. (eds) (1994), *Legal Issues of the Maastricht Treaty*, Chancery Publications.

Grant, C., 'The House that Jaques Built', *The Independent*, 29 June 1994.

Harlow, C., 'A Community of Interests? Making the Most of European Law' (1992) 55 MLR 331.

Hartley, T. C., (1994) *The Foundations of European Community Law* (3rd edn.) Clarendon Press.

Jacobs, F., 'The European Court of Justice: Some Thoughts on its Past and Future', *The European Advocate*, Winter 1994–95, p 2.

Lasok, D., and Bridge, J. W., (1989) *Law and Institutions of the European Communities*; Butterworths.

Millett, T., (1990) *The Court of First Instance of the European Communities*; Butterworths.

Noel, E., (1988) *Working Together: The Institutions of the European Community*, Office for Official Publications to the European Communities.

Nugent, N., (1994) *The Government and Politics of the European Union*, Part 2, Macmillan Press.

Pinder, J., (1991) *The European Community*, OUP.

Toth, A. G., (1990) *The Oxford Encyclopaedia of European Law* (vol 1), Clarendon Press.

Weatherill, S., (1994) *Cases and Materials on EC Law*, (2nd edn.) Blackstone Press.

Weatherill, S., and Beaumont, P., (1995) *EC Law*, Chapters 2, 3 and 4, Penguin Books.

3 The decision-making process

Decision making is central to the effective functioning of the Community. Decisions made by Community institutions may relate to the implementation of a policy, such as enlargement of the Community, or the adoption of a trade agreement with other states, or they may be part of a number of different legislative programmes.The type of process will be determined by the subject-matter of the decision, as interpreted by the European Commission, which will then choose the appropriate legislative base in the Treaties. That choice will decide what institutions and other bodies will be involved in the process, the voting system used in the Council of Ministers and the extent to which the Parliament will be able to influence the content of the measure and, in some cases, whether it is approved at all. Although, as we have seen in Chapter 2, while the European Council plays a growing role in setting policy goals, the task of translating those goals into specific policy decisions and into legislation still belongs almost exclusively to the Commission. The European Parliament does now have the power under Art 138b of the Treaty to suggest new areas for legislation, but the decision on whether or not to bring forward such legislation and in what form is for the Commission alone. Apart from a few exceptional situations where the Council may act on its own initiative (i.e., Arts 109 (b), 154 EC), in most cases the EC Treaty provides that it shall act on a proposal from the Commission.

DIALOGUE BETWEEN COMMISSION, COUNCIL AND PARLIAMENT

The virtual monopoly which the Commission enjoys over the legislative process could cause serious problems. If it submits no proposals, the Council is paralysed and the progress of the Community comes to a halt, whether in the field of agriculture, transport, commercial policy or the environment. However, except for a period of relative stagnation during the economic crisis of the seventies, the Commission has always been active in promoting the development of the Community through a series of legislative programmes. As we have seen in Chapter 2, the Commission outlines its annual work programme early in the year. The programme provides a framework of policy and legislative objectives. The Commission then brings forward a series of proposals within that programme. Once a proposal is lodged, a dialogue begins between Commission officials and the representatives of the Council in COREPER. This will continue until the legislation has passed through all its stages and it has finally been approved by the Council.

LEGISLATIVE PROPOSALS

Legislative proposals may result from the implementation a wide programme of action, such as that laid down in the plans for a single European market, or the Social Chapter, or in response to particular circumstances calling for specific legislation. The appropriate Directorate-General, assisted by one of the Commission's advisory committees, will prepare the first draft, which will, initially be approved by the appropriate Commissioner holding the relevant portfolio. The views of these advisory committees, which will contain representatives of industrial, commercial and social interests in member states, are not in any sense binding on the Commission. The proposal will then be passed for consideration by the Commission voting as a collegiate body.

VOTING PROCEDURES

The Commission

Decisions by the Commission on whether or not to adopt a proposal are taken by a simple majority of the Commissioners. Although the initiative for specific measures will be taken up by the appropriate Directorate-General, other Commissioners have no power to delegate approval of the details of that measure to that Commissioner. The Court made the position clear in Case *Commission* v *BASF and Others* (case C-137/92):

> The functioning of the Commission is governed by the principle of collegiate responsibility. The principle of collegiate responsibility is based on the equal participation of the Commissioners in the adoption of decisions, from which it follows in particular that decisions should be the subject of collective deliberation and that all the members of the college of Commissioners should bear collective responsibility at political level for all decisions adopted.

The European Parliament

Except as otherwise provided in the Treaties, the EP acts by an absolute majority of the votes cast (Arts 141 EC, 111 Euratom). A quorum exists when one third of the current MEPs are present in the Chamber. However, all votes are valid whatever the number of voters unless the President of the Parliament, acting on a request made by at least 13 MEPs, ascertains that the quorum is not present. In that case, the vote is placed on the agenda of the next sitting (Rule 89 Rules of Procedure 1993).The right to vote is a personal right. There is no voting by proxy. Although members of the European Council and Commissioners have the right to attend debates of the EP and to participate in the discussion, they have no right to vote (Arts 23 ECSC, 140 EC, 110 Euratom).

The Council of Ministers

The Treaties set up three voting methods in the Council:

1 Simple majority;
2 Qualified majority; and
3 Unanimity.

All three methods have been in existence since the earliest days of the Community.

1 *Simple majority voting.* Although Art 148 (1) provides that simple majority voting is the system to be used unless otherwise provided in the Treaty, which it almost invariably does. Under the system, one vote is allocated to each member state, and the decision is simply made in favour of the largest number of votes cast. It is largely used for the establishment of sub- committees of the Council and for procedural matters.
2 *Qualified majority voting* is a system of voting, weighted according to the population size of the member state (Art 148 (2)). Under this system votes are allocated as follows:

France, Germany, Italy and UK	10
Spain	8
Netherlands, Portugal, Greece and Belgium	5
Sweden and Austria	4
Denmark, Ireland and Finland	3
Luxembourg	2

To secure approval by a qualified majority, a measure proposed by the Commission will need to be supported by at least 62 votes. In other cases the 62 votes in favour must be cast by at least 10 member states (Art 148 (2) EC, Art 15 Act of Accession, Art 8 Decision 95/1/ 1 EC OJ 1995 L1 1.1.95 p 1). Conversely, to block a proposal, opponents need to secure more than 25 votes. Following the accession of Austria, Finland and Sweden, the number of members who have to be present to enable the Council to vote has been increased from six to eight (OJ

L 31, 10.2.95). Since the largest member states can muster only 40 votes between them, they are not in a position to force through legislation which tends to favour them, without the support of some, at least, of the smaller states. The majority of decisions were made by qualified majority vote even before the SEA. There was, however, a substantial increase in qualified majority voting following the inclusion of Art 100a, which was intended to secure more rapid decision making in the run up to the single market (see below).

3 *Unanimity* is reserved for the most important decisions, or those for which member states are least prepared to pool their national sovereignty. Although this effectively gives member states a veto, that veto must be exercised for a measure to be blocked. Abstention by members present or represented does not prevent the adoption of an act which requires unanimity (Art 148 (2)). Unanimity is, for example, required for the admission of new states (Art O EC as amended by TEU), and for approval of any other matter within the competence of the Community for which the Treaty does not provide a legal base (Art 235 EC).

THE LUXEMBOURG ACCORDS

The Accords, or the Luxembourg Compromise, were the result of an impasse between France and the other member states in relation to farm prices in 1965. The decision had to be determined, under the Treaty, by a qualified majority vote. The French insisted on the right to secure a unanimous decision in cases such as this, where a vital national interest was at stake. The other member states could not agree. France then remained absent from all but technical meetings of the Council for seven months, and important decision making in the Community virtually drew to a halt. The Accords were negotiated in a reconvened meeting of the Council in January 1996. The three points that emerged from this meeting, as far as voting procedures are concerned, were as follows:

1 Where, in the case of decisions which may be taken by majority vote on a proposal of the Commission, very important interests of one or more partners are at stake, the members of Council will endeavour, within a reasonable time, to reach solutions which can be adopted by all the members of the Council while respecting their mutual interests and those of the Community, in accordance with Art 2 of the Treaty.

2 With regard to the preceding paragraph, the French delegation considers that where very important interests are at stake the discussion must be continued until unanimous agreement is reached.

3 The six delegates note that there is a divergence of views on what should be done in the event of a failure to reach complete agreement.

The six delegations concluded by observing that the divergence noted in point 3 did not prevent the Community's work from being resumed in accordance with the normal procedure. There are a number of things to be said about the Accords. In the first place, the title 'accord' is inappropriate. There was, in fact, no agreement, only an agreement to disagree. Secondly, the Accords have no standing in law. In so far as they purport to amend the voting procedure laid down by the Treaty in certain circumstances, they cannot be effective. Changes to the text and substance of the EC Treaty have to be accomplished in the appropriate form, after consultation with the Parliament and the Commission (formerly under Art 236, now under Art N, added by TEU). This was not done in the case of the Accords. The Commission has never accepted that the Accords had any validity, and disassociated itself from them (Bull EC 5 1982, p 8).

Pierre Pescatore, a former judge of the ECJ has described the Accords as 'a mere press release', without the least force of law (Pescatore, P., 'Some Critical Remarks on the Single European Act' (1987) *CML Rev* 9, 13). The Court has, moreover, stated (but not in the context of the Accords) that 'the rules regarding the manner in which the Community institutions arrive at their decisions [i.e. by a majority vote or by unanimity] are laid down in the Treaty and are not at the disposal of the member states or of the institutions themselves' *United Kingdom* v *Council* (case 68/86). Successive British Governments have, however, from the time of British entry in 1973 until the conclusion of the Maastricht negotiations on TEU, and after, assured the British public that 'on issues of vital national interest, Britain retains the right to veto any legislation' (Sir Geoffrey Howe, HC Deb Vol 96 Col 320 23 April 1986). There is, however, no right to veto proposed legislation. What there has been is a willingness, in some cases where member states appear to be in difficulties in relation to a domestic political situation, to refrain from pressing to a majority vote where the Treaty authorises it.

The Accords have undoubtedly encouraged member states to reach a compromise wherever possible. The formal invocation of the Accords has been rare, and has not always achieved the desired result. In 1982, for example, when the United Kingdom sought to block the adoption of an agricultural price package in order to put pressure on the other member states to agree a reduction of the British contributions, its purported 'veto' was ignored and a vote was taken. However, in 1985, Germany invoked the Accords to forestall an increase in cereal prices, and was successful. It is, perhaps, significant, that no state which has been overridden, following an appeal to the Accords, has ever taken the decision to the Court of Justice. The trend in voting procedures in recent Treaty changes has been, as we shall see, to more majority voting and less unanimous decision taking, and it is likely that appeals to vital national interests under the Accords will become even rarer than at present.

THE IOANNINO DECLARATION

Some recognition of the continuing need to take into account the genuine difficulties of some member states when a majority vote is to be taken was shown early in 1994. Under a declaration made in March 1994 at the Ioannino Summit, if members of the Council representing a total of between 23 and 26 votes indicate their intention to oppose the adoption by the Council of a decision by a qualified majority vote, the Council is committed to do all in its power to reach, within a reasonable time, and without infringing the obligatory times limits in Art 189b and 189c procedures (*see* below), a satisfactory solution that could be adopted by at least 65 votes (Bull EU 3 1994 p 65:OJ C 105 29.3.94 p 1 as amended by Council Decision of 1 January 1995).

This does no more than provide an opportunity to delay a qualified majority vote, but cannot prevent one from being held, because the new Treaty time limits are still to be respected, and the declaration does not, like the Luxembourg Accords, have the force of law. It is intended to continue to apply until the amendments to the Treaties following the Intergovernmental Conference of 1996 come into effect.

THE CONSULTATION PROCEDURE

From the earliest days of the Community, this was the commonest legislative procedure in the Treaty, and the only one which gave the Parliament a significant role in the process. New procedures were introduced by both the SEA and the TEU to give the Parliament a greater involvement. Article 189, as now amended by TEU, refers to the making of regulations and directives, the taking of decisions, the making of recommendations or the delivery of opinions, as a joint function of the Parliament and the Council, and the Council and the Commission. However, the Parliament is still far from being a joint legislator in the sense known to national legislatures. The consultation procedure remains the appropriate method for decisions on the Common Agricultural Policy (Art 43 EC, harmonisation of indirect taxation and environmental law: Art 130s). Under this procedure, measures are proposed by the Commission, the Parliament is consulted and delivers an opinion and the Council of Ministers makes the final decision. The opinion is prepared by the rapporteur of one of the Parliament's specialist committees. Its preparation follows the hearing of evidence by the Committee from specialist advisers, interested individuals and organisations, and members of the officials of the Directorate-General originally responsible for the drafting of the proposal. Although the Council of Ministers is free not to follow the opinion of Parliament, the consultation must be genuine. Parliament must have a proper opportunity to respond to the proposal. This was recognised as an essential procedural requirement by the Court in *Roquette Frères* v *Council* (case 138/79):

> The consultation provided for in...the Treaty is the means which allows the Parliament to play an actual part in the legislative process of the Community. Such power represents an essential factor in the institutional balance intended by the Treaty. Although limited, it reflects at Community level the fundamental principle that the peoples should take part in the exercise of power through the intermediary of a representative assembly. Due consultation of the Parliament in the cases provided for by the Treaty therefore constitutes an essential formality disregard of which means that the measure concerned is void. ([1980] ECR 3333 at 3360)

This principle was further developed to require re-consultation when a measure on which Parliament had already given an opinion was subsequently changed. In *European Parliament* v *Council* (case C-65/90) the Court said that further consultation was required unless the amendments essentially corresponded to the wishes already expressed by the Parliament. In *European Parliament* v *Council* (case C-388/92) the Court held that the obligation arose to reconsult 'on each occasion when the text finally adopted, viewed as a whole, departs substantially from the text on which Parliament has already been consulted'. On that basis the Court found that the Council had disregarded the prerogatives of Parliament and annulled a Regulation on the operation by non-resident carriers of transport services in member states (Reg 2454/92 EC). However, consultation is a two-way process. Where Parliament wilfully fails to respond it cannot, subsequently complain that its views have not been taken into account. In *Parliament* v *Council* (case C-65/93), the Council had informed the Parliament of the urgent need for approval of draft regulations on tariff preference relating to agricultural products and to be made under Article 43, EC Treaty. Having agreed to deal with the draft regulations as a matter of urgency, Parliament then decided to adjourn discussion of them for reasons wholly unconnected with their content. They were subsequently adopted by the Council without having received the Parliament's opinion. The Parliament sought to annul the Regulations on the grounds of failure of consultation. The Court rejected the application:

> ... Inter-institutional dialogue, on which the consultation procedure in particular is based, is subject to the same mutual duties of sincere cooperation as those which govern relations between member states and the Community institutions. By adopting that course of action [adjournment of consideration of the draft regulation] the Parliament failed to discharge its obligation to cooperate sincerely with the Council. ... In those circumstances the Parliament is not entitled to complain of the Council's failure to await its opinion before adopting the contested regulation ...

Although the Council should not come to a final decision without giving the Parliament an opportunity to respond, it does not have to suspend all discussion until it receives that opinion (*European Parliament* v *Council* (case C-417/93)).

THE CO-OPERATION PROCEDURE

The election of a European Parliament by direct franchise for the first time in 1979 produced pressure to address the Community's 'democratic deficit'. The Community institutions were seen as essentially undemocratic, in that the only body that was directly accountable to an electorate played only a peripheral part in the legislative process. Parliament attacked the issue by commissioning a report on wholesale constitutional reform of the Community. That report, the Spinelli Report, appeared in 1984 and although many of the recommendations were not taken up by the Commission, an attempt was made in the SEA to address the issue of lack of significant Parliamentary input. This was the co-operation procedure, now called, rather obscurely in the Treaty since TEU, the 'procedure referred to in Art 189c', but still widely known as 'the co-operation procedure' (originally Art 149 (2), now Art 189c).

Unlike the consultation procedure, the co-operation procedure requires two readings by the Parliament. The first reading corresponds to the consultation procedure, but the outcome, at this stage, is not the approval of the proposal by the Council, but the adoption of a 'common position on the measure'. Voting on the common position is by qualified majority vote. If the Council wishes, at this stage, to amend the Council's proposal, it must do so unanimously. The common position, together with the Council's views on the proposal is then passed back to the Parliament. Parliament then has three months in which to respond in one of four ways (Art 189c (b) and (c)).

It may approve the common position or it may take no further action. In either of these cases the Council must simply confirm its common position and the measure will be enacted. It may propose amendments to the Council's common position or it may reject it. In either case, the Council and Commission must be informed. In the case of a rejection by the Parliament, the Council can only proceed to approve the measure by a unanimous vote. In the case of amendments by the Parliament, which is its commonest response, the Commission must re-examine the proposal and submit its view on the amendments to the Council. The Council may adopt amendments made by the Parliament, but of which the Commission disapproves, but only by a unanimous vote. It must approve the proposal as amended by the Commission by a qualified majority vote. It can only reject such Commission-approved amendments by a unanimous vote. This elaborate procedure was intended to make positive decision making easier and a great deal of single market legislation was approved in this way. The TEU has moved the co-operation procedure onto other fields. Much of the harmonising legislation is now to be based on the new Art 189b procedure, considered below. But new uses for the co-operation procedure has been found in relation to the common transport policy, development co-operation, vocational training and the Social Fund (Art 125 EC).

Article 189b Procedure ; the new Conciliation Procedure

The Treaty on European Union introduced a new legislative procedure, which was referred to in the negotiations at Maastricht as 'co-decision making' and became Art 189b EC Treaty. That title is more appropriate to the assent procedure (below), because the procedure under Art 189b still allows the Council the final word in certain circumstances. The Art 189b procedure could, more aptly, be described as the new Conciliation Procedure.

The Art 189b procedure starts in much the same way as the Co-operation Procedure, except that, instead of the proposal coming to the Parliament after the Council has adopted its common position on it, it arrives at both Parliament and Council simultaneously. At the second reading, the Parliament is again faced with the choice of accepting the proposal, rejecting it, amending it or doing nothing.

The consequences of rejecting the proposal or amending it are, however, rather different in the Art 189b procedure. If the Parliament indicates by a vote of an absolute majority of its members that it wishes to reject the common position of the Council, the Council must be informed at once, so that it can, if it wishes, convene a meeting of the Conciliation Committee. If the Parliament amends the common position by an absolute majority of its members, the amended text is forwarded to the Council and the Commission, which delivers an opinion on the amendments. The Council has three months to accept the amendments which the Commission has approved, and can do so by a qualified majority vote. It can also approve the amendments on which the Commission has responded negatively, but must do so unanimously. If the Council rejects the proposal, the President of the Council, in agreement with the President of the EP, convenes a meeting of the Conciliation Committee.

The Conciliation Committee consists of members of the Council or their representatives and an equal number of representatives of the EP. The Committee must reach an agreement on a joint text, the Parliamentarians by a majority and the Council side by a qualified majority. They have six weeks in which to do so. The Commission acts as a broker, attempting to get both sides to agree.

If the Conciliation Committee agrees a joint text, the text must be put to both the Council and the Parliament. The Council may approve it by a qualified majority, and the Parliament by an absolute majority. If either institution rejects the proposal, it fails and is deemed not to be adopted. If the Committee cannot agree on a text in the six weeks, the proposal will again fail, unless the Council, acting by a qualified majority, confirms the common position to which it agreed before the Conciliation Procedure was initiated. In this case, the measure will be enacted, unless the Parliament rejects the text adopted by the Council within six weeks of it having approved it. If the Parliament does this, the measure will be lost.

The new Conciliation Procedure is used in relation to co-operation in employment services between member states: Art 49 EC, the abolition of restrictions on freedom of establishment : Art 54 EC, incentive measures in relation to public health : Art 129 (4) , consumer protection : Art 129a, in addition to all the Single

Market measures previously dealt with under the co-operation procedure created by Art 100a.

THE ASSENT PROCEDURE

This could truly be said to be co-decision making. Under this procedure, the Council acts on a proposal by the Commission after obtaining the assent of the EP. The procedure was introduced by the SEA. It was limited to decisions concerning the admission of new states to the Community under Art 237 (now Art O EC), and in relation to the conclusion with association agreements with other states under Art 238 (now Art 228 (3)).

The TEU extended the assent procedure to decisions enlarging the free movement rights of EU citizens and their families (Arts 8a (2), 8e) and to the application of structural funds under Art 130d and the Cohesion Fund. It will also be required in relation to legislation on elections to the EP (Art 138 (3)), and for amendments to legislation concerning the European System of Central Banks (Art 138 (3), and *see* above, Chapter 2).

THE INVOLVEMENT OF THE BRITISH PARLIAMENT

National parliaments become involved in the decision making process at two, or sometimes three points in the process. In the first place, draft Directives and Regulations are sent for scrutiny by national parliaments at the same time as they are sent to the EP. They are examined at Westminster by a Select Committee on European legislation which reports to the House of Commons on their political and legal consequences. In addition, more general discussion takes place about Community legislative proposals before the biennial meetings of the European Council.

Where the Select Committee recommends that further consideration should be given to any particular proposal, it will be referred to one of two recently created Standing Committees. Committee A takes matters relating to the Departments of Agriculture, Fisheries, Food, Environment and Forestry, while Committee B deals with all other matters (Select Committee on Procedure (HC 622 1988/89)). The UK government has given an undertaking to Parliament that they will not approve proposals for legislation in the Council of Ministers if they are awaiting consideration by the House or are still subject to scrutiny. However, ministers may agree to proposals which:

1 are subject to scrutiny if they are confidential, routine, trivial or substantially the same as an item which has already been scrutinised;

2   are awaiting consideration but the Select Committee has indicated that
    agreement could be given; or
3   are either awaiting consideration or are still subject to scrutiny, and the minister
    has special reasons why agreement should be given, provided that these reasons
    are given at the first opportunity (HC Debates Vol 178 Col 399 (24 October
    1990)).

By a Declaration annexed to the TEU, member states committed themselves to
ensuring that 'national parliaments receive Commission proposals for legislation in
good time for information or possible examination' (Declaration 13 TEU). According
to a recent report of the Select Committee, this is not happening. Decisions are often
made by the Council of Ministers on the basis of a French text for which no English
translation is available, and the Select Committee frequently only sees the English
translation *after* the measure has been approved by the Council of Ministers.
Members of the Select Committee expressed concern that the Brussels legislative
process was operating beyond the scrutiny of national parliaments. They demanded
that there should be a mimimum four weeks' notice period between an official text
of a document being available in the appropriate language in every national capital
and a decision being taken on the document by the Council of Ministers: *The
Intergovernmental Conference 1996: The Agenda; Democracy and Efficiency: the Role of
National Parliaments,* 24th report, Vol. 1, Select Committee on European Legislation:
Session 1994–1995, HMSO.

THE APPROPRIATE LEGISLATIVE BASE

In almost every case, as the initiator of the legislative process, the choice of
legislative base is made by the Commission. It is not always clear, especially in
relation to proposals which touch on a number of different activities, which Treaty
provision, and hence, which decision making process, is appropriate. Article 3b
provides that the Community shall act within the limits of the powers conferred on
it by the Treaty and the objectives of the Treaty. When legislating, the Commission
is bound to give reasons for its proposal, the legal basis on which it is made and the
process through which it passed, including the institutions and other bodies who
participated in the decision (Art 190). This information is normally contained in the
preamble to the measure. Prior to the SEA, the choice of legislative base rarely gave
rise to controversy. However, disputes have arisen subsequently, largely because
member states contested either the competence of the Community to legislate at all
or because a basis was chosen allowing for a qualified majority vote, when some
states demanded a basis requiring unanimity and the opportunity to block the
measure by a national veto.

Defects in the legal base may be one of three kinds :

1 Lack of competence of the Community;
2 Lack of competence of an institution;
3 Inappropriate Treaty provision for the subject-matter of the legislation.

The Court has not yet found that a proposed action is without a Community base, but some challenges to the powers of institutions to take action have been successful. In *Germany* v *Commission* (Case 281/85) Germany, France, the Netherlands and the United Kingdom sought to annul a decision made by the Commission in relation to migration policy from non-member states. Although free movement of persons is central to the working of the Community, the law is, as we shall see, (Chapter 10) directed at the facilitation of free movement by EU citizens and their families (but see, now the limited powers of the Community under Art K 3 (2) in relation to immigration from outside the Community). It was argued by the applicant states that neither Art 118 (which relates to social policy) nor any other Treaty provision empowered the Commission to adopt a binding decision. The Court held that the Commission did have the power to consult with member states on the impact of third state immigration on the employment market, and how this was affecting Community workers, but that it did not have the power to make a binding measure restricting the way in which member states could regulate immigration into their territories from outside the Community. The Commission will generally choose the legislative base offering the best chance of approval for a measure, if there is at least an arguable alternative. The Court stated in *Commission* v *Council* (*Generalised Tariff Preferences*) (Case 45/86) that:

> The choice of a legal base for a measure may not depend simply on an institution's conviction as to the objective pursued but must be based on objective factors which are amenable to judicial review.

In *Commission* v *Council* (Case C-300/89), a conflict arose between the Council on the one hand and the Parliament and the Commission on the other, as to the choice of the appropriate legislative base. The Commission (supported by the Parliament) applied to the Court for the annulment of Directive 89/428 on procedures for harmonising the programmes for the reduction and elimination of pollution caused by waste from the titanium dioxide industry. The Commission had proposed that the directive be based on Art 100a, which involved the Council acting by a qualified majority in co-operation with the Parliament. However, despite the Parliament's objections, the Council adopted the directive on the basis of the environmental policy, Art 130s. This article provided at the time (but *see,* Art 130s (1)) that decisions in Council should be taken unanimously, and only after consultation with the EP. The Court decided that Art 100a, which provided that decisions should be taken by qualified majority in Council, in co-operation with the EP, was the appropriate legal basis. Although the directive had the dual objectives of environ- mental protection and the removal of distortions of competition by establishing harmonised production conditions, it was not possible to have recourse to two legislative bases, and the unanimity rule in Art 130s was incompatible with the co-operation procedure in Article 130a. The decision has a strong political flavour:

> The very purpose of the co-operation procedure, which is to increase the involvement of the European Parliament in the legislative process of the Community would thus be jeopardised. As the Court stated in its judgment in *Roquette Frères* v *Council* (Case 138/79) and *Maizena* v *Council* (Case C-139/79), para 34, that participation reflects a fundamental democratic principle that the peoples should take part in the exercise of power through the intermediary of a representative assembly. (para [20] of judgment)

The Commission has continued to show a disinclination to use Treaty provisions, on which decisions in the Council are to be taken unanimously, and a preference for articles for which qualified majority voting is the appropriate procedure in the Council of Ministers. An example can be found in the field of higher education. The European Court of Justice had decided in *Gravier* v *City of Liège* (Case 293/83) that Art 128 EC Treaty, which contained some fairly general provisions on the promotion of a common vocational training policy, created a directly enforceable right to access to vocational training in other member states. As a Treaty right, it was to be delivered in accordance with the principles of equality contained in Art 7 EC (now Art 6 EC).

Articles 7 and 128 were, therefore, taken as the basis for a new directive on student mobility (Directive 90/366). Article 7 provided for measures to eliminate discrimination on grounds of nationality to be decided by a qualified majority vote, and it was on this basis that the measure was proposed. The Council of Ministers substituted Art 235 as the legal base, on the grounds that since Art 128 contained no voting procedure, the residual voting system in Art 235 (a unanimous vote) was more appropriate. Although the directive was then, unanimously approved by the Council of Ministers, its legal base was challenged by the Parliament, since it did not want to see a precedent established of unanimous decision making in relation to future educational measures. The Court upheld the challenge on the basis that the measure was, fundamentally, about equal access to vocational training, and that Art 7, which required only a qualified majority vote, was the proper legal basis. The Court ordered that directive be annulled and a new measure be proposed with Art 7 as the legislative base (*Parliament* v *Council* (Case C-295/90); *see*, Directive 93/96 EC).

SUBSIDIARITY

A relatively new feature of Community law is the recognition in the Treaty, following amendment by TEU, of a national dimension to the decision making process. Article 3b now provides that :

The Community shall act within the limits of the powers conferred upon it by this Treaty and of the objectives assigned to it therein. In areas which do not fall within its exclusive competence, the Community shall take action, in accordance with the principle of subsidiarity, only if and in so far as the objectives of the proposed action cannot be sufficiently achieved by the member states and can, therefore, by reason of the scale or effects of the proposed action, be better achieved by the Community. Any action by the Community shall not go beyond what is necessary to achieve the objectives of this Treaty.

Although subsidiarity is not a new concept for the Community, the TEU made it a central criterion to be applied by the Commission in proposing new legislation. Hitherto, subsidiarity had been implicit in Art 189 in relation to the implementation of directives, where the Community set the objectives, and the member states chose the 'manner and form of implementation'. It was first made specific by Art 130, r (4) in relation to the environment, where legislation was only to be introduced where the environmental objectives could 'be attained better at Community level than at the level of individual member states'. Article 3b makes the principle applicable to all new legislation where the issue of competing competences arises.

At the Edinburgh European Council Meeting of October 1993, it was decided that the Commission should consult more widely before proposing legislation and should include in the recitals to any new measure, besides the legislative base, its justification for initiating the measure, under the subsidiarity principle. If legislation had to be made at Community level, directives were to be preferred to regulations and 'framework directives' (allowing member states considerable leeway in the manner of implementation) to specific and detailed directives (Toth, A. G., 'A Legal Analysis of Subsidiarity' in O'Keefe and Twomey (eds) *Legal Issues of the Maastricht Treaty* (1994)).

As part of the process of implementing the new subsidiarity principle, the Commission embarked on a so called 'bonfire of measures' and the abandonment of some legislative programmes, with a view to the policies which they were intended to implement being carried out at national level. It announced the withdrawal of proposals for more than 15 directives, including proposals on the liability of suppliers of services (COM (90) 482), minimum standards for the keeping of animals in zoos, the advertising of tobacco products, speed limits for motor vehicles and maximum alcohol levels for vehicle drivers (Bull EU 6 1994, p 26).

There are, however, both legal and practical limits to the implementing of policies at national level, as envisaged in Art 3b. The Article refers to matters which are not within the exclusive competence of the Community, implying that there are matters of shared competence. Such a concept is fundamentally at odds with basic principles of Community law. The Community either has competence, in which case it has the power to legislate in a way in which must take precedence over national legislation, or it has no competence, in which case the question of whether or not the decision should be taken at Communty or national level does not arise. Essentially, the issue is about how Community policies are to be implemented and enforced, and how much discretion is to be given to national governments. It is, however, arguable, that the inclusion of the new areas of competence in TEU, at the same time as the recognition of a joint competence of Community and member states, suggests that in the new areas of competence, questions of who is to make decisions as well as who is to implement them, and how, will arise.

It is at the national level that practical difficulties arise. Long experience has shown that there are major divergencies in the extent of implementation of Community law by member states. The briefest examination of the European Court Reports and the Annual Report of the Commission indicates the extent of the problem. The most recent Commission survey indicates that, out of the currently effective directives, Denmark has implemented 97.6 per cent, whereas Greece has implemented 86.7 per cent. The Commission initiated 89 infringement proceedings under Art 169 (see Chapter 22), 17 of these were against Greece, 12 against Ireland and Italy, 10 against Belgium and 9 against Spain (*The European*, 7 July 1995).

If more legislation and more enforcement are to take place at state level, there will be even greater local variations in the degree of regulation in each member state. The 'level playing field' for business may then become even less attainable. On a practical level, the regulation of air and water quality, which clearly may involve the environments of a number of member states, can only be carried out effectively if the same environmental quality is to be maintained at Community level. The Court may be called upon to decide, according to the effects or scale of a measure, whether its objectives could be 'sufficiently' achieved by legislation in the member states. It may have to apply conflicting criteria. Pollution control may be most effectively managed at local level, but given the extent of water and air pollution in Europe, the scale could require a Community *standard* of air and water quality and action at Community level to see that it is secured in member states. Whether a practical assessment to determine the appropriate level of action is possible, or whether it is an apposite exercise for a court of law is yet to be demonstrated.

Ironically, subsidiarity was championed by those member states, among them Britain, that were concerned about the centralising of decision making in Brussels, and the apparent movement of the Community towards a federal structure. If the Court has to determine which decisions can and should be taken at the centre, and which at national level by national parliaments, then Art 3b could become the cornerstone in the constitution of a new federal Europe. This issue will continue to be contentious and will undoubtedly be discussed at the 1996 Intergovernmental Conference.

Further reading

Bradley, K., 'Comitology and the Law: Through a Glass Darkly' (1992) 29 *CML Rev* 695.

Curtin, D., 'The Constitutional Structure of the Union : A Europe of Bits and Pieces' (1993) 30 CML Rev 17.

Duff, A., Pinder, J. and Pryce, R., (1994) *Maastricht and Beyond*, Pt III, Routledge.

Hartley, T. C., (1994) *The Foundations of the European Community*, Clarendon Press, Chapter 1.

Lang, J. Temple, 'Community Constitutional Law: Article 5 EEC Treaty' (1990) 27 CML Rev 645.

The Intergovernmental Conference 1996: The Agenda; Democracy and Efficiency; the Role of National Parliaments, 24th Report, Vol. 1, Select Committee on European Legislation: Session 1994–1995, HMSO.

Mancini, G. F., 'The Making of a Constitution for Europe' (1989) 26 CML Rev 594.

Nugent, N., (1994) *The Government and Politics of the European Union*, Macmillan, Chapters 5 and 11.

O'Keefe, D. and Twomey, P. (eds) (1994) *Legal Issues of the Maastricht Treaty*, Chancery Publications, Chapters 3–5, 11.

Pescatore, P., 'Some Critical Remarks on the Single European Act' (1987) CML Rev 9, 13.

Thompson, B., (1995) *Constitutional and Administrative Law*, (2nd edn.) Blackstone Press.

Toth, A. G., (1994) *The Oxford Encyclopaedia of European Community Law*, Clarendon Press.

Toth, A. G., 'A Legal Analysis of Subsidiarity', in O'Keefe, D. and Twomey, P. (1994) *Legal Issues of the Maastricht Treaty*, Chancery Publications.

Weatherill, S. and Beaumont, P., (1993) *EC Law*, Penguin Books, Chapters 2, 3 and 5.

4 Sources and supremacy of Community law

SOURCES

There are seven principal sources of Community law:

1   The Treaties establishing the three European Communities.
2   Secondary legislation made under the Treaties.
3   Related Treaties made between the member states.
4   International Treaties negotiated by the Community under powers conferred on it by the Treaties.
5   Decisions of the European Court of Justice.
6   General principles of law and fundamental rights upon which the constitutional laws of the member states are based.
7   Recommendations, programmes and other 'soft law', in so far as they cast light on interpretation of Community law.

The Treaties and the Community Legal Order

The Treaty establishing what was then called the European Economic Community did more than establish a trading area between the participating states. It created four institutions bound by a body of law that took precedence over the laws of the member states. The European Coal and Steel Treaty and Euratom did likewise. Member states are bound by Art 5 of the EC Treaty to:

> take all appropriate measures, whether general or particular, to ensure fulfilment of the obligations arising out of this Treaty or resulting from action taken by the institutions of the Community. They shall facilitate the achievement of the Community's tasks.

Article 5 has been called the 'good faith clause' of the Treaty, because it imposes a general obligation on member states and all their constituent institutions, including national courts, to ensure that Community law is effective in their states. The Treaty does not specifically recognise the supremacy of Community law, but the Court of Justice has recognised Art 5 as providing the source of this fundamental principle.

Breach of this or any of the specific obligations imposed by the Treaty can result in an action brought in the European Court of Justice by any other member state or by the European Commission. Although national courts retain exclusive competence over the interpretation and application of national law, this competence is now limited by Community law where there is a conflict with national law. Provisions of Community law conferring directly effective rights must be recognised in national courts, and national remedies must be adapted to ensure their effective delivery (*R v Secretary of State for Transport, ex p Factortame* (Case C-213/89)). The supremacy of Community law and its direct effect are the twin pillars of the Community legal order.

Although the Treaty does not purport to create the constitution of a federal state, it does, in some respects have that effect, and has been interpreted in that way by the Court of Justice. In Opinion 1/91 on the Draft Agreement between EEC and EFTA the Court said:

> The EEC Treaty, albeit concluded in the form of an international agreement, nonetheless constitutes the constitutional charter of a Community based on the rule of law. As the Court of Justice has consistently held, the Community Treaties established a new legal order for the benefit of which the states had limited their sovereign rights, in ever wider fields, and the subjects of which comprised not only the member states but also their nationals.
>
> The essential characteristics of the Community legal order which had thus been established were, in particular its primacy over the law of member states and the direct effect of a whole series of provisions which were applicable to their nationals and to the member states themselves. ([1991] ECR 6079)

However, the Treaty, although fulfilling many of the functions of a constitution for the Community still falls far short of creating a federal state and although Community law prevails in member states, the Community depends on the Courts and the enforcement agencies of the member states to implement it. There is no Community police or military force and defence and foreign policy remain in the hands of national governments, although important steps were taken in TEU to co-ordinate action in those areas, as well as in the area of drugs enforcement, illegal immigration and justice and home affairs (Titles V and VI TEU). These areas are, ultimately, still a matter of national policy over which member states retain final control in their territories. In a federal state, defence and foreign policy would be the sole prerogative of the central, federal government. The Community is, therefore, at the most, only an embryonic federal state.

The Treaty most nearly resembles a constitution in the way in which it defines the competence of the Community itself, and each of its constituent parts, and to a lesser extent, the rights of its citizens. Although the Treaty does not contain a complete catalogue of citizens' rights, it does confer a number of directly effective rights, which must be enforced in the national courts. Ultimately, the Court of Justice acts as guarantor of those rights and has, in fact, quite consciously used the doctrine of direct effect to empower citizens in their own courts and, if need be, against their own governments (Mancini, G. F., 'The Making of a Constitution for Europe' (1989) 26 CML Rev 595, 596; Lenaerts, K., 'Fundamental Rights to be included in a Community Catalogue' (1991) 16 EL Rev 367). A whole range of Treaty provisions have been held to create directly effective rights, among them the right not to be discriminated against on grounds of nationality (Art 6 EC), the right to equal pay for work of equal value, regardless of gender (Art 119), the right to seek work and remain as a worker in another member state (Art 48), the right to receive and provide services (Art 59), the right not to be subjected to import taxes (Art 12) and the right to take action against another undertaking for breach of the competition rules (Art 86; *Garden Cottage Foods* v *Milk Marketing Board* [1984] AC 130; and see Chapter 5).

It has been suggested by Advocate-General Jacobs that the 1996 Inter-governmental Conference might be the occasion at which the member states could draw together all the fundamental rules of the Community into a single document. The way to do this would be:

> ... To strip out from the Maastricht morass those basic Treaty provisions governing the competences of the Community, the competences of the institutions, and the funda-mental principles of the Community legal order, which could then be incorporated in a basic text as an incipient constitution, and one which could be amended only by a special procedure, so that the current allocation of competences was effectively protected against amendment by the ordinary legislative procedure; while many of the other Treaty provisions could be relegated to an instrument of a less fundamental status. (Jacobs, F., 'The European Court of Justice: some thoughts on its past and future', *The European Advocate*, Winter 1994/1995 p 2.)

The Court of Justice, in its submission to the 1996 Intergovernmental Conference, has called, more modestly, for 'a codifying and streamlining of the constitutive Treaties'. (Para 23, Report of the Court of Justice on Certain Aspects of the Treaty of European Union (May 1995))

Secondary legislation

Article 189 contains the provisions for the making of Community legislative acts:

> In order to carry out their task and in accordance with the provisions of this Treaty, the European Parliament acting jointly with the Council, the Council and the Commission, shall make regulations, issue directives, take decisions, make recommendations or deliver opinions.

The different types of act have different consequences:

- A *regulation* shall have general application. It shall be binding in its entirety and directly applicable in all member states (Art 189(2)).
- A *directive* shall be binding, as to the result to be achieved, upon each member state to which it is addressed, but shall leave to the national authorities the choice of form and methods (Art 189/3).

- A *decision* shall be binding in its entirety upon those to whom it is addressed (Art 189/4). *Recommendations* and *opinions* shall have no binding force.

Regulations are the Community equivalent of legislation produced by a national parliament, in that they are immediately binding ('directly applicable') on anyone falling within their terms in all member states. They require no further action by member states, and can be applied by the Courts of the member states as soon as they become operative.

Directives are directed at the governments of member states and are binding on them. The form in which Art 189 is drafted was intended to give member states a discretion as to how the objectives of directives were attained in national law by the date set for their implementation. They were not intended, as regulations were, to confer rights on individuals in national courts. However, the persistent failure of member states to implement directives by the target date led the European Court of Justice (the Court) to develop the doctrine of the direct effect under which individuals could, in appropriate circumstances, rely upon them in national courts. The nature and scope of this doctrine is examined in detail in Chapter 5.

Decisions are individual measures addressed to states, persons, institutions or undertakings. They are immediately effective, and do not require any further action to give them legal force.

Recommendations and opinions have no immediate legal force, but may achieve some legal effect as persuasive authority by adoption in a decision of the European Court of Justice. Measures of this kind are sometimes referred to as 'soft law' for this reason (Snyder, F., 'The Effectiveness of European Community Law: Institutions, Processes, Tools and Techniques' (1993) 56 MLR 19, 32). National courts are bound to take them into account when interpreting Community measures, where they throw light on the purpose of the legislation (Case C-322/88 *Grimaldi* v *Fonds des Maladies Professionelles* [1991] ECR 4402).

Regulations, directives and decisions adopted under Art 189b (see Chapter 3), must be signed by the President of the European Parliament and by the President of the Council of Ministers and published in the *Official Journal* of the Community. Normally a date is fixed for the measure to come into force, but if none is fixed, then it comes into effect on the twentieth day after its publication in the Journal.

Related treaties made between member states

These are treaties related to the original Treaties, either amending or enlarging upon them. Within this category, as a source of law, are the Merger Treaties of 1965, the Single European Act 1986, the Treaty on European Union 1992, as well as the Treaties of Accession of Denmark, Ireland and the UK in 1972, Greece in 1981, Spain and Portugal in 1986, and Austria, Finland and Sweden in 1994.

Like the Treaties themselves, the Treaties of Accession have been held to confer directly enforceable rights on individuals (*Rush Portugusa* v *Office National d'Immigration* (Case C-113/89)).

International treaties negotiated by the Community under powers conferred by the Treaty

This category includes not only multilateral treaties to which the Community is a party, such as the General Agreement on Tariffs and Trade, but Association Agreements concluded by the Community with individual states. The GATT agreement was held in *International Fruit* (Case 21–24/72) to be binding on the Community, and the Court has also held that undertakings which complain to the Commission of illicit commercial practices which breach the Community's commercial policy instrument may rely upon the GATT as forming part of the rules of international law to which the instrument applies (*Fediol* (Case 70/87)).

In *Kupferberg* (Case C-104/81), the Court held that Art 21 of the EEC/Portugal Association Agreement to be directly applicable. The principle of the direct effect of such agreements has enabled the nationals of the states which are parties to such agreements to enforce their provisions against member states of the Community. In *Kziber* (Case C-18/90), the Court has also held that parts of the EEC-Morocco Co-operation Agreement are directly effective (*see also, Yousfi* v *Belgium* (Case C-58/93)).

Decisions of the European Court of Justice

The jurisprudence of the Court is a major source of law. It comprises not only all the formal decisions of the Court, but also the principles enunciated by it in judgments and the opinions sought from it. The Treaties and the implementing legislation do not, between them, contain an exhaustive statement of the relevant law, and much of the work of the Court has been to put flesh on the legislative bones. The creative jurisprudence of the Court, and its willingness to interpret measures in such a way as to make them effective, to achieve the *effet utile*, has done much to help in the attainment of the general objectives of the Treaties.

The role of the Court in developing the law of the Community has already been discussed in Chapter 2.

General principles of law and fundamental rights upon which the constitutional laws of the member states are based

In interpreting primary and secondary Community legislation, the Court has developed a number of general principles of law, some based on the fundamental laws of the constitutions of the member states, some based on principles of international law and some derived directly from the European Convention on Human Rights. Although the jurisdiction of the Court of Justice is, as we have seen (*see* Chapter 2), limited by Art 164 to the interpretation of the Treaties and the subordinate legislation made under them, this is to be done in such a way as to ensure that 'the law is observed'. This has been widely interpreted to mean not only the law established by the Treaties but 'any rule of law relating to the Treaty's application' (Pescatore, 1970). The principles of the Convention are to be applied insofar as they relate to matters within the competence of the Community. It shall 'respect fundamental rights, as guaranteed by the European Convention for the Protection of Fundamental Freedom signed in Rome on 4 November 1950 and as they result from the constitutional traditions common to member states, as general principles of Community law.' (Art F (2) EC (as amended by TEU).)

'The Community cannot accept measures which are incompatible with observance of the human rights thus recognised as guaranteed.' (*Wachauf* v *Germany* (Case 5/88); *A* v *Commission* (T-10/93).)

The application of these principles is dealt with in more detail in Chapter 6, but the most important are:

(a)   Proportionality

This is a general principle imported from German law, and is often invoked to determine whether a piece of subordinate legislation or an action purported to be taken under the Treaties goes beyond what is necessary to achieve the declared, lawful objects. It holds that 'the individual should not have his freedom of action limited beyond the degree necessary for the public interest' (*Internationale Handelsgesellschaft* (Case 11/70)). The principle applies in relation to action by the Community in the sphere of legislation, to determine whether a regulation has, for example, gone beyond what was necessary to achieve the aim contained in the enabling Treaty provision, or whether a Community institution has exceeded the necessary action to be taken in relation to an infraction of Community law. It may thus be invoked to challenge fines imposed by undertakings found by the Commission to have breached the competition rules in Arts 85 and 86 EC Treaty.

It is also applicable to action by member states in relation to permitted derogations from Community law. While, for example, restrictions on imports from other member states, and also other measures having an equivalent effect, are prohibited by Art 30 EC Treaty, an exception is permitted under Art 36 in relation to action taken on the grounds of public health. A total ban on a product will, in almost every case be disproportionate, while some sampling and testing, in proportion to the degree of the perceived risk, may be legitimate. Excessive action may then be a disguised restriction on trade (*Commission* v *Germany (Re Crayfish Imports)* (Case C-131/93)). The rule applies similarly in relation to restrictions on free movement of workers. Some rules relating to registration of foreigners are permitted, including their application to EU citizens, but the imposition of penalties for breach of those rules involving deportation would be disproportionate, since they would render the exercise of the very right of free movement itself ineffective (*R* v *Pieck* (Case 157/79)).

(b)   The Principle of Equality

The Treaty includes three specific types of prohibition against discrimination:

1 the prohibition against discrimination on grounds of nationality in Art 6 EC;
2 prohibition of discrimination between producers and consumers in relation to the operation of the Common Agricultural Policy under Art 40(3) EC; and
3 entitlement to equal pay for work of equal value for both men and women under Art 119 EC.

The principle has been recognised by the Court as one of general application and requires that comparable situations should not be treated differently and different situations should not be treated in the same way unless such differentiation is objectively justified (*Graff* v *Hauptzollamt Koln-Rheinau* (Case C-351/92)). Besides the specific Treaty provisions, the Court has held that the fixing and collection of the financial charges making up the Community's own resources are governed by the general principle of equality (*Grosoli* (Case 131/73)), as has the allocation of Community tariff quotas by the member states (*Krohn* (Case 165/84)); Toth, A. G., op. cit. p 188).

The principle is also evident in the Court's requirement of equality of aims under which undertakings which are subject to investigation by the Commission for breach of competition law should have full knowledge of the allegations and evidence in the Commission's file (*Solvay SA* v *Commission* (Case T-30/91)).

(c) Legal certainty and non-retroactivity

This is a general principle of law familiar to all the legal systems of the member states. In its broadest sense, it means that 'Community legislation must be unequivocal and its application must be predictable for those who are subject to it' (*Kloppenburg* (Case 70/81)). It means, for example, that the principle of the indirect effect of directives does not apply in relation to national provisions with criminal sanctions, since the need for legal certainty requires that the effect of national criminal law should be absolutely clear to those subject to it. In *Kolpinghuis Nijmegen* (Case 80/86), the Court said that the national court's obligation to interpret domestic law to comply with EC Law was 'limited by the general principles of law which form part of Community law, and in particular, the principles of legal certainty and non-retroactivity'.

(d) Legitimate expectation

This principle is based on the concept that 'trust in the Community's legal order must be respected' (*Deuka* (Case 5/75) (A. G., Trabucchi)). Under the principle, 'assurances relied on in good faith should be honoured' (*Compagnie Continentale* v *Council* (Case 169/73) (A. G., Trabucchi)). It is closely linked to the principle of legal certainty. The relationship of the two principles is well illustrated by the case of *Mulder* (Case 120/86); Sharpston, E., 'Legitimate Expectation and Economic Reality' (1990) 15 EL Rev 103).

In order to stabilise milk production, Community rules required dairy farmers to enter into a five year non-marketing agreement, in exchange for which they were to receive a premium. In 1984, the Community introduced a system of milk quotas, under which milk producers would have to pay a super levy on milk produced in excess of their quota in any one year. Those who had entered into the non-marketing agreement for 1983 were not allowed any quota, because there was no provision for them in the regulations to do so. Having suspended production for the non-marketing period, they were effectively excluded from subsequent milk production. A farmer excluded in this way challenged the validity of the regulations. The Court held that:

> where such a producer, as in the present case, has been encouraged by a Community measure to suspend marketing for a limited period in the general interest and against payment of a premium, he may legitimately expect not to be subject, upon the expiry of his undertaking, to restrictions which specifically affect him because he has availed himself of the possibilities offered by the Community provisions.

The principle of legitimate expectation goes to ensure a fair process, however, and it cannot fetter the Community's freedom of action. The balance is not always easily struck but the issues involved in doing so were clearly formulated by Schwarze (1994) and quoted with approval by Sedley J in *R v Ministry of Agriculture and Fisheries, ex parte Hamble Fisheries*:

> The principle of legal certainty and the protection of legitimate expectation are fundamental to European Community law. Yet these principles are merely general maxims derived from the notion that the Community is based on the rule of law and can be applied to individual cases only if expressed in enforceable rules. Moreover, in most instances there are other principles which run counter to legal certainty and the protection of legitimate expectations; here the right balance will need to be struck. For instance, in the field of Community legislation the need for changes in the law can conflict with the expectation of those affected by such a change that the previous legal situation will remain in force ...

In *R v Ministry of Agriculture and Fisheries, ex parte Hamble Fisheries* the court decided that the legitimate expectations of the holders of fishing licences had not been infringed when the Ministry introduced a more restrictive fishing licensing policy to protect the remaining fish stocks allocated to Britain under the EC quota system. The Court of First Instance has recently held that operators in the Community's agricultural markets cannot have a legitimate expectation that an existing situation will prevail since the Community's intervention in these markets involves constant adjustments to meet changes in the economic situation (*O'Dwyer and Others v Council* (Cases T-466, 469, 473 and 477/93)).

(e) Natural Justice

This is a concept derived from English administrative law, but closely linked to the American 'due process'. It is sometimes used by the Court of Justice to mean no more than 'fairness', and is not always distinguishable from 'equity'. In the English administrative law sense, it implies, however, two basic principles: the right to an unbiased hearing and the right to be heard before the making of a potentially adverse decision affecting the person concerned (*see*, for example, *Ridge* v *Baldwin* [1964] AC 40). In a staff case, the Court has stated the principle as:

> a general principle of good administration to the effect that an administration which has to take decisions, even legally, which cause serious detriment to the person concerned, must allow the latter to make known their point of view, unless there is a serious reason for not doing so. (*Kuhner* (Case 33/79))

The principle is explicit in relation to decisions affecting an individual's free movement rights on public policy, public security and public health grounds, (Arts 5, 6, 7 Directive 64/221) and implicit in other decisions affecting the exercise of those rights. It involves the right to be given full reasons for the decision in order that they may be challenged. The right to natural justice is thus closely linked to the right to an effective remedy:

> Where, as in this case, it is more particularly a question of securing the effective protection of a fundamental right conferred by the Treaty on Community workers, the latter must ... be able to defend that right under the best possible conditions and have the possibility of deciding, with a full knowledge of the relevant facts, whether there is any point in their applying to the courts.

(*UNECTEF* v *Heylens and Others* (Case 222/86); para 15 of judgment). Issues of legal representation and access to justice are dealt with in more detail in relation to fundamental rights and effective remedies in Chapter 6.

SUPREMACY OF COMMUNITY LAW

Community law would be of little value if it were not able to override national law. Member states could avoid the application of Community rules disadvantageous to their interests by simply passing conflicting legislation. Although the Treaty does not contain a specific statement as to the supremacy and supra-nationality of Community law, that principle has been deduced by the European Court from the primary obligations of the Treaty. The obligation contained in Art 5 EC to ensure the effectiveness of Community law has been taken by the Court as determining the conflict between Community and national law.

In *Costa* v *ENEL* (Case 6/64), the Court declared in a landmark judgment:

> By contrast with ordinary international treaties, the Treaty has created its own legal systems which, on entry into force of the Treaty, became an integral part of the legal systems of the member states and which their courts are bound to apply. By creating a Community of unlimited duration, having its own institutions, its own personality, its

own legal capacity and capacity of representation on the international plane and more particularly, real powers stemming from a limitation of sovereignty or a transfer of powers from the States to the Community, the member states have limited their sovereign rights, albeit within limited fields, and have thus created a body of law which binds both their nationals and themselves.

On these grounds, the Court held that provisions of Italian legislation, subsequent to Italy's entry into the Community, which were incompatible with Community law, could not have effect. The *Costa* principles have been elaborated in a number of subsequent important decisions. In *Commission* v *Italy* (Case 48/71), the Court stated that Community law must be 'fully applicable at the same time and with identical effects over the whole territory of the Community without the member state being able to place any obstacles in the way.' Thus, once the European Court of Justice has declared a national law to be incompatible with Community law (under Arts 169–171, 173 EC Treaty), all competent national authorities are automatically prohibited from applying that law, without the need for the repeal of the offending legislation by the national legislature or other appropriate body.

The 'competent national authorities' include the national courts.

> … Every national court must, in a case within its jurisdiction, apply Community law in its entirety and protect rights which the latter confers on individuals and must accordingly set aside any provisons of national law which may conflict with it, whether prior or subsequent to the Community rule.

(*Simmenthal* (Case 106/77)). In the United Kingdom, this should mean that a lower court should apply the appropriate rule of Community law, even if this means not following a 'binding' precedent that points to an opposite course. The existing Community rule should, in fact, provide a good reason for 'distinguishing' the earlier case and for not following it.

Community law needs to be effectively enforced. This is mainly done in two ways: by private individuals in the national courts, and by the Commission in proceedings brought before the European Court of Justice. Once it was established by the Court that Community law is directly effective and prevails over national law, the way was open for an individual with a right under Community law to bring proceedings in the national courts and to make use of national legal remedies to enforce it. Increasingly, the Court has come to see this individual-centred law enforcement process as the way forward, both on the grounds of cost effectiveness from the Community's point of view and as a means of arming the EU citizen with Community rights which he can see are of tangible value to him (Mancini, G. F., 'The Making of a Constitution for Europe' (1989) 26 CML Rev 594). For this reason, the doctrine of supremacy applies not only to substantive national law, but also to national court processes, if these prevent the rights conferred by Community law from being realised. In *R* v *Secretary of State for Transport, ex parte Factortame* (Case 213/89), a number of companies operating fishing vessels in British waters (most of them Spanish owned) sought judicial review of the entry into force of the provisions of the Merchant Shipping Act 1988. The contested sections of the Act changed the rules for the registration of fishing vessels as British, and were alleged to breach rules of Community law relating to freedom of establishment under Art 52 EC and discrimination on grounds of nationality under Art 6. The applicants sought an injunction against the Crown to restrain the enforcement of the Act against them until the issue was resolved by the European Court of Justice. The House of Lords refused the application for interim relief, maintaining that injunctions were not available against the Crown. The ECJ, on the preliminary issue, held that such national limitations on remedies should not prevent the enforcement of Community rights, and that British rules on the availability of remedies should be overruled to provide the necessary relief for the applicants. In *Re M* [1994] 1 AC 377, the House of Lords subsequently decided that injunctive relief *was* available against the Crown, an interesting example of how national law has tended to follow Community law.

In *Marshall (No 2)* (Case C-271/91), the Court of Justice held that Art 6 of Directive 76/207 EC, which entitles those who consider themselves to be wronged by breach of the equal treatment provisions to have the means 'as are necessary ... to pursue their claims by judicial process' meant that they must have an effective remedy. A court of limited jurisdiction would, therefore, have to ignore the financial limits on its jurisdiction if this was necessary to enable the applicant to have the full compensation to which she was entitled under the Directive.

SUPREMACY AND UNITED KINGDOM LAW

Under United Kingdom law, treaties entered into by the Government do not have direct effect in United Kingdom law until they are incorporated by statute (*Blackburn* v *Attorney-General* [1971] 1 WLR 1037). Until that time, they merely have persuasive effect, and may, as is the case in the interpretation of the common law in the light of European Convention on Human Rights, be used to resolve an ambiguity in domestic law (*Derbyshire County Council* v *Times Newspapers Ltd* [1991] 4 All ER 795). Community law was incorporated by the European Communities Act 1972.

The combined effects of ss 2(1) and 3(1) is that directly effective Community law must be recognised and enforced in the UK. Section 2(1) provides that:

All such rights, powers, liabilities, obligations and restrictions from time to time created or arising by or under the Treaties, and all such remedies and procedures from time to time provided for by or under the Treaties, *as in accordance with the Treaties are without further enactment to be given legal effect* or used in the United Kingdom shall be recognised and available in law, and be enforced, allowed and followed accordingly; and the expression "enforceable Community right" and similar expressions shall be read as referring to one to which this subsection applies. (emphasis added)

It is clear that, under this section, only those Community measures which are, by the Treaty required to be given immediate effect without further enactment, such as the

Treaty provisions themselves, and Community regulations, could fall within this category and be enforced by the English Courts. The subsequent development of the European Court of Justice's doctrine of direct effect of directives has therefore raised problems of interpretation for English courts. However, the status of a Community provision and the scope of its application is a matter for the European Court of Justice, and British courts are obliged under s 3(1) to treat such a question 'as a question of law ... to be determined ... in accordance with the principles laid down by and any relevant decision of the European Court'.

Whatever questions might arise about the scope of the primacy of Community law, it had become part of national law.

> The EEC Treaty and all its provisions are now part of the law of England: that is clear from the European Communities Act 1972. We have to give force to the Treaty as being incorporated lock, stock and barrel into our law here. (*Re Westinghouse Uranium Contract* [1978] AC 547 at 564 (Lord Denning))

The major difficulty for English courts has been acceptance of the obligation to give effect to earlier Community legislation or Treaty provisions in preference to later national legislation. Under English constitutional doctrine, Community law was incorporated as it then was by the 1972 Act. If there is subsequent English legislation that directly conflicts with Community law, the doctrine of implied repeal would require the courts to give effect to Parliamentary sovereignty, and assume that Parliament had, impliedly, repealed the 1972 Act, to the extent that the later English legislation was inconsistent with Community law. The English courts coped with this problem in the earlier days of British membership by interpreting English law in such a way as to ensure compliance.

In *R* v *Secretary of State for Transport, ex p Factortame Ltd* [1991] 1 AC 603, where the Act of 1988 (see above) was clearly inconsistent with Art 7 and 52 EC Treaty, following the judgment of the European Court of Justice, Lord Bridge said the terms of the European Communities Act 1972 made it clear that 'it was the duty of United Kingdom court, when delivering final judgment, to override any rule of national law found to be in conflict with any directly enforceable rule of Community law' (*Factortame*, p 659).

The implication that this obligation to override national law only arose following an adverse reference to the European Justice was not taken up by the House of Lords in *Equal Opportunities Commission* v *Secretary of State for Employment* [1994] 1 All ER 910, where the House of Lords had to consider whether the limitations on claiming unfair dismissal imposed by the Employment Protection (Consolidation) Act 1978 on part-time workers was consistent with Art 119 EC Treaty, and the equal treatment Directive 76/207. Ninety per cent of such workers are women, and the House decided that that the five year employment period which qualified part-time workers for a claim, was unfairly discriminatory in comparison to the two year qualifying period for the (largely male) full-time workers, and could not be objectively justified. The House rejected the need for any reference to the Court of Justice and the suggestion that it had no power to declare that the statute was in breach of Community law:

> A declaration that the threshold provisions of the 1978 Act are incompatible with Community law would suffice for the purposes [of] … the EOC and is capable of being granted consistently with the precedent afforded by *Factortame*.

It thereupon granted a declaration that the relevant provisions of the 1978 Act were incompatible with Art 119 EC Treaty, and Directives 75/117 (equal pay) and 76/207 (equal treatment).

Where there is such an incompatibilty, it is not sufficient for the member state to rely upon the judgment of its own courts, or even of the European Court of Justice, to that effect. Such inconsistent provisions must be amended or repealed in the interests of the transparency of national law. This is an aspect of the wider principle of legal certainty. In *Commission* v *France* (Case 167/73), the Court had found part of the French Code de Travail Maritime incompatible with Art 48 EC Treaty of free movement of workers. The French Government maintained that in practice the Government exempted EC nationals from the Code, and that there was no actual infringement. The Court disagreed, and said that the maintenance of the discriminatory provisions created uncertainty and 'an ambiguous state of affairs', and constituted, in itself, an infringement of Community law.

Further reading

Collins, L., (1990) *European Community Law in the United Kingdom* (4th edn), Butterworths, Chapters 1 and 2.

Curtin, D. and Meyers, H., 'The Principle of Open Government in Schengen and the European Union: Democratic Retrogression' (1993) 32 CML Rev 391.

Hartley, T. C., (1994) *The Foundations of European Community Law* (3rd edn) Clarendon Press, Chapter 5.

Lasok, D. and Bridge, J. W., (1989) *Law and Institutions of the European Communities* Butterworths, Chapter 4.

Lenaerts, K., 'Fundamental Rights to be included in a Community Catalogue' (1991) 16 EL Rev 367.

Mancini, G. F., 'The Making of a Constitution for Europe' (1989) 26 CML Rev 595.

Pescatore, P., 'Fundamental Rights and Freedoms in the System of the European Communities' [1970] AJIL 343.

Schwarze, J., (1992) *European Administrative Law*, Sweet & Maxwell.

Sharpston, E., 'Legitimate Expectation and Economic Reality' (1990) 15 EL Rev 103.

Snyder, F., 'The Effectiveness of European Community Law: Institutions, Processes, Tools and Techniques' (1993) 56 MLR 19.

Steiner, J., (1994) *Textbook on EC Law* (4th edn), Blackstone Press, Chapters 1 and 2.

Toth, A. G., (1990) *The Oxford Encyclopaedia of European Law*, Clarendon Press.

Weiler, J. and Lockhart, N., 'Taking Rights Seriously': The European Court of Justice and its Fundamental Rights Jurisprudence' (1995) 32 CML Rev 579.

Weatherill, S. and Beaumont, P., (1993) *EC Law*, Penguin Books, pp 220–31.

Wyatt, D. and Dashwood, A., (1993) *Substantive European Community Law* (3rd edn), Sweet & Maxwell, pp 88–103.

5 Direct applicability and direct effect

The primary sources of Community law include, as we have seen, the EC Treaty and the related Treaties. Their provisions are elaborated in secondary legislation. The effect in the member states of the different types of Community law will depend upon the type of measure concerned, according to whether they are articles of the Treaties, regulations, directives or decisions.

REGULATIONS

The EC Treaty provides in Art 189 (2) that 'A regulation shall have general application. It shall be binding in its entirety and directly applicable.' The reference to 'directly applicable' means that no domestic legislation is needed to incorporate or transpose that type of Community law into national law. Community regulations are thus part of UK law without any further need of implementation. Indeed, any attempt at express incorporation is illegal, unless it is explicitly or implicitly required by the regulation itself (*Fratelli Variola Sp A* v *Amministrazione Italiana delle Finanze* (Case 34/73)). Whether or not a directly applicable measure is 'directly effective' (i.e., is capable of creating individual rights which a national court must recognise) will depend on the terms of the regulation. In practice, many do and are a fruitful source of individual rights (*see* for example, Regulation 1612/68 on employment rights of migrant workers, and Regulation 1408/71 on social security benefits for those employed and self-employed in other member states; *see* also Chapters 8 and 10).

TREATY ARTICLES

As a general principle, treaties and international agreements are not capable, in international law, of conferring rights on individuals in the courts of their own state.

The Treaty has, however, created, in the words of the European Court of Justice, 'its own legal system which…became an integral part of the legal systems of the member states'. (*Costa* v *ENEL* (Case 6/64)). The effect of this on the rights of individuals in relation to Treaty provisions was considered by the Court of Justice in relation to Art 12 in a historic judgment (*Van Gend en Loos* v *Nederlandse Administratie der Belastingen* (Case 26/62)). The facts are quite mundane, but the consequences of the decision have been highly significant in the development of Community law.

Van Gend en Loos had imported ureaformaldehyde from Germany into the Netherlands. It had been charged a customs duty. This breached the rules on the free movement of goods between member states, and in particular Art 12 EC Treaty. Van Gend claimed reimbursement from the Dutch Government in the Dutch courts. The court referred the question of whether or not the plaintiff could rely on Art 12 in the national court to the European Court of Justice.

The Court first of all addressed the general question of whether Treaty provisions could confer directly effective rights on individuals. It decided that they could:

> … The Community constitutes a new legal order of international law for the benefit of which the states have limited their sovereign rights, albeit within limited fields, and the subjects of which comprise not only the member states but also their nationals. *Independently of the legislation of member states Community law therefore not only imposes obligations on individuals but is also intended to confer on them rights which become part of their legal heritage. These rights arise not only where they are expressly granted by the Treaty, but also by reason of obligations which the Treaty imposes in a clearly defined way upon individuals as well as upon member states* and upon institutions of the Community. (emphasis added)

The Court dismissed the suggestion that, because there existed machinery under Art 169 of the Treaty to bring offending states before the Court of Justice, this must preclude the possibility of the use of Treaty provisions before national courts.

> A restriction of the guarantees against infringement … by member states…would remove all direct legal protection of the individual rights of their nationals. The vigilance of individuals concerned to protect their rights amounts to an effective supervision in addition to the supervision entrusted by Arts 169 and 170 to the diligence of the Commission and of the member states.

The Court then moved on to the more specific question of whether or not Art 12 could be directly effective in a national court. The Court decided that it could be:

> The wording of Art 12 contains a clear and unconditional prohibition … which is not qualified by any reservation on the part of states which would make its implementation conditional upon a positive legislative measure enacted under national law. The very nature of this prohibition makes it ideally adapted to produce direct effects in the legal relationship between member states and their subjects.

The decision is important because it set the process in motion for creating what has been called 'a judicial liability system' (*see* Snyder, F., 'The Effectiveness of European Community Law: Institutions, Processes, Tools and Techniques' (1993) 56 MLR 19). Under such a system, two objectives are established. In the first place, member states are to be pursued in their own courts by their own citizens where they fail to meet the obligations imposed on them by Community law. Secondly, Community citizens are to be endowed with new, directly enforceable, rights protected in their own courts.

The principle had been established in *Van Gend* but its application was still unclear. Certain Treaty provisions were to be enforceable against member states, provided that the obligations imposed were 'clear' and 'unconditional'. These were necessary preconditions, because many Treaty provisions are set out in the most general terms and do not appear to impose a commitment to do anything. Sometimes they express no more than a statement or an aspiration. Art 138a, for example, provides that 'Political parties at European level are important as a factor for integration within the Union.' Following *Van Gend*, and largely on the basis of chance appearance of appropriate cases before it, the Court has developed its criteria for determining whether particular Treaty provisions had direct effect, and if so, against whom.

In *Van Gend* the Court had found that Art 12 EC was directly effective against the state. It had reached this position to some extent, at least, on the basis that the state had entered into a commitment when it signed the Treaty. That commitment was owed not only to the other member states as parties, but also to its own citizens as actual or potential beneficiaries of the Treaty. However, the decision left unresolved the status of Treaty provisions between private citizens. Could a private citizen rely on an article of the Treaty, provided that it was sufficiently clear, precise and unconditional, against another private citizen or undertaking? The Court did not give an unequivocal reply to this question until 13 years later in *Defrenne* v *SABENA* (Case 43/75).

The case involved a claim by an air hostess against her employer for equal pay to that received by male stewards. Article 119 EC provides that 'Each member state shall during the first stage ensure and subsequently maintain the application of the principle that men and women should receive equal pay for equal work.' Belgium had not enacted legislation to bring this about. Could the claimant rely on Art 119 in her national court? The case was referred to the Court on a reference under Art 177 (*see* Chapter 24).

The Court dismissed the suggestion that the wording of the article confined the obligation to the member state itself:

> [35] In its reference to 'member states', Art 119 is alluding to those states in the exercise of all those of their functions which may usefully contribute to the implementation of the principle of equal pay ... Thus ... this provision is far from merely referring the matter to the powers of the national legislative authorities. Therefore, the reference to 'member states' in Art 119 cannot be interpreted as excluding the intervention of the

courts in the direct application of the Treaty ... Since Art 119 is mandatory in nature, the prohibition on discrimination between men and women applies not only to the action of public authorities, *but also extends to all agreements which are intended to regulate paid labour collectively, as well as to contracts between individuals.'* (emphasis added)

The effect of the decision in *Defrenne* was, therefore, that Art 119 could be used between individuals in relation to a contract of employment. Some Articles of the Treaty could thus be vertically effective (i.e., directly effective against the state, as in *Van Gend*) or both vertically and horizontally effective (i.e., directly effective between private individuals and undertakings) according to their wording and the context. In the ensuing years the Court has found Art 7 (now Art 6 EC, prohibiting discrimination on grounds of nationality) both vertically and horizontally effective. It was held in *Cowan* v *The French Treasury* (Case 186/87) to enable a British tourist, who had been attacked and injured in Paris, to obtain equal treatment in relation to payments of criminal injuries compensation by the French Government. In *Walrave and Koch* v *Association Union Cycliste Internationale* (Case 36/74), the Court held that:

> prohibition of such discrimination does not only apply to the acts of public authorities, but extends likewise to rules of any other nature aimed at regulating in a collective manner gainful employment and the provision of services.

Other Treaty provisions have also been held to be both horizontally and vertically effective, including Arts 30 and 34 (prohibiting the imposition of restrictions on the export and import of goods: *Dansk Supermarked* (Case 58/80)), Art 48 (free movement of workers: *Donà* v *Mantero* (Case 13/76)), Arts 52 and 59 (the right of establishment of businesses and professions and the right to provide services: *Thieffrey* v *Paris Bar Association* (Case 71/76)), Arts 85 and 86, the prohibition of restrictive agreements and the abuse of a monopoly position: *Brasseries de Haecht* (Case 48/72); *Marty* (Case 37/79), Art 128 (access to vocational education: *Gravier* v *City of Liège* (Case 293/83). The accumulation of case law in relation to a number of these provisions has resulted in a subtle change in the terminology of the Court. In the jurisprudence of the Court, many of these Treaty provisions, especially those relating to freedom of movement, have come to be regarded not merely as directly effective Treaty provisions at the suit of individuals in national courts, but also as fundamental rights of Community citizens. Direct effect has come to be regarded as fundamentally important to the development of the Community. As a judge of the Court of Justice has declared: Without direct effect, we should have a very different Community today – a more obscure, more remote Community barely distinguishable from so many other international organizations whose existence passes unnoticed by ordinary citizens. (Mancini, G. F. and Keeling, D. T., 'Democracy and the European Court of Justice' (1994) 57 MLR 175, 183).

THE IMPLEMENTATION OF DIRECTIVES

Directives were not originally seen as being capable of creating directly effective rights. In contrast to regulations, they are not described as directly applicable:

> A directive shall be binding, as to the result to be achieved, upon each member state to which it is addressed, but shall leave to the national authorities the choice of form and method. (Art 189 (third indent))

Directives are thus not directed, like regulations, at the world at large, but at member states. That did not, of course, in the case of Treaty articles in *Defrenne*, deter the Court from finding that individuals could also be bound by them. But, unlike Treaty articles, directives are always conditional. They depend, under Art 189, on the member state giving effect to them. They have, since the inception of the Treaty, been a form of legislative subsidiarity, giving the member state the option of the way in which it will legislate to meet to the Community's objectives. The problem, as it became clear to both the Commission and the Court, was that member states either simply did not implement directives by the date set for them, or implemented them in such a way as to fail, in whole or in part, to achieve their objectives.

Implementation does not mean that a directive must be directly transposed into national law. The Court described the member states obligations in *Commission v Germany (Re Nursing Directives)* (Case 29/84), para 23 of judgment:

> The implementation of a directive does not necessarily require legislative action in each member state. In particular, the existence of general principles of constitutional and administrative law may render the implementation by specific legislation superfluous, provided, however, that those principles guarantee that the national authorities will, in fact, apply the directive fully, and where the directive is intended to create rights for individuals, the legal position arising from those principles is sufficiently clear and precise, and the persons concerned are made fully aware of their rights, and where appropriate, are afforded the possibilty of relying upon them before national courts.

Although legislation may not always be necessary in relation to directives which are not intended to confer rights on individuals, the vast majority have either that intention, or at least, that effect if implemented. In such cases, the issue of circular letters, urging a change of policy, or a change in administrative practice, will not constitute implementation. Such practices, which may alter from time to time at the whim of the authority, and be quite unknown to the ordinary citizen, completely lack the certainty and transparency which Community law demands (*Commission v Belgium* (Case 102/79)).

A failure to implement fully often results in a complaint by interested individuals and groups to the relevant Directorate-General in the Commission. This will usually be followed by protracted correspondence between the Commission and the offending state. If this is unsuccessful, formal Art 169 proceedings may be instituted by the Commission in the European Court of Justice. Finally, if non-implementation persists, the case may come to a hearing before the Court and the Court may impose a penalty on the member state if its judgment is not complied with (Arts 169, 171 EC; *see* Chapter 22). The process, from first complaint to judgment, may take several years. Enforcement procedures, given the limited resources of the Commission, can only be a partial solution to the problem. Until all member states have implemented a directive, however, those states who fail to do so may gain an unfair competitive advantage. Many directives, particularly those aimed at reducing environmental pollution, can significantly increase business costs. In addition, individuals may be deprived of rights which Community law has been enacted to create for them. It is this situation to which the Court responded in its approach to unimplemented directives.

DIRECT EFFECT OF DIRECTIVES

It is clear from Art 189 that directives were not to be directly applicable in the same way as regulations. They required member states to act to give the directives effect in their territories. However, in *Grad* (Case 9/70), the Court suggested, in a case turning on the effect of a regulation, that a directive might have some effect in a state where it had not been implemented by the due date. In *Van Duyn* v *Home Office* (Case 41/74), the Court took its first important step towards recognising the direct effect of a directive.

The plaintiff in the case, Ms Van Duyn, a Dutch national, was a member of the Church of Scientology. She wished to enter the UK to work at the headquarters of the organisation. She was refused leave to enter. The UK government had decided some years previously that the Church of Scientology was an undesirable organisation, although no steps had been taken against it, except to publicise the government's view.

Prima facie, Ms Van Duyn, as a worker, had a right of entry under Art 48 EC Treaty. That right was, and remains, subject to the right of the host state to exclude and expel on public policy and public security grounds. The limits of the powers of the host state to derogate from its Treaty obligation on these grounds, and the extent of the procedural rights of those affected by such a decision, are set out in Directive 64/221. In particular, Art 3(1) of the directive provided that a decision should be based 'exclusively on the personal conduct of the individual concerned'. Ms Van Duyn argued that membership of an organisation could not be 'personal conduct' under Art 3(1). The UK government maintained that its power to refuse entry could not be limited in this way, because UK had not yet implemented Directive 64/221 (it remained unimplemented for another 20 years: Immigration (European Economic

Area) Order 1994, Chapter 12). The case was referred to the European Court of Justice under Art 177 where the Court refused to accept the position taken by the UK government:

> The United Kingdom observes that, since Art 189 of the Treaty distinguishes between the effects ascribed to regulations, directives and decisions, it must therefore be presumed that the Council, in issuing a directive rather than making a regulation, must have intended that the directive should have had an effect other than that of a regulation and accordingly that the former should not be directly applicable ... However ... it does not follow from this that other categories of acts mentioned in that article can never have similar effects. It would be incompatible with the binding effect attributed to a directive by Art 189 to exclude, in principle, the possibility that the obligation which it imposes may be invoked by those concerned. In particular, where the Community authorities have, by directive, imposed on member states the obligation to pursue a particular course of conduct, the useful effect of such an act would be weakened if individuals were prevented from relying on it before their national courts and if the latter were prevented from taking it into consideration as an element of Community law.

The guiding principle adopted in *Van Duyn* is that of ensuring the *effet utile* (the useful effect) of a measure in the territories and courts of member states. In addition to this pragmatic approach, there was another, implied principle that is known to continenental as well as to common lawyers, but was not mentioned in the case. That is the equitable doctrine of estoppel or the continental doctrine of the impermissibility of reliance on one's own turpitude. On this principle, it is not open to a member state to defend itself against a claim by an individual by raising its own failure to implement a directive as a defence (Advocate-General van Gerven in *Barber* (Case C-262/88)). Once the deadline for implementing a directive had passed, and not before (*see Ratti* (Case 148/78)) an individual could enforce the directive against the government of the state which had failed to implement it. It was thus vertically effective.

Not every directive is, however, effective in this way. As the Court said in *Van Duyn*, 'it is necessary to examine in every case, whether the nature, general scheme and wording of the provision in question are capable of having direct effects.' Are the provisions 'unconditional and sufficiently precise'? (*Becker* (Case 8/81)). If these criteria are met, the individual can enforce the unimplemented directive against the state. But what constitutes 'the state' ? Under Art 5, the obligation to implement Community law binds the member states. The Court has been prepared to give that term a broad interpretation. Initially, it referred to the state exercising various functions and it was not necessary that it should be engaged in activities normally carried on by the state, such as operating immigration controls, collecting taxes, enforcing public health measures. Directives were enforceable against it, in addition, when it was, say, simply acting as an employer.

In *Marshall* v *Southampton etc Health Authority* (Case 152/84), the complainant was employed by the Health Authority. She wished to retire at 65, the same age as her male colleagues. The rules of the authority required her to retire at the age of 60. She was dismissed on the grounds of her age at 62, and brought proceedings against the authority on grounds of unfair dismissal. Discrimination on grounds of sex in relation to conditions of employment is prohibited by Directive 76/207. The Sex Discrimination Act 1975, which had been enacted to implement the directive while it was still in draft form, contained an exception, allowing differential male and female retirement ages. There was no such exception in the directive. To that extent, therefore, the United Kingdom had failed to implement the directive. Could Ms Marshall enforce it against the Health Authority? The European Court of Justice, on a referral under Art 177 EC, held that she could.

The Court decided that the Health Authority in this case was bound:

> Where a person involved in legal proceedings is able to rely on a directive as against the state, he may do so regardless of the capacity in which the latter is acting, whether employer or public authority. In either case it is necessary to prevent the state from taking advantage of its own failure to comply with Community law.

The Court added that it was for the national courts to determine the status of a body for the purposes of determining whether a directive can be directly effective against it. It has, however, continued to give guidance. It decided in *Costanza* v *Commune di Milano* (Case 103/88) that 'the state' included 'all organs of the administration, including decentralised authorities such as municipalities'. How 'decentralised' a body could be and still be bound was considered by the Court in *Foster* v *British Gas* (Case C-188/189).

The case involved another dispute about the application of Directive 76/207 to retirement ages for women. The complaint was brought against British Gas in relation to a period before its privatisation. Was Directive 76/207 vertically effective against it? The case turned on the status of British Gas at the time. Was it an 'emanation (organ) of the State'? The Court held that it was because the directive may be relied upon against a body

> whatever its legal form, which has been made responsible, pursuant to a measure adopted by the state, for providing a public service under the control of the state, and had, for that purpose, special powers beyond those which result from the normal rules applicable in relations between individuals, is included in any event among the bodies against which the provisions of a directive capable of having direct effect may be relied upon (para [20] of judgment).

In subsequent cases courts of England and Wales, applying these principles, have decided that the then publicly owned Rolls Royce was not a public body providing a public service against which a directive could be enforced (*Doughty* v *Rolls Royce* [1992] ICR 538). However, in *Griffin* v *South West Water Services* [1995] *Current Law Week* Vol 3, January 20, a privatised water authority was held to be within the *Foster* definition. The Court said that the question is not 'whether the body in question is under the control of the state. The legal form of the body is irrelevant ... It is irrelevant, too, that the state does not possess day-to-day control over the activities of the body.'

Finally, it should be noted that the fact that an unimplemented directive can be enforced vertically against the state and emanations of the state does not mean that the state is thereby absolved from implementing it by incorporating it into national law. Only by doing so can a directive that creates rights, for example, by enabling undertakings in other member states to put in bids for public works contracts, provide the intended beneficiaries with full information and the means to enforce those rights effectively (*Commission* v *Germany (Re Public Works and Public Supply Contracts)* (Case C-433/93)).

DIRECTIVES: HORIZONTAL EFFECT?

It was thus clear that directives had vertical effect against the state and emanations of the state. But could a directive have horizontal effect, that is, between individuals, after the due date for implementation had passed? Applying the reasoning that the Court used in relation to Treaty provisions, especially those used in support of the direct horizontal effect of Art 119 in relation to the application of equal pay to private contracts between individuals, it might be thought that this was the logical next step for directives. It seemed unfair, to say the least, that whether or not two employees, one in the state sector and the other privately employed, could enforce an unimplemented directive, depended on the status of the employer. The Court, however, did not take that step. Although powerful arguments were deployed by at least two Advocates-General for the Court to hold directives horizontally effective, it declined to do.

Its reluctance was partly political as national courts were already showing some resistance to giving vertical effect to directives. One supreme administrative court had quite flatly refused to follow *Van Duyn* in a case involving the same directive (*Minister for the Interior* v *Cohn-Bendit* [1980]1 CMLR 543). So, in *Marshall* (above) the Court stated quite clearly that

> ... it must be emphasised that, according to Art 189 of the EEC Treaty the binding nature of a directive, which constitutes the basis for the possibility of relying on the directive before a national court, exists only in relation to 'each member state to which it is addressed'. It follows that a directive may not of itself impose obligations on an individual and that a provision of a directive may not be relied upon as such against such a person.

There were other legal reasons for rejecting the horizontal effect of directives. To give them almost the same effect as regulations was seen as unfair, because, unlike regulations, they did not have to be published in the *Official Journal*. The government could not plead lack of knowledge, because the directive was addressed to it, but an individual on whom it might impose an obligation could legitimately argue that he had had no notice of it. The principle of legal certainty demanded that individuals should not be bound by legal provisions of which they were unaware. This argument lost some of its force when the Treaty on European Union came into effect on 1 November 1993. Under the amended Art 191(2) directives as well as regulations must now be published in the Official Journal. They enter into force on the day specified, or if there is no date fixed, then on the twentieth day following that of their publication.

The fact that directives were to be published was one of the arguments marshalled by Advocate-General Lenz in *Faccini Dori* v *Recreb s.r.l.* (Case C-91/92), paras [43] to [73]. He also argued that failure to implement a directive in one member state gave an undeserved competitive advantage to that state. Nevertheless, the Court insisted that to give horizontal effect to directives would make them practically indistinguishable from regulations, and that clearly was not the intention of Art 189. There were, in any event, now two possibilities open to an individual where a government had failed to implement a directive which was intended to confer a benefit on him. In suitable cases, the national court could be called upon to 'interpret' national legislation in conformity with the directive, the principle of 'indirect effect'. If this was not possible, the individual could claim compensation against the offending government for non-implementation (*see Francovich* v *Italy* (Cases C-6 & C-9/90)). Both these alternatives will be discussed.

INDIRECT EFFECT

The obvious limitation of the application of vertical effect is that, however generously the Court has interpreted 'emanation of the state' in favour of individual litigants, the term clearly cannot apply to the private commercial employer. The anomaly created between public and private employment in relation to the direct effect of Directive 76/207 on equal employment rights was most starkly thrown into relief by two cases which came before the Court in 1984 (*Von Colson* (Case 14/83), and *Harz* v *Deutsche Tradax* (Case 79/83)). Ms Von Colson was employed by the prison service and Ms Harz by a private company. Both cases were referred to the European Court of Justice by the West German Labour Court. Germany had implemented directive 76/207, but the German law only provided nominal and not proper compensation as required by the directive (*see Marshall (No 2)* (Case C-271/91). Clearly, Ms Von Colson could enforce the directive vertically against her employer and obtain full compensation for the discrimination she had suffered, but Ms Harz could not. The Court adopted a novel approach that would have the effect of enabling both claimants to compensation.

The Court's starting point was Art 5 EC Treaty, the obligation of member states to take all appropriate measures to give effect to Community law 'is binding on all the authorities of member states including, for matters within their jurisdiction, the courts. It follows that, in applying the national law … national courts are required to interpret their national law in the light of the wording and the purpose of the directive in order to achieve the result referred to in the third paragraph of Art 189.' The German courts therefore had to 'interpret' the national law on sexual discrimination in such a way so that there was no limit on proper compensation to which injured parties were entitled. On this basis, the German court which had referred the case could award proper compensation to both litigants. *Von Colson* dealt with a case which turned on the interpretation of legislation put into place to implement the directive in question. Was this new interpretative doctrine confined to cases where the member state had implemented the directive but had done so incorrectly? The Court answered this question in the negative in *Marleasing SA v La Commercial SA* (Case C-106/89). In *Marleasing* a Spanish court was confronted with a national law on the constitution of companies which conflicted with an EC Company Directive 68/71. The directive had not been implemented in Spain. The Court of Justice, nevertheless, held that:

> in applying national law, whether the provisions concerned pre-date or post-date the directive, the national court asked to interpret national law is bound to do so in every way possible in the light of the text and the aims of the directive to achieve the results envisaged by it and thus comply with Art 189(3) of the Treaty.

A national court, might, therefore, be required to 'interpret' a provision of national law that preceded the directive by many years, and which had been enacted with quite different considerations in mind. The extent of this interpretative obligation has caused particular problems for the UK courts. These are considered below. The Court has recently made it clear that the courts of member states should act on the presumption that relevant national legislation, whether passed before or after the relevant directive, was intended to implement it. However, whether this is in fact possible, in the light of the wording of the national provision, is essentially a matter of interpretation by those courts (*Wagner Miret*) Case 343/92)).

There is one exception to the obligation to interpret national law in conformity with an unimplemented directive. That is where the national measure, which ought to be interpreted in this way, imposes criminal liability. The Court held in *Officier van Justitie* v *Kolpinghuis Nijmegen* (Case 80/86), that the obligation of the national court is limited by:

> the general principles of law which form part of Community law and in particular the principles of certainty and non-retroactivity … A directive cannot, of itself and independently of a national law adopted by a member state for its implementation, have the effect of determining or aggravating the liability in criminal law of persons who act in contravention of the provisions of that directive.

A RIGHT TO COMPENSATION FOR NON-IMPLEMENTATION

The possibility of taking action against the state for failing to implement a directive arose in *Francovich and Bonifaci* v *Republic of Italy* (Cases C-6 & C9/90). The case arose after an Italian company went into liquidation, leaving Mr Francovich and other employees with unpaid arrears of salary. Directive 80/987 EC required member states to set up a compensation scheme for employees in these circumstances, but Italy had not established one. Mr Francovich therefore wanted compensation from the Italian government. The case was referred to the Court of Justice. The Court was asked whether the directive had direct effect, whether the member state was liable for the damage arising from its failure to implement the directive, and to what extent it was liable for damages for violation of its obligations under Community law.

The Court decided that the directive was insufficiently precise to have direct effect. However, it emphasised that the EC Treaty creates a legal order which is binding upon member states and citizens. The *effet utile* of Community law would be diminished if individuals were not able to obtain damages after suffering loss incurred because of a violation of Community law by a member state. There was an implied obligation under Art 5 EC to compensate individuals affected by such a violation. The Court held that, in cases such as this, where there was a violation of the states obligation to implement Community law under Art 189, there was a right to compensation from the state, provided that three conditions were satisfied:

1   The result which had to be attained by the directive involved rights conferred on individuals.
2   The content of those rights could be identified from the provisions of the directive.
3   There must exist a causal link between the failure by the member state to fulfil its obligations and the damage suffered by the person affected.

The Court did not decide how the extent of liability was to be determined as this was to be a matter for national law. National procedures had, however, 'to ensure the full protection of rights which individuals might derive from Community law'. In this particular case, the failure of Italy to implement the directive in question had already been established by the Court. Generally, there will not be a defence to simple non-implementation because, whatever practical difficulties there may be, the obligation to implement is strict (*Commission* v *Belgium* (Case 1/86)). Problems will, however, arise in determining the liability of a state where it believes, in good faith, that it has taken all the necessary steps to implement a directive into national law, but a subsequent judgment of the Court of Justice decides that it has not, in fact, done so. This remains an area still to be elaborated by decisions of the Court. An important indicator is the recent opinion of Advocate-General Leger in *R* v *Ministry of Agriculture, Fisheries and Food, ex parte Hedley Lomas (Ireland) Ltd* (Case C-59/94). The opinion considers the principle and scope of state liability under

Francovich, not only in the context of unimplemented Directives but for other breaches of Community law too.

In *Lomas* the English High Court referred three questions to the Court of Justice relating to the refusal of MAFF to grant licences for the export of live sheep to Spain because of concerns about the treatment of animals in Spanish slaughterhouses. The first two questions concerned whether or not these restrictions were in breach of Art 34 EC (which prohibits restrictions on exports to other member states), and if so, whether the restrictions were justified under Art 36 (which allows such restrictions in the interest, inter alia of animal health, Chapter 15). The third question concerned the question of damages against the Government if the restrictions were unlawful. The Advocate-General said that damages in *Francovich* were not restricted to breaches of Community law by failing to implement directives. *Francovich* had created a general principle of state liability. There should be liability where the state was 'seriously' at fault.

Fault is 'serious' where, for example, a state acts in clear contravention of a decision of the Court. So, too, would the adoption by the state of legislation which is clearly at odds with the Treaty. In the instant case the Advocate-General concluded that the fault was serious enough to attract damages liability. First, export licences were refused on the ground that slaughterhouses in Spain did not comply with Community requirements, yet the UK was unable to furnish proof of such a breach of Community law and relied merely on a risk of mistreatment. Second, the Commission had advised MAFF several months previously that such retaliatory action would be contrary to Community law.

The Opinion of the Advocate-General is not, of course, binding on the Court. Its general approach has, however, been substantially followed in two other cases, in a judgment delivered by the Court in March 1996 (*Brasserie du Pêcheur SA v Germany* (Case C-46/93) and *R v Secretary of State for Transport, ex parte Factortame (No 4)* (Case C-48/93)).

DIRECT EFFECT IN UNITED KINGDOM COURTS

Treaty provisions

Under the law and practice within the UK, the Treaty of Rome, like any other Treaty, is only effective in that country after it is enacted, and only to the extent of its enactment by the Westminster Parliament (*Blackburn v Attorney-General* [1971] 2 All ER 1380 at 1382; Lord Denning MR). Britain's accession to the European Community was given effect in national law by the European Communities Act 1972. The implementation of Community rights will, therefore, depend on the extent to which Community law has been fully incorporated by the Act, and the extent to which the British courts are prepared to interpret national law in conformity with Community obligations (*R v Secretary for Foreign and Commonwealth*

Office, ex parte Rees-Mogg (QBD) [1994] 1 CMLR 101; European Communities Act 1972, s. 2(1), *see* Chapter 4, above).

Only those provisions which 'in accordance with the Treaties are *without further enactment* to be given legal effect' in the courts of England and Wales, Scotland and Northern Ireland (European Communities Act 1972 s 2(1)).

Section 3 (1) of the 1972 Act provides that:

> For the purposes of all legal proceedings any question as to the meaning or effect of any of the Treaties, or as to the validity, meaning or effect of any Community instrument, shall be treated as a question of law and, if not referred to the European Court, be for determination as such in accordance with the principles laid down by and any relevant decision of the European Court or of any Court attached thereto.

Under s. 2 (1), British Courts have not had any difficulty in giving effect to Treaty provisions or regulations, since 'in accordance with the Treaties' both are to be given legal effect without further legislative enactment. Thus, the directly effective provisions of Art 119 on equal pay were, in *Macarthys Ltd* v *Smith* (Case 129/79) held to prevail over the Equal Pay Act 1970. The Court of Appeal held that it was bound to give effect to Art 119 because it was directly applicable. Lord Denning MR expressed the position in this way:

> The provisions of Art 119 of the EEC Treaty take priority over anything in our English statute on equal pay which is inconsistent with Art 119. *That priority is given by our law. It is given by the European Communities Act 1972 itself.* ([1981] QB 180 at 200–1) (emphasis added)

There was no difficulty where the legislation of the United Kingdom Parliament could be construed in accordance with Community law. The problem came where national law had been enacted after British membership in a way that clearly conflicted with a directly effective Treaty provision. In *Macarthys* Lord Denning had said that:

> If the time should come when our parliament deliberately passes an Act with the intention of repudiating the Treaty or any provision in it – and says so in express terms – then I should have thought that it would be the duty of our courts to follow the statute of our Parliament. ([1979] ICR 785 at 789)

When the House of Lords was confronted with the Merchant Shipping Act 1988, which had been enacted to prevent Spanish fishermen from 'quota hopping' into British fishing areas, the moment seemed to have arrived. It was fairly clear that these measures discriminated on grounds of nationality against the right of Spanish fishing businesses to establish themselves in the United Kingdom in accordance with the directly effective Arts 7 and 52 EC Treaty. The House of Lords was, however, prepared, following a reference to the European Court of Justice, to hold the Act to be without effect to the extent of the conflict. 'It is the duty of a United Kingdom court', said Lord Bridge in his speech, 'when delivering final judgment, to override any rule of national law found to be in conflict with any directly enforceable rule of Community law' (*R* v *Secretary of State for Transport, ex parte Factortame* [1991] 1 AC 603 at 659).

Directly effective directives

British courts have had more difficulty with directly effective directives. As we have seen, prima facie, directives are not directly applicable, and so do not fall into that category of Community provisions which, without further enactment, are to be given legal effect under the European Communities Act s 2(1). However, where they have been held by the Court of Justice to create directly effective rights they have been applied vertically against emanations of the state by the British courts, following references to the Court of Justice, as in *Marshall and Foster* v *British Gas* (above). The House of Lords has even held parts of the Trade Union and Labour Relations Act 1978 to be incompatible with a directly effective Directive 76/207 in *Equal Opportunities Commission* v *Secretary of State for Employment* [1994] 1 All ER 910. The courts have experienced the most difficulty with the *Von Colson* doctrine of indirect effect, where it is accepted that the directive in question is not directly effective, that is, horizontally, between private parties.

Where a statute has been enacted to implement a directive, the courts have shown themselves capable of creative interpretation, on the basis that parliament would have intended that the statute be interpreted in conformity with the directive, even if it had been misunderstood at the time of enactment. In *Litster* v *Forth Dry Dock* [1989] 2 WLR 634, the House of Lords had to consider Directive 77/187, which is intended to protect workers dismissed in connection with a business transfer. The directive had been implemented by the Transfer of Undertakings (Protection of Employment) Regulations (SI 1981/1794). The UK regulations did not, however, protect employees who had been dismissed immediately before the transfer of the undertaking. Several decisions of the Court had held that workers dismissed immediately before the transfer were to be treated as having been employed by the undertaking at the time when it took place. The House of Lords decided that it was the duty of the UK court to give the UK regulation 'a construction which accords with the decisions of the European Court upon the corresponding provisions of the directive to which the regulation was intended to give effect'. (Lord Keith)

Indirect effect

The House of Lords took a different line in *Duke* v *GEC Reliance* [1988] 2 WLR 359. The case turned on the legality of differental retirement ages for men and women, the same point as in *Marshall*, above. In this case, though, the employer was a private undertaking, and the question of vertical effect could not arise. Did the Court have to interpret the Sex Discrimination Act 1975 in accordance with the equal treatment directive dated 9 February 1976? The House of Lords decided that it did not. Parliament had passed the Act in the belief that it was entitled to have discriminatory retirement ages even when the directive (which was then in draft) came into effect.

> Of course a UK court will always be willing and anxious to conclude that United Kingdom law is consistent with Community law. Where an Act is passed for the purpose of giving effect to an obligation imposed by a directive or other instrument a British court will seldom encounter difficulty in concluding that the language of the Act is effective for the intended purpose. But the construction of a British Act of Parliament is a matter of judgment to be determined by British courts and to be derived from the language of the legislation considered in the light of the circumstances prevailing at the date of the enactment ... It would be most unfair to the respondent to distort the construction of the Sex Discrimination Act 1975 in order to accommodate the Equal Treatment Directive 1976 as construed by the European Court of Justice in the 1986 Marshall case. (Lord Templeman)

This decision has been criticised, but its approach was again followed in *Webb* v *Emo Air Cargo* [1993] 1 WLR 49, in which the House of Lords arrived at the same conclusion, despite the clear words of the Court of Justice in *Marleasing* (above). The courts of member states were required to interpret national legislation in the light of the directive, whether the national provisions 'pre-date or post-date the directive'. Lord Keith seized on the words in the Court of Justice's judgment 'as far as possible, in the light of the wording and purpose of the directive' to conclude that UK courts were only obliged to do so where the domestic law is 'open to an interpretation consistent with it': (*Webb* v *Emo Air Cargo*).

It seems clear that the House of Lords feels that to do more than 'interpret' national legislation by, for example, substituting words or adding words which are not there, moves the function of the courts, from the realm of interpretation into the role of legislating, which is, essentially, a matter for Parliament. This reluctance is reflected in other, later, decisions by other courts and tribunals (*see*, for example: *Finnegan* v *Clowney Youth Training Programme Ltd* [1990] 2 All ER 546; *Wychavon District Council* v *Secretary of State for the Environment*, *The Times*, 7 January 1994; *Gould & Cullen* v *Commissioners of Customs and Excise* (VAT Tribunal) [1994] 1 CMLR 347). Lord Slynn, a former Lord Advocate, and now a Lord of Appeal, has expressed the anxiety of British judges on the issue:

> I find it difficult to say that a statute of 1870 must be interpreted in the light of a 1991 directive. If the former is in conflict with the latter, it is not for the judges to strain language but for Governments to introduce new legislation.

(*Introducing a European Legal Order* (1992) p 124) Although this observation is consistent with English constitutional principles, it is at odds with the judgment of the Court of Justice in *Simmenthal* (case 106/77):

> ... Every national court must, in a case within its jurisdiction, apply Community law in its entirety and protect rights which the latter confers on individuals and must accordingly set aside any provision of national law which may conflict with it, whether prior or subsequent to the Community rule.

This apparent incompatability between British constitutional law and Community principles has yet to be resolved.

Unimplemented directives: a continuing problem

The approach adopted by the Court to individuals affected by the non-implementation of directives was, as we have seen, a pragmatic response to a perceived problem of inequality between member states. Those states which failed to implement directives on time might actually enjoy an advantage over those states which had shouldered the burden which the directive had imposed. Individuals in the non-implementing state would be deprived of the benefits which the directive was intended to confer upon them. Despite the increase in Art 169 proceedings, bringing defaulting member states before the Court is a slow and only partial solution to the problem (*see* Chapter 22). Even if it achieves belated implementation of the directive, it cannot provide compensation to those individuals who have been deprived for many years of its beneficial effect. The creation, in the first instance, of the doctrine of vertical effect, the right to enforce the directive against the defaulting member state, and a gradual enlargement of that right by the Court so that enforcement is now possible against a whole range of state or state-sponsored bodies, has provided a valuable weapon in the hands of intended beneficiaries.

The failure of the Court to grasp the nettle and to give directives horizontal direct effect between individuals in *Marshall* and *Dori* has only partly been mitigated by the development of the interpretative obligation of indirect effect expounded in *Harz* and *Marleasing*. This approach depends very much on the willingness of national courts to engage in creative interpretation of national legislation. As we have seen, there is a marked reluctance, most notably by the English courts, to do this, especially where the national legislation has preceded the directive. At the present time the Court seems reluctant, as it demonstrated in *Wagner Miret* to be more specific in defining the nature of the national court's interpretative obligation. The Court has made it clear that it expects that individuals who cannot establish the vertical effect of a directive, or who are unsuccessful in persuading a national court to give it interpretative effect, to claim damages against their own member state. This will involve a direct claim against the member state for its failure to implement on the basis of the Court's decision in *Francovich*. It may, as in *Faccini Dori*, require the individual to commence a whole new legal action, after having failed to establish the interpretative effect of the directive against another individual.

The criteria for determining the extent of fault of a member state for non-implementation are still being worked out by the Court. However, a claim against a member state cannot be regarded as a wholly satisfactory substitute for the enforcement of a directive against those who were intended to be bound by it. The member state may have believed, in good faith, that it had taken all necessary steps to implement the directive, and it may be hard to establish fault. These issues are more fully explored in Chapter 24. Even if fault is established, damages may not constitute a satisfactory remedy for, say, the failure to set up an area of environmental protection, as required by an unimplemented directive. The losers may be the local community as a whole rather than an individual and it may be impossible to establish any causal link, as required by *Francovich*, between the failure to implement the directive and any specific loss suffered by an individual. These difficulties will probably remain unless and until the Court accepts that unimplemented directives may have horizontal as well as vertical direct effect.

Further reading

Bebr, G., 'Case note on *Francovich*' (1992) 29 CML Rev 557.

De Burca, G., 'Giving Effect to European Community Directives' (1992) 55 MLR 215.

Caranta, R., 'Government Liability after *Francovich* (1993) 52 CLJ 272.

Curtin, D., 'The Province of Goverment: Delimiting the Direct Effect of Directives in the Common Law Context' (1990) 15 EL Rev 195.

Coppel, J., 'Rights, Duties and the End of Marshall' (1994) 57 MLR 859.

Demetriou, M., 'Are Member States being led to the Slaughter?' New Law Journal, Vol 145 No 6075, p 1102 (21 July 1995).

Hartley, T. C., (1994) *The Foundations of European Community Law* (3rd edn), Clarendon Press, Chapter 7.

Howells, 'European Directives: The Emerging Dilemmas' (1991) *MLR* 456.

Mancini, G. F. and Keeling, D., 'Democracy and the European Court of Justice' (1994) 57 MLR 175, 183.

Mead, P., 'The Obligation to Apply European Law: Is Duke Dead?' (1991) 16 El Rev 490.

Robinson, W., 'Annotations on Case C-91/92 *Paola Faccini Dora* v *Recrec s.r.l.*' (1995) 32 CML Rev 629.

Slynn, G., (1992) *Introducing a New Legal Order*, Sweet & Maxwell.

Snyder, F., 'The Effectiveness of European Community Law: Institutions, Processes, Tools and Techniques' (1993) 56 MLR 19.

Steiner, J., 'From Direct Effects of *Francovich*: Shifting Means of Enforcement of Community Law' (1993) 18 El Rev 3.

Tridimas, T., 'Horizontal Effect of Directives: A Missed Opportunity' (1994) 19 EL Rev 621.

Wyatt, D. and Dashwood, A., *European Community Law*, (1993) (3rd edn), Sweet & Maxwell, Chapter 4.

6 Fundamental rights and the European Convention on Human Rights in the Community

Article F.2 EC Treaty, as amended by TEU, provides that :

> The Union shall respect fundamental rights, as guaranteed by the European Convention for the Protection of Human Rights and Fundamental Freedoms signed in Rome on 4 November 1950 and as they result from the constitutional traditions common to the member states.

The effect of Art F. 2 is to give formal recognition in the Treaty to what has been part of the jurisprudence of the Court since *Stauder* (Case 29/69). In that case the Court declared that 'fundamental human rights are enshrined in the general principles of Community law and protected by the Court.' In *A v Commission* (Case T–10/93) the Court of First Instance noted the commitment in Art F. 2 to respect the fundamental rights guaranteed by the Convention and said, repeating the words of the Court of Justice in the *ERT* case (Case C–260/89), '... the Court draws inspiration from the constitutional traditions common to member states and from the guidelines supplied by international treaties for the protection of human rights on which member states have collaborated or of which they are signatories' (*see*, in particular, the judgment in *Nold v Commission* (Case 4/73)). The European Convention on Human Rights has special significance in that respect (*see*, in particular *Johnston v Chief Constable of the Royal Ulster Constabulary* (Case 221/84)). It follows that, as the Court held in its judgment in *Wachauf v Germany* (Case 5/88), the Community cannot accept measures which are incompatible with observance of the human rights thus recognised and guaranteed.'

What this means is that when there is a conflict between a national law which is, for example, intended to implement Community law, but does so in such a way as to breach the Convention, the Court will rule the national measure as contrary to Community law. In the *Johnston* case, national measures intended to prohibit sexual discrimination in Northern Ireland and to provide a remedy for those alleging discriminatory behaviour, were held contrary to Community law because the Court held that they did not give complainants an effective remedy as required by Art 13 of the Convention. It must, however, be emphasised, that the European Court of Justice can only rule on compatibility between the Convention and Community law or those areas of national law affected by Community law. It could not, for example, rule on the rights of citizens convicted in a member state of offences against the person or, for example, of assisting in or promoting the carrying out of abortions in a member state where these are prohibited, since criminal law of this kind is wholly outside Community competence: *SPUC* v *Grogan* (Case C–159/90), and *see* Shaw in O'Keeffe and Twomey (1994). The Court defined the limits of its powers in *Demirel* v *Stadt Schwabisch Gmund* (Case 12/86). The Court, it said:

> has no power to examine the *compatability with the European Convention on Human Rights of national legislation lying outside the scope of Community law.* (emphasis added)

See also, *Cinétheque* v *Féderation Nationale des Cinemas Français* (Case 60-1/84).

The application of the Convention and the development of the jurisprudence of fundamental rights has been a somewhat erratic process, depending very much on the kind of cases which have come before the Court. Some provisions of the Convention, particularly those relating to due process under Art 6, have been discussed frequently by the Court while others, such as that relating to the right to life, hardly at all. Fundamental rights have been drawn both from the Convention and from the constitutions of the member states. Rights and freedoms recognised by national constitutions as being 'fundamental' both in the sense that they protect and promote the most essential human values, such as the dignity, the personality, the intellectual and physical integrity, or the economic and social well-being of the individual, and in the sense that they are inseparably attached to the person. The Court has emphasised its commitment to human rights in general on several occasions, over a period of 25 years, starting with *Stauder* (Case 29/69). In that case, the Court declared that 'fundamantal human rights are enshrined in the general principles of Community law and protected by the Court'. However, until the Treaty on European Union came into effect in 1993, there were no specific provisions for the protection of human rights as such, in the Treaties. It is arguable that the Court has been reluctant to take on the protection of fundamental rights, and did so largely to protect the supremacy of its jurisdiction:

> Reading an unwritten bill of rights into Community law is indeed the most striking contribution the Court made to the development of a new constitution for Europe. This statement should be qualified in two respects. First ... that contribution was forced on the court from outside, by the German and, later, the Italian Constitutional Courts. Second, the court's effort to safeguard the fundamental rights of the Community citizens stopped at the threshold of national legislations (Mancini (1989)).

Even where a right is recognised by the Court as a fundamental Community right, that recognition is not conclusive. The designation by the Court of a right as 'fundamental' does not always mean that all other rules must give way before it. In some circumstances, one 'fundamental' right may have to give way to another which the Court regards as even more important. Much will depend on the context in which the 'fundamental' right is called upon, and the nature of the right itself.

FUNDAMENTAL RIGHTS

The right to property and the freedom to choose a trade or profession

(Article 1 First Protocol ECHR 1952 Cmd 9221, and *see Nold* v *Commission* (Case 4/73)). The Court has declared 'The right to property is guaranteed in the Community legal order' (*Hauer* v *Land Rheinland-Pfalz* (Case 44/79)). In *Wachauf* (Case 5/88), a German tenant farmer was deprived of his right to compensation under Regulation 857/84 for loss of a milk quota, as a result of the way in which the German Government had interpreted the regulation. He argued that this amounted to expropriation without compensation. The case was referred to the Court of Justice which held :

> It must be observed that Community rules which, upon the expiry of the lease, had the effect of depriving the lessee, without compensation, of the fruits of his labour and of his investments in the tenanted holding would be incompatible with the requirements of the protection of fundamental rights in the Community legal order. Since those requirements are also binding on member states when they implement Community rules, the member states must, as far as possible, apply those rules in accordance with those requirements.

However, the Court held in *R* v *Ministry of Agriculture, ex parte Bostock* (Case C-2/92), that where a lessor 'inherited' the benefit of a milk quota, neither the milk quota scheme itself nor the Community principles of fundamental rights required a member state to introduce a scheme for compensation for the outgoing lessee nor did they confer directly on the lessee a right to such compensation.

In *Commission* v *Germany* (Case C-280/93), the Court affirmed that both the right to property and the freedom to pursue a trade or business formed part of the general principles of Community law. But those principles were not absolute, and

> had to be viewed in relation to their social function. Consequently, the exercise of the right to property and the freedom to pursue a trade or profession could be restricted, particularly in the context of a common organisation of a market, provided that those restrictions in fact corresponded to objectives of general interest pursued by the Community and did not constitute a disproportionate and intolerable interference, impairing the very substance of the rights guaranteed.

In relation to access to a trade or profession, the principle of equality should ensure equal access to available employment and the professions between Community citizens and nationals of the host state (*see, Thieffry* (Case 71/76)). In

UNECTEF v *Heylens* (Case 222/86), the Court said that '... free access to employment is a fundamental right which the Treaty confers individually on each worker of the Community'. ([1987] ECR 4098 at p 4117).

The right to carry on an economic activity

This is closely tied to the right to property. The Court has held that the right to property is guaranteed in the Community legal order. However, it has also decided that a Community-imposed restriction on the planting of vines constitutes a legitimate exception to the principle, which is recognised in the constitutions of member states (*see Hauer* (Case 44/79); *Eridania* (Case 230/78) and *S M Winsersett* v *Land Rheinland-Pfatz* (Case C-306/93)).

Freedom of trade

In *Procureur de la République* v *ADBHU* (Case 240/83), the Court said that:

> It should be born in mind that the principles of free movement of goods and freedom of competition, together with freedom of trade as a fundamental right, are general principles of Community law of which the Court ensures observance. ([1985] ECR 520 of 531)

The Court has held on several occasions that the right for goods to be allowed access to markets in other member states under Art 30 EC is, subject to the exceptions in Art 36, a directly effective right. This decision elevates that right to a fundamental principle, in the face of which inconsistent Community and national legislation must generally give way. But, the freedom to trade is not absolute, and may have to give way to the imperatives of the single market (*see Commission* v *Germany* (above)).

The right to an effective judicial remedy before national courts (Arts 6, 13 ECHR).

This has become one of the most developed fundamental principles in the jurisprudence of the Court of Justice. In *Johnston* v *Chief Constable of RUC* (Case 222/84), the RUC maintained a general policy of refraining from issuing firearms to female members of the force. The policy was defended on the ground, inter alia, that Art 53 of the Sex Discrimination (Northern Ireland) Order 1976 (SI 1976/1042 (NI 15) permitted sex discrimination for the purpose of 'safeguarding national security or of protecting public safety or public order'. A certificate issued by the Secretary of State was to be 'conclusive evidence' that the action was necessary on security grounds. The complainant argued that the rule effectively barred her promotion, and that Directive 76/207 EC should take priority over national law. Article 6 of the directive provided that complainants should be able to 'pursue their claims by judicial process'. On a reference to the ECJ, the Court held that the national tribunal had to be given enough information to determine whether or not the policy of the

Chief Constable was objectively justified. This was necessary in the interests of effective judicial control.

> The requirements of judicial control stipulated by that Art [Art 6 Dir 76/207] reflects a general principle of law which underlines the constitutional traditions common to the member states. That principle is also laid down in Arts 6 and 13 of the European Convention of Human Rights and Fundamental Freedoms ... As the European Parliament, Council and Commission recognised in their joint declaration of 5 April 1977 (OJ 1977 C 103 p 1) and as the Court has recognised in its own decisions, the principles on which the Convention is based must be taken into consideration in Community law. (*Johnstone* v *Chief Constable of the R.U.C.* (Case 222/84))

The principle of effective judicial control and effective remedies underlies several decisions relating to difficulties encountered by individuals in seeking to establish themselves in businesses and professions in other member states. These require that sufficient reasons must be given for official decisions, to enable them to be challenged in court, should the need arise. Where

> it is ... a question of securing the effective protection of a fundamental right conferred by the Treaty on Community workers, the latter must ... be able to defend that right under the best possible conditions and have the possibility of deciding, with a full knowledge of the relevant facts, whether there is any point in their applying to the courts. (*see, UNECTEF* v *Heylens* (Case 222/86) and *Pecastaing* (Case 98/79) (A-G Capotorti))

The right to due judicial process also involves a fair investigative process in accordance with the Convention when the European Commission is investigating alleged breaches of competition law. In interpreting its investigative powers under Regulation 17/62 the Commission has to have regard to the Convention and, particularly, the rights of the defence to be informed of the matters under investigation (*see, Hoechst* v *Commission* (Case 46/87)). This principle has come to be known as 'equality of arms' (*Solray SA* v *Commission* (Case T-30/91)). The same principle entitles protection to be given to certain communications between the person under investigation and his lawyer (*see, Australia Mining & Smelting Ltd* v *Commission* (Case 155/79)).

The protection of family life, home and family correspondence (Art 8 ECHR)

In *National Panasonic* (Case 136/79), the Court held that the principles of Art 8 ECHR were applicable to an investigation by the Commission of an alleged anti-competitive practice, but held that the exception in Art 8(2) justified the action taken by the Commission under Regulation 17/62.

In *X* v *Commission* (Case C-404/92), the applicant had applied for an appointment as a temporary member of the Commission's staff. He had agreed to undergo the normal medical examination but had refused to be subjected to a test which might disclose whether or not he carried the AIDS virus. The Court of Justice held that he was entitled to do so:

> The right to respect for private life, embodied in Art 8 ECHR and deriving from the common constitutional traditions of the member states, is one of the fundamental rights protected by the legal order of the Community. It includes in particular a person's right to keep his state of health secret.

The right of Community citizens in other member states to have only those restrictions imposed on them in other member states as are necessary in the interests of national security or public safety in a democratic society (Art 2 Fourth Protocol to the Convention, 1963 Cmnd 2309)

This right has a wide application. The position of European Union citizens in other member states, in relation to their human rights, has been described in the most comprehensive terms by Advocate-General Jacobs in *Christos Konstantinidis* v *Stadt Altensteig-Standesamt* (Case C-168/91):

> In my opinion, a Community national who goes to another member state as a worker or a self-employed person under Arts 48, 52 or 59 of the Treaty is entitled ... to assume that, wherever he goes to earn his living in the European Community, he will be treated in accordance with a common code of fundamental values, in particular those laid down in the European Convention on Human Rights. In other words, he is entitled to say 'civis Europeus sum' and to invoke that status in order to oppose any violation of his fundamental rights.'

The principle applies, a fortiori, since the creation of European Union citizenship by Art 8 EC Treaty, as this carries with it, under Art 8a, a general right of residence anywhere in the Community for those holding it, subject only to the limitations contained in the Treaty and in the implementing legislation (*see* Chapter 7).

Prohibition of discrimination on the grounds of sex in relation to pay and working conditions (Art 14 ECHR)

This is incorporated into Community law by virtue of Art 119, which is a directly effective, as we have seen in Chapter 5 (*see, Defrenne* (Case 149/77). In *Sabbatini* v *The European Parliament* (Case 20/71), the Court held that sex equality was a general principle of Community law.

Freedom of expression (Art 10 ECHR)

The relationship to freedom of expression has been considered on several occasions by the Court in the context of freedom to provide and receive services, and in relation to the establishment of businesses in other member states. In *Elleneki Radiophonia Tileorasi* (ERT) (Case 260/89) the Court had to consider a challenge by an independent broadcasting company to the monopoly of the state broadcasting company. Greek law forbade any party other than the State Television Company from broadcasting television programmes within Greek territory. The defendant company defied the ban and when prosecuted, pleaded in their defence that the television monopoly was contrary both to Community law (inter alia, on the free movement of goods and services) and to Art 10 of ECHR. The Greek government defended the television monopoly as a public policy derogation from the free movement of goods and services under Art 66 EC Treaty. The Court accepted that these derogations were subject to the Convention and said:

> When a member state invokes Arts 56 and 66 of the Treaty in order to justify rules which hinder the free movement of services, this justification, which is provided for in Community law, must be interpreted in the light of general principles of law, notably fundamental rights … The limitations imposed on the power of member states to apply the provisions of Arts 66 and 56 of the Treaty, for reasons of public order, public security and public health must be understood in the light of the general principles of freedom of expression, enshrined in Art 10 of the Convention. (para 45 of judgment)

The right to free expresssion only applies where there is a Community element in the activity. In *SPUC* v *Grogan* (Case C-159/90), the defendants supplied information in Ireland on abortion clinics in the United Kingdom. They had no connection with those clinics. The Court of Justice held that no question of freedom of expression arose in this case, because, although the provision of abortion could be a lawful service in a member state, according to its own domestic laws, there was no cross-border element here. The defendants were not arranging the service for clinics in the United Kingdom. The issue remained a purely domestic one for the law of the Republic of Ireland.

Freedom of religion (Art 9 ECHR)

In *Prais* v *The Council* (Case 130/75), the question of religious discrimination came before the Court. It concerned a woman of Jewish faith who wished to obtain a post as a Community official. She did not mention her faith in her application form, but when she was informed that she would have to sit a competitive examination on a particular day, she explained that she could not do so because it was an important Jewish festival. She asked to be able to take the examination on another day. She was refused, because the Council decided that it was essential for all candidates to sit the examination on the same day. The Court upheld the decision of the Council, because it had not been told, in advance, about the difficulty. The Court accepted, as did the Council, that freedom of religion was a general principle of Community law, but decided that it had not been breached in this case.

Freedom of trade union activity including the right to join and form staff associations

Union Syndicale v *Council* (Case 175/73), recognised the right to trade union membership. It is doubtful if this right extends to a right to engage in industrial action, although Art 13 of the Community Charter of the Fundamental Social Rights of Workers of 1989 provides that the worker shall have the right

> to resort to collective action in the event of a conflict of interests and shall have the right to strike, subject to the obligations arising under national regulations and collective agreements.

(*see* Art 2(6) of the Protocol on Social Policy (TEU) signed by 11 of the then 12 member states). Individuals benefiting from the protection of Community law are, however, entitled to participate equally in trade unions and staff associations, and should not be penalised for taking part in legitimate trade union activity (*see, Rutili* (Case 36/75), and *Association de Soutien aux Traveilleurs Immigrés* (Case C-213/90)). This includes the right to vote and stand for office in such bodies (*Commission* v *Luxembourg* (Case C-118/92)). The European Court of Human Rights, in *Schmidt and Dahlstom*, held that the European Convention on Human Rights safeguards the freedom to protect the occupational interests of trade union members by trade union action, but leaves each state a free choice of the means to be used to this end. Art 8 of Regulation 1612/68 which gives migrant workers equal rights with national workers as far as membership of trade unions and the election to office in them is concerned, refers only to 'the rights attaching' to such membership, without further elaboration.

Further reading

Hartley, T. C., (1994) *The Foundations of European Community Law* (3rd edn) Clarendon Press, pp 139–64.

Dauses, M., 'The Protection of Fundamental Rights in the Community Legal Order' (1985) 10 EL Rev 398.

Coppel, J. and O'Neill, A., (1992) 'The European Court of Justice: Taking Rights Seriously?' [1992] Legal Studies, 227.

Hall, 'The European Convention on Human Rights and Public Exceptions to the Free Movement of Workers under the EEC Treaty' (1991) 10 EL Rev 466.

Lenaerts, K., 'Fundamental Rights to be Included in a Community Catalogue' (1991) 16 EL Rev 367.

Schermers, H., 'The European Communities Bound by Fundamental Human Rights' (1990) 27 CML Rev 249.

Schermers, H., 'Is there a Fundamental Human Right to Strike?' (1989) 9 YEL 225.

Shaw, J., 'Twin-track Social Europe – the Inside Track' in O'Keefe, D. and Twomey P. (eds) (1994) *Legal Issues of the Maastricht Treaty*, Wiley Chancery Laws.

Toth, A. G., (1990) *The Oxford Encyclopaedia of European Community Law*, Clarendon Press, Vol 1, p 284.

Part II

THE FREE MOVEMENT OF PERSONS AND SERVICES AND RIGHTS OF ESTABLISHMENT

7 European citizenship and free movement rights

The free movement of persons has been a cornerstone of the European Community since its inception. Article 3(c) EC Treaty requires 'the abolition, as between member states, of obstacles to freedom of movement of persons'. That freedom was not, initially, an entitlement for citizens of member states to move anywhere in the Community for any purpose, but was linked to a number of specific economic activities (Arts 48–51 (workers), Arts 52–58 (rights of establishment) and Arts 59–66 (services)). Each of these Treaty provisions has been elaborated by detailed secondary legislation. The rights of individuals and undertakings in the three principal categories are examined in more detail in Chapter 8 (workers) and Chapter 9 (services and establishment).

Free movement rights must be seen in the context of three important developments of recent years. The first of these are the measures taken to create the Single European Market which shall, under Art 7a EC Treaty, 'comprise an area without internal frontiers in which the free movement of goods, persons, services and capital is ensured'. Although Art 7a creates a commitment for the Community to remove border restrictions, it is not clear whether the provision has direct effect. In *R v Secretary of State for the Home Dept ex parte Flynn The Times*, 23 March 1995, McCullough J. held that it did not match the criteria for having direct effect. It imposed no obligation on member states, 'let alone one which is clear and precise'. He therefore refused a claim by the applicant, an EU citizen, that he had been unlawfully detained for questioning at Dover. This decision was subsequently upheld in the Court of Appeal.

The second development is the European Economic Area Agreement, under which all the free movement rights enjoyed under the Treaty of Rome were extended to the remaining states of EFTA (except Switzerland), under the agreement which came into effect on 1 January 1994. Citizens of the Union and their families and citizens of the participating EFTA states (currently Norway and Iceland) and their families enjoy the full free movement rights of the Treaty and of the implementing legislation in all the territories of the EC and the participating EFTA states. The third, and most significant, development, is the creation of EU citizenship by the Treaty on European Union (Art 8 EC Treaty).

> Under Art 8a, 'every citizen of the Union shall have the right to move and to reside freely within the territory of the member states, *subject to the limitations and conditions laid down in this Treaty and by the measures adopted to give it effect'*. (emphasis added)

The words in italics, which have been added for emphasis, make it clear that the citizenship of the Union does not bring any new free movement rights into being, but formally attaches the existing rights, with all the qualifications and exceptions, to the new citizenship. The most that might be said about EU citizenship and free movement, is that possession of such citizenship raises a presumption of a right of entry or residence which will have to be rebutted by the host state if those rights are to be refused or terminated. The Treaty envisages the existing rights as a basis for further development, and authorises further measures 'to strengthen or add to the rights' (Art 8e). The effect of the new citizenship has not yet been considered by the European Court of Justice. It was, however, a central issue in a recent case in the Divisional Court (*R* v *Home Secretary, ex parte Vitale and Do Amaral, New Law Journal Law Report*, 5 May 1995). The applicants, both EU citizens, had been in receipt of income support for a number of months. They had not found work and, in the view of the Department of Employment, they were not seeking it. They were therefore asked to leave the country. They argued that, irrespective of the truth of the allegations, they were entitled to remain simply as EU citizens. Judge J. rejected this argument:

> Article 8a provides two distinct rights, the right to move freely within the territory and the right to reside freely. Neither right is free-standing nor absolute. It is expressly and unequivocally subject to the limitations and conditions contained in the Treaty. Moreover it is clear from the provisions in Art 8a(2) and, more significantly, Art 8e, that provisions may be adopted in due course 'to strengthen or add to the rights laid down' in the part of the Treaty devoted to 'citizenship'. In effect, therefore, the existence of limitations and the potential for extending the rights of citizens are acknowledged in Art 8e as well as Art 8a. So Art 8a does not provide every citizen of the Union with an open-ended right to reside freely within every member state.

Whether Art 8a does provide any rights of movement and residence additional to those available before the TEU came into effect is currently the subject of a reference to the Court under Art 177 EC Treaty in *R* v *Secretary of State for the Home Office, ex parte Adams* (1995).

Freedom of movement was seen, in the early days of the Community, as the means by which labour and skills shortages in one member state could be met out of a surplus of labour and skills in another. That approach was subsequently modified, both in later implementing legislation, and by decisions of the European Court of Justice. The Court has interpreted the Treaty and the implementing provisions generously. The application of Art 48(3)(a), which appears to confer a right to go to another member state only on those able to 'accept offers of employment *actually made*' (emphasis added), to work-seekers is, perhaps one of the most remarkable examples of creative interpretation (*Procureur du Roi* v *Royer* (Case 48/75)). Although each of the free movement rights has depended, until recently (see the new general right of residence created by Directive 90/364, Chapter 9), on a specific economic activity, the Court has tended to develop a body of general principles applicable to all those exercising free movement rights.

Most importantly, all free movement rights, are directly effective and enforceable in the courts of member states as fundamental rights. The entry or residence of those exercising them is not dependant upon any consent or leave given by the host state. Provided that an individual is engaged in an activity which confers Community rights of entry or residence, the host state cannot terminate that right of residence (*R v Pieck* (Case 157/79)). There are exceptions to rights of entry and residence in cases where the individual constitutes a threat to public policy, public security and public health under Art 48(3), 56(1) and Directive 64/221. These powers of member states to derogate from individual rights of free movement have, however, been interpreted strictly by the Court (*Adoui and Cornuaille* v *Belgian State* (Cases 115 & 116/81), and Chapter 11).

Since free movement rights are fundamental rights, the Court has held that they must be transparent in national legislation. Incompatible provisions of national law which, for example, exclude the employment of foreign nationals, even though they are not, in practice, applied in the case of EU citizens, must be amended to make it absolutely clear that EU citizens enjoy equal access (*Commission* v *France (Re French Merchant Seamen)* (Case 167/73)). It is not sufficient that Community rights should be enjoyed by virtue of administrative concessions. Those enjoying such rights must be made aware of them, and be able, should the need arise, to rely upon them before a court of law (*Commission* v *Germany (Re Nursing Directives)* (Case 29/84)).

Decisions affecting the exercise by an individual of free movement rights should spell out the reasons for them, to enable an effective legal challenge to be made. The procedures for challenging any denial of such rights, whether on the basis of public policy, public security or public health, under Directive 64/221 (see Chapter 13), or on any other ground, should follow the Community principles of fairness and the provisions of the European Convention on Human Rights (*UNECTEF* v *Heylens and Others* (Case 222/86)). The provisions of the Convention are now directly applicable to the exercise of Community rights (Art F(2)). Non-discrimination on grounds of nationality (Art 6 EC Treaty) is another fundamental principle of Community law that is important in the exercise of free movement rights. The detailed provisions of Regulation 1612/68 relating to equal access to employment and to other benefits enable the worker and his family to integrate into the host state, but there is no parallel legislation relating to the self-employed and to those giving and receiving services. Decisions of the Court relating to access to housing and the criminal process, which have been secured for workers under Regulation 1612/68, (Arts 7(2) and 9), have, however, been achieved for the self-employed and the recipients of services by a creative use of Art 6 EC Treaty (*see Commission* v *Italy* (Case 63/86), and *Cowan* v *Le Trésor Public* (Case 186/87)). Article 6 does, however, only apply to matters covered by the Treaty, and any aspect of an individual's life which may affect his entry into or residence in another member state as a beneficiary of Community law.

Although discrimination in relation to both employment and self-employment is generally prohibited, restrictions on the employment of EU nationals in 'the public service' are permitted by Art 48(4). There are similar provisions relating to the self-employed who may be refused participation in activities which '… are connected, even occasionally, with the exercise of official authority' in Art 55. There is no definition in the Treaty or the secondary legislation of either 'the public service' or 'the exercise of official authority' but both exceptions have been narrowly interpreted by the Court. The mere fact that the employer is the state is not conclusive. It is the nature of the employment which is the determining factor (*Lawrie-Blum* v *Land Baden-Württemberg* (Case 66/85); *see* Chapters 8 and 9).

To benefit from Community free movement rights, a person must be, or have been, a migrant in some sense or other. A person who has not left his own state, and does not intend to do so, cannot be a beneficiary (*Iorio* (Case 298/84)). He can, however, be a worker or a self-employed person vis-à-vis his own state if he works abroad for a period and then returns home. He may then enjoy the family rights of a Community migrant against his own state, which will override the more restrictive national provisions (*Morson* v *Netherlands* (Case 35/82); *R* v *IAT ex parte Surinder Singh* (Case C-370/90)). A person who has not left his own state may still benefit from free movement rights if, for example, he has arranged employment in another member state, or wishes to establish a business there. He will be entitled to be issued with a travel document and cannot, subject to the public policy/public security exception, be prevented from leaving (Art 2(1) and (2), Directives 68/360 and 73/148; Chapters 8, 9 and 11).

OTHER RIGHTS DERIVED FROM CITIZENSHIP OF THE UNION

The creation of EU citizenship is part of a broader programme of enhancement of individual political and social rights in the European context called a 'Peoples' Europe' (Second Addonino Report on a Peoples' Europe, Supplement 7/85 Bull EC p 18). As part of that programme, which is intended to give European citizens both a greater sense of identity as Europeans and a number of new tangible rights, EU citizenship confers other benefits in addition to the general right of residence. It is not possible to discuss them in detail here, but broadly, they comprise: a right to vote and stand as a candidate in local (but not national) and European Parliamentary elections in other member states where the EU citizen is resident, a right to diplomatic representation outside the Community from any of the other member states in territories where the citizen's own state has no consulate or embassy, a right to petition the European Parliament and a right to apply for assistance to the newly-appointed European Parliamentary Ombudsman. The right to apply to the Ombudsman is not confined to EU citizens, but is open to 'any natural or legal person residing or having its registered office in a member state' (Art 138e EC Treaty).

Although European citizenship has created a general right of entry and residence for all those holding the nationality of a member state, that right is defined by reference to the existing miscellany of largely economically related rights of free movement contained in the EC Treaty and elaborated in secondary legislation. The subsequent chapters will examine the scope of those rights, identify the beneficiaries and the extent which member states are permitted to derogate from them. European citizenship is the primary avenue by which those rights are acquired, but Community law also confers more limited rights on those who are not citizens of the Union.

FREE MOVEMENT RIGHTS OF NON-UNION CITIZENS

Nationals of third states outside the Community can enjoy a number of important free movement rights under Treaties made with it. Besides the full range of free movement rights enjoyed by Norway and Iceland under the EEA Agreement discussed above, family members of Community workers, the self-employed and other beneficiaries of free movement rights who are nationals of other states have the right to install themselves with the person entitled to the free movement right. Host states may demand that such individuals obtain a visa, but 'every facility' should be given to enable them to obtain one (Art 3(2), Directive 68/360). Once installed with the principal beneficiary, the spouse or other family member is entitled to access to employment and equal treatment as if he or she were a European Union citizen (*Gül v Regierungspräsident Düsseldorf* (Case 131/85)).

More limited rights are enjoyed by the beneficiaries of Association Agreements made with the Community. Such agreements have been held by the Court to be directly effective (*Kupferberg* (Case 104/81)). The rights in these cases are normally limited to equal treatment in employment and social security after admission, but they do not entitle the beneficiaries to enter. Such rights have been recognised in this way under the EC-Turkey Agreement (*Kus v Landeshauptstadt Wiesbaden* (Case C-237/91); *Eroglu v Baden-Württemberg*, (Case C-355/93)), and under the EC-Morocco Co-operation Agreement (*Bahia Kziber v ONEM* (Case C-18/90); *Yousfi v Belgium* (Case C-58/93)). There are other agreements with Tunisia, Algeria, Poland, the Czech Republic, Hungary, Romania, Slovakia and Cyprus which contain provisions which could be used by nationals of those states while working in the Community.

Other third state nationals may benefit from Community free movement rights in a different way. As we shall see, undertakings established in one member state have the right to go to another, either to provide a service or to become established there

(Arts 52,59 EC Treaty). To enable the undertaking to carry out its activities in the host state it is entitled to take its workforce with it whatever their nationality. Such employees should be admitted without any requirement of a work permit in the host state and should be enabled to remain there until the business of the undertaking is complete. On this basis, the French immigration authorities have been obliged to allow non-EC workers employed by Portuguese and Belgian companies to work without any further restrictions than those already imposed in the state of origin of the undertaking (*Rush Portugesa Ldc* (Case C-113/89); *Vander Elst* v *OMI* (Case C-43/93)). This right is, in essence, the right of the undertaking rather than the right of the worker and, if challenged, should, in principle, have to be asserted by the undertaking in the courts of the member state. Advocate-General Tesauro, in his opinion in *Vander Elst*, above, did, however, describe the workers in the *Rush Portugesa* case as having a *derived* right in relation to entry and employment, although he did not argue that it could be asserted by them personally (p 3813). Somewhat surprisingly, the Immigration Appeal Tribunal has held that the right of the employing company in the United Kingdom can be the subject of an application for judicial review by the employee (*Pasha* v *Home Office* [1993] 2 CMLR 350).

Third state nationals given leave to enter any member state may, under a new regulation, be issued with a EU visa and be able to travel anywhere in the EU for a period of up to three months. The visa may be issued by any member state, but it is in a standard form for use in all the member states (Art 100c EC, Council Reg 1683/95, OJ L 164 14.7.95).

Further reading

Anderson, M., den Boer, M. and Miller, G., European Citizenship and Co-operation in Justice and Home Affairs' in Duff, A. *et al.* (eds) (1994) *Maastricht and Beyond*, Routledge.

Close, C., 'The Concept of Citizenship in the Treaty of European Union' (1992) 29 CML Rev 1137.

Close, C., 'Citizenship of the Union and Nationality of Member States' (1995) 32 CML Rev 487.

Handoll, J., (1995) *Free Movement of Persons in the European Union,* Wiley, Chapter 9.

Hartley, T.C., 'Free Movement of Persons' Pt II in Green, N., Hartley, T.C., and Usher, J.A. (1991) *The Legal Foundation of the Single European Market*, Clarendon Press.

Hedemann-Robinson, M., 'New Electoral and Political Rights in the Community', New Law Journal, 9 April 1994, p 564.

Immigration Law Practitioners' Association, (1995) *The Movement of Aliens in the European Arena*.

O'Keefe, D., 'Union Citizenship' in O'Keefe, D. and Twomey, P. (eds.), (1994) *Legal Issues of the Maastricht Treaty*, Wiley Chancery Laws.

O'Keefe, D., 'The Emergence of a European Immigration Policy' (1995) 20 EL Rev 20.

O'Keefe, D., 'The Free Movement of Persons in the Single Market' (1992) 13 EL Rev 3.

O'Leary, S., 'The Relationship Between Community Citizenship and the Protection of Fundamental Rights in Community Law' (1995) 32 CML Rev 487.

Vincenzi, C., 'European Citizenship and Free Movement Rights in the United Kingdom', *Public Law*, Summer 1995, p 259.

8 Free movement of workers

The free movement of workers is of great economic and social importance to the Community. Although the right to move to other member states in an employed capacity was originally seen as no more than an economic function whereby a surplus of labour and skills in one part of the Community could meet a shortage in another, the worker was soon recognised in the Community's legislation, and in the decisions of the European Court of Justice, as more than merely a unit of labour. The right to move was seen as 'a fundamental right' which was to be 'exercised in freedom and dignity' (Preamble to Regulation 1612/68). 'The migrant worker is not to be viewed as a mere source of labour, but as a human being' (Advocate-General Trabuchi in *Fracas* v *Belgium* (Case 7/75)).

The exercise of the migrant worker's rights is to be facilitated in the work-place and in the broader social context of the host member state. The implementing legislation and the jurisprudence of the Court is directed at securing the worker's departure from his state of origin and entry, residence and integration, in the widest sense, into the economic and social fabric of the member state. The meaning of the term 'worker' and each stage of the process of entry, residence and integration is examined in turn in this chapter.

SCOPE OF THE TERM 'WORKER'

Article 48(1) EC provides that freedom of movement of workers shall be secured within the Community. It entails the abolition of any discrimination based on nationality in relation to access to employment, remuneration and other conditions of work (Art 48(2)). Although the exercise of workers' rights may be made subject to national rules relating to public policy, public security and public health (as limited by the provisions of Directive 64/221), it should involve the right:

1   to accept offers of employment actually made;
2   to move freely within the territory of member states for this purpose;
3   to stay in the member state for the purpose of employment; and

4   to remain in the territory of a member state after having been employed in that state.

Implementing legislation has given detailed effect to these provisions. Directive 68/360 defines the rights of workers and the obligations of the immigration authorities of member states in relation to entry, residence and the issue and revocation of residence permits. Regulation 1612/69 deals with matters relating to equal access to employment, equality of terms of employment, family, housing, educational and social rights. Regulation 1408/71 ensures that workers who are entitled to contributory and related benefits continue to enjoy them in the host state and on return to their own state. Regulation 1251/70 contains detailed provisions on rights of retirement in the state where the worker has been employed, and Directive 90/365 confers a right of retirement on employees and the self-employed in member states other than those where the person has been employed. All of these provisions create directly effective rights and will be considered in the context of the exercise by the worker of those rights.

Neither the EC Treaty, nor the implementing legislation, defines the term 'worker', and so the Court of Justice has been left to elaborate its meaning. In *Lawrie-Blum* v *Land Baden-Württemberg* (Case 66/85) the Court said that:

> Objectively defined, a 'worker' is a person who is obliged to provide services for another in return for monetary reward and who is subject to the direction and control of the other person as regards the way in which the work is to be done.
> (para [14] of judgment)

What activities confer worker status is a matter of Community law. The Court emphasised in *Levin* v *Staatsecretaris van Justitie* (Case 53/81) that it is not a matter to be determined by the law of the member state. In *Levin* the host state argued that the term could only be applied to a person who did sufficient work to bring her up to the minimum subsistence level of the state concerned. The Court refused to accept such a state-determined criterion. The Court held that part-time work is not excluded. However, Community rules on the acquisition of worker status did not apply to 'activities on such a small scale as to be regarded as purely marginal and ancillary'. Even if a person earns insufficient funds from the work he does, so that he has to rely partly on social assistance, that does not, per se, deprive him of worker status, provided that the 'effective and genuine nature of his work is established' (*Kempf* v *Staatssecretaris van Justitie* (Case 139/85)).

The Court has not laid down any criteria as to how much, or how little, or what kind of work, is 'effective and genuine' and not 'marginal and ancillary', although some guidance can be gained from the cases. In *Steymann* (Case 196/87), the individual was engaged in maintenance and repair work for a religious community. He received his keep, but no wages. Despite the fact that his reward was in kind rather than in cash, the Court held that he was to be considered a 'worker' under Community law. In *Bettray* (Case 344/87) however, the person concerned was engaged in paid work as part of a form of therapy. It was, therefore, ancillary.

Surprisingly small amounts of work can, however, be regarded as 'sufficient'. In *Raulin* (Case 357/89), the person claiming worker status had been on an 'on call' contract for a period of eight months. During that period she actually worked as a waitress for a total of 60 hours. Nonetheless, the Court held that the brevity of her employment period did not exclude her from qualifying for worker status.

WORK SEEKERS

Not every individual wishing to go to another member state to work will already have a job arranged. On a first impression of Art 48(3), people in this category would not seem to qualify to a right of free movement, since the beneficiaries are described as those in a position 'to accept offers of employment actually made'. The Court of Justice decided, however, in a remarkably creative judgment, in *Royer* (Case 48/75) that

> the right of nationals of a member state to enter the territory of another member state and reside there for the purposes intended by the Treaty – in particular to look for or pursue an occupation or activities as employed or self-employed persons, or to rejoin their spouse or family – is a right conferred directly by the Treaty, or, as the case may be, by the provisions adopted for its implementation.

In elaborating on this decision in *R v Immigration Appeal Tribunal, ex parte Antonissen,* (Case C-292/89) the Court said that 'a strict interpretation of Art 48(3) would jeopardise the actual chances that a national of a member state who is seeking employment will find it in another member state, and would, as a result, make that provision ineffective.' (paras 12 and 13 of judgment).

Work-seekers are entitled to entry and limited rights of residence but not the full range of benefits enjoyed by those who have full worker status. Their differing entitlements are examined below.

THE EXERCISE OF WORKERS RIGHTS

Departure from the Home State

A person cannot benefit from free movement rights as a worker until he has taken steps to leave his home state. Thus, in *Iorio* (Case 298/84), an Italian national from Southern Italy who complained of unequal treatment in relation to travel arrangements compared to local workers in the North, was held unable to rely on Community law, because the matter was wholly internal to Italy. A worker cannot rely on Art 48 unless he or she has exercised the right to free movement, or is seeking to do so. The possibility that a person may do so at some time in the future is insufficient (*Moser* (Case 180/83)). However, if he wishes to go to work in another member state, his own state is obliged to allow him to leave and to issue him with a valid identity card or passport to enable him to do so. It cannot demand that he first obtain an exit visa or equivalent document (Art 2(1), (2) and (3), Directive 68/360). British nationals are, therefore, entitled to be issued with a passport, and the directive will override the discretion of the Foreign Secretary under the royal prerogative to withhold it (*R* v *Secretary of State for Foreign and Commonwealth Affairs, ex parte Everett* [1989] QB 811). Limitations on departure may, however, be imposed where they are justified on grounds of public policy or public security, as defined by Community law (*see* Chapter 11).

Entry

Since the creation of the Single European Market at the beginning of 1993, national frontier controls on the movement of European Citizens and their families should have been removed (Art 7a EC Treaty). The removal of controls envisaged by Art 7a has not been realised. An attempt to challenge the remaining restrictions on the basis of Art 7a was, however, unsuccessful in the English High Court and the Court of Appeal in *R* v *Secretary of State for the Home Office*, in 1995 (*ex parte Flynn*, above, Chapter 7). It was not intended that there would be no frontier supervision, but that routine checking of individual travel documents would be discontinued. Only where there was some basis for suspicion, justifying action on grounds of public policy, public security or public health would the individual examination of passengers be justified. In several member states this point has not been reached, particularly in the United Kingdom, where there is anxiety about relaxation of port controls. The permitted limitations on public policy, public security and public health are considered in Chapter 11. Some states have implemented an open frontier policy under the Schengen Agreement. This agreement has been made outside the structure of the Community, although all member states have signed it except Ireland and the United Kingdom (*see*, Editorial (1995) 32 CML Rev 673).

Under Art 3(1), Directive 68/360, workers and their families are entitled to enter 'simply on production of a valid identity card or passport. No entry visa or equivalent document may be demanded save from members of the family who are not nationals of a member state.' The directive says that the member state shall 'allow' them to enter, but the Court of Justice held in *R* v *Pieck* (Case 157/79), that beneficiaries of free movement did not require 'leave' from the host state, since the rights conferred by Art 48 EC Treaty are directly effective. Indeed, any process of granting 'leave' amounts to the imposition of an additional requirement on entry, contrary to the express words of Art 3(1) of the Directive. Furthermore, questioning of passengers coming to work in another member state in relation to their ability to support themselves while there, is also prohibited by Art 3(1) (*Commission* v *Netherlands* (C-68/89)). Family members who are not European Union citizens may have to obtain a visa, but the host state is expected 'to accord to such persons every facility for obtaining any necessary visas' (Art 3(2)).

Residence rights and residence permits

The right of residence of a worker derives from the direct effect of Art 48. It cannot be subject to limitations imposed by the state, other than those justified by Community law. In effect, it means that, provided that he does nothing to warrant his expulsion, a worker has a right of residence as long as he continues in employment, or at least, retains worker status. However, he is entitled, as soon as he has found work, to apply for a residence permit. That permit, the Court stated in *Echternach and Moritz* v *Netherlands Minister for Education and Science* (Cases 389 & 390/87), 'does not create the rights guaranteed by Community law and the lack of a permit cannot affect the exercise of those rights' (para [25] of judgment).

Residence permits should be issued by the host state in such a way as to distinguish them from other permits issued to foreign nationals. Such permits should say that they are issued under Directives 68/360 and Regulation 1612/68 and should be free of charge, or if there is a charge, it should not amount to any more than that charged to nationals of the host state for identity cards (Arts 4(2), 9(1)). A worker is entitled to be issued with a residence permit on production of (1) the document with which he entered the territory and (2) a confirmation of engagement issued by the employer (Art 4(3)). Despite the clear words of this provision, the Court has held that a worker who no longer holds the original document with which he entered the country is entitled to be issued with a permit on the basis of a valid national identity card (*Giagounidis* (Case C-376/89)). Family members are entitled to be issued with a residence permit on production of the document with which they entered the territory and a document issued by the country of origin proving their relationship to the worker. In most cases these will be marriage and birth certificates, although for remoter relations a sworn declaration may be required. This will be the case where there is also an issue of whether or not they are dependent on the worker (Art 4(3)(e), Directive 68/360 and Art 10(2), Regulation 1612/68).

Workers do not have to wait until the permit is issued before they begin work (Art 5 Directive 68/360). The residence permit must be valid for the whole territory of the member state which issued it, must be valid for at least five years from the date of issue and be automatically renewable (Art 6(1)). Whether or not the worker holds a residence permit, he cannot, in any event, have his residence limited to any area in the member state (*Rutili* (Case 36/75)). Workers who are to be employed for less than a year, but for more than three months, may be issued with a permit that is valid only for the expected period of employment (Art 6(3)). Residence permits cannot be withdrawn from the worker on the grounds that he is no longer in employment, either because he is involuntarily unemployed or is incapable of employment as a result of illness or accident. Whether or not an individual's unemployment is involuntary or not is a matter for the 'competent employment office' (Art 7(1)).

Rights of residence of work-seekers

Work-seekers have no right to be issued with a residence permit until they have found work. Although the Court had decided in *Royer* (above) that work-seekers were entitled to enter another member state and look for work, it had not given any indication of how long that right should continue. For a number of years it was thought that the appropriate period was three months, partly because that was the limit of the entitlement to payment of unemployment benefit under Art 1408/71 (*see* Chapter 10), and partly because the Council of Ministers had made a declaration to that effect at the time of approval of Regulation 1612/68 and Directive 68/360 (*see* the opinion of Advocate-General Lenz in *Centre Public d'Aide Sociale* v *Lebon* (Case C-316/85)). The Court rejected both bases for limiting the rights of residence of work-seekers. In *R* v *Immigration Appeal Tribunal, ex parte Antonissen* (Case C-292/89), the Court said that there was no 'necessary link between the right to unemployment benefit in the member state of origin and the right to stay in the host state' (para 20 of judgment). The declaration had 'no legal significance', since it was not part of any binding legislative provision (para [18] of judgment).

The way seemed clear for an unequivocal statement by the Court on how long an individual may look for work in another member state. The Court's response to the question only marginally clarified the issue. The British Immigration Rules had laid down a period of six months in which a Community national had to obtain employment or leave the country (para 72 HC 251). The Court held that:

> In the absence of a Community provision prescribing the period during which Community nationals seeking employment in a member state may stay there, a period of six months ... does not appear in principle to be insufficient to enable the persons concerned to apprise themselves, in the host member state, of offers of employment corresponding to their occupational qualifications and to take, where appropriate, the necessary steps in order to be engaged and, therefore, does not jeopardise the effectiveness of the principle of free movement. However, if after the expiry of that period, the person concerned provides evidence that he is continuing to seek employment and that he has genuine chances of being engaged, he cannot be required to leave the territory of the member state. (para [21] of judgment)

It would appear, therefore, that six months is a reasonable period within which a work-seeker can be expected to find work, but he may remain longer if he can show that he is continuing to seek work and has 'genuine chances' of finding it.

Loss of worker status on cessation of employment

As we have seen, a person remains a worker as long as he continues in employment. However, that status is not automatically lost when a person ceases to work. The provisions of the Treaty and the implementing legislation give little guidance on how long worker status is retained after cessation of employment. Article 48(3)(d) EC refers to the right 'to remain in the territory of a member state after having been employed in that state, subject to conditions which shall be embodied in implementing legislation'. This is generally taken to mean the right to remain after retirement, or when the worker has become incapable of employment. Regulations have been made to that effect (Regulation 1251/70). The Court of Justice in *Lair* v *University of Hannover* (Case 39/86), referred to Art 48(3)(d) in more general terms, saying that 'migrant workers are granted certain rights linked to their status of worker even when they are no longer in the employment relationship'. It did not, however, indicate how long that status might continue. Since the right of residence is not dependent on the possession of a residence permit, it must be assumed that the provisions of Art 7(1), which exclude the loss of a residence permit, except in the event of 'voluntary' unemployment, apply no less to someone who has no such permit. This, at least, was the view of the United Kingdom Immigration Appeal Tribunal in *Lubbersen* v *Secretary of State for the Home Department* [1984] 3 CMLR 77.

The concept of 'voluntary' unemployment has had little attention from the European Court of Justice, except in the context of the availability of 'social advantages' to those who retain worker status (Art 7(2), Regulation 1612/68, *see* below). In connection with obtaining access to educational 'social advantages' the Court has held that a worker who leaves employment to take up a vocational course linked to his previous employment retains his status as a worker, even though he has voluntarily left that employment (*Raulin* (Case C-357/89), para [21]). It is, further, likely that a worker who is voluntarily unemployed may become a work-seeker, but it would seem likely that the competent employment office under Art 7(1), Directive 68/360 may properly conclude that a person who refuses a reasonable offer of employment cannot genuinely be seeking work. Such a person would no longer have a right of residence, unless he has sufficient resources to bring him within the residual category of general residence rights conferred by Directive 90/364 (*see* Chapter 9).

EQUAL ACCESS TO EMPLOYMENT, HOUSING, EDUCATION AND SOCIAL RIGHTS UNDER REGULATION 1612/68

Equal access to employment

Regulation 1612/68 provides a wide range of directly enforceable rights designed to enable the migrant worker to obtain employment, and to provide the means

> by which the worker is guaranteed the possibility of improving his living and working conditions and promoting his social advancement. The right of freedom of movement, in order that it may be exercised by objective standards, in freedom and dignity, requires that equality of treatment in fact and law in respect of all matters relating to the actual pursuit of activities as employed persons ... eligibility for housing ... the right to be joined by his family and the conditions for the integration of that family into the host country. (Preamble)

Articles 1, 3 and 4 of the regulation require equal treatment in relation to applications for employment by those entitled to free movement rights and prohibit national quotas and other systems of limiting access to employment by foreign nationals. Where these exist, it is not sufficient for the member state to issue instructions that they are not to be applied in relation European Union citizens. They must be repealed or amended so that Community workers are fully aware of their right to have access to that type of employment. In *Commission* v *France (Re French Merchant Seamen)* (Case 167/73), the Court held that a quota system excluding foreign deck officers from French ships, under the Code Maritime was unlawful under both Arts 1–4, Reg 1612/68 and Art 7 EC Treaty. The Court refused to accept an assurance that it was not operated against Community nationals. Individuals needed to be able to see a clear statement of their rights in the national legislation. The Court came to a similar decision in relation to the reservation of seamen's jobs for Belgian nationals (*Commission* v *Belgium* (Case C-37/93)). The same principle of transparency was applied by the Court in relation to nursing posts in the German health service (*Commission* v *Germany (Re Nursing Directives)* (Case 29/84), para [23] of judgment). The only exception to this rule is the right given to member states by Art 48(3) EC to exclude foreign nationals (including EU citizens) from the public service. This exception is, however, very narrowly construed by the Court of Justice (*see* below). It is permissible to make a knowledge of the language a pre-condition of appointment, provided that it is necessary for the kind of post to be filled. This may be so, even if it is a language which the applicant will not be required to use to carry out the job. In *Groener* v *Minister of Education* (Case 397/87), the Court of Justice held that a requirement of Irish law that teachers in vocational schools in Ireland should be able to speak Gaelic was permissible under Art 3(1), because of the national policy to maintain and promote the national language as a means of sustaining national education and culture.

Community work-seekers are entitled to receive the same assistance as that offered to national workers from the state's employment offices (Art 5). Recruitment should not depend on medical, vocational and other criteria which are discriminatory on grounds of nationality (Art 6). The Court of Justice has recently held that refusal by a government department in one member state to take into account the employment experience of a job applicant in the government service of another state amounted to unlawful discrimination (*Scholz* v *Opera Universitaria di Cagliari* (Case C-419/92)). Those entitled to Community free movement rights are also entitled to equal access to any form of employment on an equal basis, even that requiring official authorisation (*Gül* v *Regierungspräsident Düsseldorf* (Case 131/85)). The only exception to this is in relation to the public service under Art 48(4) EC Treaty (*see* below).

The general prohibition on discrimination contained in Art 48(2) EC covers not only measures that directly impact on the rights of access to employment, but any conditions which may make the engagement of Community workers more difficult or result in their employment on less favourable terms. In *Allué and Others* v *Università degli studi di Venezia*, the applicants challenged national legislation under which foreign language assistants' contracts at Italian universities were limited to one year, where no such limitation applied to other university teachers' contracts. There was evidence that about a quarter of those effected were from other Community states. On a preliminary reference under Art 177 EC the Court held that, while it was permissible to adopt measures 'applying without distinction in order to ensure the sound management of universities … such measures have to observe the principle of proportionality'. It concluded that the limitation constituted 'an insecurity factor' and was precluded by Art 48(2) EC Treaty.

Under Art 7(1) and (4), Regulation 1612/68 Community workers are entitled to the same treatment in relation all conditions of employment, including pay, dismissal, reinstatement and re-employment, and they should benefit equally from the terms of any collective agreement negotiated with the management. They are entitled to participate equally in trade unions and staff associations, and should not be penalised for taking part in legitimate trade union activities (*Rutili* v *Ministre de l'Interieur* (Case 36/75); *Association de Soutien aux Traveilleurs Immigrés* (Case C-213/90)).

The public service exception

Although, as a general rule, member states are not entitled to restrict access to any type of employment on grounds of nationality (Arts 6, 48(3), EC Treaty and Arts 1, 3, 4 and 6 Regulation 1612/68), there is one important exception. Under Art 48(4), EC Treaty, the right of equal access 'shall not apply to employment in the public service'. The term 'public service' is not defined in the Treaty or the implementing legislation and its definition has been left to the Court. The Court has sought to limit its application, in order to give the widest employment opportunities to migrant workers.

In *Sotgiu* v *Deutsche Bundespost* (Case 152/73), Advocate-General Mayras offered a definition in his Opinion which has largely been adopted in subsequent judgments of the Court. He said:

> It is clear … that for the interpretation of Art 48(4) the concept of employment in the public service cannot be defined in terms of the legal status of the holder of the post. A Community interpretation which would allow a uniform application of the exception provided for by this provision requires us therefore to have resort to factual criteria based on the duties which the post held within the administration entails and the activities actually performed by the holder of the post.
>
> The exception will only be applicable if this person possesses a power of discretion with regard to individuals or *if his activity involves national interests – in particular those which are concerned with the internal or external security of the state*. (emphasis added)

In *Commission* v *Belgium* (Case 149/79), the Court elaborated on the two central criteria proposed by Advocate-General Mayras. It held that Art 48(4)

> removes from the ambit of Art 48 (1)–(3) a series of posts which involve direct or indirect participation in the exercise of powers conferred by public law and duties

designed to safeguard the general interests of the state or of other public authorities. Such posts in fact presume on the part of those occupying them the existence of a special relationship of allegiance to the state and reciprocity of rights and duties which form the foundation of the bond of nationality.

The Court, in fact, adopted a somewhat looser definition than that offered by Advocate-General Mayras. Instead of the limitation applying to a person with a power of discretion over individuals, the Court held that it applied to posts participating in the exercise of such powers. In other words, only those who acted under the instructions of the person vested with the public powers would be included in the exception. On this basis, the Court seems to have accepted that the posts of head technical office supervisor, principal supervisor, works supervisor, stock controller and night-watchman with the municipalities of Brussels and Auderghem fell within the exception. It is clear that a person with specific statutory powers, such as an environmental health officer, a registrar of births and deaths and a police officer would all be posts in the United Kingdom falling within the exception relating to the exercise of public powers. In relation to national security and allegiance, appointments with the defence ministry dealing with issues relating to national defence, would fall within the 'allegiance' aspect of the exception. Some posts, such as a policeman at a defence establishment, would seem to fall within both.

The essential factor is the nature of the work, not the status of the employer or of the employee. In *Lawrie- Blum* v *Land Baden-Württemberg* (Case 66/85) the applicant was a trainee teacher employed by the Ministry of Education, with the status of a civil servant. The local state government argued that she came within the exception in Art 48(4), since she performed 'powers conferred by public law', including the preparation of lessons, the awarding of marks, and the participation in the decision of whether or not the pupils should move to a higher class. The Court rejected this argument. It held that the exception in Art 48(4) must be construed in such a way as to limit its scope to what is strictly necessary for safeguarding the interests which that provision allows member states to protect. Access to posts could not be limited simply because the host state designated them as civil servants (*Bleis* v *Ministre de l'Education Nationale* (Case C-4/91)). To allow that would be to accept the power of the member states to determine who fell within the exception of Art 48(4). The derogation permitted by Art 48(4) applies only to access to employment. It does not apply to the terms of the employment once access has been permitted. It would not therefore be permissible for national and Community citizens to be engaged in the same work, but on different contractual terms or conditions (*Sotgiu* v *Deutsche Bundespost* (Case 152/73); *Allué and Coonan* v *Universita di Venezia* (Case 33/88)).

The Court did not elaborate in *Lawrie-Blum* on the special qualities of public employment to which Art 48(4) is applicable, except to repeat, almost verbatim, its formulation in *Commission* v *Belgium* (above). It added that 'Those very strict conditions are not fulfilled in the case of a trainee teacher, even if he does in fact take the decisions described by the [government of] Baden-Wurttemberg.' (para

[28]). Doubtless senior officers in the Government Education Service would take major public policy decisions affecting education. It is, however, not clear at what level the Art 48(4) exception would start to apply. Only further decisions of the Court of Justice on specific cases can provide more detailed criteria for the application of this exception. In the meantime, the Commission has issued a Notice in 1988 which indicates, provisionally at least, its view of a number of occupations in public employment which do not fall within the Art 48(4) exception. This includes posts in public health care, teaching in state education, non-military research, and public bodies involved in the administrative services. This is a far from exhaustive list, and does not, of course, have the force of law.

The public service in the United Kingdom

Until May 1991, all Civil Service posts in the United Kingdom were unavailable to all Community nationals, except Irish citizens (who are not classified as aliens under the Aliens Employment Act 1955). The 1955 Act did permit some limited exceptions, but it was far too sweeping to comply with Art 48(4), as interpreted by the Court of Justice in *Commission* v *Belgium* (above). The European Communities (Employment in the Civil Service) Order 1991 (1991 S I No 1221) was brought into effect to enable citizens of member states and their families to have access to Civil Service posts in accordance with Community law. It does not specify the posts which are to be opened up, but an internal Civil Service Circular (GC/378) lists a large number of jobs which are now open to EU citizens. The list includes bookbinders, catering staff, civil researchers, cleaners, dentists, porters, plumbers, teachers, translators and typists. However, the posts of curators in such museums as the National Gallery, the Tate Gallery, and the National Galleries of Scotland all remain closed to EU citizens.

The circular acknowledges that the criteria for identifying posts that fall within Art 48(4) according to the concept of powers conferred by public law is difficult to apply in the United Kingdom, where it does not have the same meaning as in other member states. Neverthless, many of the posts which are still unavailable, such as that of clerical officer in the Department of Health, and museum curators, are clearly not within the narrow core of state activities envisaged by the Court of Justice in *Commission* v *Belgium* (above).

Social advantages

Article 7(2) Regulation 1612/68 provides simply that the migrant worker 'shall enjoy the same social and tax advantages as national workers'. This provision has been a very fruitful source of rights for Community workers and their families. 'Social advantages' has been given the broadest of interpretations by the European Court of Justice. In Case 207/78 *Ministere Public* v *Even* [1979] ECR 2019, the Court said that

> 'social advantages' were all those advantages which, whether or not [they] are linked to a contract of employment, are generally granted to national workers, *primarily because of*

their objective status as workers or by virtue of the mere fact of their residence on the national territory and the extension of which to workers who are nationals of other member states therefore seems suitable to facilitate their mobility. (at p 2034, emphasis added)

Advocate-General Mancini in his opinion in *Gül* above (at p1579) also emphasised that the equal treatment provisions of Regulation 1612/68 are not confined to the employment relationship:

The migrant worker is not regarded by Community law – nor is he by the internal legal systems – as a mere source of labour but is viewed as a human being. In this context the Community legislature is not concerned solely to guarantee him the right to equal pay and social benefits in connection with the employer–employee relationship, it also emphasised the need to eliminate obstacles to the mobility of the worker … ' (and *see, Mr and Mrs F v Belgium* (Case 7/75), Opinion of Advocate-General Trabucchi)

Adopting an approach of facilitating removal of obstacles, and assisting the worker in the process of integrating into the social fabric of the member state, the Court has held a very diverse range of benefits to be within the term 'social advantages'. In *Cristini v SNCF* (Case 32/75) SNCF, the French railway company, offered a fare reduction for large families. The applicant, an Italian national resident in France, and the widow of an Italian national who had worked in France, was refused the reduction card on the basis of nationality. SNCF argued that Art 7(2) covered only advantages connected with the contract of employment. The Court denied that such advantages were so linked, and held that they could be claimed by the widow, even after his death. In *Mutsch* (Case 137/84), the applicant was a German national working in Belgium. He was charged with a criminal offence. In that part of Belgium German-speaking Belgian nationals were allowed to have proceedings conducted in German. Mutsch was denied this right as a non-Belgian citizen, but the Court of Justice, held that he was entitled to this facility as a 'social advantage' under Art 7(2). In *Netherlands v Reed* (Case 59/85) the applicant, a UK national, sought to establish the right of a Community worker to be joined by a cohabitee. Under Dutch immigration law, Dutch nationals who had worked abroad and were in a long-standing relationship with a foreign national, were entitled to be joined by their partners. The Court held that, although this relationship did not fall within the family relationships defined by Art 10 Regulation 1612/68, it was a social advantage within Art 7(2).

The advantages to which migrant workers are entitled continue even after they have ceased employment, provided that they retain worker status. Thus, a worker who is not voluntarily unemployed can claim payments of 'social assistance' from the state. He is excluded from claiming them as social security benefits under Regulation 1408/71 (Art 4(4), *see* Chapter 10), but the Court held in *Scrivner v Centre Public d'Aide Sociale de Chastre* (Case 122/84) that 'a social benefit guaranteeing a minimum means of subsistence in a general manner' constituted a social advantage and the applicant was, therefore, entitled to the Belgian payment, MINIMEX, on this basis, despite the fact that national rules restricted it to Belgian citizens. Similarly, a person who loses her job and takes up an educational course is entitled to an educational grant as a social advantage (*Lair* v *University of Hannover* (Case 39/86)). This will be the case even if the worker gives up her job voluntarily, provided that there is a link between the job and the course that is undertaken (*Raulin* (Case C-357/89); paras [18], [22]).

The tax advantages referred to in Art 7(2) of Regulation 1612/68 were held in *Biehl* (Case C-175/88) and *Schumacker* (Case C-279/93), to require that different rates of tax payable by residents and non-residents could not be applied to workers from other member states.

Social advantages for work seekers

Access to social advantages is, however, conditional upon the acquisition of worker status. A person who has never worked in the host state will not be eligible. In *Centre Public d'Aide Sociale de Courcelles* v *Lebon* (Case 316/85), the applicant, a French national living in Belgium, claimed MINIMEX. She lived with her father, also French, who was a retired migrant worker. She was no longer dependent, but had never found employment. The Court held in this case, that, since she was no longer dependent, she was not entitled to a social advantage as a member of his family and could not claim such an advantage as a work-seeker, in her own right. The decision is, in some ways, surprising. The Court held that she was not entitled to social advantages because these are payable only to 'workers', as compared to the benefits in Title I Regulation 1612/68, which are available to all 'nationals' of other member states. This is certainly in keeping with the text of the regulation. However, Ms Lebon, in seeking work, was exercising a right conferred by Art 48(3) EC Treaty and in doing so, she was entitled to expect that she would be treated by the national authorities in the same way as a fellow Belgian work-seeker, who would be entitled to be paid MINIMEX. The Court did not deal with this aspect, nor did the opinion of Advocate-General Lenz. It is likely that the decision was motivated as much by policy as by legal considerations. Some of the submissions by member states indicated an anxiety about 'social tourism' and abuse of national welfare systems.

Education and vocational training

Migrant workers are entitled, by virtue of Art 7(3) of the regulation, to equal access with local workers to vocational schools and retraining centres. Article 12 also provides that the workers children are to be admitted to the host state's 'general, educational, apprenticeship and vocational training conditions under the same conditions as nationals of that state.'

Neither the Treaty or any implementing measures define the meaning of vocational training, but the Court of Justice in *Gravier* v *City of Liège* (Case 293/83) said that 'any form of education which prepares for a qualification for a particular profession, trade or employment or which provides the necessary skills for such a profession, trade or employment is vocational training whatever the age and level of the pupil or student'. The applicant's course in *Gravier*, that of strip cartoon design, clearly fell into that category. The Court held in *Blaizot* (Case 24/86), that whether all, or part of a course was 'vocational' was for the national court to decide on the facts. Academic work at university level was not excluded, provided either that the final academic examination gave the required qualification for a particular trade, profession or employment or where

> the studies in question provide specific training and skills ... [which] ... the student needs for the pursuit of a profession, trade or employment, even if no legislative or administrative provisions make the acquisition of that knowledge a prerequisite for that purpose. (para [19] of judgment)

Despite the need for a course of study with at least some career-orientated skills, the Court, in *Lair* v *University of Hannover* (Case 39/86), did not appear to doubt that a course in Romance and Germanic languages, that had no immediate vocational orientation was, nonetheless, a 'vocational course' (*see* Flynn, J., 'Vocational Training in Community Law and Practice' [1988] YEL 59).

The entitlement to equal access includes non-discrimination in relation to course fees (*Gravier*, above), so that, on any distinctions drawn by the host state between 'home' and 'foreign' students, European Union citizens and their families exercising free movement rights should be classified as 'home' students. In addition, equal access applies to courses not only in the host state, but also to courses in other states, where the host state assists its own nationals in relation to attendance at foreign universities and colleges (*Matteucci* (Case 235/87)).

The educational rights of workers' children extend to a right to be admitted to the host state's primary and secondary schooling system, as well as to vocational courses in further and higher education (*Casagrande* (Case 9/74)). Besides equal treatment in relation to course fees, students are entitled to equal access to educational grants. In the case of the children of workers, this right is dependent on the child continuing as a dependent of the worker (Arts 10, 12, Regulation 1612/68), who must remain resident in the host state, or alternatively, the student must have acquired the status of worker himself. Both possibilities were discussed in the important case of *Brown* v *Secretary of State for Scotland* (Case 197/86).

Brown, who was a French national of Anglo-French origin, had applied for a discretionary grant from the Scottish Education Department to attend an electrical engineering course at Cambridge. Prior to the commencement of the course, he had obtained employment with an engineering company in Edinburgh for eight months. This job was described as 'pre-university industrial training'. Although he did not qualify for a grant under the Scottish regulations, he argued that he was entitled to receive one either as a social advantage in his capacity of a worker, under Art 7(2), Regulation 1612/68 or, alternatively, as a child of a worker under Art 12, since his parent, although no longer resident in Scotland, had worked there as his last place of employment. He was refused on both counts and the case was referred to the Court under Art 177.

Although the Court emphasised that it was for the national court to decide whether or not a particular course was 'vocational', there seems little doubt that this course met the criteria which the Court had laid down in *Blaizot* (above). It held that, although access to education, in terms of admission fees and admission criteria, was within the Treaty (and thus within the prohibition against discrimination under Art 7 EC Treaty), access to educational grants was not. Art 7 did not, therefore, assist the applicant unless he qualified either as a worker or a child of a worker. The Court, in a somewhat ambivalent decision, held that a person who

> enters into an employment relationship in the host state for a period of eight months with a view to subsequently taking up university studies there in the same field of activity ... is to be regarded as a worker within the meaning of Art 7(2) of Regulation 1612/68.

That should have concluded the issue, but the Court then added, in answer to the fourth question raised by the national court

> it cannot be inferred from that finding that a national of a member state will be entitled to a grant for studies in another member state by virtue of his status as a worker where it is established that he acquired that status exclusively as a result of his being accepted for admission to university to undertake the studies in question. In such circumstances, *the employment relationship, which is the only basis for the rights deriving from Regulation No. 1612/68, is merely ancillary to the studies to be financed by the grant.* (para [27]) (emphasis added)

As we have seen, where the employment is 'ancillary' to some other purpose, for example, therapy, as in the case of *Bettray* ((Case 344/87), above), the individual may not be regarded, although engaged in some kind of work, as a worker, either under Art 48 EC Treaty, or Art 7(2), Regulation 1612/68, for the purpose of social advantages. On that basis the Court, and the Advocate-General, could well have concluded that Brown was not a worker at all. His entitlement to social advantages would not, therefore, have arisen, as in the case of *Lebon*, above. It chose, however, to hold that he was both a worker and disentitled to the social advantages to which workers would normally be entitled in these circumstances! The Court had less difficulty in concluding that he could not be a child of a worker either, because he was born after his parents had ceased to work and reside in the host state.

Family rights

Regulation 1612/68 confers extensive family rights on the worker. Once he is in employment, he may either be accompanied by, or be joined by, his spouse and their descendants who are under the age of 21 or who are dependent, and his own dependant relatives in the ascending line and those of his spouse. That means that dependent children, grandchildren, and even great-grandchildren have the right to install themselves with the worker. Likewise, parents and grandparents of both spouses, if dependent, could join the worker. Other family members not coming within the ascending or descending lines, such as aunts and uncles and nephews and nieces, if dependent on the worker, or living under his roof, should have their entry 'facilitated' (Art 10(1), (2)). 'Facilitation' might seem to fall short of a right to admission. However, read in conjunction with Art 1, Directive 68/360, which requires the abolition of restrictions on the free movement of workers and of 'members of their families *to whom Regulation 1612/68 applies*', (emphasis added), and Art 3 Directive 68/360, which confers a right of entry on the worker and the family members defined in Art 1 of the same directive, it would seem that they also have a right of entry. In the case of family members who are not nationals of a member state, it is permissible that they should obtain visas before being admitted. In such cases member states should 'accord to such persons every facility for obtaining any necessary visa' (Art 3(2), Directive 68/360).

There should be no need to prove the relationship at the point of entry, although, for the purpose of acquisition of a residence permit, proof of the relationship, normally in the form of marriage and birth certificates, and proof of the dependency in the form of documentary evidence from the state of origin, will have to be produced when the application for a residence permit is made (Art 4 (3) (c) (d) and (e), Directive 68/360). Rights of residence of spouses do not depend on their continuing cohabitation. In *Diatta* v *Land Berlin* (Case 267/83), the Court of Justice held that the right of residence subsisted as long as the marriage continued, irrespective of whether or not the parties to the marriage were still together. Once the marriage is dissolved, the spouses right of residence in that capacity would appear to terminate. That was the decision of the House of Lords in *R* v *Secretary of State, ex parte Sandhu, The Times*, 10th May 1985, although Community free movement rights must be read in the light of Art 8 of the European Convention on Human Rights (respect for family life). In *Berrehab*, judgment of European Court of Human Rights, 21 June 1988, series A, No. 138, pp.15, 16, the Court held that the expulsion of a divorced husband whose child remained in Belgium, breached Art 8. The Court held that expulsion in such circumstances did not, however, automatically breach the Convention for it depended on the degree of contact between the divorced parent and the child. Thus, the person whose marriage has terminated, does not automatically lose the right of residence. It will depend on whether he or she would leave children or other relatives in the state in question, and the extent to which they were, in fact, part of a close family unit (*see* Schermers, H., *Human Rights and Free Movement of Persons* in *Free Movement of Persons in Europe: Legal Problems and Experiences* (1993)). The European Court of Justice has yet to consider the position arising on the divorce of the worker and spouse. In the context of rights of residence of a Turkish national under the EEC-Turkey Association Agreement, the Court has held that where a Turkish national is working lawfully in a member state, the fact that his marriage to a Community national, the original basis of his right of residence, had been dissolved did not affect the legality of his continuing residence (*Kus* v *Landeshaupt stadt Wiesbaden* (Case C-237/91); *Buyukyilmas* v *Secretary of State for the Home Department* (11769) 19 January 1995 (Immigration Appeal Tribunal) (unreported)).

Family free movement rights derive directly from Community law. They apply not only to European Union citizens who work in other member states in relation to those states, but also in relation to their own state where they have returned to it after having worked abroad. In *R* v *Immigration Appeal Tribunal, ex parte Singh* (Case C- 370/90), the Court of Justice held that a national of a member state who has gone to another member state in order to work there as an employed person under Art 48 EC Treaty, and returns to establish himself as a self-employed person in the territory of the member state of which he is a national has the right to return to that state under the same conditions as are laid down by Regulation 1612/68 or Directive 68/360. That meant that the obligation under United Kingdom immigration law for a spouse to establish that the 'primary purpose' of his entry was the marriage and not to secure entry or residence to the United Kingdom did not apply (for the current UK Rules, see para 281 HC 395, 23 May 1994). It is, therefore, not open to member states to impose additional requirements for the entry and residence of family members. However, in *Kwong* (11 February 1994) (10661), the Immigration Appeal Tribunal held that a marriage to a Community national, even if it was a valid marriage under national law, could be found to be an empty 'shell' if it was entered into 'specifically to achieve the benefits of residence'. (at p. 10, *see* Art 2 (2), Immigration (European Economic Area) Order 1994 (SI 1994 No. 1895)). It may well be desirable to prevent abuses of Community law, but as Community law stands at present, it is not open to member states to add qualifications to access of rights conferred by Community law (*Roux* (Case C-363/89); *Commission* v *Belgium* (Case C-326/90)). Any attempt to put a non-EU spouse through a process of interrogation to establish whether or not the spouse has contracted the marriage to secure entry to the country, would certainly not amount to the granting of 'every facility' for the issue of the visa, as demanded by Art 3(2), Directive 68/360.

Members of the family have a right to work in the host state. Under Art 11 Regulation 1612/68, the worker's spouse and those of his children who are under the age of 21 or dependent on him, are entitled to take up any activity as an employed person throughout the territory of the host state, even if they are not nationals of any member state. In Gül (Case 131/85), the applicant sought to rely on Art 11. He was a Turkish-Cypriot doctor, married to an Englishwoman working as a hairdresser in Germany. When he applied for authorisation to practise medicine in Germany he was refused on account of his nationality. On a reference under Art 177, the Court held that, provided that he had the qualifications necessary to practise in the host state, according to national legislation, he was entitled to practise his profession in that state by virtue of Art 11 of Regulation 1612/68.

Housing provisions

The entry of family members is conditional upon the worker having available for them 'housing considered as normal for national workers in the region where he is employed' (Art 10(3), Regulation 1612/68). This condition is only operative at the time of the family's entry. An attempt by the German authorities to make access to reasonable housing provisions a precondition for the renewal of a resident permit was held by the Court of Justice in *Re Housing of Migrant Workers: EC Commission* v *Germany* (Case 249/86) to be unlawful. The reference to adequate housing in Art

10(3) related only to the 'installation' of the worker's family. The Court emphasised the importance of family re-union, as guaranteed by Art 8 of the European Convention on Human Rights, and the need to 'facilitate … the integration of the worker and his family into the host member state without any difference in treatment in relation to nationals of that state.' (para [10], [11] of judgment).

The need for equal treatment in the housing field is dealt with in Art 9, Regulation 1612/68. Under this provision, the 'worker shall enjoy all the rights and benefits accorded to national workers in matters of housing, including ownership of the housing he needs. If his family has remained in the country whence he came, they shall be considered for this purpose as residing' in the region where he is working. On this basis, the worker is entitled to be treated both for the purpose of applications for public housing, and the purchase of a private house, as having his family with him. If he loses the housing which he initially obtained for his family, through no fault of his own, he is entitled to equal access, for example, to emergency housing provision under Housing Act 1985 Pt III, in the United Kingdom. Even if he has housing in his country of origin, provided that he organised adequate housing on the arrival of the family, the family cannot be expected to return to the country of origin (*Compare, De Falco* v *Crawley Borough Council* [1980] QB 460 and *R* v *Hillingdon LBC, ex parte Islam* [1981] 3 WLR 942 at 953 (HL)). The Court of Justice held in *Commission* v *Germany* (above) that the acquisition of housing solely to secure a residence permit could be penalised, if the family then moved into less suitable accommodation, but that any penalty should fall short of measures leading to expulsion (para [14] of judgment).

Retirement

Article 48(3) confers on the worker the right to remain in the host member state, with his family, after having been employed there. The conditions under which this right is exercisable following retirement, or premature cessation of work due to an accident at work, or to a disease contracted while working, are laid down in Regulation 1251/70. The worker must have been employed for at least a year in the host state, before he is entitled to retire there on reaching the age at which the state retirement pension becomes payable (Art 2(1)(a)). If the worker becomes incapable of working after working more than two years in the host state, he can stay on there for as long as he likes. He can remain, irrespective of his period of residence, if he is incapacitated by an accident or disease contracted at work (Art 2(1)(b)). His family, as defined in Art 10, Regulation 1612/68, are entitled to remain as long as he does.

If the worker should die before retirement, his family is entitled to remain in the host state, provided the deceased worker had lived continuously there for more than two years. If he died as a result of an industrial accident, or occupational disease, there is no qualifying period to satisfy to enable the family to remain, nor is there such a qualifying period if the widow or widower either is a national of the host state, or was one before his or her marriage (Arts 2, 3, Regulation 1251/70). The families of deceased workers are entitled to all the social advantages that are available to the families of active and retired workers (*Cristini* v *SNCF* (Case 32/75) (see above)). They must also be issued with a residence permit on application, valid for a period of five years, which is automatically renewable (Art 6, Regulation 1251/71).

The entitlement to retire to another member state is not limited to those who have worked there. Under Directive 90/365, European Union citizens who have worked either as employees or in a self-employed capacity in one member state are entitled to retire to another member state. The directive is made possible by the fact that, under Art 10 of Regulation 1408/71, recipients of invalidity or old age cash benefits or pensions for accidents at work or occupational diseases are entitled to continue to receive those benefits and pensions even if they reside in the territory of a member state other than the one that pays the benefits (see recitals of Directive 90/365, and Chapter 10). It has a more limited application, however, than Regulation 1251/70, and could result in unwary individuals getting into difficulties, especially those who retire to a member state with a Mediterranean climate but a less developed welfare state than in their country of origin.

The right of residence is dependent on the retired person having, firstly, a retirement or other pension, of an amount sufficient to avoid becoming a burden on the social security system of the host state, and secondly, an all-risks sickness insurance scheme. Pensioners are entitled to be accompanied by their families, who are, in this case, limited to spouse and dependent children and grandchildren, and dependent relatives in the ascending line of the pensioner and his spouse. Unlike under Art 10(2), Regulation 1612/68, there are no provisions for the entry of collateral relatives (Art 1(2), Directive 90/365). Pensioners are entitled to be issued with residence permits, but the period of validity can be limited to two years. On application and on renewal the host state is entitled to demand proof that the individual continues to meet the subsistence and insurance criteria (Art 2(1)). Unlike those who retire in the state where they worked, the beneficiaries of this directive are not entitled to social advantages under Art 7 (2), Regulation 1612/68, so will have to meet payments for medical treatment either under their sickness insurance policy or from their own resources.

Further reading

Farmer, P., 'Article 48 EC and the Taxation of Frontier Workers' (1995) 32 CML Rev 310.

Flynn J., 'Vocational Training in Community Law and Practice' [1988] 8 YEL 60.

Green N., Hartley T.C., and Usher, J., (1991) *The Legal Foundations of the Single European Market*, Pt II, OUP.

Handoll, J., 'Article 48(4) EEC and Non-National Access to Public Employment' (1988) 13 EL Rev 223.

Lonbay, J., 'Education and Law: The Community Context' (1989) 14 EL Rev 363.

Morgan, 'Migrant Workers and Social Security' (1987) 24 CML Rev 498.

Pickup, D., 'Reverse Discrimination and Freedom of Movement of Workers' (1986) 23 CML Rev 135.

Schermers (ed) (1993) *Free Movement of Persons in Europe.*

Steiner, J., (1994) *Textbook on EC Law*, (4th edn),Blackstone Press, Chapter 18.

Watson, P., Notes on Free Movement of Workers (1985) 9 EL Rev 335; (1989) 14 EL Rev 415.

Weatherill, S. and Beaumont, P., (1993) *EEC Law*, Penguin Books, Chapter 18.

Wyatt, D., and Dashwood, A., (1993) *European Community Law*, (3rd edn), Sweet & Maxwell, Chapter 9.

9 Freedom of establishment and the provision and receipt of services

Individuals will frequently wish to move to another member state to engage in a business or profession in a self-employed capacity. Articles 59 and 60 EC Treaty provide for the abolition of restrictions on individuals to provide services in a member state other than that in which they are established. Article 60 provides that services shall be considered to be 'services' within the meaning of the Treaty 'where they are normally provided for remuneration'. Article 60 lists such services as including activities of an industrial and commercial character, activities of craftsmen and activities of the professions. This is, however, far from being an exhaustive list. The person providing the service 'may, in order to do so, temporarily pursue his activity in the state where the service is provided'. This is 'without prejudice to the right of establishment'. There is, in fact, a close link to the right of establishment. The right to provide the service confers a right of residence as long as the service is provided.

If, however, the service provider wishes to provide that service in the host state on a long-term basis, he may, under Art 52, become established in that state. 'Establishment' is not defined in the Treaty or the implementing legislation. However, Art 52 requires the abolition of restrictions on the freedom of establishment of nationals of a member state in the territory of another member state. Freedom of establishment includes the right to take up and pursue activities as a self-employed person and to set up and manage undertakings. The crucial element that differentiates the service provider from the established business is the process of 'setting up'. This may involve anything from leasing or buying business premises, or acquiring a licence to run a company in the host state (*see, Steinhauser* v *City of Biarritz* (Case 197/84) and *R* v *Secretary of State for Transport, ex parte Factortame* (Case C-213/89)). The Court of Justice referred to 'establishment' in the *Factortame* case as 'the actual pursuit of an economic activity through a fixed establishment for an indefinite period' (at para [20]).

None of the Treaty provisions confer a right to go to another member state to *receive* services, but Directive 73/148 is more wide-ranging than Arts 52, 59 and 60. It provides for the abolition of restrictions on the movement and residence of:

1   nationals of a member state who are established or who wish to establish them-
    selves in another member state in order to pursue activities as self-employed
    persons or who wish to provide services in that state; and
2   nationals of member states wishing to go to another member state as recipients
    of services;

The scope of the Treaty provisions and the directive in relation to the provision of
services, the receipt of services and the right of establishment will be examined in
turn.

THE PROVISION OF SERVICES

Only those services which are provided for remuneration entitle the providers and
recipients to move to another member state to provide and receive them. The Court
of Justice in *Belgium* v *Humbel* (case 263/86) said that 'the essential characteristic of
remuneration is that it constitutes the countervailing financial advantage for the
services in question and is normally fixed between the supplier and the recipient of
the service'. It held, on this basis, that courses of study provided in the framework
of a national educational system were not provided for remuneration. The situation
was not affected by the facts that students had to pay a registration fee or some
other charge. By establishing and maintaining a national educational system, 'the
state does not intend to engage in activities for which remuneration is received, but
is fulfilling its duty to its people in the social, cultural and educational fields' (para
[17] and [18] of judgment). Education can, however, be a service if it is provided by
a private body on a commercial basis (*see, Luisi and Carbone* v *Ministero del Tesoro*
(Case 286/83)). The services are, therefore, either of a commercial character, or they
are, at least provided in exchange for money or money's worth.

The Court considered the meaning of a 'service' in *Schindler* (Case C-275/92).

In this case, the undertakings concerned were agents of four local state lotteries in Germany.
They sent letters from the Netherlands to the United Kingdom enclosing application forms with
invitations to participate in the German lotteries. The letters were confiscated by Customs and
Excise on the grounds that they infringed national legislation on lotteries and gaming. The
Court held that the letters were not 'goods', so the restrictions did not fall to be considered
under Art 39 EC Treaty.

Were they, then, a service? The Court decided that they were. The services provided
by the operators of the lottery enabled purchasers of tickets to participate in a game
of chance with the hope of winning, by arranging for that purpose for the stakes to
be collected, the draws to be organised and the prizes for winnings to be ascertained
and paid out. The services were 'normally provided for remuneration', represented
by the price of the lottery ticket. They were cross-border, since they were offered in

the member state other than that in which the lottery operator was established. The Court recently reached a similar conclusion in relation to the offer of financial services by telephone to potential recipients in another state (*Alpine Investments BV* v *Minister van Financiën* (Case C-348/93)).

The provision of services may be by sole traders, companies or partnerships. If they are companies, they do not need to be owned or controlled by nationals of the member state in which they are based, nor do the employees of the company providing a service in another member state have to be EU citizens. They should be able to operate in other member states without restriction. In *Vander Elst* v *OMI* (Case C-43/93),

the complainant operated a demolition company which was established in Belgium. He employed a number of foreign workers, many of them from Morocco. They had work permits and were lawfully employed in Belgium. The company was engaged to carry out a demolition contract in France. Foreign employees were not permitted by the French authorities to work on the contract without French work permits. On an Art 177 reference, the Court of Justice held that the Belgian undertaking was providing a service under Arts 59 and 60, and that it could bring its workforce of whatever nationality to perform that task. Any attempt to impose further controls on its workforce would amount to a restriction on the provision on services and would be unlawful. The imposition of further workpermit requirements would, the Court said, amount to the duplication of the procedures the company had already gone through in its home state.

As one of the fundamental principles of the Treaty, freedom to provide services may be restricted only by rules which are justified by overriding reasons in the general interest and are applied to all persons and undertakings operating in the territory of the state where the service is provided, in so far as that interest is not safeguarded by the rules to which the provider of such a service is subject in the member state where he is established (*see*, in particular, Case C-180/89 *Commission* v *Italy* [1991] ECR I-709, para 17, and in Case C-198/89 *Commission* v *Greece* [1991] ECR I-727, para 18). While the Court is reluctant to recognise new 'overriding intersts in the general interest', it will, in exceptional circumstances, accept that such interests enable a state to impose a total ban on the import of the service in question, even when it is permitted, within strict limitations, in the state imposing the ban (*Schindler*, above).

RECIPIENTS OF SERVICES

It was originally thought by many commentators that the right of entry for receipt of services had to be associated with a specific service. Thus, for example, a private patient who goes to another member state to be examined by a consultant, or the owner of an antique who takes it to another state for a valuation would be within the context, but a tourist who went walking in the Alps, and incidentally used hotel and transport services would not. In other words, the receipt of the service had to be the *reason* for the individual's entry into the other state. It could not merely be incidental to it. However, in *Luisi and Carbone* (above) the Court held that tourism itself was a service which was covered by Art 59, and in Case 186/87 *Cowan* v *Le Tresor Public* (1986) ECR 195, that tourists were entitled to full equal treatment under Art 6 of the Treaty, and that equal treatment included access to the criminal process and to national provisions on criminal injuries compensation (*see* Weatherill, S., 'Note on *Cowan* v *Le Tresor Public*' (1989) 25 *CML Rev* 563; Van der Woude and Mead, 'Free Movement of Tourists in European Community Law' (1988) 25 *CML Rev* 117).

Recipients of services are, like providers, only entitled to remain as long as the service is received. Given the breadth of the concept of 'services' it would seem that any EU Citizen or national of an EEA state can remain in another member state for as long as he is paying for a service. He may, for example, be paying for accommodation out of his own resources. As long as he is relying exclusively on his own resources, however modest, he is providing 'remuneration' and would seem to be entitled to remain under Arts 59, 60 EC, and Directive 73/148; and *see The State* v *Humbel* (Case 263/86). There is a somewhat unclear dividing line between this situation and that to which the general right of residence Directive 90/364 is applicable.

Directive 90/364 confers a right of residence on nationals of member states who do not enjoy such a right under any other provision of Community law, and to spouses and descendents and relatives in the ascending line of the main beneficiary and his spouse who are dependent. This right of residence is only open to those who have sufficient resources to avoid becoming a burden on the social assistance system of the host state and who hold an 'all risks' sickness insurance policy (Art 1). There is no obvious distinction between individuals in this residual category and recipients of services. It may be that a person who has adequate resources can survive in another member state without paying for services, such as by staying with a friend. But in most cases, self-sufficient individuals will also be recipients of services. It is clearly in their interest to remain in this category, because if they are identifiable as beneficiaries under Directive 90/364 they will have to provide evidence of 'all risks' health insurance, a facility which appears to be currently unavailable from any insurance company! (Vincenzi, C., 'Welcoming the Well and Wealthy: the Implementation of Directive 90/364 in the United Kingdom' in Daintith, T., *Implementing EC Law in the United Kingdom: Structures for Direct Rule* (1995).

THE PROVISION OF SERVICES AND RIGHTS OF ESTABLISHMENT

As we have seen, there is a close link between the provision of services by the self-employed and by undertakings and the establishment of businesses in another member state. The one frequently precedes the other. Thus, provisions under Arts 52 to 58 dealing with establishment, particularly the preliminaries to becoming established, will often overlap with the provision of services. Freedom of establishment includes:

> the right to take up and pursue activities as self-employed persons and to set up and manage undertakings, in particular companies and firms … under the conditions laid down for its own nationals by the law of the country where such establishment is effected (Art 52).

'Companies and firms' means companies and firms constituted under civil or commercial law, including co-operative societies, and other legal persons governed by public or private law, save for those which are non profit-making (Art 58). Although the inclusive term 'other legal persons' would seem to exclude the English partnership, since this has no legal personality, this is not, in fact the case. The rights to both provision of services and to establishment belong to both natural and legal persons. In practice, it matters not whether a partnership enjoys the right to set up branches in another member state by virtue of being a 'legal person', or a collection of 'natural persons', provided that both have their registered office, central administration or principal place of business within the Community.

Article 52 draws a distinction between nationals of member states, and those already established in the territory of a member state. Each state defines its own nationals, thereby giving them the benefits enjoyed by EU citizenship (*see* Chapter 7). However, an undertaking which does not have its principal office in the Community, if it is established in one of the member states, may, nonetheless set up agencies and branches in other member states.

OBSTACLES TO ESTABLISHMENT

Article 54 of the Treaty provided for the drawing up of a general programme for the abolition of restrictions on freedom of establishment within the Community. The Council and Commission were to give priority treatment to activities where freedom of establishment made a particularly valuable contribution to the development of production and trade, and were to abolish administrative procedures and practices forming obstacles to establishment, and enable nationals of member states to acquire and use land and buildings. Existing necessary safeguards for the operation of businesses and the professions were to be harmonised and co-ordinated.

The General Programme made under Art 54 was approved in December 1961. Title III of the Programme called for the abolition of discriminatory measures which might impair access to non-wage-earning activities of Community nationals. The measures to be abolished included:

1   Provisions which made access to a non-wage-earning activity conditional upon the issue of an official authoriastion or the issue of a document, such as a foreign merchant's card or a foreign professional's card;

2   The imposition of taxes or other charges which would make access to a business or profession in another member state more difficult and costly. In Case C-20/92 *Hubbard* v *Hamburger,* judgment of 1 July 1993 (unreported) where the Court of Justice held that a demand made in German proceedings for an English solicitor/executor who was a party to the proceedings brought in connection with a deceased's estate to make a deposit for costs was unlawful and discriminatory. No such demand was made of German lawyers;

3   Provisions which barred or limited membership in companies, particularly with regard to the activities of their members;

4   Restrictions imposed on foreign nationals in relation to entry into various commercial and other contracts, the right to tender or participate in public works contracts, to borrow and have access to various forms of credit and to have access to loans and grants provided by state agencies.

To give effect to the programme, the Commission drew up a wide range of directives which were intended to facilitate access to a great variety of activities, including itinerant traders, film producers, hairdressers and the providers of gas, water and electricity services. Some of these require specific periods of academic training and practical experience, while others simply require a period of self-employment and a certificate of good character (compare the provisions in Directive 86/653 on self-employed commercial agents with Directive 87/540 on carriers of goods by waterway). It was thought, initially, that until an appropriate directive was in place, national measures would continue to apply and, in many cases, would have the effect of excluding Community nationals from participating in the relevant business or occupation. The right to equality of opportunity provided in Art 52(2) in relation to establishment and Art 60(3) in relation to the provision of services relates to the conditions for establishment and self-employment in the host state. These may, in many instances, be more difficult for Community nationals to satisfy, despite their overt application to local nationals and Community nationals on the same terms.

However, the right of establishment and the right to provide services have been described by the Court of Justice as 'fundamental rights', and it has been active in asserting that businesses and the self-employed should have access to activities in member states without hindrance or open or covert discrimination, even where there were no implementing Community measures. The difficulty, in many of these cases, is that perfectly proper national measures to protect consumers and users of professional services, or to achieve other legitimate objectives, have, in the same way as they have in the national context, been used by practitioners to exclude competitors from other member states. The Court has often had to judge whether a national measure could be objectively justified, or whether it operated as an unlawful restriction. In *Commission* v *Italy* (*Re Freedom of Establishment*) (Case

168/85), it held that national provisions on tourism, the operation of pharmacies and access to the occupation of journalism, which denied access to those not holding Italian nationality, were incompatible with Arts 48, 52 and 59 of the Treaty. It was not sufficient that instructions should be issued disapplying them to Community citizens. They had to be repealed.

In *Reyners* v *Belgian State* (Case 2/74), the Court held that, like Art 48, Art 52 was directly effective. The fact that it was to be given effect over a period did not affect the right of the beneficiaries to enjoy immediate protection.

> Article 52 … imposes an obligation to attain a precise result, the fulfilment of which had to be made easier by, but not made dependent on, the implementation of a programme of progressive measures. The fact that this progression has not been adhered to leaves the obligation itself intact beyond the end of the period provided for its fulfilment.
> (paras [26] and [27] of judgment)

On this basis, the Court held that rules, under which a Dutchman, who had been born and educated in Belgium, who was resident there, and who held a doctorate in Belgian law, had been excluded from legal practice because he was not a Belgian, were incompatible with Arts 7 and 52 of the Treaty.

Less direct provisions than national restrictions may also infringe the rights conferred by Arts 52, 59 and 60. In a series of cases brought by the Commission under Art 169, local restrictions on the operation of insurance services were challenged in the Court. In each of the four states concerned insurance undertakings were required to conduct their business in those states through individuals already established and authorised to practise there (*Commission* v *Denmark* (Case 252/83); *Commission* v *France* (Case 220/83); *Commission* v *Germany* (Case 205/84); *Commission* v *Ireland* (Case 206/84)). The Court accepted that, in the state of Community law prevailing at the time, the authorisation and licensing of insurance services was still a matter of the law of the host state. However, in operating its national system, the host state may not duplicate equivalent statutory conditions which have already been satisfied in the state where the business has originally been established. However, until such time as national rules on company taxation are harmonised throughout the Community, it is permissible for a member state to impose a restriction on companies, so that they cannot move their principal place of business without the consent of the national tax authorities (*R* v *HM Treasury, ex parte Daily Mail and General Trust plc* (Case 81/87)). The retention of national company taxation rules should not, however, allow member states to operate discriminatory tax rules which operate as a barrier to the establishment of branches of foreign undertakings in their territories (*R* v *IRC, ex parte Commerzbank AG* (Case 330/91)). A similar principle applies, pending the adoption of a common visa policy, in the case of companies which operate in other member states and employ third state nationals (*Van der Elst* (Case C-43/93)).

RIGHTS OF ENTRY AND RESIDENCE

Directive 73/148 was adopted under Title II of the General Programme for the abolition of restrictions on the right of establishment and the provision of services. Its provisions are similar to Directive 68/360 in relation to the entry and residence of workers. The Court of Justice does not, in fact, always draw a clear distinction between the rights of entry and residence enjoyed on the basis of being a giver or receiver of services or being a worker (*Royer* (Case 48/75); *Watson and Belmann* (Case 118/75)). Indeed, where a person enters another member state, he may not immediately know whether he will set up in business, provide a service or enter into employment. The latter status has, however, some distinct benefits, particularly in the area of social advantages, which are not enjoyed by the self- employed.

The beneficiaries of the directive, are, as indicated above, those establishing themselves or wishing to do so, those providing and those receiving services. The family members entitled to move are the spouse of the main beneficiary, their children under the age of 21, and ascending and descending relatives of beneficiary and spouse who are dependent on the beneficiary. Member states are also obliged to 'favour the admission' of any other member of the family of the beneficiary who are either dependent or are living under the same roof in the country of origin (Art 1). Despite the difference in terminology in relation to collateral and other relatives, Art 3, like the equivalent provision of Directive 68/360 (Art 3), provides that all the family members should have the right to enter the territory of the host state simply on production of a valid identity card or passport. Visas can be demanded for non-EU family members, but 'every facility' should be afforded to them for obtaining one (Art 3(1)).

Those giving or receiving services are entitled to remain for as long as the services are being given or received. The right is not, as with the right of workers, dependent on the issue of a residence permit (Art 4 (2); *Royer* (Case 48/75)). However, it is useful to have a residence permit as proof of the right of residence. In the case of a provider or recipient of services there is no residence permit, only a 'right of abode', which is similar to a temporary residence permit issued under Art 6 (3), Directive 68/360 to workers. Those who have become established are entitled to be issued with a permit valid for at least five years, which is automatically renewable. The provisions for the issue and renewal of permits are very similar to those with regard to workers. There is, however, an important distinction. Although a residence permit cannot be lost where the self-employed worker becomes temporarily incapable of working because of sickness or accident (Art 4(1), Directive 73/148), it can, however, be withdrawn where the self-employed person's business fails through no fault of his own, and he becomes 'involuntarily' unemployed (compare Art 7, Directive 68/360).

EQUAL TREATMENT

Neither the providers nor recipients of services have the benefit of Art 7(2), Regulation 1612/68 (social advantages), nor the provisions of Arts 7(1), 9, 10, 11 and 12 of the same regulation in relation to vocational education, housing, and employment rights of family members, since the regulation only applies to workers. On the face of it, this is an important difference, since social advantages have played an important part in the jurisprudence of the Court in relation to the integration of workers and their families into the host state (*see* Chapter 8). There are no equivalent provisions in Directive 73/148, and its beneficiaries are obliged to look to Art 6 of the Treaty to be put on an equal footing with local nationals. The Court considerably mitigated the difference by a creative application of Art 6 EC. It has, however, drawn the line at equality of treatment in relation to social assistance and educational grants.

In *Commission* v *Italy (Re Housing Aid)* (Case 63/86), a cheap mortgage facility which was by Italian law, confined to Italian nationals, was held by the Court of Justice to contravene Art 7 (now Art 6) EC Treaty. In *Cowan* v *Le Tresor Public* (Case 186/87), Mr Cowan, a British citizen, was visiting Paris as a tourist, when he was assaulted in the exit of a Metro station. He was held to be entitled to the same rights in relation to criminal injuries compensation as a French national. The Court confined itself to considering the availability of the compensation scheme to non-French nationals. Rather on the same basis that it had decided that equal access to the criminal process was a necessary pre-condition to the vindication of the rights of the worker in the criminal process (and could thus be seen to be a 'social advantage' in *Mutsch* (Case 137/84) it decided that the criminal injuries scheme should be similarly available to Mr Cowan. Presumably it would have come to the same conclusion if his attackers had been identified, and his application had been for legal aid to bring proceedings against them for assault (*see*, Weatherill op. cit., p 575). It is, however, difficult to predict this with confidence. Although the Court has been quick to use Art 7 to enable an individual to overcome obstacles, either overt or covert, to the exercise of rights conferred by Arts 52, 59 and 60, it has been more reluctant to do so when the obstacle is the individual's shortage of resources.

In *Gravier* v *City of Liège* (Case 293/83), the Court held that Ms Gravier was exercising a right to receive education under Art 128 EC Treaty. In the course of exercising such a right, she was entitled to benefit from Art 7 (now Art 6) EC Treaty. On that basis she should receive equal treatment in relation to payment of the university admission fee, the minerval, so that she would only have to pay the same amount as 'home' students (*see* also, *Commission* v *Belgium (Re University Fees)* (Case C-47/93)). In *Commission* v *Spain* (Case C-45-93), the Court held that the principle of equal treatment extended to the right of visitors from other EU states to free admission to museums, where this facility was availale to Spanish nationals. The right to equal treatment in relation to access to vocational education did not, however, extend to financial assistance to enable an individual to go to another member state and receive a grant to support him while at a vocational school or on a vocational course. Such a right did not exist under Art 128, nor under Art 7 (*Lair* v *University of Hannover* (Case 39/86)). Indeed, the right to receive education as a 'service' under Art 59 depended on the individual providing 'remuneration' for it *Humbel* (Case 263/86); paras 8–13 of judgment: *see* now Directive 93/96, under which students have a right to receive vocational educational in another member state, provided that they have sufficient resources to avoid becoming a burden on the social assistance scheme of the host state (Art 1). The directive expressly excludes any entitlement to a maintenance grant from the host state, although a maintenance grant paid by the state of origin could, of course, constitute the 'resources' which would enable the student to exercise the right.

THE OFFICIAL AUTHORITY EXCEPTION

As with Art 48, the rights of entry and residence of those entering to provide and receive services are subject to the right of the host state to derogate on grounds of public policy, public security and public health (Art 56(1), 66 EC Treaty). The scope of these provisions will be examined in Chapter 11. In addition, the rights enjoyed by virtue of Arts 52, 59 and 60 EC Treaty 'shall not apply … to activities … connected, even occasionally, with the exercise of official authority' (Art 55 EC Treaty). Like 'the public service ' exception in Art 48(4), 'the exercise of official authority' is not defined in the Treaty, but its scope was considered by the Court of Justice in *Reyners* v *Belgian State* (Case 2/74). The defendant in this case argued that the profession of avocat was exempted from the chapter of the Treaty on rights of establishment because it sometimes involved the exercise of official authority. The Court rejected the idea that an avocat, despite his occasional official duties, was necessarily concerned with the exercise of official authority:

> An extension of the exception allowed by Art 55 to a whole profession would be possible only in cases where such activities were linked with that profession in such a way that freedom of establishment would result in imposing on the member state concerned the obligation to allow the exercise, even occasionally, by nationals of functions appertaining to official authority. This extension is on the other hand not possible when, within the framework of an independent profession, the activities connected with the exercise of official authority are separable from the professional activity in question taken as a whole. (paras [46] and [47] of judgment)

The 'exercise of official authority' would seem to be analagous to the exercise of 'public service' under Art 48(4) (*Commission* v *Belgium* (Case 149/79), *see* above, Chapter 8), and is likely to be as narrowly construed by the Court (*see*, for example,

Commission v *Greece* (Case C-306/89) (road traffic experts not within Art 55 exception); *Commission* v *Italy* (Case C-272/9), the provision of computer services for the state lottery not within Art 55). More decisions of the Court are required before the full scope of this exception can be determined.

PROFESSIONAL QUALIFICATIONS

As we have seen, the lack of common qualifications in the Community, and an unwillingness to recognise diplomas and other qualifications from other states proved a major obstacle to the exercise of free movement rights, especially those with specialist skills. The problem was addressed by the General Programme, which resulted in the production of a whole range of harmonising directives relating to a wide range of activities. Little progress was, however, made in relation to the traditional professions. It is generally accepted that in such professions as law, accountancy, medicine, banking and insurance the public needs to be protected against those who might misrepresent their skills and qualifications. To protect both public and professionals many such professions are regulated by law. Regulation will cover such matters as education and training, professional conduct and disciplinary proceedings. In some member states the regulatory process is entirely in the hands of Government. In the United Kingdom and Ireland it is largely in the hands of professional bodies, operating within a statutory framework. Individuals and undertakings providing financial services will also work within a framework of self and state regulation, although the trend in the United Kingdom in recent years has been towards self-regulation and deregulation. From the point of view of the consuming public, the self-regulation process by professionals has sometimes been seen to be as much concerned with the protection of professionals from competition as with protection of the public from abuse. It could also be perceived in a single market as a covert form of protectionism in relation to the delivery of professional services by citizens of other member states.

The reluctance of national professional bodies to agree harmonised standards for particular occupations led the Commission to adopt a new approch in 1985, following publication of the white paper on the single market. That approach acknowledged the need

> to provide a rapid response to the expectations of nationals of Community countries who hold higher-education diplomas awarded on completion of professional education and training issued in a member state other than that in which they wish to pursue their profession. (Preamble to Directive 89/48)

The new approach involved both general educational criteria and the mutual recognition of educational diplomas and relevant practical experience. Directive 89/48 opened the way for entry into professional practice in other member states for a whole new range of activities. In the United Kingdom these occupations include:

actuaries, auditors, barristers, chiropodists, dietitians, physiotherapists, optomotrists, civil engineers, marine architects, town planners, solicitors and teachers. There are more than 30 regulated professions listed by the Department of Trade and Industry (*see* Department of Trade and Industry, EC Professional Qualifications Directive : Guidance for Competent Authorities (1989)).

Directive 89/48 is essentially a 'residual' directive, in the sense that it does not apply to professions which are the subject of a separate directive establishing arrangements for the mutual recognition of diplomas by member states (Art 2). It applies to 'regulated professional activity', that is, 'a professional activity, in so far as the taking up or pursuit of such an activity or one of its modes of pursuit in a member state is subject, directly or indirectly by virtue of laws, regulations or administrative provisions, to the possession of a diploma'. (Art 1). Beneficiaries of the directive are those who can show the following:

1 Possession of a diploma indicating that the holder has the professional qualifications required for the taking up or pursuit of a regulated profession in one of the member states.
2 Completion of a post-secondary course of at least three years duration, or of an equivalent duration part-time, at a university or establishment of higher education or another establishment of similar level.
3 Where appropriate, that the holder of the diploma has successfully completed the professional training required in addition to the post-secondary course.

The host state may also require the holder of the diploma to provide evidence of professional experience of not more than four years where the period of education and training falls short by more than one year compared to that required in the host state. Where the education and training received by the individual in his home state differ substantially from those required in the host state, or where there is a substantial mismatch between the regulated activities in the home and host states, the host state can require the holder of the diploma to complete either an adaptation period of not more than three years or take an aptitude test. Except in those cases where the holder would need a precise knowledge of the law of the host state to carry on the profession, the choice of whether to undergo an adaptation period or an aptitude test belongs to the diploma holder.

Directive 89/48 has been implemented in the United Kingdom by the European Communities (Recognition of Professional Qualifications) Regulations 1991 (S I 1991 No. 824). Under the regulations, professionals bodies are obliged to recognise the qualifications of other Community professionals, to provide full reasons where this is not done in individual cases, and to set up an independent appeal tribunal before which any refusal of recognition can be challenged.

Recognition of diplomas for other professional activities

Directive 89/48 applies only to regulated professional activities where the holder has completed at least three years in higher education. There still remained a great many professional and other activities for which some further education was required, but which do not fall within the ambit of Directive 89/48. A further directive was, therefore, approved in 1992, Directive 92/51 to deal with the remaining areas of professional education and training. Directive 92/51 applies to holders of diplomas which show that the holder has either successfully completed a post- secondary course of at least a year or the equivalent on a part-time basis, entry to which is on the same basis as entry into university or higher education or the holder has been succesful in completing one of the recognised education and training courses listed in the directive. In the same way as Directive 89/48, the host state may require the diploma holder to complete an adaptation period of not more than three years or to take an aptitude test (Art 4 (1) (b)).

OTHER QUALIFICATIONS

In the case of qualifications which do not fall within the specific directives which have been adopted, or the general Directives 89/48 and 92/51 described above, the basic rules on recognition and the investigation of the equivalence of qualifications will continue to apply. In *Colegio Oficial de Agentes de la Propriedad Inmobiliara* v *Aguirre, Newman and Others*, (Case C-104/91),

the defendant Newman was prosecuted for practising as an estate agent in Spain without being a member of the Colegio. He had applied for membership but had received no response. He was a member of the Royal Institute of Chartered Surveyors in the United Kingdom. It should be noted that the prosecution took place before 4 January 1991, the date by which Directive 89/48 should have been implemented in member states. The Spanish court referred the question of how far the Colegio was obliged to take into account the defendant's United Kingdom qualifications to the Court of Justice. The Court held that, in the absence of harmonisation of the conditions of access to a particular profession, member states were entitled to lay down the knowledge and qualifications needed in order to pursue it and to require the production of a diploma certifying that the holder had the relevant knowledge and qualifications. In this case, the member state was required to carry out a comparative examination of professional qualifications, taking into account the differences between the national legal systems concerned.

If the comparison shows that the knowledge and qualifications correspond to the national provisions of the host state, then it is bound to accept their equivalence. If, on the other hand, the examination reveals only partial equivalence, the host state has the right to require that the person concerned should demonstrate that he has acquired the additional knowledge and qualifications needed. The host state is under an obligation to give full reasons as to the lack of equivalence. This is to enable the person to takes steps to remedy the deficiency, or if he disagrees with the decision, to challenge it in a court of law (*UNECTEF* v *Heylens* (Case 222/86); *Vlassopoulou* (Case C-340/89)).

RETIREMENT

There is no equivalent right to remain in the host state after a person has become established there under Art 52, in comparison to that enjoyed by workers under Art 48 (3) and Regulation 1251/71. However, Directive 75/34 is intended to put the self-employed person on the same basis:

> The nature of establishment, together with the attachments formed to the countries in which they have pursued their activities, means that such persons have a definite interest in enjoying the same right to remain as that granted to workers. (Preamble)

The right to remain is to be enjoyed by all those who have pursued an activity as a self-employed person in another member state and who have reached the age at which an old-age pension becomes payable in that state. They must have pursued the activity for at least the previous 12 months, and have lived in the state for more than three years. If no pension is payable to the self-employed in that state, then the retirement age is to be 65 (Art 2 (1) (a)).

The qualifying period is shorter for a self-employed person who has worked in another state and who become permanently incapacitated. In such cases, he has a right to remain if he has lived in the state for two years. If he ceased to work as a result of an accident at work or an occupational disease, there is no qualifying period, provided that he is entitled to an industrial injuries or similar pension payable by the host state (Art 2 (1) (b)).

Those enjoying this right are entitled to retain with them those members of their family who were living with them at the date on which their right to remain became effective (Art 3 (1)). Members of the family can remain after the death of the self-employed person, even if he dies before his own entitlement to remain has taken effect, provided that the individual who would have had the right, had lived there for at least two years (Art 3 (2)).

The self-employed while both active and retired, are not entitled to the 'social advantages' conferred by Art 7 (2), Regulation 1612/68, but they will be entitled to equal treatment under Art 6 EC Treaty and this will, in this case, entitle them to a number of benefits available in the host state. Given the reluctance of the Court to extend the principle of equal treatment to benefits, such as grants, for recipients of services (*see Lair* (case 39/86)) it is not clear how far this principle extends. However, since Directive 75/34 is modelled closely on Regulation 1251/70, it seems likely that the retired self-employed and their families will be treated no less favourably than the beneficiaries of Regulation 1251/70 (*see*, for example, *Cristini* v *SNCF* (Case 32/75) Chapter 8).

Further reading

Capelli, F., 'The Free Movement of Professionals in the European Community' in Schermers, H., (ed) (1993) *Free Movement of Persons in Europe*, p 437.

Department of Trade and Industry, EC Professional Qualifications Directive: Guidance for Competent Authorities (1989).

Eidenmüller, H., 'Deregulating the Market for Legal Services in the European Community' (1990) 53 MLR 604.

Green, N., Hartley, T.C., and Usher, J., (1991) *The Legal Foundations of the Single European Market*, OUP, Chapter 12.

Marenco, M., 'The Notion of Restriction on Freedom of Establishment and Provision of Services in the Case Law of the Court' (1991) 11 YEL 111.

Peers, S., 'Indirect Rights for Third-Country Service Providers Confirmed' (1995) 32 CML Rev 311.

Rawlinson, W. and Cornwell-Kelly, M., (1994) *European Community Law*, Chapter 10.

Steiner, J., (1994) *Textbook on EC Law*, (4th edn), Blackstone Press, Chapter 19.

Van der Woude, M., and Mead, P., 'Free Movement of the Tourist in Community Law' (1988) 25 CML Rev 117.

Vincenzi, C., 'Welcoming the Well and Wealthy: the Implementation of Directive 90/364 in the United Kingdom, in Daintith T., *Implementing EC Law in the United Kingdom: Structures for Direct Rule* (1995).

Weatherill, S., 'Note on *Cowan* v *Le Tresor Public* (1989) 26 CML Rev 563.

Weatherill, S., (1994) *Cases and Materials on EC Law*, (2nd edn), Blackstone Press, Chapter 10.

Weatherill, S., and Beaumont, P., (1993) *EC Law*, Penguin Books, Chapter 19.

Wyatt, D., and Dashwood, A., (1993) *European Community Law*, (3rd edn), Sweet & Maxwell, Chapter 10.

10 Social security

All member states of the Community have contributory social security systems, but they vary greatly in the quantity and quality of benefits which they provide. This is, potentially, a major barrier to the mobility of the employed and self-employed. A person moving to another member state may suffer the double disadvantage of losing out on the contributions to his own national insurance scheme, with a consequent loss of benefits in his home state, and he may also find that he is not entitled to benefits in the host state because he has not contributed sufficiently or for long enough. The founders of the Community were clearly aware of this difficulty and provision was made to deal with it in Art 51 EC Treaty. This facilitates the adoption of such measures in the field of social security as are necessary to provide freedom of movement for workers; to this end it shall make arrangements to secure for migrant workers and their dependants:

1 aggregation, for the purpose of acquiring and retaining the right to benefit and of calculating the amount of benefit, of all periods taken into account under the laws of the several countries;
2 payment of benefits to persons resident in the territories of member states.

Art 51 is thus aimed at enabling the migrant worker to take his accrued rights with him, in the sense that his contributions and period of contribution in his home state will be taken into account in the host state, and his contributions in the host state will be taken into account in calculating his level of benefits when he returns to the home state. Given the variation in level and type of contribution in each member state, and the dissimilarity of social security schemes, this is a complex task. It must, however, be emphasised that the scheme is not intended to equalise the level of social security benefits throughout the Community. It is simply directed at ensuring that the migrant worker gets, as far as possible, equal treatment within local social security schemes, and does not lose out in relation to entitlements due from his home state. The Court of Justice has recently declared that, when applying national social security law to migrant workers, the host state should interpret its own legislation in the light of the aims of Art 48 to 51 of the Treaty. It should, as far as possible, avoid interpreting it in such a way as to discourage migrant workers from exercising their rights to freedom of movement (*Van Munster* (Case C-165/91)).

Because there are such large discrepancies between national security schemes, this area of Community law has been highly productive of litigation and the case law is considerable and complicated. This chapter will do no more than outline the general principles and provide some examples of their interpretation by the Court of Justice and their application in the United Kingdom.

The current Community rules enacted to give effect to the principles laid down in Art 51 are to be found in Regulations 1408/71, 574/72 as amended by Regulation 2001/83. Regulation 1408/71 as amended by Regulation 2001/83 contains the substantive provisions. Regulation 574/72 deals with the procedures for the operation and interrelation of national social security schemes. The most recent important legislation, Regulation 1247/92, limits the availability of national welfare provisions, and will be looked at in the context of United Kingdom legislation. The scope of Regulation 1408/71, as amended, will first be examined.

THE BENEFICIARIES OF THE REGULATIONS

The regulations cover the European Union citizens who are employed or self-employed and who are, or who have been, subject to social security legislation in more than one of the member states. Their families are also covered, together with any survivors of the worker or self-employed person after his death, provided that they were, at some stage, covered by the the social security legislation of more than one member state (Arts 1, 2, Regulation 1408/71). It also applies to refugees, stateless persons, and their families, as defined by Art 1 of the Geneva Convention on the Status of Refugees 1951 and Art 1 of the Convention on Stateless Persons 1954, and civil servants who are treated as such by national legislation. The term 'employed person' is much wider in scope than 'worker' under Art 48 EC Treaty and it includes any person who is insured either voluntarily or compulsorily against one of the contingencies covered by the regulation. The fourth recital of Regulation 1408/71 refers to the wide variations in applicability of various national social security schemes, which made it desirable to establish the principle that the regulation applied to all nationals of a member state insured under social security schemes for employed persons.

In relation to the self-employed, they are classified as such, because, like the the employed, they are included in a national scheme set up for the benefit of the self-employed, not because they might enjoy that status under Arts 52 and 59 EC Treaty. In *Van Roosmalen* (Case 300/84), the Court considered the meaning of 'self-employment' in the context of Regulation 1408/71.

The case concerned a missionary priest who had worked from 1955 until 1980 in what is now Zaire. He was not paid by the religious order of which he was a member but was maintained by his parishioners. The Court held that the concept of a self-employed person encompasses any person who pursues, other than under a contract of employment, the exercise of an independent trade or profession in respect of which he receives income permitting him to meet some some or all of his needs. The situation is not affected by the fact that the income may be supplied by a third party, the parishioners, in this case.

The determining factor is the making of contributions to the national social security scheme. Thus, a person who goes to another member state, not in the capacity as a worker, may still fall within the scope of the regulation. Thus, in *Hoekstra (née Unger)* (Case 75/63), a person subject to Netherlands social security legislation who fell ill during a visit to her parents in Germany was entitled to claim the cost of treatment received in that country on her return. Similarly, in *Hessische Knappschaft* v *Maison Singer et Fils* (Case 44/65) a German worker was killed in a road accident while on holiday in France. It was argued that the rights arising under Art 51 EC Treaty were intended to promote the freedom of movement of workers, not holiday-makers, but the Court rejected this argument. It held that nothing in Art 51 required the concept of workers to be limited strictly to that of migrant workers as such. In *Brack* v *Insurance Officer* (Case 17/76), the Court held that the term 'employed persons' must be applied taking into account the objectives and spirit of the regulation and Arts 48 to 51 on which it is based. The claimant had been covered by the British social security scheme, first as an employed person and then in a self-employed capacity. He had gone to France for health reasons, but had fallen seriously ill there. The Court held that he retained the status of an employed/self-employed person for the purposes of Art 1 (a) (ii) during his stay in France.

Family members

Unlike the provisions relating to the exercise of free movement rights for workers under Regulation 1612/68 (Art 10) and the self-employed under Directive 73/148, Art 1(1)(c) and (d) the scope of family membership is not defined by Community law, but is left to the member state. Under Art 1(f) of the Regulation, a member of the family is any person defined or recognised as a member of the family or 'designated as a member of the household by the legislation under which benefits are provided … Where the said legislations regard as a member of the family or a member of the household only a person living under the same roof as the worker, this condition shall be considered satisfied if the worker in question is mainly dependent on that worker'. Although the definition of family entitlement is left to the state concerned, where the definition could constitute a barrier to worker mobility, the Court has preferred a broader definition. In *Angelo Marie Fracas* (Case 7/75), the Belgian social security scheme provided a benefit payable to parents of handicapped children. This was only payable to parents of Belgian nationality and until the age of the majority of the child. The Court held that neither condition should be applied to the child of an employed person covered by Regulation 1408/71.

An exception to the general rule has been introduced by Regulation 1247/92, amending Art 1(f), which provides a Community definition of 'family members' in the case of benefits for people with disabilities. The Court had already adopted a more liberal definition of 'family members' to include adult handicapped members who had never worked and could not do so (*Inzirillo* (Case 63/76)).

Equality of treatment

The beneficiaries of the regulation who are resident in the territory of one of the member states 'shall be subject to the same obligations and enjoy the same benefits under the legislation of any member state as the nationals of that state' except where the regulation provides otherwise (Art 3(1)). The effect of this provision is to prohibit indirect or covert discrimination. In *Commission* v *Belgium*, (Case C-326/90), the Court held that the Belgian authorities had breached Art 3(1) by maintaining a requirement of a period of residence on Belgian territory which workers from other member states subject to Belgian legislation had to fulfil in order to qualify for the grant of allowances for handicapped people, the guaranteed income for the elderly and for payment of the minimum subsistence allowance (MINIMEX). An even more direct form of discrimination occurred in *Palermo* (Case 237/78).

The case concerned a claim by an Italian woman to an allowance payable under the French Social Security Code to French women of at least 65 years of age and without sufficient means, who were married and who had brought up at least five dependent children of French nationality during a period of at least nine years before their sixteenth birthday. The French authorities did not insist on the nationality requirement in the case of the applicant herself, but refused the benefit because five of the seven children were Italian and not French. The Court held that payment of a benefit could not be made conditional on the nationality of the claimant or her children, provided that both she and the children held the nationality of a member state.

Discrimination may occur not only in relation to entitlement to social security benefits but also in relation to contributions. In *Allué and Coonan* (Case 33/88) a number of Community nationals employed as university teachers were obliged, as a consequence of Italian legislation, to pay their own social security contributions, whereas in the case of the ordinary salaried employees of the university, this burden was largely carried by the employer. The Court held that the practice violated Art 3(1). The Court has also said that a system of calculation of social security contributions that works less favourably in relation to trainee workers coming from another member state in comparison to workers who come under the national educational system is also discriminatory *URSSAGF* v *Societe a Responsabilite Limitée Hostellerie Le Manoir* (Case C-27/91).

Another aspect of equality of treatment in the regulation is specifically dealt with in relation to mobility and receipt of benefits. Art 10(1) of the regulation provides:

> Save as otherwise provided in this regulation, invalidity, old-age or survivors cash benefits, pensions for accidents at work or occupational diseases and death grants acquired under the legislation of one or more member state shall not be subject to any

reduction, modification, suspension, withdrawal or confiscation by reason of the fact that the recipient resides in the territory of a member state other than that in which the institution responsible for payment is situated.

The effect of Art 10(1) is that a worker or self-employed person who has, for example, contributed all his working life to a national insurance scheme in one member state, will be entitled to have that pension paid to him at the full rate, should he choose to retire to another member state. It should be noted, however, that the right of equal treatment as it affects payment of social security and the mobility of the employed and self-employed only applies to those benefits specifically covered by Art 10(1) that is, to benefits which are 'exportable', that is, payable by the state where the contributions have been made to the recipient in the member state in which he or she now lives.

The principle of equality is also reflected in Directive 79/7 under which there is a prohibition against any kind of discrimination on ground of sex (Art 4(1)). The principle applies in relation to access to social security schemes, the obligation to contribute and the calculation of contributions and the calculation of benefits. This directive applies both to migrant workers and their families and to domestic claimants for social security who do not leave their own state. The equality requirement is, however, limited to schemes which relate to sickness, invalidity, old age, accidents at work and occupational diseases, unemployment and social assistance, so far as the social assistance is intended to supplement or replace one of the schemes included. The directive does not, for example, cover housing benefits (*R v Secretary of State for Social Security, ex parte Smithson* (Case C-243/90). However, where a benefit is linked to employment, as, for example, family credit in the UK, which is intended to bring low wages for family wage earners up to a minimum level, the position is different. The Court of Justice has recently held that benefits of this kind are concerned with improving access to employment. They are therefore subject to the prohibitions against discrimination in employment in Directive 76/207 (*Meyers* v *Adjudication Officer* (Case C-116/94)).

THE PRINCIPLES OF ARTICLE 51 EC TREATY

The principles underlying Art 51 have been elaborated by Regulation 1408/71 and by decisions of the Court.

1 Aggregation of contributions and periods of contribution

The Court has held on a number occasions that all the provisions of Regulation 1408/71 are to be interpreted in the light of Art 51 (*see*, for example, *Reichling* v *INAMI* (Case C-406/93)). The purpose of Art 51 was to facilitate freedom of movement for workers by securing for migrant workers and their dependants 'aggregation, for the purpose of acquiring and retaining the right to benefit and of calculating the amount of benefit of all periods taken into acccount under the laws of the several countries' (Art 51(a)).

Art 18(b) of the regulation contains specific provisions on aggregation in relation to sickness and maternity benefits:

> The competent institution of a member state whose legislation makes the acquisition, retention or recovery of the right to benefits conditional upon the completion of periods of insurance, employment or residence shall, to the extent necessary, take account of periods of insurance, employment or residence completed under the legislation of any other member state as if they were periods completed under the legislation which it administers (as amended by the Act of Accession and Regulation 2864/72).

In *Reichling* for example, above, the Art 177 proceedings concerned the way in which the amount of invalidity benefit to which the claimant was entitled should be calculated under Art 46(2)(a) of the regulation. The legislation of the state where he claimed the benefit required the amount to be calculated on the basis of the amount of his remuneration which he last received in that state. He was not, in fact working in that state when the invalidity occurred. The Court held that the competent institution of the state in which he made the claim must calculate it on the basis of the remuneration he received in the state where he last worked. In *Paraschi* v *Handelsversicherungs anstalt Württemberg* (Case C-349/87), the failure of the host member state to take account of the circumstances of the claimant in the state of origin in calculating the qualifying period for a benefit was held to constitute both discrimination in breach of Art 48(2) and of the aggregation provisions of Art 51 EC Treaty.

2 Exportability of benefits

Exportability is often more expressively described as 'the portability principle'. It requires that the right to receive a benefit, usually from the state of origin, attaches to a worker as he or she travels around the Community, irrespective of national boundaries. It also enables individuals to have benefits remitted to dependants who live in other member states. It does not, however, apply to all types of benefit, but, as a general rule, only to those payable on a long-term basis. The benefits which are exportable are: invalidity, old-age or survivors' cash benefits, pensions for accidents at work or occupational diseases, death grants and lump sum benefits granted in case of re-marriage of a surviving spouse: Art 10(1) Regulation 1408/71. Other benefits linked to the above may also be exportable. In *Re an Emigre to the Canary Islands* (1994) for example, the UK Social Security Commissioners decided that a constant attendance allowance that was payable to a recipient of an invalidity allowance should be treated in the same way, and be payable to the claimant who had emigrated from the UK to the Canary Islands.

3 Prevention of overlapping of benefits

The concept of overlapping benefits is closely related to exportability. It is intended to prevent a worker or a self-employed person who has qualified for an exportable benefit from receiving it from both his country of origin and the state to which he or she has emigrated.

Article 12(1) provides that the Regulation:

> Can neither confer nor maintain the right to several benefits of the same kind for one and the same period of compulsory insurance.

This provision does not, however, apply to invalidity, old age, death or occupational diseases payments which are awarded by the institutions of two or more member states (Arts 41, 43(2) and (3), Arts 46, 50, 51 and 60(1)(b)).

In relation to those cases to which the rule against overlapping benefits applies, the position can be illustrated by a claim to unemployment benefit. A worker who is, for example, intermittently unemployed in the host state, may not claim unemployment benefit as long as he is entitled to receive it from his state of origin (Art 71(2)). National legislation prohibiting the receipt of overlapping benefits is lawful, provided that it does not work more unfavourably for the claimant than Community law. Whether or not two benefits are of the same kind and do, in fact, overlap is a matter of interpretation of the national legislation by the national court (*Union National des Mutualit Socialistes* v *Aldo Del Grosso* (Case C-325/93)).

In the case of old age, invalidity and the other benefits which may be paid on an overlapping basis, it is still permissible for the state paying the largest amount of benefit to set off against what it would normally pay the amount which the beneficiary actually receives in the state where he is living. In *Bogana* v *UNMS* (Case C-193/92) the claimant, an Italian national, had worked in both Italy and Belgium. When he became incapable of working, he returned to Italy, and became entitled in both states to invalidity benefits. He was paid the Belgian benefit, less the Italian benefit, on a pro rata basis. The Court of Justice accepted this as a proper course. However, it did not accept that when an increase in payment was made in Italy to compensate beneficiaries for the deterioration in the value of the Italian currency that the Belgian payments could be decreased. To allow that to happen would depreciate the real value of the claimant's total pension.

4 The types of benefit covered

Article 4(1) of Regulation 1408/71 provides that:

> This regulation shall apply to all legislation concerning the following branches of social security:
>
> (a) sickness and maternity benefits;
> (b) invalidity benefits, including those intended for the maintenance or improvement of earning capacity;
> (c) old-age benefits;

(d) survivors' benefits;
(e) benefits in respect of accidents at work and occupational diseases;
(f) death grants;
(g) unemployment benefits;
(h) family benefits.

The terms 'benefits', which is used throughout Art 4(1), and 'pensions' are defined in Art 1(t) as 'all benefits and pensions ... payable out of public funds, revalorisation increases and supplementary allowances, ... as also lump sum benefits which may be paid in lieu of pensions, and payments made by way of reimbursement of contributions'.

Not all benefits are, however, covered by the regulation. Article 4(4) expressly excludes three types:

1 social and medical assistance;
2 benefit schemes for victims of war and its consequences;
3 special schemes for civil servants and persons treated as such.

The effect of these exclusions is that migrant workers and the self-employed in other member states will not be entitled to the benefits listed in Art 4(1), except where they are linked to other benefits to which they are entitled under the 'double function test' (*see* below).

The regulation does not provide any criteria for differentiating between 'social security' and 'social assistance'. The Court of Justice has held that benefits must satisfy two tests to come within the regulation. Firstly, the legislation granting the benefit must place claimants in a legally defined position as a result of which they have an absolute right to benefits as opposed to a conditional right dependent upon the exercise of a discretionary power in their favour. Secondly, the benefit must cover one of the risks referred to in Art 4(1) of the regulation. The characteristic feature of social assistance is that it is discretionary and will be payable according some nationally defined criteria indicating need. In the UK, for example, a payment such as unemployment benefit, is dependent on contributions and other qualifying criteria. Once they are established, there is, as a general rule, an entitlement to payment. Payment of Income Support will depend on an assessment of means, and may be withheld in certain circumstances, even when the criteria are satisfied (if for example, a claimant is classed as voluntarily unemployed, even if available for work: see criteria for new 'jobseekers allowance'). Under Directives 90/364 a claim for social assistance will be indicative that an individual no longer has a right of residence under that directive.

The Commission, reflecting the jurisprudence of the Court of Justice, has laid down the following criteria for identifying social assistance:

1 The benefit must be designed to alleviate a manifest condition of need in the person concerned, established after a proper investigation into his resources and bearing in mind the standard of living in the country of residence. If cash

benefits are concerned, the amount must be set, case by case, on the basis of the individual situation and means of likelihood of the person concerned.

2   The award of benefit should not be subject to any condition of length of employment or length of residence.

3   The fact that a benefit is non-contributory does not determine its nature as a social assistance benefit or exempt it from the rules laid down in Regulation 1408/71. In the same way, the fact that a benefit is linked to a means test is not sufficient in itself to give it the nature of a social assistance benefit: Commentary on Regulation 1408/71 in Compendium of Community Provisions on Social Security (1980) Commission of the European Communities, para 4084, p 235.

Although the Court has emphasised that the list of benefits enumerated in Art 4(1) is exhaustive (*see Scrivner* v *Centre Public d'Aide Sociale de Chastre* (Case 122/84) some benefits may, according to the circumstances, qualify as both social assistance and social security under the 'double-function' test.

5   The double-function test

Although the Court held in *Scrivner* that discretionary social assistance type-benefits would fall outside the scope of Regulation 1408/71, as a result of the exclusion contained in Art 4(4), it had tended to be generous in its interpretation of the scope of Regulation 1408/71. The discretionary element which the Court established as the primary differentiation between social security and social assistance did not exclude many benefits, even though they were not within the list set out in Art 4(1), and benefits which have been described as 'of extremely dubious status as social security benefits' (Steiner op. cit., p 240) were accepted as within the scope of the Regulation (*Inzirillo* (Case 63/76); *Vigier* (Case 70/80); *Palermo* (Case 237/78). Following *Scrivner*, in which the Court emphasised the exhaustive nature of the list in Art 4(1) Regulation 1408/71, and, instead, turned to Art 7(2), the 'social advantages' route in Regulation 1612/68 as an alternative basis for entitlement (*see* below) as an alternative basis for entitlement, the opportunities for claiming benefits not listed in Art 4(1) as social security benefits would seem to have diminished.

However, the 'double function-test', which was one aspect of the earlier case law would seem to have survived. It remains important, because, unlike 'social advantages', a benefit which can be brought within Regulation 1408/71 will be 'exportable', whereas 'social advantages' (*see* below) are only available in the host state and are only open to those who have the status of worker or are members of his family. The 'double function' test was established by the Court in *Frilli* (Case 1/72). In this case, the Court held that even a means-tested discretionary payment could become 'social security' rather than 'social assistance' where it was used to *supplement* a contributory old age benefit. Thus a supplement, which, when it stood alone, might be considered to be 'social assistance', could come within regulation where it could be regarded as a supplement to one of the listed benefits. In *Giletti* (Cases 379, 380, 381/85 and 93/96), the Court held that Community social security benefits could include supplements to inadequate old age, widows' and invalidity pensions.

The 'double-function' aspect of welfare benefits, as developed in the jurisprudence of the Court, has been recognised in recent Community legislation. The preamble to Regulation 1247/92 states that it is 'necessary to take account of this (case) law', and that changes are necessary which 'take account of the special characteristics of the benefits concerned ... in order to protect the interests of migrant workers in accordance with the provisions of Art 51 of the Treaty.' Social assistance-type benefits may, therefore, continue to be treated as social security where they are linked to a recognised benefit under Art 4(1), Regulation 1408/71. Where there is no such linkage, a person may only have an entitlement to it, if at all, as a social advantage under Art 7(2), Regulation 1612/68, in the host state where he or she works or has worked.

The problem of classification of non-contributory benefits has partly been alleviated as a result of the extension of the scope of Regulation 1247/92 to cover a wide range of non-contributory social security benefits.

SOCIAL ASSISTANCE AND SOCIAL ADVANTAGES

The exclusion of social and medical assistance from the scope of the regulation was, potentially, a major obstacle to social mobility, but it reflected the anxiety of member states about 'social tourism'. Now that new European citizenship confers a right to live anywhere in the Community, it would seem arguable, at least, that the new citizens, like the old citizens of the nation states, should be able to do so regardless of means. This argument, as HC Taschner, a Commission official, has observed 'overlooks the fact that the social security systems of member states still differ enormously, and any effort to harmonise these systems is met with formidable resistance, mainly by those member states that have highly developed social security systems financed by their taxpayers ... the fear of an uncontrolled flow of persons seeking residence for no other reason than to become beneficiaries of better social security than at home was, and is, completely justified'. 'Free Movement of Students, Retired Persons and other European Citizens' in *Free Movement of Persons in Europe*, Schermers, H. (ed.) (1993). There is, in fact, no evidence that 'social tourism' is a major factor in the decision to move to another member state, but in matters of political sensitivity of this kind, the perception is more important than the reality.

Although Regulation 1408/71 excluded social assistance, the narrow definition given to that term, and the generous interpretation of the listed benefits in the ways described above, did somewhat diminish the problems caused by that exclusion. Where 'social assistance' payments could not, by the double function test, be linked to a social security benefit, the court developed the scope of social advantages under Art 7(2), Regulation 1612/68 to plug the gap. The scope of social advantages has already been examined in some detail in Chapter 8, but something needs to be said about Art 7(2), Regulation 1612/68 in the context of social assistance.

In *Scrivner* v *Centre Public d'Aide Sociale de Chastre* (Case 122/84), the Court had to consider the relationship between 'social assistance' which is excluded from the application of Regulation 1408/71 by Art 4(4), and 'social advantages' under Art 7(2), Regulation 1612/68.

Mr and Mrs Scrivner settled in Belgium in 1978, with their six children. In June 1982 Mr Scrivner left his employment 'for personal reasons'. It is not stated in the report what they were, but the Court seems to have assumed that they were not such as to make Mr Scrivner 'voluntarily unemployed' and therefore deprive him of his worker status (See *Raulin* (Case C-357/89) para [22]). Mr Scrivner and his family were refused payment of MINIMEX (a grant to provide the minimum means of subsistence) because it was only available to those who had been resident in Belgium for at least five years. The claimants argued that the benefit fell within Regulation 1408/71, and that they should, therefore, be protected from discrimination under Art 3(1) of the Regulation. The question was referred to the Court of Justice under Art 177.

The Court, on this occasion adopting a more restrictive approach, held that MINIMEX did not fall within the regulation:

> The Court has stated in a number of decisions that the distinction between benefits which are excluded from the scope of Regulation 1408/71 and benefits which come within it rests entirely on factors relating to each benefit, in particular its purpose and the condition for its grant, and not whether the national legislation describes the benefit as a social security benefit or not. (para [11])

The list of risks contained in Art 4(1) is exhaustive. Thus, a branch of social security not mentioned in the list does not fall within that category 'even if it confers upon individuals a legally defined position entitling them to benefits'. Furthermore, MINIMEX 'adopts "need" as an essential criterion for its application and *does not make any stipulations as to periods of work, contribution or affiliation to any particular social security body covering a specific risk*'. (para [13], emphasis added).

The Court was, however, prepared to accept that MINIMEX was a social advantage under Art 7(2) Regulation 1612/68 and found that it could be seen to be an advantage granted to national workers 'primarily because of their objective status as workers or by virtue of the mere fact of their residence on the national territory', drawing on the analogy of the guaranteed old peoples' income in *Castelli* v *ONPTS* (Case 261/83), which the Court had also found to be a social advantage under Art 7(2).

It must be emphasised that the right to subsistence grants of the MINIMEX type under Art 7(2) is only available to *workers* and not to *work-seekers* since the provisions of Title I apply to all Community nationals, whereas Titles II and III of Regulation 1612/68 (including Art 7(2)) are confined explicitly to workers (*Centre*

Public d'Aide Sociale de Courcelles v *Lebon* (Case 316/85), para [26]). However, as we have seen, the term 'worker' is wide enough to cover anyone who is working, or who has worked but has lost his employment other than voluntarily. In relation to education grants for vocational education, even voluntary unemployment may not deprive an individual of worker status, provided there is a link between the work that has been abandoned and the course which the student has embarked upon (*Raulin* above, Chapter 8).

Self-employed workers are not entitled to receive subsistence payments, or social assistance, as a social advantage since Regulation 1612/68 is only applicable to workers and their families. The equal treatment provisions of Art 6 EC Treaty are not likely to assist here, because the Court has held that grants and other such benefits are outside the scope of equal treatment of recipients of services (*Lair* (Case 39/86)). However, the distinction between having equal access to facilities to enable a person to pursue a business or a profession and equal access to grants and benefits is not always clear. In *Commission* v *Italy* (Case 63/86), the Court held that denial of housing aid to a self-employed person claiming under Arts 52 and 59 EC Treaty was unlawful as an 'obstacle to the pursuit of the occupation itself'. (para 16 of judgment)

The scope of the benefits covered

The range of social security schemes listed in Art 4(1), Regulation 1408/71 has been the subject of extensive litigation in the Court of Justice. A selection of cases on the main benefits will give some idea of the scope of each benefit.

(a) Sickness and maternity benefits

The Court in *Heinze* v *Landesversicherunganstalt Rheinprovinz* (Case 14/72) held that 'sickness benefits' are not confined to benefits paid to a sick person when he is incapcitated. They included social security benefits which, without being related to earning capacity on the part of the insured person, are also granted to members of his family and which are designed principally for healing the sick person and protecting those around him. In *Commission* v *Luxembourg* (Case C-118/91), the Court held that a maternity benefit was covered by both Art 4, Regulation 1408/71 and Art 7(2), Regulation 1612/68 as a social advantage. Residence requirements breached both the principle of aggregation under Art 51 and the prohibition against discrimination.

(b) Invalidity benefits

Invalidity benefit normally means a long-term contributory benefit for adults who are unfit to work (*see*, for example, Social Security Contributions and Benefits Act 1992 ss 20, 33 and 34). The Administrative Commission set up under Community social security rules considers that the term 'invalidity benefits' must be interpreted broadly so as to include all benefits granted to a person who is an invalid (*Re Invalidity Benefits* [1988] CMLR 1). In *Biason* (Case 24/74), the Court held that the term included a supplementary allowance, paid by a national solidarity fund, which could be awarded to individuals receiving a life pension provided by virtue of an invalidity that reduced the worker's working or earning capacity by two thirds. In *Newton* v *Chief Adjudication Officer* (Case C-358/89) the Court held that an allowance paid under the legislation of a member state which is granted on the basis of objective criteria to persons suffering from physical disablement affecting their mobility and to the grant of which the individuals concerned have a legally protected right must be treated as an invalidity benefit.

Old age benefits

These are pensions payable by the state in which the pensioner has been employed, according to the law of the state in which he retired and claimed a pension (Arts 44, 45). There are complex rules under Arts 46 and 47 on the calculation of the amount payable in respect of each member state to which the retired worker has paid contributions. An old age benefit will normally be a personal retirement pension 'intended to ensure that a worker has an adequate income from the date on which he or she ... retires' (*Schmidt* v *Rijksdienst voor Pensioenen* (Case C-98/94).

Unemployment benefits

A worker who is wholly unemployed and who satifies the conditions of the legislation of a member state for entitlement to benefits, and who goes to one or more member state seeking employment, retains his right to benefit. He will, however, have had to register as unemployed in his home state, and have remained available for work there for at least four weeks (Art 69(1)). He has to register as a person seeking work with the employment services of each of the member states to which he goes and must subject himself to the procedures of that system. He will be entitled to benefit for three months after he last registered with the employment office of his home state (Art 69(1)(b) and (c)).

The Court held in *Kuyken* (Case 66/77), that the provisions of Arts 69 and 70 have no application to an unemployed person who has never been in employment and never been treated as an unemployed person under the relevant national legislation. However, in *Bonaffini* v *INPS* (Case 27/75), the Court held that:

> Art 69 ... is intended solely to ensure for the migrant worker the limited and conditional preservation of the unemployment benefits of the competent state even if he goes to another member state and this other member state cannot, therefore, rely on mere failure to comply with the conditions prescribed under that Art to deny the worker entitlement to the benefit which he may claim under the national legislation of that state.

SOCIAL SECURITY AND SOCIAL ASSISTANCE IN THE UNITED KINGDOM

Social Security

The full range of benefits falling within Art 4(1) is available in the UK. The terms on which these benefits are available are complicated but it is possible to match a number of contributory and non-contributory benefits which will be available to Community migrant workers, assuming that the qualifying provisions under both UK and EC law are met.

The UK benefits falling within Art 4(1) currently comprise: unemployment benefit, statutory sick pay and sickness benefit, maternity allowances, benefits relating to invalidity and disability, widow's benefits, retirement pensions, industrial injuries benefits and benefits for children. In *Re an Emigré to Canary Islands* 1 CMLR 717, the Social Security Commissioner held that attendance allowance was equivalent to invalidity benefit, and should therefore, as a benefit payable under Regulation 1408/71, continue to be paid to a claimant after he had moved to another member state.

Social Assistance

Since both Income Support and Family Credit are calculated according to need, they would appear to fall outside the social security criteria (see above). In relation to Family Credit, however, the Court has stated, in relation to the form of family credit payable in Northern Ireland, that it is a Community social security benefit (*Hughes* (Case C-78/91)). The position should now be viewed in the light of the United Kingdom's declaration annexed to Regulation 1247/92, Annex II, sIII L. It will continue to be the case that inclusion of a benefit in a declaration will be conclusive evidence that a benefit is within the Community social security scheme. However, the new regulation enables member states to specify in the annex non-contributory benefits which are excluded from Community law. These exclusions by a member state are only permissible when the validity of the benefit excluded 'is confined to part of its territory'. The UK's declaration excludes the following benefits:

Mobility allowance, invalid care allowance, family credit, attendance allowance, income support, disability living allowance and disability working allowance. The declaration also lists separately the same provisions made under Northern Ireland legislation. Whether the United Kingdom declaration is in fact only in relation to part of its territory, as required, is certainly open to argument (*see* Morris, P., Rahal and Storey, H., p 289). The effect of the declaration will have to be determined by the Court of Justice. It should, however, be remembered that, even if an entitlement to the above benefits does not arise as a social security benefit, there can be no doubt that all those benefits should be paid to a European Union citizen, or other beneficiary of free movement rights, under Art 7(2), Regulation 1612/68 as a social advantage in the same circumstances in which they would be payable to a British citizen. The fact that the benefit is included in the list lodged by the British Government in relation to social security benefits will have no bearing on the availability of the benefit as a social advantage.

Income Support

United Kingdom law is more generous than it is required to be in relation to Income Support which, as we have seen, except where it is supplementing a social security benefit listed in Art 4(1), Regulation 1408/71, does not have to be paid to an individual who has not yet reached worker status. The Court of Justice decided in *Lebon* (Case 316/85), that work-seekers, as opposed to workers, were not entitled to the social advantages conferred by Art 7(2), Regulation 1612/68. Income Support can be a social advantage, but only for a person who has, say, worked, but lost his job involuntarily and thus retains his worker status (*see* above, Chapter 8). In the UK, a European Union citizen, or other national of an EEA State, who arrives to look for work can sign on here. If he has paid sufficient contributions in his home state, he may qualify for unemployment benefit and, under Regulation 1408/71, Art 69(1)(c), will be entitled to receive it for three months. He may, as he is entitled, remain to look for work for as long as six months, or even longer (*R v Immigration Appeal Tribunal, ex parte Antonissen* (Case 292/89)). In the latter half of that six month period he may be compelled to rely on Income Support.

The practice in the UK is that EU citizens and EEA nationals who come here to seek work and who have not previously worked in the UK are eligible for Income Support for a period of up to six months. After that period, if in the opinion of the Employment Services Claimant Adviser they are no longer actively looking for work, they may be declared no longer lawfully present in the UK by the Home Office and required to leave. His case will be then referred to an adjudication officer and payment of Income Support will cease (*Report by the Social Security Advisory Committee on the Income-related Benefits Schemes (Miscellaneous Amendments) (No. 3) Regulations 1994*, (SI 1994 No. 1807) Cm 2609, para 9).

Other EU citizens who come to the UK to retire, on social visits, as students or in some other non-economically active capacity will fall under the three new Directives 90/364 (economically self-sufficient), 90/365 (retired people) and 93/96 (students). All three categories have a right of residence on condition that they do not become a burden on the social assistance system of the host state. In the UK, if an EU citizen or an EEA national who is living here under the terms of one of the directives makes a claim for Income Support, he may be declared by the Home Office to be no longer lawfully present in the country and required to leave (*Report of the Social Security Advisory Committee*, op. cit. para 8).

In addition, since 1994, a European Union citizen, an EEA national or a member of their families will not be entitled to receive Income Support, Council Tax Benefit or Housing Benefit unless he can show that he is 'ordinarily resident' in the UK. This provision does not apply to workers 'for the purposes of Regulation 1612/68' or a person with a right of residence under Directive 68/360 or Directive 73/148 or as a refugee under the Geneva Convention on the Status of Refugees 1951 (*paras 2, 3 and 4, Income-related Benefits Schemes (Miscellaneous Amendments) (No 3) Regulations 1994*) (SI 1994 No. 1807).

These new rules mean that an EU national who does not fall within one of the categories defined by the above Community provisions, will have to satisfy the residence test. This test will involve proof by the claimant that his centre of interest lies in the UK, that he has stable employment, his reasons for coming to this country, the length and continuity of his residence outside the UK and his future intentions (para 6, *Report of Social Security Advisory Committee*). There is some doubt as to the legality of this test under Community law. If Community nationals are to be allowed these benefits while in the UK, they should receive them on the same basis as local nationals, without discrimination. Such equal treatment should operate at least in relation to those individuals who are exercising a right of residence under Community provisions and it should not be open to member states to impose additional requirements that discriminate covertly against Community nationals. Residence qualifications operated in relation to all applicants, both EU and non-EU, may however, represent indirect discrimination where it is obvious that local nationals will find them much easier to satisfy than Community nationals (*Lair* (Case 39/86); *Commission* v *Belgium* (Case C-326/90)).

Where a person ceases to benefit from the free movement rights conferred by Community law, he may become subject to the national rules. Under British immigration law, a foreign national can be required to leave as a result of 'becoming a charge on public funds' i.e., being in receipt of Income Support, Family Credit, Council Tax Benefit, Housing Benefit and emergency housing under (Pt III, Housing Act 1985; paras 6, 322(4) HC 395 (23 May 1994)). The relationship between claims to benefit and the exercise of free movement rights in the United Kingdom will be examined in Chapter 12.

Further reading

Morris, P., Rahal, I. and Storey, H., (1993) *Ethnic Minorities Benefits Handbook Pt III*, Child Poverty Action Group.

Schermers, H., (ed) (1993) *Free Movement of Persons in Europe.*

Steiner, J., 'The Right to Welfare: Equality and Equity under Community Law' (1985) 10 EL Rev 21.

Steiner, J., (1994) *Textbook on EC Law*, (4th edn) Blackstone Press, Ch 21.

Taschner, H., 'Free Movement of Students, Retired Persons and Other European Citizens – A Difficult Legislative Process, in Schermers, H. et al. (eds) *Free Movement of Persons in Europe* (Dordrecht, Nijhoff Publications, 1993).

Watson, P., 'Minimum Income Benefits: Social Security or Social Assistance?' (1985) 10 El Rev 335.

Wikeley, N.J., 'Migrant Workers and Unemployment Benefit in the European Community' (1988) 5 Journal of Social Welfare Law, 300.

Wyatt, D. and Dashwood, A., (1993) *European Community Law*, (3rd edn), Sweet & Maxwell, Ch 11.

11 Limitations on the freedom of movement

All the Treaty provisions conferring free movement rights are subject to the power of national derogation on the grounds of public policy, public security and public health (Art 48(3) and 56(1) EC Treaty, Directives 68/360 Art 10, Directive 73/148 Art 8). There is no Community definition of any of those grounds, but Directive 64/221 is intended, firstly, to limit the extent to which member states are entitled to restrict rights of free movement and, secondly, to provide minimum standards of procedural protection for the individuals affected when member states take such restrictive action. The scope of both aspects of the directive will be examined.

PUBLIC POLICY

The directive does not attempt to define 'public policy'. It is a term that is also found in relation to permitted restrictions on the import and export of goods under Art 36 (*see* Chapter 14). Member states are free to determine the scope of public policy in their territory, which may be different in each member state. It is, for example, permissible for the Republic of Ireland to prohibit abortions on its territory, and equally acceptable under Community law for the United Kingdom to permit them. It would, however, probably not be compatible with Community law for a person to be prevented from receiving information in Ireland issued by an abortion clinic in the United Kingdom or from going to the United Kingdom to have an abortion. In *Society for the Protection of the Unborn Child Ireland Ltd* v *Grogan* (Case C-159/90), the Court held that medical termination of pregnancy, performed in accordance with the law of the state where it was carried out, constituted a service within Art 60. However, the distribution of information about the clinics in the UK was not carried out on their behalf and the Court did not adjudicate on whether the lawful public policy restrictions in one state could legitimately interfere with access to a lawful service in another. The same issue was raised in *Attorney General* v *X and Others* [1992] 2 CMLR 277, but the case was decided by the Supreme Court of the Republic of Ireland on the basis that the young woman who wished to go to the UK for an abortion had 'an unenumerated constitutional right to travel' under Irish law, and did not, therefore, need to rely on her Community right to travel to receive a service (pp 303, 306). Different public policy requirements in different states may result in the quite lawful prohibition of cross-border services, even where they are legitimate in one of the states concerned, provided that the prohibition is proportionate to the risk and provided it is applied equally in the receiving state to local citizens and EU citizens alike (*Customs and Excise Commissioners* v *Schindler* (Case C- 275/92). 'Public policy' and 'public security' are used interchangeably, and they seem to be regarded by the Court of Justice as overlapping concepts. However, although the Court accepted in *Van Duyn* (Case 41/74) that 'the concept of public policy may vary from one country to another and from one period to another and it is, therefore, necessary … to allow the competent national authorities an area of discretion within the limits imposed by the Treaty', in more recent years it has tended to emphasise the limitations imposed by Community law and the need for equality of treatment between local nationals and EU citizens and their families (*Commission* v *Germany Re Housing of Migrant Workers* (Case 294/86), paras [18] and [19] of judgment.

The discretion retained by member states in identifying the areas of public policy which may result in the restriction of free movement rights, has been substantially limited by the substantive provisions of Directive 64/221.

Scope of Directive 64/221

The Directive applies to any national of a member state or a state in the European Economic Area, and his family, who reside in or travel to another member state either in order to pursue an activity as an employed or self-employed person or as a recipient of services (Art 1). It covers all measures concerning entry into their territory, issue or renewal of residence permits, or expulsion from their territory taken by member states on grounds of public policy, public security or public health (Art. 2). It is not confined to restricting or limiting national legislation regulating entry and residence, but the directive also applies to all administrative decisions made by states in relation to individuals exercising free movement rights on their territory (Case 36/75 *Rutili* v *Minister of the Interior* [1975] ECR 1219).

The directive does not refer to departure from the home state and it is not immediately clear whether national measures taken to restrict individuals from leaving the home territory to go to another member state fall within the directive. However, individuals have a right to depart from their own state which is specifically dealt with in Art 2, Directive 68/360 in the case of workers, and Art 2 of Directive 73/148 in the case of the self-employed. Both directives have been held to be directly effective (*Royer* (Case 48/75)). The exercise of all the rights conferred by both directives is made subject to the power of the member states to derogate from them on grounds of public policy, public security and public health (Art 10 Directive 68/360) and it does, therefore, seem that the exercise of all the rights conferred by the directives are protected by Directive 64/221, including the right to depart, and the right to be issued with a travel document.

The directive refers only to public policy, public security and public health measures. Member states may decide, in some cases, that an individual, although a European Union citizen, is not exercising rights conferred by the Treaty or the implementing legislation. This is a decision taken on the facts of the case. The Court of Justice has, on a number of occasions, declared that whether or not a person is a worker or a recipient of services is to be determined according to principles laid down by Community law (*see*, for example, *Levin v Staatsecretaris van Justitie*, (Case 53/81) para [11] of judgment). In *Commission v Netherlands* (Case C-68/89), the Court held that this was a decision which could not be made by the national authorities at the point of entry, but had to be determined subsequently on the basis of activities undertaken by the individual. It seems likely that a decision say, that an individual is not economically active and does not have sufficient resources to fall within the residual right of residence under Directive 90/364 will not be a decision made on public policy or public security grounds. It will, however, be a decision affecting the exercise of an individual's free movement rights and should therefore confer at least the minimum procedural protection guaranteed by the general principles of Community law (*UNECTEF v Heylens* (Case 222/86); and *see R v Secretary of State v The Home Department, ex parte Vitali and Do Amaral*, NLJ 5 May 1995. If an individual does enjoy the protection of Community law, but has been a recipient of welfare benefits because of incapacity or some other reason beyond his control, expulsion to relieve the burden on public funds is prohibited by Art 2(2), Directive 64/221, which excludes any action by national authorities falling within the Directive 'to service economic ends.'

Article 3(1) provides that measures taken shall be 'based exclusively on the personal conduct of the individual concerned'. Although member states have a wide discretion in determining the type of 'personal conduct' which may form the basis for action, the Court of Justice has laid down a number of criteria by which such national restrictions must be judged. In the first place, the Court has said that the action of member states must be assessed in the light of the European Convention on Human Rights. In *Rutili* (above) an Italian national working in France had, following political and trade union activity, been confined by a ministerial order to certain areas of France. He challenged this restriction and the case was referred to the Court under Art 177. The Court held that:

> The concept of public policy must, in the Community context and where, in particular, it is used as a justification for derogating from the fundamental principles of equality of treatment and freedom of movement of workers, be interpreted strictly, so that its scope cannot be interpreted unilaterally by each member state without being subject to control by the institutions of the Community. Accordingly, restrictions cannot be imposed on the right of a national of any member state to enter the territory of another member state, to stay there and to move within it unless his presence constitutes a genuine and sufficiently serious threat to public policy ... Nor, under Art 8 of Regulation 1612/68,

which ensures equality of treatment as regards membership of trades unions and the exercise of rights attached thereto, may the reservation relating to public policy be invoked on grounds arising from the exercise of those rights. Taken as a whole, these limitations placed on the powers of member states in respect of control of aliens are a specfic manifestation of the more general principle, enshrined in Arts 8, 9, 10 and 11 of the Convention for the Protection of Human Rights ... which provide in identical terms, that no restrictions in the interests of national security or public safety shall be placed on the rights secured by the above-quoted articles other than such as are necessary for the protection of those interests 'in a democratic society'.

The Court held in this case that free movement rights entailed a right of entry and residence in the whole territory of the host state, and the restrictions imposed in this case could not be justified in the case of Community nationals exercising free movement rights unless they were also applicable in similar circumstances to nationals of the host state.

Secondly, the conduct must be both 'personal' and 'a genuine and serious threat' to public policy. The concepts of 'personal conduct' and 'genuine and serious threat to public policy' were explored by the Court in *Van Duyn* v *Home Office* (Case 41/74). It was in this case, it may be remembered, that the Court established the principle that directives, and Directive 64/221 in particular, are vertically effective against the state which has failed to implement them (*see* Chapter 5).

Yvonne van Duyn, a Dutch national, was a member of the Church of Scientology. She wished to enter the UK to work for the organisation. The British Government had decided in 1968 that membership of the Church was 'socially harmful', but had not taken any steps to ban or restrict the activities which it carried on at its headquarters in East Grinstead, Sussex. Other Dutch nationals who wished to work for the organisation had, however, been excluded before British membership of the Community (*Schmidt* v *Home Office* [1969] 2 Ch 149). Ms Van Duyn was refused entry on the grounds that her membership of the organisation constituted a threat to public policy. She challenged the refusal on the grounds that membership of an organisation could not be 'personal conduct' within Art 3(1), Directive 64/221. The case was referred to the Court of Justice. The Court held that membership of an organisation could constitute 'personal conduct'.

Although a person's past associations cannot in general, justify a decision refusing him the right to move freely within the Community, it is nevertheless the case that present association, which reflects participation in the activities of the body or of the organisation as well as identification with its aims and designs, may be considered a voluntary act of the person concerned and, consequently, as part of his personal conduct within the meaning of the provision cited. (para 17).

As to whether such an organisation could be regarded as a threat to public policy when no action had been taken against it and when it operated without restriction in the United Kingdom, the Court said:

The particular circumstances justifying recourse to the concept of public policy may vary from one country to another and from one period to another ... It follows from the above that where the competent authorities of a member state have clearly defined their standpoint as regards the activities of a particular organisation and where, considering it to be socially harmful, they have taken administrative measures to counteract their activities the member state cannot be required, before it can rely on the concept of public policy, to make such activities unlawful, if recourse to such a measure is not thought appropriate in the circumstances. (paras 18 and 19 of judgment).

This decision was somewhat anomolous. Member states were apparently justified in excluding or expelling Community citizens for belonging to an organisation engaged in activities which were both 'a serious threat to public policy' and, which were, at the same time, thought by the host state not serious enough to merit even the mildest criminal sanctions when they were engaged in by the citizens of the host state. Indeed, the Church of Scientology had, and still has, charitable status, and so enjoys considerable relief from taxation! Whilst membership of an organisation committed to activities which clearly breach the criminal law, such as a terrorist organisation, would seem to fall clearly within the concept of 'personal conduct constituting a serious threat to public policy' (*see* for example *Astrid Proll (No. 2)* [1988] 2 CMLR 387, IAT), membership of an organisation enjoying the full protection of the law would hardly seem to fall within the same category. Nor would such a decision seem to be compatible with the right to freedom of thought, conscience and religion and freedom of expression enshrined in Arts 9 and 10 of the European Convention on Human Rights which should, as the Court made clear in *Rutili* (above) inform all decisions made by member states in relation to the exercise of free movement rights.

The wide discretion which the Court seemed to accept that member states enjoyed in *Van Duyn* in relation to the type of prohibited conduct was subsequently limited by the Court in an important decision in *Adoui and Cornuaille* v *Belgian State* (Cases 115 & 116/81). The applicants in this case were French nationals who worked in a Belgian café with a somewhat dubious reputation. They were refused residence in Belgium on public policy grounds. The case was referred to the Court, because 'prostitution as such is not prohibited by Belgian legislation, although the law does prohibit certain incidental activities, such as the exploitation of prostitution by third parties and various forms of incitement to debauchery' (para [6]). On this occasion the Court emphasised the need, as far as possible, for equality of treatment between nationals and non-nationals exercising Community rights. Having pointed out that member states cannot exclude or expel their own nationals, it said:

Although that difference of treatment, which bears upon the nature of the measures available, must therefore be allowed, it must nevertheless be stressed that, in a member state, the authority empowered to adopt [public policy/public security] measures must not base the exercise of its powers on assessment of certain conduct which would have the effect of applying an arbitrary distinction to the detriment of nationals of other member states ... Although Community law does not impose upon the member states a uniform scale of values as regards the assessment of conduct which may be considered as contrary to public policy, it should nevertheless be stated that conduct may not be considered as being of a sufficiently serious nature to justify restrictions on the

admission to or residence within the territory of a member state of a national of another member state in a case *where the former member state does not adopt, with respect to the same conduct on the part of its own nationals repressive measures or other genuine and* effective measures intended to combat such conduct. (paras [7] and [8] of judgment) (emphasis added)

It seems unlikely that, had this test been imposed in the *Van Duyn* case, the outcome would have been the same since, although the government had 'clearly defined its standpoint' on Scientology, it had, in fact, taken no 'repressive or other genuine and effective measures to combat it.' This new approach, reflecting both a standard of equality of treatment and proportionality of response, is also to be found in decisions of the Court in relation to measures taken by national authorities restricting the importation of goods, where reliance is placed on the 'public morality' derogation permitted by Art 36 EC Treaty (*Conegate Ltd* v *Customs and Excise Commissioners* (Case 121/85); *see* Chapter 15.

'Personal conduct' justifying action must relate exclusively to the individual on whom the restriction is imposed. In *Bonsignore* v *Oberstadtdirektor der Stadt Köln* (Case 67/74), Bonsignore, an Italian national working in Germany, had been found guilty of causing the death of his brother by the negligent handling of a firearm. Following the conviction, he was ordered by the aliens authority to be deported. It was accepted by the German authorities that there was little likelihood of the commission of further offences by the defendant. They were, however, concerned to use the deportation for its deterrent effect 'which the deportation of an alien found in illegal possession of a firearm would have in immigrant circles having regard to the resurgance of violence in large urban areas' (para [4] of judgment). The matter was referred to the Court of Justice. Advocate-General Mayras emphasised, in his opinion, that 'it is not permissible for a Community worker, even when convicted of a criminal offence, to be made into a "scapegoat" in order to deter other aliens from acting in the same way … the concept of personal conduct must be examined not only in the light of the offences committed but also in view of the "potential criminality" of the offender.' The Court agreed with this view and held that Art 3(1), Directive 64/221 means that action taken against an individual on public policy or public security grounds 'cannot be justified on grounds extraneous to the individual case', and thus deportation as a deterrent or as a general preventive measure is prohibited.

The effect of criminal convictions

Previous criminal convictions should not 'in themselves constitute grounds' for exclusion or expulsion (Art 3(2) Directive 64/221). The Court of Justice, in *R v Bouchereau* (Case 30/77), was asked by Marlborough Street Magistrates' Court 'whether the wording of Art 3(2) of Directive 64/221 EEC, namely that previous criminal convictions shall not "in themselves" constitute grounds for the taking of measures based on public policy or public security means that previous criminal convictions are solely relevant in so far as they manifest a present or future propensity to act in a manner contrary to public policy or public security; alternatively, the meaning to be attached to "in themselves" in Art 3(2) of Directive 64/221'.

In its reply, the Court said that Art 3(2):

> must be understood as requiring the national authorities to carry out a specific appraisal from the point of view of the interests inherent in protecting requirements of public policy which does not necessarily coincide with the appraisals which formed the basis of the criminal conviction.
>
> The existence of a previous criminal conviction can, therefore, only be taken into account in so far as the circumstances which gave rise to that conviction are evidence of personal conduct constituting a present threat to the requirements of public policy.
>
> Although, in general, a finding that *such a threat exists implies the existence in the individual concerned of a propensity to act in the same way in the future, it is possible that past conduct alone may constitute such a threat to the requirements of public policy.*
> (emphasis added)

It would seem, from this somewhat obscure judgment, and the words emphasised, that what the national authorities making the decision relating to a European Union citizen should be looking for is indications of whether or not the person concerned is likely to be a future threat. Or, in other words, is there a likelihood of re-offending? That would seem to be the purpose of the assessment. Some commentators, in interpreting this passage have sought to emphasise the opinion of the Advocate-General in the case (*see*, for example, Wyatt, D. and Dashwood, A., op. cit. p 267). Advocate-General Warner had referred to 'circumstances when cases do arise, exceptionally, where the personal conduct of the alien has been such that, whilst not necessarily evincing any clear propensity on his part, has caused such deep revulsion that public policy requires his departure'. ([1977] ECR 1999 at 2022). However, there is no indication that the Court agreed with Advocate-General Warner in this regard and indeed, it had agreed with Advocate-General Mayras in an earlier case when he warned against the use of deportation to mollify public opinion: 'one cannot avoid the impression that the deportation of a foreign worker, even a national of the Common Market, satisfies the feeling of hostility, sometimes verging on xenophobia, which the commission of an offence by an alien generally causes or revives in the indigenous population'. (*Bonsignore*, above).

There is very little to be said, in terms of the limitations imposed by the directive, for making a decision on the basis of public reaction to an offence. Setting aside the frequent misreporting of the circumstances of offences in the press which may well provoke a quite inappropriate response, the requirement in Art 3(1) that the decision should 'based exclusively on the personal conduct of the offender' would seem to exclude the taking into account of such extraneous factors as the public response to the offence. What, then, did the Court mean when it said that 'past conduct alone may constitute such a threat'? A 'threat' must indicate something that may happen. A reasonable interpretation of this exceptional circumstance in which

past conduct constitutes a future threat might be where the offence itself indicates some kind of mental or other disorder importing the risk of recurrent offending. As we shall see, however, the authorities will have to decide at the time when the decision is taken, by making an assessment, whether the individual still constitutes a threat at the time when the exclusion or expulsion is given effect, 'as the factors to be taken into account, particularly those concerning his conduct, are likely to change in the course of time' (*R* v *Secretary of State for the Home Department, ex parte Santillo* (Case 131/79); para [18] of judgment).

Whilst it is permissible to penalise individuals exercising free movement rights who do not comply with national provisions on registration and notification of their removal to a different place, any penalties for not renewing a passport or identity card should not include expulsion from the territory or even imprisonment (Art 3(3) 'Such penalties should not be so severe as to cause an obstacle to the freedom of entry and residence provided for in the Treaty' (*Sagulo, Brenca and Bakhouche* (Case 8/77); at para [12] of judgment).

Public health measures

Article 4, Directive 64/221 permits exclusion of European Union citizens and their families where they are suffering from the diseases listed in the annex to the directive. The list includes diseases subject to quarantine under World Health regulations, tuberculosis in an active state, syphilis, and other infectious diseases subject to notification under the legislation of the host state. There is a separate category of diseases and disabilities which might threaten public policy and public security. These are: drug addiction, profound mental disturbance and manifest conditions of psychotic disturbance with agitation, delirium, hallucinations or confusion.

It is not permissible to carry out routine medical examinations for any of these conditions, since to do so would be to impose an additional requirement on entry prohibited by Art 3(1), Directive 68/360 (*Commission* v *Netherlands* (Case C-68/89)). Nor would it be open to a state to require production of medical or other certificates to confirm that individuals are free from infection, since this, too, would constitute a further restriction. A medical examination would, however, be lawful, if a person were to be manifesting obvious symptoms of sickness which might indicate that he was suffering from one of the conditions listed in the Annex to Directive 64/221. Such a situation might constitute a case where there is 'sufficient justification for imposing restrictions' (*Commission* v *Belgium (Re Belgian Passport Controls)* (Case 321/87); para [10] of judgment).

Once a person has entered the member state, the development of one of the listed diseases cannot be a ground for expulsion. Art 4(1), Directive 64/221 provides that diseases or disabilities occurring after a first residence permit has been issued shall not justify refusal to renew the residence permit or expulsion from the territory. It might, however, be implied from this, that a person who contracts a listed illness before being issued with a residence permit, or where none has been applied for, can be expelled on this ground. Such a conclusion would not be compatible with the Court's frequent affirmation that the residence permit is merely proof of the right of residence, not the basis for it (*see*, for example, *Echternach* (Case 389/87)).

> The issue of such a permit does not create the rights guaranteed by Community law.
> (para 25)

It would also seem that expulsion following the development of an infectious disease could be regarded as a measure of a 'general preventive nature', that is, one not relating to the personal conduct of the individual. It was for this reason, inter alia, that the Court held that occupation by a family of overcrowded or insanitary housing could not justify expulsion *Commission* v *Germany (Re Housing of Migrant Workers)* (Case 249/86); para [18] of judgment).

Procedural Protection

Arts 5, 6, 7, 8 and 9 of Directive 64/221 are intended to ensure that when action is taken against European Union citizens or others exercising Community free movement rights it is taken in accordance with minimal standards of due process. In addition, in 'each member state nationals of other member states should have adequate legal remedies available to them in respect of decisions of the administration' (preamble to Directive 64/221). Article 5 provides that a decision to give or refuse a residence permit should be taken as soon as possible and in any event not later than six months from the date of application. In the meantime, 'the person concerned shall be allowed to remain temporarily in the territory pending a decision either to grant or refuse a residence permit. The language of this provision sits somewhat awkwardly with the often repeated pronouncement of the Court that 'the issue of the permit does not create the rights guaranteed by Community law.' (*see Echternach*, above). However, it is plain that a European Union citizen, has, prima facie, a right of entry and residence under Art 8a EC Treaty. Since the onus is on the member state to justify the denial of that right on public policy, public security or public health grounds, the individual continues to enjoy that right until he has been notified that grounds exist warranting his exclusion or expulsion, and the member state has provided sufficient evidence to justify its actions.

Under Art 6, the person concerned shall be informed of the grounds of public policy, public security or public health upon which the decision taken in his case is based, unless this is contrary to the interests of the security of the state involved. Where a decision has been taken to refuse the issue or renewal of a residence permit or to expel a person from the territory, he must be officially notified of the decision. The period allowed for leaving the territory must be stated in the notification and except in cases of urgency, the period should not be less than 15 days if a person has not yet been granted a residence permit and not less than a month in all other cases (Art 7). The person concerned is entitled to have the same legal remedies in respect of any decision concerning entry, or refusing the issue or refusal of a residence permit, or ordering expulsion from the territory, as are available to nationals of the host state in relation to acts of the administration (Art 8).

The giving of sufficient reasons

To enable an effective judicial challenge to be mounted, it is important that adequate reasons are given where a person is excluded or expelled on public policy or public security grounds (Arts 5, 6 Directive 64/221). The reasons will need to address the relevant aspects of public policy or public security on which the decision is based. The Court in *Rutili* v *Minister of the Interior* (Case 36/75) (para [39] of the judgment), held that

> this requirement means that the state concerned must, when notifying an individual of a restrictive measure adopted in his case, *give him a precise and comprehensive statement of the grounds for the decision, to enable him to take effective steps to prepare his defence.*
> (emphasis added)

To be comprehensive, the statement will have to indicate the way in which a person continues to constitute a threat to public policy or public security. In determining whether or not to act against an individual, national authorities must 'carry out a specific appraisal from the point of view of the interests inherent in protecting the requirements of public policy' (*R* v *Bouchereau* (Case 30/77); at para [27] of judgment). It is the result of that appraisal that the authorities must communicate to the individual against whom they have decided to act. If the communication does not meet these requirements, then it will invalidate the decision (*R* v *Secretary of State for the Home Department, ex parte Dannenberg* [1984] 2 CMLR 456 (CA)).

Although Art 6 of Directive 64/221 provides that an individual need not be given the reasons for a decision where this is contrary to the interests of the security of the state involved, it would probably not satisfy the Community's principle of a minimum of effective judicial control if the authority does not at least provide some justification as to why the giving of reasons would threaten national security. The Court, in *Johnston* v *RUC* (Case 222/84) (a sex discrimination case), held that the mere issue of a certificate by the authorities to the effect that the disclosure of information would be prejudicial to national security was not sufficient without some indication of why this should be the case. Although the decision was given in the context of the need for an effective judicial process in Art 6 Directive 76/207, the Court emphasised that it was part of a broader principle of effective judicial control ([1986] ECR 1651 at 1663). However, the English Court of Appeal in *R* v *Home Secretary, ex parte Gallagher* [1994] 3 CMLR 295, thought that a recital of the relevant section of the Prevention of Terrorism (Temporary Provisions) Act 1989 as the basis of an exclusion from the United Kingdom, without more, would meet the requirements of Art 6 (*per* Steyn LJ at p 307). (See also, *R* v *Secretary of State for the Home Department, ex parte McQuillan* [1995] 4 All ER 400 (QBD).)

The need for effective remedies

Article 9 deals with the refusal to renew a residence permit or a decision to order the expulsion of the holder of a residence permit. It provides, in three cases, where the decision must not be taken, except in cases of urgency, until an opinion has been obtained from a competent authority of the host country before which the person concerned enjoys such rights of defence and representation as are provided by domestic law. The three types of cases are, firstly, where there is no right of appeal to a court of law, secondly, where such an appeal lies only in respect of the legal validity of the decision and thirdly, where the appeal cannot have suspensory effect. The object of these provisions, collectively, is to enable an individual either to have an appeal to an appeal body, where this exists, so that it may consider the full circumstances of an individual's case and be obliged to suspend expulsion until it has made a decision, or where no such appeal body exists, for a competent authority to give an opinion before a decision is put into effect. Article 9(2) provides that '*the person concerned shall then be entitled to submit his defence in person*, except where this would be contrary to the interests of national security'. (emphasis added)

The Court considered the relationship between Arts 8 and 9 in *The State* v *Royer* (Case 48/75). The defendant, a French national, was charged with having entered Belgium illegally. He had no residence permit, nor, it seems from the facts of the case, had he applied for one. In an Art 177 reference from the national court the Court of Justice was asked, inter alia, whether a decision ordering expulsion or a refusal to issue a residence or establishment permit may be put into effect immediately or only after remedies before national courts have been exhausted. The Court ruled that:

> Under Art 8 of Directive 64/221 any person subject to an order of expulsion from the territory shall have the same legal remedies in respect of those decisions as are available to nationals in respect of acts of the administration (para [53]). In default of this *the person concerned must, under Art 9, at the very least, be able to exercise his right of defence before a competent authority which must not be the same as that which adopted the measure restricting his freedom* [54]. It is appropriate to state in this respect that *all steps must be taken by the member state to ensure that the safeguard of the right of appeals is in fact available to anyone against whom a restrictive measure of this kind has been adopted.*
>
> *However, this guarantee would become illusory if the member state could by the immediate execution of a decision ordering expulsion, deprive the person concerned of the opportunity of effectively making use of the remedies which he is guaranteed by Directive 64/221.* In the case of the legal remedies referred to in Art 8 of Directive 64/221, the party concerned must have at least the opportunity of lodging an appeal and thus obtaining a stay of execution before the expulsion order is carried out [57]. This conclusion also follows from the link established by the directive between Arts 8 and 9 thereof in view of the fact that the procedure set out in the latter provision is obligatory, inter alia, where the legal remedies referred to in Art 8 'cannot have suspensory effect.' [58].
>
> Under Art 9, the procedure of appeal to a competent authority must precede the decision ordering expulsion, except in cases of urgency [59]. Consequently, where a legal remedy referred to in Art 8 is available the decision ordering expulsion may not be

executed before the party concerned is able to avail himself of the remedy [59]. Where no such remedy is available, or where it is available but cannot have suspensory effect, the decision cannot be taken – save in cases of urgency which have been properly justified – until the party concerned has had the opportunity of appealing to the authority designated in Art 9 of the Directive 64/221 and until that authority has reached a decision [61]. (emphasis is added)

Where an individual is relying on the national remedies referred to in Art 8, it might be though that, since there is no provision in that Article entitling the individual to remain to present his case, there is no right in such cases to remain until the appeal authority has reached a decision, unless, of course, national law provides otherwise (*see* Wyatt, D. and Dashwood, A. op. cit. p 270). This would seem to be a possible interpretation of the Court's decision in *Pecastaing* (Case 98/79). However, the relationship between Arts 8 and 9, as the Court said in *Royer* (above) is that Art 9 is complementary to Art 8 (para [12] of judgment). Although Art 8 refers, ostensibly, to all those exercising free movement rights, whereas Art 9 refers only to those refused renewal of a residence permit, the Court has not used these apparent limitations to distinguish between the two provisions. Indeed, neither *Royer*, nor *Adoui, Cornuaille* or *Santillo* were holders of residence permits, but the Court, nonetheless, indicated that they might have recourse to Art 9, without commenting on their lack of permits. This approach accords with that of the Court in *Giagounidis* (Case C-376/89), where it disregarded the requirement of Directive 68/360 to produce the document with which he entered the country, and declared that since 'freedom of movement of workers forms one of the foundations of the Community … the provisions laying down that freedom must be given a broad interpretation.' (para [20] of judgment). It was, of course, in *Royer* that the Court declared that the right of residence did not depend on the issue of a permit. It would, therefore, seem anomalous to make the procedural rights of those exercising free movement rights conditional upon the possession of a permit. Art 9 is, therefore, to be read as being available to remedy any deficiencies in national legislation relating to the exercise of any free movement rights under which acts of the administration can be challenged. The provisions of the Article are 'to ensure a minimum procedural safeguard for persons affected by one of the measures referred to in the three cases described in para (1) of that Article' (para [12] of judgment in *Santillo*). If, therefore, there is no right to remain until a decision is given, under national law, then such a right will be conferred by Art 9.

Article 9(1) refers to the requirement, before a final decision is taken, to obtain the opinion 'of a competent authority before which the person concerned enjoys such rights of defence and of assistance or representation as the domestic law of that country provides for'. In *Santillo* (above) the Court of Justice considered the meaning of 'competent authority'. It refers to an authority which must be independent of the administration, but it gives member states a margin of discretion in regard to the nature of the authority (para [15]). It accepted that a criminal court in Britain was such an independent authority. Whether or not an an adviser appointed by the Home Secretary whose decision is under review is similarly independent was doubted by the majority of the Court of Appeal in *R* v *Home Secretary, ex parte Gallagher* [1994] 3 CMLR 295. The Court, having taken into account the observation of Advocate-General Capotorti in *Pecastaing* that 'the advisory authority should have no links whatsoever with the authority required to take the decision' referred the question to the European Court of Justice under Art 177. The ECJ did not exclude the possibility of the competent authority being appointed by the administrative authority, provided that it is able to 'perform its duties in absolute independence' (Case C-175/94).

Article 9 does not provide that the opinion is binding on the administrative authority. The Court of Appeal in *Gallagher*, (p 308 *per* Steyn LJ) considered that the better view is that it is not. However, in *UNECTEF* v *Heylens* (Case 222/86) the Court declared, in the context of the exercise of the right of migrant workers to equal access to employment,

> ... *the existence of a remedy of a judicial nature* against any decision of a national authority refusing the benefit of that right is *essential in order to secure for the individual effective protection for his right.* (emphasis added)

The concept of 'effectiveness' means that the national court must 'have the power to do everything ... to set aside national legislative provisions which might prevent ... Community rules from having full force and effect' (*R* v *Secretary of State for Transport, ex parte Factortame* (Case C-213/89), para [20] of judgment). There would, therefore, be little point in obtaining such an opinion if the administrative authority was free to ignore it. The nature of remedies generally under Arts 8 and 9 of Directive 64/221 must also be considered in the light of Art 13 of the European Convention on Human Rights, which provides that 'Everyone whose rights and freedoms ... are violated shall have an effective remedy before a national authority notwithstanding that the violation has been committed by persons acting in an official capacity.' In *Johnston* v *RUC* (Case 222/84), the Court declared that Art 13 is to be applied when rights conferred by Community law are at issue, and it emphasised that the existence of effective judicial protection is a general principle of Community law.

Further reading

Arnull, A., (1990) *The General Principles of EEC Law and the Individual*, Leicester University Press, pp 92–99.

Barav, A., 'Court Recommendations to Deport and the Free Movement of Workers in EEC Law' (1981) 6 EL Rev 139.

Handall, J., (1995) *Free Movement of Persons in the European Union*, J. Wiley & Son, Chapter 7.

Vincenzi, C., 'Freedom of Movement in the Single Market : An Irish Solution?' (1990) New Law Journal 664.

Vincenzi, C., 'Deportation in Disarray : the Case of EC Nationals' (1994) Crim LR 163.

Wyatt, D. and Dashwood, A., (1993) *European Community Law*, (3rd edn), Sweet & Maxwell, pp 265–275

Wyatt, D., 'Note on Bouchereau' (1978) 15 CML Rev. 221.

12 Free movement rights in the United Kingdom

THE BRITISH APPROACH TO FREE MOVEMENT: THE ISLAND PROBLEM

The maintenance of strict immigration controls at the ports and airports of the United Kingdom has characterised British immigration policy since the First World War. Even after the effective date for the creation of the single market at the beginning of 1993 had passed, the Government continued to maintain the need for strict frontier controls and nationality checks on all passengers coming from within the Community. This has involved a rejection of the Commission's view of Art 7a that the creation of an area 'without internal frontiers' necessarily meant the abandonment of such routine checks. The British government has stated that it is essential that such controls are maintained and it has promised 'to take whatever steps are necessary to ensure that ... controls are not dismantled and remain in place' (The Home Secretary, *The Times*, 23 March 1995). A recent decision of the Divisional Court, confirmed on appeal, has supported the view that Art 7a does not create a directly effective right to entry without submission to routine immigration controls (*R* v *Secretary of State for the Home Department, ex parte Flynn* (1995) NLJ 5 May) *The Times*, 20 July 1995 (CA). The Commission is, however, committed to moving ahead with a directive to open the remaining national frontiers, but this will undoubtedly be opposed by the United Kingdom.

The UK government has not participated in the Schengen Agreement, an agreement made by all the member states on the mainland of Europe except Denmark, but outside the decision making processes of the Community. The agreement came into effect at the end of March 1995. Under it, the member states undertake to maintain strict checks on people coming from outside the Community, but once within it, they will be able to move freely between other Schengen States (Schengen Pros and Cons Editorial, (1995) 32 CML Rev 673). The UK has, however, agreed to accept a Community common visa regime which allows those issued with a visa by any member state to remain for up to three months in any other member state (see Art 100C EC Treaty; *The Guardian*, 8 March 1995).

Successive UK Governments have used the port control system to give effect to Community law and in some areas, such as registration with the police under the Immigration (Registration with the Police) Regulations 1972 (SI 1972 No. 1758), Community nationals benefit from a more relaxed regime. Community law would permit such registration, although not as a condition of residence (*Watson and Belmann* (Case 118/75)). The more relaxed internal system reflects a less intrusive policy of internal controls when compared to mainland Europe. In most Continental member states immigration controls have, for a great many years, been of a post-entry type, involving registration and identity cards, because borders with other member states were largely unpoliced, except at road crossing points. The effect of Britain's island geography has, however, been that the emphasis has been very much on the entry process and the granting or refusing of leave at the point of entry.

Control of entry and the granting of 'leave'

United Kingdom entry to the Community on 1 January 1973 coincided with the coming into force of the Immigration Act 1971. The Act largely assimilated the position of Commonwealth citizens with that of aliens, who had been subject to the most stringent controls since the outbreak of the First World War. Surprisingly, although Community nationals (with the exception of the Irish) are aliens under British law, the Act remained unamended by the European Communities Act 1972 and no provision was made giving Community citizens a right of entry. The need for Community citizens to obtain 'leave' to enter, although found by the Court of Justice to be contrary to Art 3 Directive 68/360 in *R* v *Pieck* (Case 157/79), continued until July 1994, when the Immigration Act 1988 s 7 was brought into effect (Immigration Act 1988 (Commencement No 3) Order 1994, SI 1994 No. 1923). In practice, however, the requirement was waived by immigration officers. Of more practical importance was the failure to implement Directive 64/221, for which the Court of Justice had held the UK to be at fault in *Van Duyn* v *Home Office* [1974] ECR 1337. The procedural rights guaranteed by the Directive (*see* Chapter 11) were allowed as concessions, or, in some cases, not acknowledged or only inadequately provided for. There was no right of appeal against refusal of a residence permit until 1994 (*see Rubruck* v *Home Secretary* [1984] 2 CMLR 499 (establishing a non-binding review procedure)).

The Immigration (European Economic Area) Order 1994

The distinct position of those exercising Community free movement rights was finally addressed more than 20 years after British entry by the Immigration (European Economic Area) Order 1994, (the 'EEA Order') which came into effect in July 1994 (SI 1994/1895; Statement of Changes in Immigration Rules HC 395 (23 May 1994)). The Order was made under European Communities Act 1972 s 2(2) and was intended to implement the free movement rights conferred by all the directives relating to entry and residence, including Directives 64/221, 68/360, 73/148, 90/364, 90/365 and 93/96 (Explanatory Note to the Order).

SCOPE OF THE ORDER

Nationality of beneficiaries

The order applies to all 'EEA Nationals', that is, to all nationals of states who were parties to the European Economic Area Agreement of 1992, which was incorporated into British law by the European Economic Area Act 1993. Nationals of Liechtenstein are excluded until Liechtenstein ratifies the agreement. The nationals of all the other EEA states are covered, that is, all the member states of the Community together with Iceland and Norway, except the UK. British citizens were excluded, it would appear, because they already have an unqualified right of entry and residence under British law (Immigration Act 1971 s 1, para 12 HC 395). This is unfortunate, because Community law confers certain rights on European Union citizens which are more beneficial to British citizens than the provisions of national law.

Rather surprisingly, there is no mention of European Union citizenship at all. Since this confers a right of residence, prima facie, on all citizens, under Art 8a, they should be distinguishable from EEA nationals from Iceland and Norway who have rights of residence when engaged in one of the activities referred to by the Treaty or the enabling legislation, but no general right of residence.

In the first place, it will be recalled from Chapters 8 and 9 that workers and the self-employed have the right to be issued with a travel document and to leave the territory of the home state (Art 2, Directives 68/360, 73/148). The exclusion of British citizens effectively excludes these rights, although they are, of course, directly effective against the Government. Under English law, there is no entitlement to a passport and there is no constitutional or other right to leave the country (*Secretary of State* v *Lakdawalla* [1972] Imm AR 26; *R* v *Secretary of State for Foreign and Commonwealth Affairs, ex parte Everett* [1989] QB 811; *compare Kent* v *Dulles* 357 US 116 (1958) and *Attorney-General* v *X* [1992] 2 CMLR 277 (an 'unenumerated constitutional right' to leave Ireland (Finlay CJ) at p 303)).

Secondly, Community family rights may be more beneficial than national provisions to individuals returning to their own states after having worked elsewhere in the Community. In *R Immigration Appeal Tribunal and Singh, ex parte Secretary of State for the Home Department* (Case C-370/90), a British national, who had been working in a self-employed capacity in Germany, was held by the Court of Justice to be entitled to be accompanied by her spouse when returning to her home state, without having to meet *national* criteria for the entry and residence of foreign spouses. The Court held that the foreign spouse was entitled to the same rights of entry and residence in the UK under Community law as if the self-employed UK national to whom he was married had continued to work in Germany (para 23 of judgment). British citizens should, therefore, be able to enjoy under national law the rights of entry conferred by Community law. These righs should be reflected in the EEA Order.

Other nationalities may benefit from more limited free movement rights under Community law. These include employees of companies based in other member states which carry on economic activities here (*Vander Elst* v *OMI* (Case C-43/93)), and nationals of states which have association agreements with the Community (*Kziber* v *ONEM* (Case C-18/90); *see*, above, Chapter 7). These are not covered by the order, and the beneficiaries will have to rely upon the direct effect of the relevant provisions of the Treaties. In the case of association agreements with Poland and Hungary, there are provisions for the granting of leave to enter to nationals under the Immigration Rules for those intending to establish themselves in business here. The Immigration Appeal Tribunal has indicated that such individuals will only be able to rely on appeal rights conferred by the Immigration Act 1971 in so far as those Treaty provisions have been incorporated into English law. However, there would be a strong case for arguing that the Act should be interpreted to comply with Community law (*Pasha* v *Home Office* [1993] 2 CMLR 350 at 355; *compare Marleasing* v *La Commercial* (Case C-106/89)).

Family rights

The order applies to the beneficiary's spouse, descendants of the beneficiary or his spouse who are under 21 or dependent, and ascendants (parents, grandparents) of the beneficiary or his spouse who are dependent on them. This definition excludes some of the family members covered by Art 10(2) Regulation 1612/68 and Art 1(2) Directive 68/360. Although these two provisions, covering other family members dependent on the worker or self-employed person who are dependent on him or who live under his roof in the country of origin, only require that the host state must 'facilitate' their admission, rather than conferring on them a right of entry, Art 3 Directives 68/360 and Directive 73/148 make it clear that all family members have a right of entry. They should, similarly, have a right under the EEA Order, and it should, following *Marleasing*, be interpreted accordingly.

The term 'spouse' in the EEA Order 'does not include a party to a marriage of convenience' (Art 2(2)). There is no definition of a 'marriage of convenience' in the order, but, during the debate on the draft order in the House of Lords, Earl Ferrers, on behalf of the Government, described such a marriage as 'entirely bogus, the purpose of which is simply to circumvent immigration control' (HL debates Vol. 557 No. 120 Col. 116 (18 July 1994)). Governments may properly be concerned about abuses of Community free movement rights, but it is doubtful if it is open to member states to act unilaterally in this way by adding further qualifications to existing categories of Community beneficiaries. To benefit as a spouse of a Community worker, there simply has to be a subsisting marriage (*Diatta* v *Land*

Berlin (Case 267/83)). It does not matter if the parties are no longer cohabiting and are even likely to divorce (*see Singh*, above). Whether or not a marriage is subsisting is a matter for national law and it would seem that, under UK law, at least, a marriage entered into purely for the purposes of remaining in England and to evade extradition may still be valid as a marriage (*Puttick* v *Attorney General* [1979] 3 WLR 542 at 556). The Immigration Appeal Tribunal has however, decided that a marriage entered into with a Community worker for the purpose of remaining in the UK did not confer a right to remain under Community law (*Kwong* (1994) (10661) 11 February 1994 (unreported)).

It is unlikely that such an interpretation would be supported by the Court of Justice as its approach is generally objective. It tends, for example, not to attempt to determine *why* a person entered a member state, but looks objectively, at the amount of work a person is doing to decide whether or not he or she meets the Community definition of 'a worker' (*see*, for example, *Levin* (Case 53/81); *Kempf* (Case 139/85)). National attempts to add further qualifications before worker status will be recognised have been resisted (*Roux* (Case C-363/89)). Most recently, in *Landesamt für Ausbildungsforderung Nordrhein-Westfalen* v *Gaal* (Case C-7/94), the Court held that the definition of 'child' in Art 12 Regulation 1612/68 could not be made subject to age limits or conditions connected with the status of the child which are not included in that article and to do so would conflict not only with the letter of the provision but also with its spirit. It is likely that the British attempt to qualify the position of 'spouses' in Art 10 of the same regulation will meet a similar response from the Court.

The exercise of free movement rights in the UK: Entry

All British ports and airports now have a route for British and EEA nationals and those arriving through the Channel Tunnel will be examined in transit (Channel Tunnel (Fire Services, Immigration and Prevention of Terrorism) Order, SI 1990 No. 2227). Examination will generally be confined to ensuring that a person is an EU Citizen or a national of an EEA State and any EU citizen or EEA national should be admitted simply on production of a valid identity card or passport (Art 3(1), (2) EEA Order). People who enter as a family member of a worker or self-employed person and who are not themselves EU citizens or EEA nationals will have to produce a 'family permit' issued in the member state from which they have come (Art 2(1) and Art 3(3) EEA Order). Article 3(2) Directive 68/360 permits a visa requirement for non-EU nationals, but states that 'every facility' should be provided for obtaining such visas. Someone who arrived with only proof of the relationship could probably, under Community law, insist on being granted a visa at the port of entry, but they could well risk refusal of entry by doing so! Family members who are EU Citizens or EEA nationals (Iceland and Norway) may be called upon to produce evidence of their relationship (Art 3(2) EEA Order). This is an additional requirement over and above the identity card or passport required by Art 3(1) Directive 68/360. Adult family members will, in any event, have an entitlement to entry in their own right. Refusal to produce such evidence will, again, probably result in refusal of admission and any challenge to such a practice would prudently, be mounted after entry, rather than on arrival.

The Immigration Service retains full powers of examination of EU and EEA citizens on entry. This can, under the EEA Order and the Immigration Act 1971, involve detention in custody, an oral examination, and a full, physical (and medical) examination (Art 20(2) EEA Order; Schedule 2, Immigration Act 1971) although this will be a vary rare occurrence and indeed millions of Community nationals enter annually without examination. However, the power of examination is without precondition and there is no requirement under British law for there to be a perceived threat, in an individual case, to public policy, public security or public health, and the powers are, probably, much wider than permitted by Community law (*Commission* v *Belgium* (*Re Belgian Passport Controls*) (Case 321/87); *Commission* v *Netherlands* (Case C-68/89)).

Residence

Under the EEA Order, a 'qualified person' is entitled to reside in the UK without the need to have 'leave' under British law, as long as he remains a 'qualified person' (Art 4(1) EEA Order). The expression 'qualified person' means anyone falling within one of the classes of beneficiaries of free movement rights under either the EC Treaty or under secondary legislation. It covers, workers, self-employed people, providers of services, recipients of services, the self-employed who have ceased economic activity, retired people, students and the economically self-sufficient (Art 6(1) EEA Order). Work-seekers are not distinguished from workers. The order simply refers to 'a worker within the meaning of Art 48 EC Treaty'. Workers clearly have a right to remain for the duration of that status and the order makes specific provision for loss of employment, and confirms that a worker does not lose that status by virtue of temporary incapacity to work as a result of illness or accident, or involuntary unemployment (Art 7 (1)). As far as work-seekers are concerned, Community law provides no time limit for that status. The Court has merely observed that six months is a reasonable period for a person to find work, but a longer time may, in some circumstances, be appropriate (*Antonissen* (Case C-292/88)). No attempt is made to reflect this ruling in the order. Generally, however, the provisions of the order in this context, do reflect Community law. There are, however, some omissions where individuals will have to rely on the direct effect of Community law.

'Students' are, for example, defined only with regard to those undertaking vocational courses. They have to show that they have sufficient funds to maintain themselves and that they are covered by all-risks sickness insurance (Art 6(2)(h) EEA Order). This is in accordance with Directive 93/96. However, students who enter to take non-vocational courses also have a right of entry and residence, provided that they are studying outside the state system and are paying the full cost of the course. They should be treated as recipients of services and, as such, do not have to meet the means and insurance requirements (*Luisi* (Case 286/83); *The State* v *Humbel* (case 263/86)).

Retired people have to show that they have an invalidity, old age, survivor's or industrial pension which is sufficient to enable them to avoid becoming a burden on the social security system of the UK. Although this meets the requirement of Directive 90/365 Art 1, which relates to those who have spent their working life outside the UK, it makes no exception for those EU citizens and EEA nationals who have worked in the UK for more than three years. They benefit from Regulation 1251/70 and do not have to have sufficient funds to maintain themselves. Under the Immigration Rules, they may be granted 'permission to remain in the United Kingdom indefinitely' (paras 255, 257). Since they have a right to remain under Community law, the 'permission' is redundant, but it is a useful way of being relieved of renewing any residence permit the beneficiary may have.

Residence permits

Residence permits must be granted to those who are qualified to reside in the UK as a 'qualified person' (Art 5(1) EEA Order). The order does not specify what proof a person who claims that they have a right to reside must produce, except a valid identity card or passport and, in the case of the worker, confirmation from the employer. There is no need to produce the document with which the applicant entered the country (*compare* Art 3 (3) Directive 68/360). It would seem that the order takes into account the decision of the Court in *Giagounidis* (Case C-376/89) that, despite the clear wording of the directive, this is not required. The periods for the grant of residence permits and the terms on which they are to be granted, generally five years, reflect the requirements laid down in Arts 4, 5, 6, 7 and 8 of Directives 68/360 and 73/148 (Arts 10, 11, 12, 13 and 14 EEA Order; *see* Chapters 8 and 9, above). Family members are entitled to permits on the bases laid down in the same Directives (Art 5(2) EEA Order).

Exclusion and removal

EU citizens and EEA nationals may be excluded from the UK if that exclusion is justified on grounds of public policy, public security or public health. In addition, EU citizens and EEA nationals may be removed from the UK on ceasing to have a right of residence as a qualified person or if the removal is justified on public policy, public security or public health grounds (Art 15(1) and (2) EEA Order). Residence permits may also be refused on public policy, public security or public health grounds under the order, and withdrawn on the same grounds. They may also be revoked on the same grounds when a person ceases to be qualified to remain under Community law (Art 16(1) EEA Order). For the first time, the limitations on state action based on public policy, public security and public health set out in Arts 2, 3, 4 and 5 of Directive 64/221 are set out, in extenso, in English law (Art 17 EEA Order).

Most of the provisions concerning exclusion and removal accurately reflect

Directive 64/221. However, it is clear from the directive that a residence permit may not be revoked nor may a person be removed on public health grounds, and in that respect, Art 16(2) of the order conflicts with Community law. Nor does the fact that a person who is an EU citizen no longer 'qualify' as a person engaged in an economic activity, *per se*, mean that his right of residence is terminated. Unlike EEA nationals, EU citizens have a presumptive right of residence under Art 8a of the EC Treaty. The onus is cast on the state to prove the public security or public health grounds authorising the state to derogate from that right are met. However, in *R* v *Secretary of State for the Home Department, ex parte Do Amaral and Vitale* (1995) *Times*, 21 March, the applicants, a Portuguese and an Italian national, were asked to leave by the Home Office because they were claiming income support and found not to be seeking work. The Court (Judge J) rejected the argument that Art 8a provided EU citizens with 'an open-ended right' to remain. The issue is very likely to be appealed and will, in all probability, be referred to the Court of Justice. The scope of the extra rights conferred by Art 8a is already the subject of a reference to the Court in *R* v *Secretary of State for the Home Department, ex parte Adams* [1995] All ER 177.

THE EFFECT OF CLAIMS TO SOCIAL ASSISTANCE

Prior to the coming into force of the EEA Order in July 1994, the residence rights of European Union citizens and their families were made dependent upon them not claiming public funds (para 72 Immigration Rules HC 251) which were defined to include emergency housing provision, housing benefit, family credit and income support. These conditions were too wide and consequently breached Community law. Many Community citizens will, after they have worked and gained worker status, be entitled to such benefits as 'social advantages' under Regulation 1612/68 or, in some cases, under Regulation 1408/71 (*see* Chapter 10). Others, although not entitled under Community law to the benefits they claimed, should not have been required to leave. Expulsions of this kind are contrary to Art 2(2) of Directive 64/221, which prohibits expulsions 'to service economic ends'.

Although there is no longer any such condition attached to the rights of residence recognised in the EEA Order, there remains an important link between claims to public funds, as defined in the current Immigration Rules (HC 395 October 1994 para 6), and the rights of residence of EU citizens. The link may operate in two separate, but related, ways. Firstly, by denying the financial support which a Community national may require when he has insufficient resources to maintain himself, and secondly, by providing evidence that he cannot support himself without recourse to social assistance.

Prima facie, as a work-seeker or a beneficiary of the general right of residence under Directive 90/364, or as a retired person under Directive 90/365, he will have a right to remain as long as he satisfies the relevent requirements of Community law. He cannot, however, look to the United Kingdom's welfare system for any kind of assistance, unless it be for contributory benefits to which he may be entitled under Regulation 1408/71 (*see* Chapter 10). Income support, housing benefit and council tax benefit are now conditional upon proof by a claimant who is a national of an EEA State or an EU citizen that he is 'habitually resident in the UK or the Republic of Ireland' (Income-related Benefits Schemes (Miscellaneous Amendments) (No. 3) Regulations 1994). The test is not applied to those who have worker status or to the first six months in which a worker is looking for work (Reg 21(3)(h), Income Support (General) Regulations 1987/1967), or to a person who has a right of residence as a self-employed person or a recipient of services under Directice 73/148.

The second way in which the social assistance system may jeopardise a person's right to remain is by providing evidence that he is no longer self-sufficient. The new residence rights conferred on students, retired people who have worked in another member state and people relying on their own resources are all conditional upon the beneficiaries not becoming a burden on the social assistance system of the host state (Art 1 Directives 90/364, 90/365 and 93/96). A claim to income support or to one of the benefits named in the above regulations is almost certain to fail, because the habitual residence test is difficult to satisfy. The details of the claim will, however, be forwarded to the Home Office and if the individual is not a worker or a self-employed person, or otherwise entitled to remain under the EEA, then he will be required to leave under Art 15(2)(a) EEA as someone who has 'ceased to be a qualified person'.

DEPORTATIONS

Deportations in the UK are either carried out by the Home Secretary on his own initiative or following a recommendation of the Courts at the time when a sentence is imposed on an offender (Immigration Act 1971 ss 3(5)(6), 5. The Home Secretary has a general power to deport a foreign national where he 'deems his deportation to be conducive to the public good' (the Immigration Act 1971 s 3(5)(b)). It was on this basis that deportations of Community nationals have been carried out, although both the Home Secretary and the Courts have been obliged to make decisions on whether or not to deport or recommend deportation within the limits laid down by Directive 64/221. The Community criteria are much narrower than those allowed under British immigration law, and the EEA Order now lays down both the circumstances for removal and deportation and the Community criteria. The Court of Appeal has, however, said that Community law in this area 'simply mirrors the law and practice of this country' (*Escauriaza* (1987) 87 Cr App R 344 at 349).

It will be remembered that action can only be taken against individuals in relation to their personal conduct, which the Court in *Bonsignore* (Case 67/74) held to exclude deterrent or general preventive action (Chapter 11, above). Criminal convictions cannot in themselves provide grounds for action and there must be evidence that the individual continues to constitute a threat to public policy, although, exceptionally, one such conviction may provide evidence of such a continuing threat (*R v Bouchereau* (Case 30/77)). UK law permits deportation following a criminal conviction where that conviction is serious and where the individual's continuing presence will be a detriment to this country. The Court of Criminal Appeal has now arrived at a position at which evidence must be adduced to show that a person has a continuing propensity to offend or, that he represents a continuing threat to public policy (*Kraus* (1982) 4 Cr App R(S) 113; *Spura* (1988) 10 Cr App R (S) 376). The Court of Appeal (Civil Division), dealing with appeals on applications for judicial review where there has been no recommendation for deportation, and where the Home Secretary has taken the initiative to deport someone on public policy grounds, has taken a different approach. Even where there is evidence before the Court, which the Court accepts, that indicates a European Union citizen is not likely to commit further offences, the Court has felt free to uphold deportation on public policy grounds if the offence is sufficiently serious.

In *R v Secretary of State for the Home Department, ex parte Marchon* [1993] 2 CMLR 132, the appellant, a Portuguese national, who had been a general practitioner, was convicted of dealing in drugs. He was sentenced to a long term of imprisonment but not recommended for deportation by the trial court. The Home Secretary, nonetheless, issued notice of an intention to deport him. The Court of Appeal upheld the decision on the ground that 'the offence merits deportation ... it involves a disregard of the basic or fundamental tenets of society' (Dillon LJ). Concurring, Beldam LJ added that there should be no hint that society was prepared to tolerate the importation and dealing in drugs: 'I say this *not simply because refusal to do so would act as a deterrent to others but rather because it serves to emphasise the grave and present danger from this threat*' (emphasis added). The decision is surprising, not least because it is clearly not wholly based on the conduct of the offender and the likelihood of his future offending, but on a clear intention by the Court to take deterrent or general preventive action because of a concern about offences of this type. Such an approach obviously conflicts with Art 3 (1) Directive 64/221 and the decision of the Court of Justice in *Bonsignore*, above, Chapter 11.

APPEALS

A refusal of entry on grounds of public policy, public security or public health is subject to a right of appeal to an adjudicator, and from thence, if unsuccessful, but only on a point of law, and with leave, to the Immigration Appeal Tribunal (Art

15(1) EEA Order; s 13(1), Immigration Act 1971). Appeals against a refusal of entry on these grounds may, however, not be made until the person excluded has left the UK. It would seem, however, that a person who is a family member but is not himself a EU citizen, and who has a family permit, can remain to challenge such a decision. This is because such non-EU family members must present themselves with a 'family permit' which is described in the order as 'entry clearance', and holders of 'entry clearance' are entitled to remain to challenge their refusal (Art 2(1) EEA Order; Immigration Act 1971, s 13(3)). Ironically, EU citizens cannot be issued with such prior entry clearance, and cannot, therefore, bring themselves within this statutory provision. (No prior clearance can be demanded of EU citizens: Art 3(1) Directive 68/360; *R* v *Pieck* (Case 157/79), *see* Chapter 8.)

Refusal or revocation of a residence permit, removal or deportation where a criminal court has not recommended it are also subject to a two-stage right of appeal (Arts 15(2) EEA Order; Immigration Act 1971, s 14(1)). A successful appeal will result in a direction by the adjudicator or the Immigration Appeal Tribunal which is binding on the Home Secretary. Appeals normally involve a full oral hearing before an adjudicator at which all the facts and all the issues can be fully examined. Exceptionally, however, where the exclusion has been personally ordered by the Home Secretary on the grounds that it is not conducive to the public good there is no appeal at all (Immigration Act 1971, s 13(5)). In the late sixties, the early seventies and the eighties the power of exclusion was used to stop a variety of individuals of whose views the Government of the day disapproved, including North Vietnamese politicians, European student leaders, Marxist professors and American radicals (Robertson, G. *Freedom, the Individual and the Law* (1989)). Political deportations of this kind are subject to a limited 'appeal' to three advisers (*R* v *Secretary of State for the Home Department, ex parte Cheblak* [1991] 1 WLR 890). The decision of the advisers, like that of the single adviser in the case of exclusion orders made under the Prevention of Terrorism (Temporary Provisions) Act 1989, is not made known to the appellant and is not binding on the Home Secretary (*R* v *Secretary of State for the Home Department, ex parte Gallagher* [1994] 3 CMLR 295). In this kind of non-statutory procedure, the person proposed to be deported will be informed, 'so far as possible, of the nature of the allegations against him and will be given the opportunity to appear before the advisers, and to make representations to them before they tender advice to the Secretary of State' para 374 Immigration Rules, HC 395 (23 May 1994)). The information may not, in practice, be sufficient to enable him to know the allegations against him or to attempt to answer them effectively (*R* v *Secretary of State for the Home Department, ex parte Hosenball* [1977] 1 WLR 766). Where a decision is to deport a person because 'it is deemed that his expulsion will be conducive to the public good on other than security or political grounds' there is a right of appeal direct to the Immigration Appeal Tribunal, without a first hearing before an adjudicator (Immigration Act 1971 s 15(7)(a)).

How far do these procedure meet the procedural requirements of Community law and, specifically, of Arts 5, 6, 7, 8 and 9 of Directive 64/221? As far as in-state appeals for those threatened with removal or deportation in the general run of cases are concerned, they are very satisfactory. The appeals have suspensory effect; the appellants are entitled to challenge decisions with a full statement of the grounds of the refusal and have an opportunity to put their cases in person (Art 9(1) Directive 64/221; *Royer* (Case 48/75)). They also have a right to remain until the appeal is decided and, indeed, to stay in the UK until the appeal process is exhausted. Decisions of both the adjudicator and the tribunal are binding on the responsible administrative body, the Home Office. There are, however, three kinds of decision for which the appeal rights fall short of what is required by Community law.

The first problem arises in connection with appeals in relation to refusal on entry. As noted above, such appeals can only be launched from abroad. The appellant has no right to attend the appeal and will have to rely on someone to present his case for him in his absence. No legal aid is available for this process. The difficulty of doing this for someone with limited resources and with little or no knowledge of the English language can be well imagined and these difficulties will be exacerbated by the fact that there is, currently, no requirement that a refusal be given in a language with which the individual is familiar, although the rules state that 'If he has difficulty understanding the notice [of refusal] its meaning should be explained to him' (HC 395 (23 May 1994)).

Under Art 6, individuals should be given the public policy, public security or public health grounds for refusal and no decision should, under Art 9 (1) be put into effect until the individual has had the chance of putting his case to a competent authority and the competent authority has reached a decision (*Royer*, para [62] of judgment). The fact that an applicant for entry does not have a residence permit, should not be a bar to a suspension of his expulsion. It should be remembered that *Royer* had neither applied for or been granted such a permit and in any event, since residence permits are proof only of a right of residence, there seems to be little logic in making possession of such a permit a pre-condition to the exercise of appeal rights concerning a claimed right of residence. This applies, *a fortiori*, when the rights of entry and residence depend on EU citizenship (Art 8a EC Treaty). It should also be borne in mind that those exercising free movement rights should have the same rights 'as are available to nationals of the state concerned in respect of acts of the administration' (Art 8 Directive 64/221). Someone who holds a British passport carrying a right of abode under English law has an in-state right of appeal if he is refused entry on the ground he is, for example, impersonating the individual to whom the document was issued (Immigration Act 1971 s 3(1)). Those exercising free movement rights should be entitled to no less an effective remedy. An attempt to remove a person before the conclusion of an appeal could therefore be unlawful, unless it was justified on security grounds or some other reason requiring urgent removal. The individual could also rely on the direct effect of the directive to secure an effective remedy (*Van Duyn* v *The Home Office* (Case 41/74)). A denial of an appeal could also form the basis for a claim for damages against the national authorites under *Francovich* v *Italian Republic* (Case C-6/90).

The second problem arises in relation to refusals of entry on policy grounds. In cases where the Home Secretary has personally directed refusal, there is no appeal at all. The power to make exclusions of this kind in relation to EU citizens, EEA nationals and their families has been specifically retained (Art 20(2)(b), EEA Order). Nor is there an appeal against expulsion on similar grounds (Art 20(2)(c), EEA Order; Immigration Act 1971 s 14(3)). Here there is no remedy of any kind having suspensory effect. Decisions can, of course, be challenged in judicial review proceedings but such challenges only determine whether the decision-maker had the power to make the decision, not whether a particular individual constitutes a threat to public policy. Some of the individuals excluded on these grounds have been engaged in political activity which did not attract any kind of 'repressive measures' when engaged in by British nationals and would, consequently, not be justified in relation to a person exercising Community free movement rights (*Rutili* (Case 36/75)). The lack of effective procedural rights where a deportation was ordered in relation to an Italian national was held by the European Commission for Human Rights to be a prima facie breach of Art 13 of the Convention (*Caprino* (1980) 4 EHRR 97). The same argument of lack of procedural protection, as well as a lack of an independent 'competent authority', applies to the limited 'appeal' to advisors provided for in relation to deportation on these grounds. It remains to be seen whether or not the similar process which was subject to an Art 177 reference to the European Court in the *Gallagher* case (above), will be seen as meeting the Community's minimum procedural requirements, when the decision of the Court is applied by the Court of Appeal.

The third difficulty with regard to British appeal rights relates to the situation which follows a recommendation by a criminal court after conviction of a EU citizen. The Court of Justice decided in *R* v *Secretary of State, ex parte Santillo* (Case 131/79) that the recommendation could be the 'opinion' of a 'competent authority' under Art 9(1) which is necessary before the expulsion takes effect, even though it precedes the decision of the Home Secretary to expel the individual concerned. The Court, however, emphasised that such an opinion must be sufficiently proximate in time to the decision to deport to enable the competent authority to make an asessment that remained relevant when the recommendation of the criminal court was put into effect by the Home Secretary. If, for example, it was acted upon at the conclusion of a long prison sentence, during which time the behaviour of the individual may have significantly changed, then it would cease to meet the requirements of Art 9(1) Directive 64/221:

> A lapse of time amounting to several years between the recommendation for deportation and the decision by the administration is liable to deprive the recommendation of its function as an opinion within the meaning of Art 9. *It is indeed essential that the social danger resulting from a foreigner's presence should be assessed at the very time when the decision ordering expulsion is made against him as the factors to be taken into account are likely to change in the course of time.* (para [18] of judgment) (emphasis added)

There remains no right of appeal against a decision to implement a deportation recommendation, although the original recommendation is appealable as a sentence of the trial court (Immigration Act 1971, s 6(5)(a)). The problem of a substantial lapse of time between recommendation and implementation continues to represent a potential breach of the Community safeguards. Although the decision to implement the decision can be judicially reviewed, judicial review does not consider the merits of an individual case only the general legality of the action taken. Ideally, the original trial court should order further reports and hear evidence on the defendant's behaviour, to determine whether or not he remains a threat to public policy or public security.

Further reading

Bevan, V., (1986) *The Development of British Immigration Law,* Groom Helm, pp 201–13.

Evans, J.M., (1983) *Immigration Law,* Sweet & Maxwell, Chapter 4.

Macdonald and Blake, (1995) *Macdonald's Immigration Law and Practice* (4th edn) Butterworths.

Robertson, G., (1989) *Freedom, the Individual and the Law*, Penguin Books, Chapter 9.

Vincenzi, C. and Marrington, M., (1991) *Immigration Law: The Rules Explained*, Sweet & Maxwell.

Vincenzi, C., 'Welcoming the Well and Wealthy: the Implementatation of Directive 90/364 in the United Kingdom' in Daintith, T. (1995) *Implementing EC Law in the United Kingdom: Structures for Indirect Rule*, John Wiley & Sons.

Part III
THE FREE MOVEMENT OF GOODS

13 The free movement of goods
The removal of customs duties and fiscal barriers to the creation of a single market

The Community originally set as one of its central tasks 'the elimination, as between member states, of customs duties and quantitive restrictions on the import and export of goods, and all other measures having equivalent effect' (Art 3 (a) EC Treaty). It also bound itself, in Art 9 EC Treaty, to the creation of 'a customs union which shall cover all trade in goods and which shall involve the prohibition between member states of customs duties on imports and exports and all charges having equivalent effect, and the adoption of a common customs tariff in their relations with third countries'. Existing customs duties on exports had to be abolished by the end of the first stage in the development of the original Common Market (Art 16). The customs union involved not only the abolition of existing duties but it also committed the member states to 'refrain from introducing between themselves any new customs duties on imports or exports or any charges having equivalent effect' (Art 12).

The object of these provisions is to create not only an internal free trade area within the Community, where there are no duties imposed on the internal borders, but also a customs union where there is a common external tariff. Goods entering the Community will be subjected to the same duty, irrespective of where they enter the Community. To ensure that member states do not use national tax systems to favour home produced products and thereby create fiscal protection of home markets, Art 95 EC Treaty provides:

> No member state shall impose, directly or indirectly, on the products of other member states any internal taxation of any kind in excess of that imposed directly or indirectly on similar domestic products. Furthermore, no such member state shall impose on the products of other member states any internal taxation of such a nature as to afford indirect protection to other products.

These measures must now be seen in the broader context of the aims of the internal market which is 'an area without internal frontiers in which the free movement of goods, persons, services and capital is ensured in accordance with the provisions of [the] Treaty'. The single market envisages the abolition not only of duties and of discriminatory fiscal legislation, but of all physical, legal and technical barriers to the free movement of goods. The latter will be examined in Chapter 14 in connection with the physical and other equivalent restrictions on the free movement of goods. However, the earliest problem which had to be addressed by the Community and one which has not wholly disappeared concerned duties and tax provisions which affected the free flow of goods.

ARTICLE 12

This Article, which, with Art 9, plays a central role in the prohibition of customs duties and similar charges, has been held by the Court to be directly applicable *Van Gend en Loos* (Case 26/62):

> With regard to the general scheme of the Treaty as it relates to customs duties and charges having equivalent effect it must be emphasised that Art 9, which bases the Community on a customs union, includes as an essential provision the prohibition of customs duties and charges. This provision is found at the beginning of the Treaty which defines the 'Foundations of the Community'. It is applied and explained by Art 12.
>
> It follows from the wording and general scheme of Art 12 of the Treaty that, in order to ascertain whether customs duties or charges having equivalent effect have been increased contrary to the said Art, regard must be had to the customs duties and charges actually applied at the entry into force of the Treaty. Such an illegal increase may arise from a re-arrangement of the tariff resulting in the classification of the product under a more highly taxed heading ... It is of little importance how the increase in customs duties occurred when, after the Treaty entered into force, the same product in the same member state was subjected to a higher rate of duty.

It does not matter how small the charge may be that is imposed on imported goods, or for what purpose. In *Social Fund for Diamond Workers* (Cases 2 & 3/69) it was submitted that a small levy imposed under Belgian law on imported diamonds could not be in breach of Arts 9 and 12 because (1) it had no protectionist purpose as Belgium did not produce diamonds and (2) the levy's purpose was to provide social security benefits for Belgian diamond workers. The Court explained the sweeping nature of these provisions:

> In prohibiting the imposition of customs duties, the Treaty does not distinguish between goods according to whether or not they enter into competition with the products of the importing country. Thus, the purpose of the abolition of customs barriers is not merely to eliminate their protective nature, as the Treaty sought on the contrary to give general scope and effect to the rule on elimination of customs duties and charges having equivalent effect in order to ensure the free movement of goods. It follows from the system as a whole and from the general and absolute nature of the prohibition of any customs duty applicable to goods moving between member states

that customs duties are prohibited independently of any consideration of the purpose for which they were introduced and the destination of the revenue obtained therefrom. *The justification for this prohibition is based on the fact that any pecuniary charge – however small – imposed on goods by reason of the fact that they cross a frontier constitutes an obstacle to the movement of such goods.* (emphasis added)

Although the Court has stated that Arts 9 and 12 of the Treaty do not apply to a charge imposed on goods crossing a frontier within the Community if the charge constitutes consideration for a specific service rendered to an undertaking on an individual basis and representing a proportionate payment for that service, charges imposed for the cost of inspections and administrative formalities carried out by customs officers, or even by private firms on their behalf under a contract, do breach Arts 19 and 12 (*Edouard Dubois et Fils SA* v *Garoner Exploitations SA* (Case C-16/94)).

ARTICLE 13

Article 13(1) requires that customs duties in force between member states at the start of the first period of the Common Market were to be progressively abolished. Article 13(2) provides an essential re-enforcement of Article 13(1). Charges 'having an effect equivalent to customs duties' were also to be abolished. The Court of Justice has declared that:

> Any pecuniary charge, however small and whatever its designation and mode of application, which is imposed unilaterally on domestic or foreign goods by reason of the fact that they cross a frontier, and which is not a customs duty in the strict sense, constitutes a charge having an equivalent effect within the meaning of Arts 9, 12, 13 and 16 of the Treaty, even if it is not imposed for the benefit of the state, is not discriminatory in effect and if the product on which the charge is imposed is not in competition with any domestic product. (*Commission* v *Italy* (Case 24/68))

Not every charge levied on a frontier on incoming goods will be a charge having an equivalent effect to a customs duty. Each case will depend very much on the facts. The Court has, however, been reluctant to accept that a charge levied at a frontier is not a disguised form of duty unless it gives a tangible benefit to the importer. Where a genuine service is provided for the benefit of the importer, the Court has held that the charge must not exceed the value or the cost of the service (*Rewe-Zentralfinanz* v *Landwirtshaftskammer* (Case 39/73)). Where a charge results from the storage of goods in connection with customs formalities carried out inland the Court held that the benefit was intended to accrue to the Community's policy of encouraging post-entry customs formailities, and that if it conferred an incidental benefit on the trader, he should not be charged for that. Such a charge would breach Art 13(2) unless the storage of the goods was carried out quite independently of the post-entry customs controls (*Commission* v *Belgium* (Case 132/82)). A medical inspection carried out in the public interest is not a service to the importer.

In *Bresciano* v *Amministrazione Italiana delle Finanze* (Case 87/75), a charge was imposed for compulsory veterinary and public health inspections carried out on the importation of raw cowhides. The Court of Justice was asked whether such a levy constituted a charge having equivalent effect to a customs duty on imports. It held that it was:

> Any pecuniary charge, whatever its designation and mode of application, which is unilaterally imposed on goods imported from another member state by reason of the fact that they cross a frontier, constitutes a charge having an effect equivalent to a customs duty. In appraising a duty of the type at issue it is ... of no importance that it is proportionate to the quantity of the imported goods and not of their value. ... Nor, in determining the effects of the duty on the free movement of goods, is it of any importance that a duty of this type at issue is proportionate to the costs of a compulsory public health inspection carried out on entry of the goods. The activity of the administration of the state intended to maintain a public health inspection system imposed in the general interest cannot be regarded as a service rendered to the importer such as to justify the imposition of a public charge. (paras [9] and [10] of judgment)

However, the Court has held that charges imposed in relation to health controls required by Community law are not to be regarded as having equivalent effect to customs duties (*Bauhuis* v *Netherlands* (Case 46/76)). It came to a similar decision in relation to charges for health controls required under an international convention, intended to facilitate the free movement of goods, to which all the member states are parties (*Commission* v *Netherlands* (Case 89/76)). In *Bauhuis* the Court held that inspections carried out under the relevant Directive were not measures prescribed by a member state to protect some interest of its own but by the Council in the general interest of the Community. They could not, therefore, be regarded as unilateral measures which hinder trade, but rather as operations intended to promote the free movement of goods, since they removed the obstacles to free movement caused by national measures which might be justified under Art 36 (*see* Chapter 15). Fees charged for inspections required by Community law before export did not constitute charges equivalent to customs duties, provided that they did not exceed the actual cost of the inspection.

Most charges which have been held to breach the prohibition in Arts 12 and 13 have been those levied directly on imported or exported goods. Charges which are levied indiscriminately on home produced and imported goods will not, generally, breach Art 12 and will be lawful, provided they do not conflict with the prohibition in Art 95 against discriminatory taxation (*see* below). A breach of Arts 12 or 13 may, however, occur if the charge on the imported product is not imposed in the same way and determined according to the same criteria as the domestic product. In *Marimex* v *Italian Finance Administration* (Case 29/72) a veterinary inspection tax imposed on imported meat to ensure that it complied with national health standards was also imposed on domestic meat. But the inspections were conducted by different bodies applying different standards.

Where the charge is in the nature of a tax, care must be taken to determine whether it is, in fact a charge in the nature of a customs duty or a provision of national taxation. If it is a charge equivalent to a duty, it is unlawful in its entirety. If it is a provision of national taxation, it is unlawful only to the extent that it is discriminatory or protective (*IGAV* v *ENCC* (Case 94/74)). The difficulty of distinguishing between charges equivalent to duties and taxation is illustrated by *Capolongo* v *Maya* (Case 77/72). In this case a charge ostensibly levied on both imported and domestic products was claimed to be used to promote domestic products. The Court emphasised that the same charge could not be both equivalent to a customs duty and be a provision of internal taxation. It held that where a charge is levied on both imports and on domestic products, it can, nevertheless, constitute a charge equivalent to a customs duty when it is intended exclusively to support activities which specifically benefit the taxed domestic product. In *IGAV* v *ENCC* (above) the Court held that this was also the case where the domestic tax was remitted on the domestic product 'wholly or in part'. The Court later modified its position in *Fratelli Cucchi* (Case 77/76), where it held that apparent internal taxation can only constitute a charge equivalent to a customs duty 'if it has the sole purpose of financing activities for the specific advantage of the taxed domestic product; if the taxed product and the domestic product benefiting from it are the same; and if the charges imposed on the domestic product are made good in full'. However, a much more probable conclusion is that a tax on imported and domestic products which gives a partial benefit to the taxed domestic product constitutes discriminatory internal taxation, contrary to Art 95, on the basis that it indirectly imposes a heavier burden on products from other member states than on domestic products (*Commission* v *Italy* (Case 73/79)).

ARTICLE 16

Art 16 required the abolition of all duties and charges having an equivalent effect on exports. Like Art 12, Art 16 has been held to be directly effective (*Eunomia di Porro* v *Italian Ministry of Education* (Case 18/71)). 'Exports' does not only include goods normally traded in commerce. In *Commission* v *Italy* (Case 7/68) the Court rejected the argument of the Italian Government that the free movement provisions of the Treaty could have no application to a charge levied on the export of goods of historic or artistic interest. The antiques and other objects covered by the Italian law resembled such goods in that they had monetary value and could constitute the object of commercial transactions. An internal duty which falls more heavily on exports than on domestic sales amounts to a charge having an equivalent effect to a customs duty (*Irish Creamery Milk Suppliers* v *Government of Ireland* (Cases 36 & 71/80)).

ARTICLE 95 AND DISCRIMINATORY INTERNAL TAXATION

In the absence of a harmonised tax system in member states, the member states are entitled to take such measures as are necessary to make that system effective, even, it would seem, at the expense of fundamental rights under the Treaty, such as the right of establishment (*R* v *HM Treasury, ex parte Daily Mail* (Case 81/87)). Article 99 provides for the enactment of measures to harmonise legislation on turnover taxes, excise duties and other forms of indirect taxation. Until a fully harmonised Community tax regime is achieved, however, member states retain their national prerogative in relation to internal taxation. This principle of national autonomy gives way to another fundamental principle, that of free movement of goods. Art 95 provides that:

> No member state shall impose, directly or indirectly, on the products of other member states any internal taxation of any kind in excess of that imposed directly or indirectly on similar domestic products.
>
> Further, no member state shall impose on the products of other member states any internal taxation of such a nature as to afford indirect protection to other products.

Since Art 95 refers to 'products of other member states' it might well be thought that discriminatory taxation levied on goods coming from another member state but originating from outside the Community was permissible. Unlike the provisions relating to the free movement of goods in Chapter 2 of the Treaty, which relate both to products originating in the Community and 'to products coming from third countries which are in free circulation in member states', there is no such application to the non-discriminatory tax rules (Art 9(2) EC Treaty). The Court therefore at first held that member states were entitled to impose such discriminatory taxes on third-state products circulating freely in the Community, provided that such taxation was compatible with any concessions made to that state in any association or other agreement (*Hansen* v *Hauptzollamt Flensburg* (Case 148/77)). It modified its position, however, in *Co-Frutta* (Case 193/85). In this case, which involved Italian taxation of bananas imported through other member states, the Court accepted that the Common Customs Tariff (CCT) and the Common Commercial Policy were intended to ensure a uniform treatment of goods imported from third states and the facilitation of the free movement of such goods once they have been legitimately imported into one of the member states. (*see* Usher, J., 'The Single Market and Goods Imported from Third Countries' (1986) YEL 159,167).

Article 95 is aimed at two distinct, but sometimes overlapping, national taxation practices namely, the taxing of the same or similar imported and home produced products in a different way and, the taxing of different but competing imported and home produced products in such a way as to afford protection to the home produced product. The two key concepts are therefore similarity and product competition (*Commission* v *France* (Case 168/78)). Many of the earlier cases in this area concerned alcoholic drinks, where the level of tax is high compared to the production cost and a drink's competitive edge will depend very much on its retail price. More recently, the focus has moved to discriminatory taxation of motor vehicles.

In assessing similarity of beverages, the Court has used method of manufacture, content, taste and alcoholic strength. On this basis, a similarity has been found between whisky and gin, and cognac and armagnac (in *Commission v France*, above) and sparkling wine matured in the cask and sparkling wine matured in the bottle (*Commission v Italy* (Case 278/83)). In *FG Roders BV ea v Inspecteur der Inverrechten en Accijnzen* (Joined Cases C-367/93 to C-377/93), importers of French wine, Spanish sherry and Italian vermouth challenged the higher rates of excise duty that were charged on those products, as compared to fruit wines produced in the Benelux countries. The Court considered whether still and sparkling fruit wines are similar to sparkling and still fruit wines, that is, wines made from fruit other than grapes. The Court decided that they are. They are made from the same kind of agricultural products, and by the same process of natural fermentation. They both possess the same kind of organoleptic properties – in particular taste and alcoholic strength and meet the same needs of consumers, since they can be consumed for the same purposes, namely both to quench thirst, to refresh, and to accompany meals. Although differential taxation on similar home produced and imported products will normally breach the first paragraph of Art 95, and the second paragraph if the tax has a protectionist effect, in some circumstances different rates of taxation may be applied if they are based on objective criteria, designed to achieve economic policy objectives which are compatible with EC law. In order not to infringe Art 95, they must also be applied in such a way as to avoid discrimination against imports or afford indirect protection to domestic products. On this basis, in the course of Art 169 proceedings brought by the Commission against France, the Court held that a more favourable tax rate applied to natural sweet wine as compared to ordinary table wine was justified. The purpose of the tax was to assist the economy of areas which were heavily reliant on such wines, and which were produced in difficult circumstances (*Commission v France* (Case 196/85)). Where such tax relief is applied, it must be operated indiscriminately, even where there is a legitimate and defensible objective. Thus, it has been held that an importer of spirits into Germany was entitled to take advantage of tax relief available, inter alia , in respect of spirits made from small businesses and collective farms. The Court accepted that such tax concessions could meet legitimate economic and social purposes, but Art 95 required that such preferential systems must be extended without discrimination to spirits coming from other member states (*Hansen v Hauptzollamt Flensburg* (Case 148/77)).

In *Commission v Greece* (Case C-105/91) the Commission brought an action under Art 169 for a declaration that, by applying higher rates of special consumer tax to private cars incorporating traditional technology imported from other member states than are applied to private cars incorporating the same technology produced or assembled in Greece, the Greek Government had infringed Art 95. In its defence the Greek Government maintained, first, that, as the production of Greek vehicles did not cover more than 10 per cent of internal demand, there was no manifest discrimination and, secondly that the provisions were justified by the concern to offset the competitive disadvantage suffered by the Greek automobile industry compared to manufacturers in other member states, and to enable it to conform to the new ecological Community rules.

The Court rejected both arguments. There was no *de minimis* rule in relation to infringements of Community provisions. It emphasised that it had consistently held that a member state was guilty of a failure to fulfil its obligations under the Treaty, regardless of the frequency or the circumstances of the alleged breach. As to the lack of manifest discrimination, the Court held that the Greek Government's actual defence constituted an admission of a protectionist intention. In *Commission* v *Greece* (Case C-327/90) the Commission proceedings concerned a special consumption tax on passenger vehicles which made provision for two methods of calculating the taxable amount, depending on whether the vehicle was imported or home produced. The consequence did not always mean that the imported vehicle paid more tax, but the Court held that it, nonetheless breached Art 95b because the way the tax was levied could not ensure that the imported product was never subject to greater taxation than the domestic product (*see also, Fazenda Pública and Others* v *Américo Tadeu* (Case C-345/93)).

In deciding whether there is an infringement of Art 95 in relation to competing rather than similar products, it is necessary to examine the nature of the market. This exercise was carried out by the Court in *Commission* v *United Kingdom* (Case 170/78) in relation to wine and beer. The Court held that, in order to determine the existence of a competitive relationship, it was necessary to consider not only the present state of the market, but also possible developments regarding the free movement of goods within the Community, 'and the further substitution of products for one another which might be revealed by intensification of trade, so as fully to develop the complementary features of the economies of the member states'. The Court concluded, on the basis of evidence submitted to it, that a competitive relationship could be established in the United Kingdom between beer and the cheapest wines. The tax burden on wine in this country was subsequently reduced. Although the Court conceded in the *Roders* case (above) that fruit wine produced in the Benelux countries was not similar to imported sherry, madeira, vermouth and champagne, it recognized that these products might, nevertheless, be in competition with the fruit wine, and the differential tax structure might, therefore, favour the home produced fruit wine. The Court observed that the existence of a competitive relationship between the products had to be considered to establish whether or not there was a breach of the second paragraph of Art 95. The essential question was whether the charge imposed was of such a kind as to have the effect on the market in question, of reducing potential consumption of the imported products. The national court that had to make the final decision, must have regard to the difference between the selling prices of the products in question and the impact of that difference on the consumer's choice, as well as to changes in the consumption of those products. The fact that tax is imposed on a product which is not produced in the importing state and for which there is no domestic equivalent may well mean that there is no breach of Art 95, since there will be no similar product in relation to which discrimination can be alleged or home market to be protected (*Fink-Frucht* v *HZA Munchen-Landsberger Strasse* (Case 27/67)).

Further reading

Easson, A. J., 'Fiscal Discrimination: New Perspectives on Article 95' (1981) 18 CML Rev 521.

Green, N., Hartley, T. C. and Usher, J., (1991) *The Legal Foundations of the Single Market*, Clarendon Press, Chapters 3 and 4.

Schwarze, J., (1988) The Member States Discretionary Powers under Tax Provisions of the EEC Treaty in Schwarze, J (ed.) *Discretionary Powers of the Member States in the Fields of Economic Policies and their Limits under the EEC Treaty* Nomos 1988.

Steiner, J., (1994) *Textbook on EC Law*, (4th edn), Blackstone Press, Chapter 7.

Weatherill, S. and Beaumont, P., (1995) *EC Law*, (2nd edn) Penguin Books, Chapter 11.

Wyatt, D. and Dashwood, A., (1993) *European Community Law* (3rd edn), Sweet & Maxwell, Chapter 7.

14 The elimination of quantitative restrictions on the movement of goods and measures having equivalent effect

The elimination of any restrictions on the free movement of goods is clearly central to the creation of an internal market in the member states of the Community, and this is one of the main objectives of the Community (Arts 1 and 2(c) EC Treaty). Art 30 provides that:

> Quantitative restrictions on imports and all measures having equivalent effect shall, without prejudice to the following provisions, be prohibited between member states.

The prohibition of restrictions on *imports* in Art 30 is reflected by a matching prohibition on *export* restrictions in Art 34. Both prohibitions are, however, qualified by the right of member states to impose limited restrictions on trade, if they can *justify* them under the criteria laid down in Art 36. The rules attempt to strike a balance in achieving a genuine free and competitive market in goods on the one hand, and the recognition of the need, in some circumstances, to protect essential public interests on the other. The process of harmonisation of national standards of consumer and environmental protection through a programme of standardising directives for goods throughout the Community is part of a programme to reduce the need for such national exceptions to the general Community right of free movement of goods. Much of the jurisprudence of the Court of Justice has been devoted to consideration of the extent to which such national measures infringe the relevant provisions of the Treaty or fall within the permitted derogations.

Articles 30 and 34 adopt the same approach shown in the prohibitions in Arts 12 and 13. They are aimed at measures which are clearly directed at imports and exports to and from other member states, but they also prohibit measures which have the same effect as such restrictions, even though there may be no intention by the member state imposing them to have that effect. The prohibition on restrictions affects all kinds of products, including agricultural produce and it applies not only to goods which originate in the member states but also to goods which come from outside the Community and are in free circulation in a member state. Such goods are in free circulation when they have crossed the Common External Tariff (CET) wall with all import formalities complied with and duties and charges paid (Art 10(1)).

For the purposes of Arts 30–36, the Court has held that 'goods' are 'manufactured material objects' (*Cinéthèque* (Cases 60 and 61/84)). The term is wide enough to include not only plants, vegetables, fruit and livestock and animal produce and even, the Court held recently, bovine semen (*Société Civile Agricole*) (Case C-323/93). The context in which an item is applied, may, however, result in it being regarded not as a product in itself subject to the provisions of Arts 30–36, but as an incident to the provision of service, and thus subject to Art 59 (*Customs and Excise Commissioners v Schindler* (Case C-275/92)) (para [23]). However, coins and banknotes or bearer cheques are not 'goods' as their transfer is subject to the rules on transfer of capital under Art 67 EC Treaty (*Aldo Bordessa and Others* (joined Cases C-358/93 & C-416/93)). However, in *R v Thompson* (Case 7/78), the Court held that old gold coins were 'goods' because they were not a normal means of payment.

The Treaty provisions which are aimed at ensuring the free movement of goods are directed at the governments of member states. Art 31 prohibits the introduction of any new quantitative restrictions by member states. We have already considered the prohibition of tariffs and discriminatory charges and taxes imposed by member states in the last chapter. Articless 30–36 form part of a larger strategy to free up trade and to prevent member states from adopting covert protectionist policies. The same strategy also includes the regulation of state monopolies of a commercial character under Art 37 and state aids to nationalised industries under Arts 92–94. It underlies Council Directives 88/95 and 89/440 on public procurement, which are intended to prevent the governments of member states from favouring national contractors in the award of public works contracts. For that reason, attempts by a private undertaking to persuade consumers to buy national products in, say a 'Buy British' advertising campaign, will not breach Art 30, although such a campaign would infringe Art 30 if promoted by a public, or publicly sponsored bodies (*Apple and Pear Development Council v KJ Lewis Ltd* (Case 222/82)). The obligation to observe Art 30 extends to private bodies which exercise powers conferred by statute, an increasingly common phenomenon in the United Kingdom and elsewhere. In *R v Royal Pharmaceutical Society, ex parte API* (case 266/87) the Court held that rules of the society which required pharmacists to supply, under a prescription, only a named branded drug were, prima facie, in breach of Art 30, although, in the circumstances, jusifiable under Art 36.

It is, of course, not only states and public bodies which may, either directly or indirectly, seek to exclude foreign competition. Articles 30–36 must also be considered in the light of Arts 85 and 86, which play an important part in preventing national cartels and national monopolies from using private economic power to keep goods from other member states from national markets. Where the private body enjoys a monopoly conferred on it by the state, which enables it to restrict the import of foreign products by virtue of that monopoly, there may be an overlap between Arts 30 and 86 (*see*, for example, *Société Civile Agricole* v *Coopérative d'Elevage de la Mayenne* (Case C- 323/93), and *see also* Chapters 18 and 19).

QUANTITATIVE RESTRICTIONS

Direct restrictions, such as quotas and bans on certain products of other member states were abolished or phased out in the early days of the Community. Limited restrictions have been permitted in the transitional period after new member states have joined, but these are also being rapidly phased out. The concept of 'quantitative restrictions' is straightforward enough:

> The prohibition on quantitative restrictions covers measures which amount to a total or partial restraint of, according to the circumstances, imports, exports, or goods in transit.
> (*Geddo* v *Ente Nazionale Risi* (case 2/73)

Some national prohibitions do survive, such as the prohibition on the importation of obscene materials into the United Kingdom under the Customs Consolidation Act 1876. It was argued by the British Government in *R* v *Henn and Darby* (Case 34/79) that a ban on the import of pornographic material under the Act was not a quantitative restriction under Art 30. The Court of Justice, in an Art 177 reference disagreed. It held that Art 30 'includes such a prohibition on imports in as much as this is the most extreme form of restriction'. The reference in Art 30 to 'quantitative restrictions' was to be read in the light of Art 36 which referred also to 'prohibitions' on imports. In the event, the Court held that the prohibition in this case was justified under Art 36. That aspect of the case will be examined below. Although a quantitative restriction is readily recognisable, measures having an equivalent effect to quantitative restrictions on imports have proved much more elusive and have resulted in a large, and growing, jurisprudence on the subject by the European Court of Justice.

MEASURES HAVING EQUIVALENT EFFECT TO QUANTITATIVE RESTRICTIONS (MEQRs)

Commission Directive 70/50

'Measures' in this context can cover a whole range of activities carried out by or on behalf of the government of a member state. As noted above, Arts 30–36 are aimed at action taken by the governments of member states. The expression 'measure' is often used with regard to some kind of legislative act, but in this context it can cover not only legislative action of any kind, but a whole range of administrative acts and even commercial, promotional activities carried on for or with the support of government (*Commission v Ireland: Re 'Buy Irish' Campaign* (case 249/81)). In *Apple and Pear Development Council v Lewis* (case 222/82), the Council had been set up by the British Government by a statutory instrument and was financed by a charge imposed on growers. The Court held that it could not enjoy the same freedom as regards methods of advertising used as that enjoyed by producers themselves or producers' associations of a voluntary character. Art 30 imposed on the Council 'a duty not to engage in any advertising intended to discourage the purchase of products from other member states or to disparage those products in the eyes of consumers. Nor must it advise consumers to purchase domestic products solely by reason of their national origin.' (para [18]).

Administrative practice by a member state can also constitute a 'measure' breaching Art 30. In *Commission v France* (Case 21/84) the Commission alleged that the Government of France had violated Art 30 by refusing to approve postal franking machines from other member states. A British manufacturer, despite repeated applications, had been unable to secure French approval for his machines. The Court of Justice accepted that the mere fact that the law of a member state did not breach Art 30 was insufficient:

> Under the cloak of a general provision permitting the approval of machines imported from other member states, the administration might very well adopt a sytematically unfavourable attitude towards imported machines, either by allowing considerable delay in replying to applications for approval or in carrying out the examination procedure, or by refusing approval on the grounds of various alleged technical faults for which no detailed explanations are given or which prove to be inaccurate. The prohibition on measures having an effect equivalent to quantitative restrictions would lose much of its useful effect if it did not cover protectionist or discriminatory practices of that type.

However, not every discriminatory administrative act will breach Art 30. Isolated acts of discrimination will not suffice. There must be some consistency in the practice:

> ... To constitute a measure prohibited under Art 30 that practice must show a certain degree of consistency and generality. (paras [11], [12] and [13] of judgment)

Nor can a practice of not implementing a national law which infringes Art 30 constitute compliance with the Treaty. In the same way that it has rejected similar arguments that the free movement rights of persons can be implemented by concessions of this kind, the Court has been unequivocal in the rejection of the 'concessionary' implementation of the equally fundamental and directly effective right to the free movement of goods:

> ... A measure caught by the prohibition provided for in Art 30 ... does not escape that prohibition simply because the competent authority is empowered to grant exemptions, even if that power is freely applied to imported products. Freedom of movement is a

right whose enjoyment may not be dependent upon a discretionary power or on a concession granted by the national administration. (*Keldermann* (Case 130/80), para [14]; *compare, Commission* v *France* (Case 167/73).)

Directive 70/50, issued in December 1969, was intended to provide guidance on the kind of acts and activities which constitute 'measures' infringing Art 30, and which were in force when the EC Treaty came into force. Although many measures will have been made since that time, and will be outside its scope, it still has value in identifying prohibited acts or conduct.

The directive covers measures 'other than those applicable equally to domestic or imported products, which hinder imports which could otherwise take place, including measures which make importation more difficult or costly than the disposal of domestic products.' It is thus concerned with national measures which apply specifically to or affect only imported products. These are often called 'distinctly applicable' measures, because they distinguish between imported and home produced products. Art 2 of the directive contains a non-exhaustive list of the sort of measures applied to imported goods which would constitute MEQRs. They include:

1   the laying down of minimum and maximum sale prices;
2   the fixing of less favourable prices for imported than for domestically produced goods;
3   the exclusion of prices for imported goods which reflect importation costs;
4   the making of access to markets in the importing state dependent upon having an agent there;
5   the laying down of conditions of payment in respect of imported products only, or the subjection of imported goods to conditions which are different from those laid down for domestic products and are more difficult to satisfy;
6   requiring for imported goods only, the giving of guarantees or the making of payment on account;
7   subjecting imported products only to conditions, in respect of shape, size, weight, composition, presentation, identification, or subjecting imported products to conditions which are different from those for domestic products and more difficult to satisfy;
8   hindering the purchase by individuals of imported products only, or encouraging, requiring or giving preference to the purchase of domestic products only;
9   the total or partial preclusion of the use of national facilities or equipment in respect of imported products only or the total or partial confinement of such facilities to national producers;
10 the prohibition of limitation of publicity in respect of imported products only, or the total or partial restriction of publicity to home produced products.

The above list is indicative of the sorts of national measures which will constitute MEQRS, but the ability of member states to introduce measures which are either intended or will have the effect of protecting domestically produced goods can neither be anticipated nor underestimated, and the court has laid down a number of general principles about measures which specifically affect imported goods and which constitute MEQRs. Each national measure will have to be assessed on these principles as and when it comes before national courts and before the Court of Justice.

Distinctly applicable measures

In *Procureur du Roi* v *Dassonville* (case 8/74), a Belgian importer of Scotch whisky was prosecuted for selling the whisky with false certificates of origin. He had imported the whisky from France and it had been difficult to obtain the certificates from the producers. He argued that the Belgian law infringed Art 30, in that it made the importation of whisky from anywhere other than the state of origin more difficult. The Court of Justice agreed. Although the case related to a specific measure affecting only importers the Court, in an Art 177 reference, gave a very broad definition of what constitutes an infringement of Art 30. The definition is wide enough to include both distinctly applicable measures affecting imports and indistinctly applicable measures affecting both imported and home produced products:

> All trading rules enacted by member states *which are capable of hindering, directly or indirectly, actually or potentially, intra-Community trade are to be considered as measures having an equivalent effect to quantitative restrictions.* (emphasis added)

There was no need to prove that trade between member states had been affected by the measure. All that was necessary was for there to be a possibility of such an effect. In *Commission* v *Ireland (Re 'Buy Irish' Campaign)* (Case 249/81), the Court of Justice conceded that the campaign had not significantly affected intra-Community trade :

> Whilst … the advertising campaign and the use of the 'Guaranteed Irish' symbol, *have not had any significant success in winning over the Irish market to domestic products, it is not possible to overlook the fact that, regardless of their efficacity those two activities form part of a government programme which is designed to achieve the substitution of domestic products for imported products* and is liable to affect the volume of trade between member states.'
> (para [25]), (emphasis added)

The Court remains very ready to assume that different treatment of imported goods may result in a reduced volume of sales. In *Lucien Ortscheit GmbH* v *Eurim-Pharm GmbH* (Case C-320/93), a German law prohibiting the advertising of foreign medicinal products which had not been authorised for sale in Germany but which could, nonetheless, still be imported into Germany, was held necessarily to fall within the scope of Art 30, since it did not have the same effect on the marketing of medicinal products from other member states as on the marketing of national medicinal products. It added that the prohibition of advertising might restrict the volume of imports of medicinal products not authorised in Germany, since it deprived pharmacists and doctors of a source of information on the existence and availability of such products. It was, therefore, equivalent to a quantitative restriction.

Similarly, any kind of licensing arrangement affecting imports or importers, however liberally operated, will be assumed to have an effect on imports. In *International Fruit Co. NV* v *Produktschap voor Groenten* (Cases 51-4/71), the Court held that national measures requiring import and export licences in intra-Community trade, even though such licences were granted automatically, infringed both Arts 30 and 34. In *Commission* v *Germany* (Case 247/81), German legislation providing that pharmaceutical products could only be placed on the market by a pharmaceutical undertaking having its headquarters in the area to which the legislation applied was held by the Court as likely to involve additional costs to the exporter and therefore constituted a barrier to trade.

The assumption that trade is affected is, however, no longer made where the measure in question impacts in exactly the same way on both imported and home produced products. In *Keck and Mithouard* (Cases C-267-268/91), French legislation prohibited the resale of goods at a loss. In an Art 177 reference the national court asked whether the measure was compatible with Art 30. The Court held that it was:

> The Court has consistently held that any measure which is capable of directly or indirectly, actually or potentially, hindering intra-Community trade constitutes a measure having equivalent effect to a quantitative restriction. [12] National legislation imposing a general prohibition on resale at a loss is not designed to regulate trade in goods between member states. [13] Such legislation may, admittedly, restrict the volume of sales, and hence the volume of sales of products from other member states, in so far as it deprives traders of a method of sales promotion. But the question remains whether such a possibility is sufficient to characterise the legislation in question as a measure having equivalent effect to a quantitative restriction. [14] In view of the increasing tendency of traders to invoke Art 30 of the Treaty as a means of challenging any rules whose effect is to limit their commercial freedom even where such rules are not aimed at products from other member states, the Court considers it necessary to re-examine and clarify its case law on this matter.
>
> ... Contrary to what has previously been decided, the application to products from other member states of national provisions restricting or prohibiting certain selling arrangements is not such as to hinder directly or indirectly, actually or potentially, trade between member states within the meaning of *Dassonville* so long as those provisions apply to all relevant traders operating within the national territory and so long as they affect in the same manner, in law and in fact, the marketing of domestic products and those from other member states. [17]. Such rules therefore fall outside the scope of Art 30 of the Treaty.

There will, therefore, be no assumption that the importation of products will be affected, provided that the measure in question affects the marketing of home and domestic products in law and in fact in the same way. Whether that is, in fact, the case will remain a key issue.

Commenting on the new test described in *Keck*, Advocate-General Jacobs has observed:

> It seems to me … that the *Dassonville* formula was indeed too broad – and illustrates the dangers in taking as a starting point a very broad proposition which subsequently has to be whittled down – but that the main body of the Court's case law on Art 30 was wholly satisfactory and that to introduce at this stage a notion of discrimination may raise more problems than it solves. (*The European Advocate* (1994/1995) 2,4)

Indistinctly applicable measures constituting a barrier to imports

Article 3 of Directive 70/50 also covers measures which affect both home produced and imported products. They do not, in other words, distinguish between goods according to their origin, and are, therefore, referred to as 'indistinctly applicable' measures. Specifically, Art 3 refers to measures relating to the marketing of products dealing with shape, size, weight, composition, presentation, or identification 'which are equally applicable to domestic and imported products where the restrictive effect of such measures on the free movement of goods exceeds the effects intrinsic to trade rules'. This will, in particular, be the case, where the restrictive effects on the free movement of goods are out of proportion to their purpose and where the same objective can be attained by other means which are less of a hindrance to trade. These criteria have been crucial in the development of the jurisprudence of the Court of Justice in relation to national measures which appear, at least, to apply indiscriminately to both imported and home produced goods.

In a landmark decision on whether such national provisions could be MEQRs the Court, in *Rewe-Zentrale AG* v *Bundesmonopolverwaltung für Branntwein* (Case 120/78) (usually called 'the *Cassis de Dijon Case*'), laid down two important principles. The case concerned the proposed importation of a blackcurrant liqueur called 'Cassis de Dijon' into the Federal Republic of Germany. The importer applied for a licence to do so from the administrative authority in Germany, but it was refused because the liqueur did not meet the Federal Republic's requirement of a minimum alcoholic content of 25 per cent which was required for domestic cassis. French cassis was only required to have an alcoholic strength of between 15 and 20 per cent. The importer challenged the decision on the basis that the rule infringed Art 30, and the case was referred to the Court of Justice under Art 177.

The Court accepted that, in the absence of any common rules in the Community relating to the production and marketing of alcohol, it was up to member states to regulate these activities in their own territories. It therefore held that:

1   Obstacles to movement within the Community resulting from disparities between the national laws relating to the marketing of the products in question must be accepted *in so far as those provisions may be recognised as necessary in order to satisfy mandatory requirements relating in particular to the effectiveness of fiscal supervision, the protection of public health, the fairness of commercial transactions and the defence of the*

:umer. (para [8]) (emphasis added. This principle is usually referred to as 'the
of reason'.)

re is no valid reason why goods which have been lawfully produced and
keted in one member state should not be introduced into any other member
?. (para [14]) (the 'rule of recognition')

Applying these principles to the French cassis, the Court did not accept that the
German minimum alcohol rules were necessary to protect consumers, because the
fact that French cassis had a lower alcoholic strength than German cassis could
easily be made known to German consumers by effective labelling and packaging.
The requirement relating to the minimum alcoholic content did not 'serve a purpose
which is in the general interest and [is] such as to take precedence over the
requirements of the free movement of goods, which constitutes one of the
fundamental rules of the Community'.

The fact that the goods in question had been lawfully produced and circulated in
another member state (the second principle) does not preclude the application of the
first principle. As with Art 36, which allows member states to derogate from Arts 30
and 36 on public policy and public health grounds (*see* below), there is a presumption
in favour of the entry and distribution of the goods which can only be rebutted by
the host state if it is able to establish the existence of the circumstances in which the
first *Cassis* principle is applicable. The Court in subsequent cases has been called
upon to consider a wide variety of legislative and other national provisions. The
scope of the *Cassis* principles can best be illustrated by an analysis of some of them.

In *Commission* v *United Kingdom* (Case 207/83) a British Order in Council required
that certain products, including woollen clothing and cutlery, be marked with the
country of origin. French manufacturers complained that goods for the British
market had to be specially origin marked, which increased production costs. The
Commission also argued that such origin marking encouraged consumers to
exercise their prejudices in favour of national products and was likely to reduce the
sale of Community produced goods. The British Government defended the origin
marking order on the grounds that the origin details gave important information to
the consumer about the nature and quality of the product, and that the requirement
of origin marking was non-discriminatory, in that it applied to both domestic and
imported products. The Court was not persuaded that origin marking was a
necessary consumer protection measure. It agreed with the Commission that it
encouraged the exercise of national prejudices. Any distinctive national quality of
the goods could be highlighted by individual retailers, and should not be the subject
of national legislation.

Another national rule that was held to have the effect of making foreign
penetration of the national market more difficult was considered by the Court in
Walter Rau Lebensmittelwerke v *De Smedt PVBA* (Cases 279 and 280/84). The plaintiffs
manufactured margarine and complained that a Belgian law, under which
margarine had to be sold in Belgium in cube-shaped packs to distinguish it from
butter, infringed Art 30. The Court, in an Art 177 reference, agreed. Although the

rule applied to all margarine sold in Belgium, foreign manufacturers wishing to import margarine into Belgium would have to establish a special production and packaging line for the Belgian market which would increase their production costs. There was no consumer protection reason for the packaging requirement. The true nature of the product could just as well be conveyed to the consumer by effective labelling and packaging.

Although individual states have a margin of discretion in deciding what level of protection to provide to consumers, the Court, in determining whether such national measures are proportionate, will take into account the extent of current knowledge, in, for example, the assessment of national provisions to protect the health of consumers. In *Proceedings against M Debus* (Cases C-13/91 and C-113/91), the defendant was prosecuted for importing and marketing in Italy beer containing sulphur dioxide in a quantity permitted by the relevant French legislation but higher than that permitted in Italy. The defendant contested the prosecution on the basis that the Italian legislation breached Art 30 and the case was referred to the Court under Art 177. The Court had little difficulty in finding that the Italian rules led to 'a general and absolute prohibition of all beers containing more than 20 mg of sulphur dioxide per litre without any exception whatsoever'. There was uncontested evidence that the level of sulphur dioxide prohibited was far less than that found to constitute a risk by the World Health Organisation. It was an indistinctly applicable measure. The Court did not accept that, since there were other methods of preserving beer, that the importing state was entitled to determine the method to be used, 'since such an interpretation of the concept of technological requirement, which leads to preference for domestic production methods, constituted a means of imposing a disguised restriction on trade between member states'. (*see* also *Sandoz BV* (Case 174/82); *Deserbais* (Case 286/86).

A similar approach was adopted by the Court in relation to a product specification in the terms for tender for a public contract. In *Commission* v *Ireland* (Case 45/87) the Commission brought an action under Art 169 EC Treaty against the Irish Government for allowing a specification relating to a water supply contract in Dundalk which, it alleged, breached Art 30. The specification stipulated for pipes which had been certified as complying with Irish Standard 188. Only one manufacturer, located in Ireland, made pipes of such a standard. Did the specification constitute a barrier to the importation of pipes for this (and other) contracts? The Court held that it did. Whilst it was perfectly reasonable to specify the quality of pipes to be used for the transmission of drinking water, the attainment of that object could as well have been achieved by pipes produced abroad to a standard equivalent to the Irish standard. A more direct restriction in a public supply contract, under which a minimum of thirty per cent of awarded contracts had to be to undertakings established in the Mezzogiorno area of Italy, was held to constitute a clear breach of Art 30 in *Laboratori Bruneau Srl* v *Unita Sanitaria di Monterotondo* (Case C-351/88).

The Court has, however, accepted a wide range of national measures, many of them going well beyond measures designed to protect consumers or the specific exceptions permitted to member states under Art 36. In *Commission* v *Denmark* (Case 302/86), for example, the Commission challenged a Danish law under which all containers for beer and soft drinks must be returnable. Prima facie, this constituted a barrier, because foreign manufacturers would not be geared up to selling drinks in such containers and would have to take special steps to do so to supply the Danish market. The Court recognised, citing the case of *Walter Rau* (above) that the rule constituted an obstacle to trade. Was it, however, a mandatory requirement? The Court accepted that protection of the environment is one of the Community's 'essential objectives', which may justify certain limitations to the principle of the free movement of goods. Those limitations must not, however, 'go beyond the inevitable restrictions which are justified by the pursuit of the objective of environmental protection'. It was, therefore, necessary to examine whether all the restrictions which the contested rules imposed on the free movement of goods were necessary to achieve the objectives pursued by those rules.

The Court has shown a willingness to accept that restrictions aimed at protecting national cultural and social values could also be mandatory requirements. In *Cinéthèque* (Cases 60 and 61/84), for example, the Court upheld a non-discriminatory French rule prohibiting the sale or hire of videos of films within a year of their first showing at a cinema. Although the rule had the effect of restricting the import of videos from other member states, the Court held the restriction to be justified and not, therefore, in breach of Art 30. The Court accepted that the protection of the French cinema was a legitimate objective, presumably (although it was not stated), as a means of protecting national culture. The case can, perhaps, be compared to a case involving the free movement of persons, *Groener* v *Minister for Education* (Case 379/87), in which the Court accepted a requirement of a knowledge of Irish imposed on a Dutch teacher seeking employment in Ireland, although it was not needed for the subject she was to teach. The Court did so in recognition of the clear national policy of maintaining and promoting the langauge as a means of promoting national identity and culture. The Court has also accepted as mandatory requirements national rules intended to protect the character of Sunday, and the limitation of workers' hours on that day, provided that national legislation did not go further than was necessary to achieve those legitimate aims. The Court laid down some general principles applicable to national restrictions on activities of this kind:

> ...It is therefore necessary in a case such as this to consider first of all whether the rules such as those at issue pursue an aim which is justified with regard to Community law. As far as that question is concerned, the Court has already stated in its judgment of 14 July 1981 in *Oebel* (Case 155/80) that national rules governing hours of work, delivery and sale in the bread and confectionary industry constitute a legitimate part of economic and social policy, consistent with the objectives of public interest pursued by the Treaty.
>
> The same consideration must apply as regards national rules governing the opening hours of retail premises. Such rules reflect certain political and economic choices in so far as their purpose is to ensure that working and non-working hours are so arranged as to accord with national or regional socio-cultural characteristics, and that, in the

present state of Community law, is a matter for the member states. Furthermore, such rules are not designed to govern the patterns of trade between member states.
(*Torfaen Borough Council* v *B & Q plc* (Case 145/88))

In some of these cases the Court appears to have taken the position that if a measure was justified to protect a mandatory requirement, it did not breach Art 30 at all. In others, however, the Court's approach appears to be to treat the mandatory requirements as justifying a measure which, prima facie does breach Art 30, in the same way as the exceptions in Art 36 (*Wurmser* (Case 25/88)). The effect of the decision in *Keck* and *Mithouad* (above) is that the issue of whether or not a measure is justifiable as a mandatory requirement does not even arise if there is equal treatment in law and in fact given to both imported and domestic goods. If this is the case, the national measures are altogether outside the scope of the Treaty. The Court has recently reaffirmed the principle in several cases in response to attempts by commercial organisations to use Art 30 to invalidate national regulatory provisions enacted for the public benefit and applied to a whole range of goods, both imported and home produced. In relation to Dutch legislation regulating the opening hours of petrol stations, the Court has applied the new principles laid down in *Keck*:

> Those conditions [in *Keck*] are fulfilled [in this case]. The rules in question relate to the times and places at which the goods in question may be sold to consumers. However, they apply to all relevant traders without distinguishing between the origin of the products in question and do not affect the marketing of products from other member states in a manner different from that in which they affect domestic products.
> (*Tankstation't Heukse* (Case C-401/92 and C-402/92))

An assessment has to be made in each case of the actual or potential effect of the national legislation, and whether, in fact, it operates in a discriminatory manner. In *Neeltje* v *Houtwipper* (Case C-293/93) the compatability with Art 30 of national legislation requiring the hall-marking of precious metals which are offered for sale was raised in criminal proceedings against the defendant. All such metals in the Netherlands, both home produced and imported, had to be hall-marked to show the content of precious metals. The measure thus appeared to be indistinctly applicable, but it meant, in practice, that it rendered importation of precious metals into the Netherlands more difficult and costly, because importers would have to have their products re-assayed and date-stamped to indicate the year of manufacture in accordance with the Dutch hallmarking law. In practice, therefore, the importers of precious metals were at a disadvantage. Although the Court accepted that hall-marking of precious metals was a mandatory requirement designed to ensure effective protection of consumers and the promotion of fair trading, it held that the way in which the system operated breached Art 30:

> ...A member state cannot require a fresh hall-mark be affixed to products imported from another member state in which they have been lawfully marketed and hall-marked in accordance with the legislation of that state, where the information

provided by that hall-mark, in whatever form, is equivalent to that prescribed by the member state of importation and intelligible to consumers of that state.

EXPORTS: ARTICLE 34

Most of the cases considered so far have involved national restrictions, or measures equivalent to restrictions, on imports. The principles applicable to restrictions on exports are, broadly, the same. The more limited case law on measures affecting exports matches that for imports. In *Procureur de la République* v *Bouhelier* (Case 53/76), for example, a quality control charge imposed only on exports and not on goods sold on the domestic market, was held to be measure equivalent to a quantitative restriction on exports. However, the Court of Justice appears to look for some element of discrimination, either formal or material, in the case of exports. It emphasised that aspect in *Groenveld* (Case 15/79):

> [Art 34(1)] concerns national measures which have as their specific object or effect the restrictions of patterns of exports and thereby the establishment of a difference in treatment between the domestic trade of a member state and its export trade in such a way as to provide a particular advantage for national production of the domestic market of the state in question at the expense of the production or of the trade of other member states. This is not so in the case of a prohibition like that in question which is applied objectively to the production of goods of a certain kind without drawing a distinction depending on whether such goods are intended for the national market or for export. (para [7])

Whether or not there is discrimination is a both a matter of national law and practice. Clearly, therefore, a national law requiring producers to deliver poultry offal to their local authority has been held, necessarily, to involve a ban on exports (*Nertsvoederfabriek Nederlandse* (Case 118/86)). However, legislation applied to all producers of cheese in the Netherlands, affecting its content and quality, which put Dutch producers at a disadvantage in comparison to foreign producers who did not have to produce their cheese to the same standards was held by the Court of Justice not to be a measure equivalent to a quantitative restriction on exports, although it made exporting more difficult for Dutch producers (*Jongeneel Kaas BV* v *Netherlands* (Case 237/82)). Here, the Court demonstrated its willingness to tolerate measures which, although not actually discriminating against exports, had an adverse effect on domestic producers, which it would not have been prepared to tolerate in relation to imports.

OVERCOMING BARRIERS CREATED BY DIFFERING NATIONAL STANDARDS

The relationship between harmonising directives and Articles 30 to 36

Much of the jurisprudence of the Court of Justice relating to MEQRs concerns national measures enacted, ostensibly at least, for the protection of consumers or to promote other national concerns. It was apparent from the inception of the Community that such national provisions, including an enormously diverse range of standards, could only be effectively tackled by creating a Community-wide minimum standard binding on all member states. In that way producers could have the advantage of large product runs, without having to go to the additional expense of having to tailor their products to the standards set in each member state. Consumers could have a wider range of products at a lower cost. Article 100 was included in the Treaty specifically for this purpose. To facilitate the approximation of national legislation on a whole range of issues affecting the development of a common market, it enables, for example, the Commission, on the advice of expert advisory committees, to draft directives on Community-wide standards on the safety of specific products, to be approved unanimously by the Council of Ministers.

Considerable difficulties were encountered in this harmonising process, not least because some member states, not unnaturally, wished to ensure that their own high national standards were reflected in the Community standard. Member states were unwilling to accept a standard that represented the lowest common denominator. Procedures for agreeing common standards were time consuming and cumbersome and since approval had to be unanimous, the opportunity for procrastination was great. The standards adopted were, in some cases, technically obsolete by the time they came into effect and the cost, in terms of lost intra-Community trade, was high.

Where, however, a common standard had been reached and the appropriate directive adopted there was no further scope for national measures in the same field, and attempts to justify them either as mandatory requirements or under the specific exceptions in Art 36 will be rejected. In *Commission* v *Germany (Re Compound Feedingstuffs)* (Case 28/84) the Commission brought proceedings against the German goverment because, the Commission contended, that Council directives adopted in 1970, 1974 and 1979 constituted a complete and exhaustive set of rules covering the whole field of production and marketing of compound animal feedstuffs. The Court agreed and consequently held that German rules on the minimum and maximum levels of certain ingredients could not apply (*see* also *Société Civile Agricole* v *Coopérative d'Elevage du Departement de la Mayenne* (Case C-323/93)).

The new approach to harmonisation

The *Cassis de Dijon* case gave a new impetus to the harmonisation process. It led to a declaration by the Commission that it would concentrate on steps for the harmonisation of national laws which could still affect inter-state trade and which would have to be justified, in the absence of harmonisation, if at all, as mandatory requirements under the first *Cassis* principle or under one of the specific exceptions provided for in Art 36. It also led to a Council Resolution of 7 May 1985 on a new approach to technical harmonisation and standards. The Resolution established four fundamental principles on which the new aproach would be based:

1 Legislative harmonisation is limited to adoption, by means of directives based on Art 100 of the EEC Treaty, of the essential safety requirements (or other requirements in the general interest) with which products put on the market must conform, and which should therefore enjoy free movement throughout the Community.
2 The task of drawing up the technical specifications needed for the production and placing on the market of products conforming to the essential requirements established by the directives, while taking into account the current stage of technology, is entrusted to organisations competent in the standardisation area.
3 These technical specifications are not mandatory and maintain their status of voluntary standards.
4 National authorities are obliged to recognise that products manufactured in conformity with harmonised standards (or, provisionally, with national standards) are presumed to conform to the 'essential requirements' established by the directive. (This signifies that the producer has the choice of not manufacturing in conformity with the standards but that in this event he has an obligation to prove that his products conform to the essential requirements of the directive.)

In order that this system may operate it is necessary:

(a) On the one hand that the standards offer a guarantee of quality with regard to the 'essential requirements' established by the directives.
(b) On the other hand that the public authorities keep intact their responsibility for the protection of safety (or other requirements envisaged) on their territory.

There is a clear link between the resolution and the *Cassis de Dijon* principles, which is most apparent in the numbered paragraphs (1) and (4). The new approach established a clear break with the past and instead of attempting to create a detailed technical specification for a 'Europroduct', which was a difficult and lengthy task, new directives would set only minimum safety and other standards (mimimum requirements) which could be satisfied in a number of different ways in member states, including different manufacturing methods. The emphasis was now on broad performance standards rather than compliance with detailed technical specifications. Once a Community directive is adopted under the new approach and after the implementation date in each member state, performance is verified at Community level under a process monitored by the Commission. Where a directive has been adopted, member states are obliged to assume that products purporting to conform to the essential requirements do, in fact, do so. Until new directives are adopted establishing Community-wide standards in other products, member states should recognise (under the second *Cassis* principle) that those products meet appropriate essential requirements, unless there are indications that they do not.

Besides the adoption of a broader approach to essential requirements, agreement between Community institutions was further facilitated by the addition of Art 100A to the Treaty by the SEA. The Council needs only now to agree, on a majority basis under Art 100A, 'codes of essential requirements' for broad, homogenous products areas or types of risk. This leaves manufacturers greater flexibility in meeting such requirements. Proof of conformity with essential requirements is satisfied by conformity with standards set by Europe-wide standards bodies, such as the European Committee for Standardisation (CEN) and the European Committee for Electrotechnical Standardisation (CENELEC). Products marked with the appropriate standards mark are presumed to conform. To satisfy those member states who were concerned about the lowering of general product standards and the effect on specific products, in exceptional circumstances member states may adopt higher standards than those laid down in the essential requirements. Under Art 100A(4):

> If, after the adoption of a harmonisation measure by the Council acting by a qualified majority, a member state deems it necessary to apply national provisions on grounds of major needs referred to in Art 36, or relating to protection of the environment or the working environment, it shall notify the Commission of these provisions.
>
> The Commission shall confirm the provisions involved after having verified that they are not a means of arbitrary discrimination or a disguised restriction on trade between member states. By way of derogation from the procedures laid down in Arts 169 and 170, the Commission or any member state may bring the matter directly before the Court of Justice if it considers that another member state is making improper use of the powers provided for in this Article.

Between 1984 and 1990 over 800 European products standards were adopted, which was three times as many as in the previous 20 years. Since 1986, when a target of more than 300 directives was set to lay the foundations for the single market in 1992, less than half-a-dozen national provisions have been approved under the exception contained in Art 100 A (4). It remains, however, a valuable safety valve to deal with national concerns over specific products. Overall, the new approach is widely regarded as having had considerable success in reducing national legal and technical barriers and in moving the Community towards a genuine single market.

Further reading

Bieber, R., et al (eds) (1992) *One European Market* Nomos, 1988.

Burrows, N., 'Harmonisation of Technical Standards' (1990) 53 MLR 597.

Cecchini, P., (1988) *The European Challenge 1992, The Benefits of a Single Market*, European Commission.

Ehlermann, C., 'The Internal Market Following the Single European Act' (1987) 24 CML Rev 361.

Gormley, L., 'Actually or Potentially, Directly or Indirectly? Obstacles to the Free Movement of Goods' (1989) 9 YEL 197.

Green, N., Hartley, T.C. and Usher, J.A., (1991) *The Legal Foundations of the Single European Market*, Clarendon Press.

McGee, A. and Weatherill, S., 'The Evolution of the Single Market – Harmonization or Liberalization?' (1990) 53 MLR 578.

Mortelmans, K., 'Article 30 of the EEC Treaty and Legislation Relating to Market Circumstances: Time to Consider a New Definition?' (1991) 28 CML Rev 115.

Pinder, J., (1991) *European Community: The Building of a Union*, OUP, Chapter 4.

Steiner, J., (1994) *Textbook on EC Law* (4th edn), Blackstone Press, Chapter 8.

Steiner, J., 'Drawing the Line: Uses and Abuses of Article 30 EEC' (1992) 29 CML Rev 749.

Tillotson, J., (1993) *European Community Law: Text, Cases and Materials*, Cavendish Publishing Ltd, Chapter 12.

Weatherill, S., (1994) *Cases and Materials on EC Law*, Blackstone Press, Chapters 7 and 8.

Weatherill, S. and Beaumont P. (1995) *EC Law* (2nd edn) Penguin Books, Chapter 15.

White, E., 'In Search of the Limits to Article 30 of the EEC Treaty' (1989) 26 CML Rev 235.

Wils, W., 'The Search for the Rule in Art 30 EEC: Much Ado About Nothing?' (1993) 18 EL Rev 475.

Wyatt, D. and Dashwood, A., (1993) *European Community Law*, Sweet and Maxwell, Chapter 8.

15 Restrictions affecting the free movement of goods permitted by Article 36

Art 36 EC Treaty permits member states to derogate from their obligation to ensure the free movement of goods. It provides:

> The provisions of Arts 30 to 34 shall not preclude prohibitions or restrictions on imports, exports or goods in transit justified on grounds of public morality, public policy or public security; the protection of health and life of humans, animals and plants; the protection of national treasures possessing artistic, historic or archeological value; or the protection of industrial and commercial property. Such prohibitions or restrictions shall not, however, constitute a means of arbitrary discrimination or a disguised restriction on trade between member states.

These derogations comprise an exhaustive list and are interpreted strictly by the Court. Unlike the mandatory requirements under the first *Cassis* principle, where the Court has shown a certain receptiveness to new arguments about national interests requiring protection, in the case of Art 36 it is much more likely to conclude that the national measures in issue are being used to protect domestic markets. Since the *Cassis* principles are only applicable to indistinctly applicable measures, Art 36 is most often pleaded by member states in defence of distinctly applicable measures (*Commission* v *Ireland* (Case 113/80)). Article 36 is, however, equally applicable to indistinctly applicable measures:

> A measure which, in regard both to domestic products and imported products, imposes an obligation to verify conformity [with the rules in force on that market] on the person who first places the product on the market is, in principle, applicable without distinction to both categories of products. It may, therefore, be justified under Art 36 and under Art 30 as interpreted by the Court [in the *Cassis* case].
> (*Wurmser* (Case 25/88))

Since the exceptions contained in Art 36 are treated as exhaustive, national measures not falling clearly within its terms are rejected by the Court. It has, therefore, refused to accept a number of grounds for national provisions which might well have qualified as mandatory provisions under the first *Cassis* principle in relation to indistinctly applicable measures. These grounds have included the protection of consumers, the fairness of commercial transactions, economic policy and the protection of creativity and cultural diversity (*Commission* v *Italy* (Case 95/81); *Commission* v *Italy* (Case 7/61); *Leclerc* (Case 229/83)).

The Art 36 exceptions can only be advanced to justify national measures in the absence of any relevant Community-wide harmonising provisions aimed at harmonising the legislation protecting the interest which the national measure seeks to protect. In *Lucien Ortscheit GmbH* v *Eurim-Pharm GmbH* (Case C-320/93), German legislation prohibited the advertising of foreign drugs which had not been authorised for use in the German market, but which could, under certain conditions, be imported into Germany. The Court was under no doubt that the measure was distinctly applicable and equivalent to a quantitative restriction. It noted that the health and life of humans ranks foremost among the interests protected by Art 36 and at the present stage of harmonisation there was no procedure for Community authorisation or mutual recognition of national authorisations. In those circumstances, it was for member states, within the limits imposed by the Treaty, to decide what degree of protection they intend to ensure. In the circumstances, the Court was satisfied that the German measures were justified under Art 36. However, if there is relevant Community legislation, there will be no scope for national measures that are incompatible with it, or the application of Art 36.

In *Société Agricole de la Crespelle* (Case C-323/93), French rules conferred a monopoly on a number of regional bovine insemination centres and, effectively, created a restrictive regime for the importation of bovine semen from other member states. The Court was satisfied that the restrictive regime amounted to an MEQR, but could it be justified under Article 36? It decided that it could not be.

> The Court has consistently held that where, in application of Art 100 of the EEC Treaty, Community Directives provide for the harmonisation of the measures necessary to ensure, *inter alia*, the protection of animal and human health and established Community procedures to check that they were observed, invoking Art 36 is no longer justified and the appropriate checks have to be carried out and protective measures adopted within the framework of the directive.

This rule applies where the Community has introduced a consistent and exhaustive set of measures to cover the type of importation in question (*Commission* v *Italy (Re Authorisation for Importation of Plants*) (Case C-296/92)). However, it does not preclude restrictions on imports where these are specifically authorised by the directive (*The State* v *Vitaret and Chambon* [1995] 1 CMLR 185 (French Cour de Cassation)).

Where Art 36 can be advanced as a justification for national measures, it is for the national government relying on it to provide evidence to support the grounds justifying their actions. This principle of casting the evidential burden on the member state taking the action applies not only in relation to the national measure itself, but also in relation to individual cases in which that national measure is applied. In *Officier van Justitie* v *Sandoz BV* (Case 174/82), Sandoz wished to sell confectionary in the Netherlands to which vitamin supplements had been added. The confectionary was freely sold in Belgium and Germany. The Dutch authorities refused permission for it to be sold, on the grounds that the vitamins were a risk to health. The case was referred to the Court of Justice under Art 177. The Court was in no doubt that the measure breached Art 30, but in the absence of Community harmonising measures on the kinds of additives which were acceptable, it was permissible under Art 36 for the member state to determine the kind and extent of protection to be given. However, the state had first to establish the existence of a risk:

> In as much as the question arises as to where the onus of proof lies when there is a request for authorisation [to market a foodstuff] ... it must be remembered that Art 36 of the Treaty creates an exception, which must be strictly interpreted, to the rule of free movement of goods within the Community which is one of the fundamental principles of the Common Market. It is therefore for the national authorities who rely on that provision in order to adopt a measure restricting intra-Community trade to check in each instance that the measure contemplated satisfies the criteria of that provision ... Community law does not permit national rules which subject authorisation to market to *proof by the importer that the product in question is not harmful to health.*
> (paras [22],[24] of judgment) (emphasis added)

Where action may be justified under Art 36, measures taken by member states will still have to meet two fundamental Community criteria. First, there must be no arbitrary discrimination between imported and domestic products and second, any national measures must be proportionate to any risk and must not restrict trade any more than is necessary to protect the legitimate public interests recognised by Art 36. The operation of these principles can best be seen by an examination of the jurisprudence of the Court of Justice in relation to the specific exceptions.

PUBLIC MORALITY

The concept of public morality will vary widely from state to state and is not elaborated in Art 36 or in any secondary legislation. The Court has, for example, refused to rule that termination of pregnancy is intrinsically immoral and cannot, therefore, constitute a service under Art 59 EC Treaty, because it is, in fact, lawfully carried out in several member states (*Society for the Protection of the Unborn Child* v *Grogan* (Case C-159/90), and in *Customs and Excise Commissioners* v *Schindler and Others* (Case C-275/92) it observed, with regard to gambling, that, 'Even if the morality of lotteries is at least questionable, it is not for the Court to substitute its assessment for that of the legislature where that activity is practised legally.' (para [32]). The Court may, however, have to assess whether or not national rules are applied proportionately and without discrimination. The issue first came before the

Court in relation to Art 36 in an Art 177 reference from the House of Lords. In *R v Henn and Darby* (Case 34/79) the defendants were convicted of being 'knowingly concerned in the fraudulent evasion of the prohibition of the importation of indecent or obscene articles' contrary to the Customs Consolidation Act 1976 s 42 and the Customs and Excise Act 1952 s 304. The articles involved in the charges formed part of a consignment of several boxes of obscene films and magazines which had been brought into the UK in 1975 on a lorry travelling on a ferry from Rotterdam. The six films and magazines referred to in the charges were all of Danish origin.

The House of Lords referred a number of questions to the Court of Justice. The first question asked whether a law of a member state prohibiting the importation of pornographic articles is a measure having equivalent effect to a quantitative restriction. The Court was in no doubt that it was since a prohibition on imports is 'the most extreme form of restriction' (para [12]). However, it emphasised that member states were free to take such action in appropriate circumstances:

> In principle, it is for each member state to determine in accordance with its own scale of values and in the form selected by it the requirements of public morality in its territory. In any event, it cannot be disputed that the statutory provisions applied by the United Kingdom in regard to the importation of articles having an indecent or obscene character come within the powers reserved to the member states by the first sentence of Art 36.

The House of Lords was also concerned to know whether the fact that the prohibition imposed on the importation of pornography was different in scope from that imposed by the criminal law on the possession and publication of such material in the United Kingdom constituted a means of arbitrary discrimination or a disguised restriction on trade between member states. In particular, there were (and are) differences in treatment of the possession and publication of pornography in different parts of the UK, and there are circumstances in which, under the Obscene Publications Act 1959, possession and publication may not be a criminal offence. The defences available in those circumstances have no application to the Customs and Excise Acts under which the defendants were prosecuted. The Court of Justice was satisfied that the differences, such as they were, were not significant:

> Whatever may be the differences between the laws on this subject in force in the different constituent parts of the United Kingdom, and notwithstanding the fact that they contain certain exceptions of limited scope, these laws, taken as a whole, have as their purpose the prohibition, or at least the restraining, of the manufacture and marketing of publications or articles of an indecent or obscene character. In these circumstances it is permissible to conclude, on a comprehensive view, that there is no lawful trade in such goods in the United Kingdom. A prohibition on imports which may in certain respects be more strict than some of the laws applied within the United Kingdom cannot, therefore, be regarded as amounting to a measure designed to give indirect protection to some national product or aimed at creating arbitrary discrimination. (para [21])

Another case under which goods had also been seized by H M Customs and Excise under s 42 of the Customs Consolidation Act 1876 came, on a reference under Art 177 from the Queen's Bench Division, to the Court of Justice in 1986. In *Conegate Ltd v HM Customs and Excise* (Case 121/85) the goods consisted of inflatable sex dolls and other erotic articles. The importers argued that the situation was different to that in *Henn and Darby*, because sex dolls, although not permitted to be publicly displayed, could be lawfully sold throughout the UK. The Court of Justice agreed:

> ... Although Community law leaves the member states free to make their own assessments of the indecent or obscene character of certain articles, it must be pointed out that the fact that the goods cause offence cannot be regarded as sufficiently serious to justify restrictions on the free movement of goods where the member state concerned does not adopt, with respect to the same goods manufactured or marketed within its territory, penal measures or other serious or effective measures intended to prevent the distribution of such goods in its territory. [15] It follows that a member state may not rely on grounds of public morality in order to prohibit the importation of goods from other member states when its legislation contains no prohibition on the manufacture or marketing of the same goods in its territory. [16]

There is a striking similarity in the language used by the Court in this case to that employed by it in *Adoui and Cornuaille* v *Belgium* (Cases 115 & 116/81). (*see* Chapter 11) That case, it may be recalled, concerned the scope of the public policy exception in Art 48(3) EC Treaty. The Court, having accepted in *Van Duyn* v *Home Office* that the public disapproval of the Church of Scientology to which Ms Van Duyn belonged was sufficient to justify her exclusion, moved away from that position in *Adoui*. It held, in that case, that a member state could not take action under the public policy exception against a European citizen unless it took some kind of 'repressive measures' against its own nationals for engaging in the same conduct on which the exclusion is based. A similar concept of equality of treatment underlies the requirement that the state excluding the goods must take 'penal measures or other serious or effective measures' in relation to the same kind of goods produced on its own territory.

PUBLIC POLICY AND PUBLIC SECURITY

Very few attempts have been made by national governments to justify restrictive measures on these grounds. Public policy, was, however, successfully advanced by the British Government in *R* v *Thompson and Others* (Case 7/78). The defendants traded in coins, some of which were old British silver coins that were no longer legal tender. They were convicted in England of being knowingly concerned in the fraudulent evasion of the prohibition on importation of gold coins into England. They argued, on appeal, that the provisions under which they had been convicted breached Arts 30–34. The British Government defended the legislation on the ground that it was an important aspect of public policy to protect the national coinage and the Court agreed. It held that a ban on destroying old coinage with a view to it being melted down or destroyed in another member state was justified on grounds of public policy under Art 36, because it was based on the need to protect the right to mint coinage which is traditionally regarded as involving the fundamental interests of the state.

It was put to the Court in *Cullet* (Case 231/83) by the French Government that national rules fixing retail selling prices for fuel was justified on grounds of public order and security which would arise in relation to retailers affected by unrestrained competition. The Advocate-General warned against the dangers of responding to public agitation:

> ... The acceptance of civil disturbance as a justification for encroachments upon the free movement of goods would ... have unacceptably drastic consequences. If road-blocks and other effective weapons of interest groups which feel threatened by the importation and sale at competitive prices of certain cheap products or services, or by immigrant workers or foreign businesses, were accepted as justification, the existence of the four freedoms of the Treaty could no longer be relied upon. Private interest groups would then, in the place of the Treaty and Community (and, within the limits laid down in the Treaty, determine the scope of those freedoms). In such cases, the concepts of public policy requires, rather, effective action on the part of the authorities to deal with the disturbances. [1985] ECR 306 at 312 (para 5.3)

The Court was equally sceptical about the incapacity of the French authorities in the face of rampaging fuel retailers on the streets of France. It remarked drily:

> In that regard, it is sufficient to state that the French Government has not shown that it would be unable, using the means at its disposal, to deal with the consequences which an amendment of the rules in question ... would have upon public order and security. (paras [32],[33] of judgment)

In response to recent attempts by animal welfare groups to block the export of live animals, the issue was seen by Simon Brown LJ, expressly adopting the Advocate-General's Opinion in *Cullet*, above, as a straightforward issue of the rule of law, both Community and national (*R* v *Coventry City Council, ex parte Phoenix Aviation* [1995] 3 All ER 37 at 67). See also *R* v *Chief Constable of Sussex, ex parte International Trader's Ferry Ltd* [1995] 4 All ER 364

The Irish Government had more success with the public security argument in *Campus Oil* v *Ministry for Industry and Energy* (Case 72/83). Irish legislation required importers of petroleum products to purchase up to 35 per cent of their requirements from Ireland's state-owned refinery at prices fixed by the Minister. There was no doubt that the requirement breached Art 30. The Government, however, argued that the measure was necessary on the ground that the importance of oil for the maintenance of the life of the country made it essential to maintain fuel capacity in Ireland. The system it had adopted was the only means by which a fuel reserve could be built up. The Court agreed that petroleum products were of fundamental importance to the country's existence, since they were needed for the country's institutions, vital services and the survival of its inhabitants, and accepted, in this instance, the public security justification. It did, however, warn the Irish Government that the purchasing obligation could only be continued if there was no less restrictive measure which was capable of achieving the same objective, nor should the quantities covered by the scheme exceed the minimum supply requirements without which the public security of the state would be affected. The scheme had, in other words, to be proportionate to the risk anticipated.

PUBLIC HEALTH

The same principle of proportionality has been prominent in the many decisions of the Court of Justice in which member states have sought to rely on the exception relating to the health of humans, animals and plants. In this context, Art 36 attempts to strike a balance between the interests involved in the creation of a single market and the protection of health, and the Court is particularly careful to determine whether or not a measure is, in fact, a disguised form of protectionism. To be capable of justication as a health measure, it must form part of 'a seriously considered health policy'.

This was lacking in *Commission* v *UK* (*Re Imports of Poultry Meat*) (Case 40/82). There was evidence before the Court of Justice that, in the two years before the ban on the import of turkeys from France in September 1981 that was the subject of the proceedings, there had been a steep rise in turkey imports for the Christmas market from France and other member states. This had been followed by a chorus of complaints about unfair competition from British poultry producers. The imposition of a sudden ban on the import of French turkeys was, ostensibly, because of the risk of the outbreak of Newcastle Disease, a serious poultry infection. There had, however, been no recent outbreak in France and the main object of the UK government's ostensible concern was imports into France of turkeys from Eastern European countries where there was a more serious risk. The Court was unconvinced by the British justification:

> Certain established facts suggest that the real aim of the 1981 measure was to block, for commercial and economic reasons, imports of poultry products from other member states, in particular from France. The United Kingdom government had been subject to pressure from British poultry producers to block these imports. It hurriedly introduced its new policy with the result that French Christmas turkeys were excluded from the British market for the 1981 season … The deduction must be made that the 1981 measures did not form part of a seriously considered health policy.
>
> Taken together, these facts are sufficient to establish that the 1981 measures constitute a disguised restriction on imports of poultry products from other member states, in particular from France, unless it can be shown that, for reasons of animal

health, the only possibility open to the United Kingdom was to apply the strict measures which are at issue in this case and that, therefore, the methods prescribed by the 1981 measures ... were not more restrictive than was necessary for the protection of poultry flocks in Great Britain.

The Court was satisfied that, on the evidence, there were much less restrictive methods available that were appropriate to the degree of risk. The United Kingdom had, therefore, breached Art 30. Subsequently, this successful action by the Commission led to a claim by an importer affected by the ban in the British courts (*Burgoin* v *MAFF* [1986] QB 716; *see* Chapter 24).

Many of the cases in which the health exception is raised turn on whether there is, in fact, any risk at all. The perception of risk may, quite genuinely, be different in different member states. The Court, in these cases, will have to assess, on the best available scientific evidence, firstly whether there is, indeed, a risk to health, and secondly, if there is, whether the state taking the restrictive measures has responded appropriately. In *Commission* v *France* [1988] ECR 793, for example, French legislation prohibited the marketing of milk substitutes. The French government attempted to justify the prohibition on the ground, first, that milk substitutes had a lower nutritional value and second, that they were harmful to some people. The Court rejected both arguments. The fact that an imported food product had a lower nutritional value than milk products hardly constituted a health risk when consumers had so many other food products to choose from. Milk products themselves could pose a risk to some individuals with certain allergies or suffering from certain diseases. Labelling would provide consumers with the necessary information to enable them to make a properly informed choice.

Milk also figured in *Commission* v *UK* (*Re UHT Milk*) (Case 124/81). In this case, the Commission brought Art 169 proceedings against the United Kingdom for imposing a requirement that UHT milk should be marketed only by approved dairies or distributors. The government argued that this was necessary to ensure that milk was free from bacterial or viral infections. The effect of the restriction was that all imported milk had to be re-packaged and re-treated. The Court rejected these measures as inappropriate and unnecessary. There was evidence that milk in all member states was of similar quality and subject to equivalent controls. The restriction was, therefore, unjustified. The Court has also held that German legislation, which prohibited the import from other member states of meat products manufactured from meat not coming from the country of manufacture of the finished product, could not be justified on health grounds since there was no reason to believe that the risk of contamination increased simply because the fresh meat crossed a Community frontier (*Commission* v *Germany* (Case 153/78)).

Although the Court has held that the fact that testing has occurred in the country of origin should give rise to a presumption that the imported goods are safe to use, this is not the universal rule (*de Peijper* (Case 104/75); *Frans-Nederlands* (Case 272/80)). In particular, differences in approach to food additives or medical products may justify additional testing by the importing state before authorisation to market the goods is given. In *Sandoz*, noted above, there was uncertainty about the point at which a large intake of vitamin additives in food could become harmful. The Court held that the importing state was entitled to carry out tests on the food before it was put on the market:

> … Community law permits national rules prohibiting without prior authorization the marketing of foodstuffs lawfully marketed in another member state to which vitamins have been added, provided that the marketing is authorised when the addition of vitamins meets a real need, especially a technical or nutritional one.
> (para [20]) [1983] ECR 2445

The position is similar for medical products. The Court has held that member states are entitled, at the present stage of harmonisation and in the absence of a procedure for Community authorisation or mutual recognition of national authorisation, to exclude medical products from other member states which have not been authorised by the competent national authorities (*Lucien Ortscheit GmbH* v *Eurim-Pharm GmbH* (Case C-320/93)).

PROTECTION OF INDUSTRIAL AND COMMERCIAL PROPERTY

Industrial and commercial property rights are valuable rights relating to the protection and distribution of goods and services. Such rights are protected by patents, trademarks, copyrights and similar devices. Each member state has devised its own system for protecting the investment, creativity and innovation which has gone into a new product or system. The period of protection may vary widely between member states, and between different kinds of industrial property rights. In the United Kingdom, for example, the exclusive rights enjoyed under a patent endure for 20 years, indefinitely for trademarks and the author's lifetime plus 50 years for copyright. Since each form of industrial property is defined under national law, it would seem, prima facie, not to be a matter within Community competence and indeed, Art 222 appears to emphasise the exclusive competence of each member state in this matter:

> This Treaty shall in no way prejudice the rules in member states governing the system of property ownership.

However, it is clear that a restrictive approach taken by the owners of industrial property rights could have a very significant effect on the free movement of goods. The different national rules on such property rights could be used, effectively, to partition the market for those products on a national basis, and prevent the achievement of one of the Community's primary aims. The Court has, therefore, drawn a distinction between rules affecting the ownership of such rights and their exercise. It has declared that the protection given to the different systems of property ownership in different member states by Art 222 EC do not allow national legislatures to adopt measures relating to industrial and commercial property which would adversely affect the principle of free movement of goods within the common market (*Spain* v *Council* (Case C-350/92). It has also emphasised that this Art 36 exception cannot 'constitute a means of arbitrary discrimination or a disguised restriction on trade between member states'. National rules protecting patents and copyrights must therefore operate without discrimination. In *Collins* v *Imtrat* (Case 92/92) the performer Phil Collins attempted to bring proceedings to stop the distribution in Germany of pirated tapes and illegal recordings taken at his concerts. Under German law, such relief was only available to German nationals. The Court of Justice held that, although member states were still free to determine the nature and extent of protection provided by national copyright rules, such rules should be applied indiscriminately. On this basis it has also held that national rules which require that a patent be exploited only on the territory where the patent is granted and which prohibit or restrict its development elsewhere, so that the patented goods may not be manufactured elsewhere and imported into the patent-granting state, breach Art 30 (*Commission* v *Italy* (Case C-235/89); *Commission* v *UK* (Case 30/90). There is a parallel here to the prohibition of discrimination in the acquisition of real property rights by those attempting to establish themselves under Art 52 EC Treaty (*Steinhauser* v *City of Biarritz* (Case 197/84); *Commission* v *Italy* (*Re Housing Aid*) (Case 63/86)).

The Court has tried to allow the property exception to operate only in relation to the essential core of property rights, although what those are in each case is sometimes difficult to determine. In the case of a patent the Court said in *Centrafarm* v *Sterling Drug* (Case 15/74):

> ... Article 36 in fact only admits of derogations from the free movement of goods where such derogations are justified for the purpose of safeguarding rights which constitute the specific subject matter of this property.
>
> In relation to patents, the specific subject matter of the industrial property is *the guarantee that the patentee, to reward the creative effort of the inventor, has the exclusive right to use an invention with a view to manufacturing industrial products and putting them into circulation for the first time*, either directly or by the grant of licences to third parties, as well as the right to oppose infringements. (emphasis added)

This right is enjoyed in the member state in which the goods are patented. The patentee, under the Art 36 exception, can exclude goods which breach his patent. However, once the patented goods are circulated in another member state, either by him or with his consent, his right to exclude those goods as the patentee is then said to be 'exhausted'. This principle is demonstrated by the facts of the *Centrafarm* case:

Sterling Drug Inc. held British and Dutch patents relating to a drug called NEGRAM. In both countries the drug was marketed either by Sterling Drug itself, or companies which it had licensed to do so. Centrafarm, an independent Dutch company, bought supplies of the drug in both Britain and Germany, where it was much cheaper, as a result of price controls, and re-sold it in the Netherlands. Sterling Drug and its subsidiaries invoked their respective patent and trade mark rights before the Dutch courts to prevent NEGRAM being marketed in the Netherlands by Centrafarm.

The Dutch Court referred a number of questions to the Court of Justice under Art 177. The Court described the limits of national patent rights in this context:

> An obstacle to the free movement of goods may arise out of the existence, within a national legislation concerning industrial and commercial property, of provisions laying down that a patentee's right is not exhausted when the product protected by the patent is marketed in another member state, with the result that the patentee can prevent importation of the product into his own member state when it has been marketed in another member state. Whereas an obstacle to the free movement of goods of this kind may be justified on the ground of the protection of industrial property where such protection is invoked against a product coming from a member state where it is not patentable and has been manufactured by third parties without the consent of the patentee and in cases where there exist patents, the original proprietors of which are legally and economically indpendent, a derogation from the principle of the free movement of goods is not, however, justified where the product has been put onto the market in a legal manner, by the patentee himself or with his consent, in the member state from which it has been imported, in particular in the case of a proprietor of parallel patents. (paras [10] and [11] of judgment)

The exhaustion of rights principle has been applied by the Court with regard not only to patent rights, but also to trade marks, copyright and industrial design. It defined the proprietorial interest in relation to trade marks in *Centrafarm* v *Winthrop* (Case 16/74):

> ... The specific subject matter of the industrial property is the guarantee that the owner of the trade mark has the exclusive right to use that trade mark for the purpose of putting products protected by the trade mark into circulation for the first time, and is therefore intended to protect him against any competitor wishing to take advantage of the status and reputation of the trade mark by selling products illegally bearing the trade mark.

Crucial to the application of the exhaustion principle is the meaning of 'consent' in this context. Consent is assumed where the owner markets the goods himself, where he does so through a subsidiary company or where the owner and the undertaking responsible for the first marketing are under common control. The limits of consent were explored in *Pharmon BV* v *Hoechst AG* (Case 19/84).

Hoechst owned a patent in Germany for the process to manufacture a drug called FRUSEMIDE. It also owned parallel patents on the process in the Netherlands and the UK. Although FRUSEMIDE was not manufactured by Hoechst or any of its subsidiaries in the UK, it was manufactured there by an independent company called DDSA under a compulsory licence granted under British legislation. As its name suggests, a compulsory licence does not require the consent of the owner of the patent, but royalties on sales are paid to him. The litigation in this case arose out of imports from the UK being placed on the Dutch market by Pharmon. Because British prices for the drug were much lower, Pharmon stood to make a considerable profit at Hoechst BV's expense. Could Hoechst resist their marketing in the Netherlands? The question turned on whether the compulsory licensing and payment of royalties to Hoechst amounted to 'consent'. The Court of Justice, in an Art 177 reference did not think that it did.

> It is necessary to point out that where, as in this instance, the competent authorities of a member state grant a third party a compulsory licence which allows him to carry out manufacturing and marketing operations which the patentee would normally have the right to prevent, the patentee cannot be deemed to have consented to the operation of that third party. Such a measure deprives the patent proprietor of his right to determine freely the conditions under which he markets his products. (para [25] of judgment)

The Court went further in *IHT Internationale Heiztechnik GmbH* v *Ideal-Standard GmbH* (Case C-9/93), holding that action by an assignee under contract (as opposed to a subsidiary in another member state) could not be regarded as carried out with 'consent' of the assignor in relation to the use of a trade mark on goods imported into another member state, and the import could be restrained under the property justification in Art 36. The decision is surprising because it could be said that the assignment itself included a right to deal generally with the trade mark and the assignment would therefore exhaust the rights of the assignor. The Court, however, stressed that the free movement of the goods would undermine the essential function of the trade mark. Consumers would no longer be able to identify for certain the origin of the marked goods and the proprietor of the trade mark could be held responsible for the poor quality of the goods for which he is in no way accountable. In this case, at least, the Court's concern for the proprietorial interest of the patentee seems to have outweighed its concern to secure the free movement of goods.

The importance of consent can be seen in two apparently similar cases involving copyright. In *Musik Vertrieb Membran GmbH* v *GEMA* (Case 55/80) the Court of Justice held that the performing rights society GEMA could not rely on its German copyright in sound recordings to prevent parallel imports of records from the UK which had been put on the market there with its consent. In *EMI Electrola* v *Patricia* (Case 341/87), the plaintiffs owned the production and distribution rights in Germany of the musical works of Cliff Richard. The defendants sold records of Cliff Richard's songs in Germany which had been imported from Denmark, where the copyright protection had expired. The plaintiffs applied for an order from the German courts to exclude these imports. The defendants resisted on the grounds that such an order would breach Art 30, since the records lawfully circulated in Denmark. The Court of Justice, in an Art 177 reference, did not agree. Lawful circulation was not equivalent to consent. The Court distinguished the GEMA case on the ground that the marketing in Denmark was due to the expiry of the protection period in another member state, and not to the consent of the copyright owner or his licensee. This was an aspect of ownership and the different rights of copyright owners in different member states. The problems caused by these difficulties would continue until these rules had been harmonised for the whole Community.

HARMONISATION OF INDUSTRIAL PROPERTY RIGHTS

The Commission has two principal aims in this field. The first is that each member state should employ, as far as possible, the same substantive industrial property rules. The second is that intellectual property monopolies should run the length and breadth of the Community, irrespective of the country of their origin. Some modest progress has been made towards both these aims (for an account, *see* Phillips, J. and Firth, A., *Introduction to Intellectual Property Law* (1995)). There are broadly similar rules in member states governing criteria for patentability and the patent term. Registration is, however, undertaken according to different rules in different states. A Community Patent Convention, which would provide that one unitary patent would cover the entire territory of the Community, and that the Community would be treated as one country under the existing rules of the European Patent Convention still awaits implementation. In the meantime, some specific measures have been approved or are being considered, to give some protection in a few areas which are regarded as particularly important in the context of the single market. A regulation has been approved to extend existing protection for pharmaceutical products (Regulation 1768/92). A draft directive on the legal protection of inventions in biotechnology is currently under discussion and a new Community Plant Variety Regulation has been approved to protect the rights of plant breeders (Regulation 2100/94).

There is more difficulty in harmonising legislation on copyright, because the United Kingdom and Ireland, as common law countries have a very different approach to copyright to that prevailing in the other civil law states of the Community. An attempt in a Community Green Paper of 1988 to reconcile the civil *droit d'auteur* with the common law concept of copyright was not well received. As with patents, some progress has been made on individual measures to harmonise the law where the need seemed most pressing and there are now, for example, copyright directives on computer software, rental and lending rights, cable and satellite (Directives 91/250, 92/100 and 93/83).

The area of industrial property law where there has been the most progress is in relation to trade marks and designs. The Trade Mark Approximation Directive 1988 laid down principles common to the Community's national or regional trade mark systems (Directive 89/104). In addition, the Community Trade Mark Regulation provides for a single standard of registrability for a trade mark which will grant protection to its proprietor throughout the Community (Regulation 40/94). Both have been implemented in the United Kingdom by the Trade Marks Act 1994. The

Community Trade Marks Office has been established and is likely to commence operations in 1996. As with directives on standards, safety and quality, the principles developed by the Court of Justice for the protection of industrial property rights, and the rules on the exhaustion of property rights will only be replaced by the Community legislation in those areas where a directive or regulation effectively replaces all the national rules. Until that time, the industrial property exception in Art 36, and the Court's jurisprudence on its application, will continue to play an important role in ensuring that national property rules do not create unnecessary barriers to the free movement of goods.

Further reading

Gormely, L., (1985) *Prohibiting Restrictions on Trade within the EEC*, Elsevier, Chapter 6.

Millet, T., 'Free Movement of Goods and Public Morality' (1987) New Law Journal, 39.

Oliver, P., (1988) *Free Movement of Goods in the EEC (Arts 30–36)*, European Law Centre.

Phillips, J. and Firth, A., (1995) *Introduction to Intellectual Property Law*, Butterworths, Chapter 27.

Steiner, J., (1994) *Textbook on EC Law* (4th edn) Blackstone Press, Chapter 9.

Tillotson, J., (1993) *European Community Law: text, cases and materials*, Cavendish Publishing, Chapters 12 and 18.

Weatherill, S., (1994) *Cases and Materials on EC Law*, Blackstone Press, Chapters 7 and 14.

Weatherill, S., and Beaumont, P., (1995) *EC Law*, (2nd edn.) Penguin Books, Chapter 16.

Whish, R., (1993) *Competition Law*, Butterworths, Chapter 19.

Wyatt, D. and Dashwood, A., (1993) *European Community Law*, Sweet & Maxwell, Chapter 8.

16 The implementation of EC rules on the free movement of goods in the United Kingdom

There are two important aspects of national implementation that need to be considered. Firstly, compliance with the primary obligations established by Art 5 and Arts 30 to 36 and secondly, the transposition and implementation of the large volume of harmonising legislation, especially that designed to remove the remaining legal and technical barriers necessary to bring the single market into operation. Much of this legislation comprises directives made under the new approach and involves implementation by a range of individuals and bodies at different levels in the civil service, local government, commerce and industry.

PRIMARY TREATY OBLIGATIONS

The European Communities Act 1972 gives effect to the primary Community law contained in the Treaties, and, in particular, in this context, to Art 30. This fundamental obligation of the United Kingdom, and of its courts, is contained in s 2(1) of the Act, in relation to the 'rights, powers, liabilities, obligations and restrictions… arising by or under the Treaties'. The Court of Appeal in *Bourgoin* v *Ministry of Agriculture, Fisheries and Food* [1986] QB 716; [1985] 3 All ER 585, accepted that Art 30 was directly effective in the courts of the United Kingdom and conferred rights which must be protected in an effective manner. National legislation which is incompatible with Community law should be repealed or amended so that it properly reflects the Community rules and should be transparent to individuals in member states. This is particularly the case with Treaty provisions (*see, Commission* v *France (Re French Merchant Seamen* (Case 167/73)).

Following judgment of the Court of Justice where the United Kingdom has been found to be in breach of its primary Treaty obligations, specific legislation has been passed to rectify the situation. After the *UHT* milk case (*see* Chapter 15, above) where the UK was held to have breached Art 30, the government secured the passage of the Importation of Milk Act 1983. Likewise, following proceedings by the Commission against the United Kingdom in relation to the Sex Discrimination Act 1975, the Sex Discrimination Act 1986 was passed to bring British law into line with Art 119 EC Treaty and Directive 76/207. Primary legislation is not always used, even where national law requires amendment to make it compatible with Treaty provisions. Following *Commission* v *United Kingdom* (Case 246/89R), in which the Court ordered the UK to suspend the Merchant Shipping Act 1988 as incompatible with Arts 7 and 52 EC Treaty, the necessary amendments to the Act were made by a statutory instrument under the European Communities Act 1972 s 2(2).

To ensure compliance with the Treaty provisions on the free movement of goods the Customs and Excise Management Act 1979 s 9 was enacted. This provides:

> For the purpose of implementing Community obligations the Commissioners shall co-operate with other customs services on matters of mutual concern, and (without prejudice to the foregoing) may for that purpose: (a) give effect, in accordance with such arrangements as they may direct or by regulation prescribe, to any Community requirement or practice as to the movement of goods between countries ... and (b) give effect to any reciprocal arrangements made between member states (with or without other countries or territories) for securing, by exchange of information or otherwise, the due administration of their customs laws and the prevention or detection of fraud or evasion.'

It is interesting to note that there has been no parallel amendment to the Immigration Act 1971, and the procedures for control and entry of persons remains specifically subject to all the requirements of national law (Art 20(2)(e), Immigration (European Economic Area) Order 1994 (SI 1994/1895)).

SECONDARY COMMUNITY LEGISLATION

The position in this case is that the United Kingdom has, essentially, four options:

1 where the requirements of a directive are already met in national law, no specific action may be necessary;
2 where there is existing UK legislation creating the power to make appropriate delegated legislation, by such delegated legislative power;
3 through regulations made under European Communities Act 1972, s 2(2).
4 through primary legislation.

Secondary Community legislation is most often implemented by secondary UK legislation, although more substantial directives have been put into effect by primary legislation (*see*, for example, the Product Liability Directive 85/374 by the Consumer Protection Act 1987). In relation to the free movement of goods, this has largely involved the great number of Community directives made under Art 100A EC Treaty and intended to harmonise national standards to secure the objectives of the Single European Market.

Effective implementation

In carrying out the implementation process, member states must follow the rules evolved by the Court of Justice on what is required. It is often argued that national law, either in its language or in the way it is applied and interpreted, adequately reflects the Community provision. In relation to a directive, the purpose of which was to abolish obstacles to the free movement of tractors that might be caused by different technical rules in the member states, the Court said that implementation must be:

> … In a way which fully meets the requirements of clarity and certainty in legal situations which the directives seek for the benefit of manufacturers established in other member states. Mere administrative practices, which by their nature can be changed as and when the authority pleases and which are not published widely enough, cannot in these circumstances be regarded as proper fulfilment of the obligation imposed by Art 189. (*Commission* v *Belgium* (Case 102/79))

The Court has, therefore, rejected arguments that directives have been properly implemented by ministerial circulars (*see, Commission* v *Netherlands* (Case 96/81)). It has also rejected claims that it is sufficient to implement in practice, but not by means of incorporation into legislation (*see Commission* v *Italy* (Case 145/82)). It is, however, clear from these cases that if national legislation of a sufficiently general nature which covers the requirements of the directive is in place and which has received sufficient publicity, then no further implementation may be necessary (*Commission* v *Netherlands* (Case C-190/90)). However, this is rarely the case, and most directives will require legislation.

Where criminal sanctions are created to ensure compliance, they must be in line with penalties in national legislation. There should be no discrimination based on nationality or on the origin of the goods or services involved. In *Cayrol* v *Rivoira* (Case 52/77), the Court held that it would be incompatible with the Treaty for national law to impose a heavier penalty for infringements of a Community regulation concerning products from other member states than for infringement of that regulation concerning domestic products. The same principle applies, of course, to directives. The Court has also held that, whilst the choice of penalties is within the discretion of the member state, they must, at the least, ensure that infringements of Community law are penalised under conditions, both procedural and substantive, which are analagous to those applicable to infringements of national law of a similar kind. They should make the penalty effective, proportionate and dissuasive (see, *Commission* v *Greece* (Case 68/88)). There may be a conflict between the need for effective penalties and equal treatment of 'Community' and 'national' offences. If, in a similar case, national law provides a defence when Community law imposes strict liability, can there be proper implementation when national law adds that defence in its implementation of the Community provision? The Commission is considering Art 169 proceedings against the UK in relation to the Product Liability Directive 85/374 by the Consumer Protection Act 1974. It is arguing that there is a difference between the 'state of the art' defence available to the manufacturers of a defective product in the wording of the directive, and that available under the Act (*see*, D'Sa, *European Community Law and Civil Remedies in England and Wales* (1994) p 166). There is a similar problem in relation to the 'due diligence' defence. The Toy Safety Directive 88/378 was implemented by the Toy (Safety) Regulations 1989, SI 1989/1275 made under powers conferred on the Secretary of State by the Consumer Protection Act 1987. The enforcement of the regulations is by Trading Standards Officers. Where there is a successful prosecution, traders who sell toys which are found to be unsafe can be fined up to £5000 or may be liable to a maximum of six months imprisonment.

Liability under the Consumer Protection Act 1987 can be avoided by the 'due diligence' defence. This is a common defence in consumer protection and safety legislation. It provides that a person charged, inter alia, with an offence against a safety regulation has a defence where that person can 'show that he took all reasonable steps and exercised all due diligence to avoid committing the offence'. In addition, there is an obligation on officers to pay compensation to traders where goods have been seized and it transpires that there has been no 'neglect or default' by the trader (s 34). Neither of these provisions is in the directive, and it may well be that their combined effect may be to deter prosecutions by Trading Standards Officers, with the result that the directive, as implemented in the UK, is not effectively enforced (*see*, Weatherill, S., 'Playing Safe: The UK's Implementation of the Toy Safety Directive' in Daintith, T., *Implementing EC Law in the United Kingdom: Structures for Indirect Rule (1995)*). The existence of these defences and remedies does not appear to enable the British legislation to meet the Community law requirement of being sufficiently effective and dissuasive, and with the necessary deterrent effect. The concept of 'effectiveness' goes to both any penalty or damages and to the criteria for judging culpability (*see*, *Dekker* (Case 177/88) and *Commission* v *United Kingdom* (Case C-383/92) (para [55] of judgment)).

It has been argued that failure to implement a directive within the prescribed time limit in the United Kingdom may not, in practice, affect the application of a directive in the United Kingdom (*see*, *Department of Trade and Industry Review of the Implementation and Enforcement of EC Law in the UK* (1993)). This argument depends on the decision of the Court of Justice in *Marleasing* v *La Commercial* (Case C-106/89). It will be remembered that the Court decided, in that case, that, in applying national law, a national court must interpret it as far as possible, in the light and purpose of any relevant EC directive, whether the national law originated before or after adoption of the directive (*see* above, Chapter 5). There are two problems with this argument. In the first place, there has to exist a provision of national law that can be interpreted in the light of the unimplemented directive. It does not have to have been made to implement the directive, but there must be some provision which has been adopted at some time in relation to the relevant area of activity to which the directive applies (*see, Paola Faccini Dori* v *Recreb Srl* (Case C-91/92)). The wording in *Dori* would seem to preclude implying the relevant provisions of the unimplemented directive into a contract. Secondly, as we have seen in Chapter 5, both the Court of Appeal and the House of Lords have shown a marked reluctance to 'interpret' statutes made before the relevant, unimplemented directive (*Duke* v *GEC Reliance* [1988] AC 618; *Webb* v *EMO Air Cargo* [1992] 4 All ER 929, HL), where they are unable to base their interpretation on the presumed intent of Parliament to implement the directive (*compare, Litster* v *Forth Dry Dock* [1990] 1 AC 546). The doctrine of indirect effect would, therefore, not be much help in these cases and the individual would be forced back onto his remedy in *Francovich* v *Italy* (Case C-6/90) against the UK Government, provided, of course, that he met the criteria laid down by the Court of Justice in that case.

The Single Market Directives

More than 300 measures were proposed in the Commission White Paper on Completing the Internal Market (COM (85) 310 (*see* Bieber, R., Dehousse, R., Pinder, J. and Weiler, J. 'Back to the Future: Policy, Strategy and Tactics of the White Paper on the Creation of a Single European Market' in Bieber, et al (eds) 1992: *One European Market*). Many of these were concerned with the harmonisation of rules about financial and other services, and were intended to facilitate the cross-border provision of those services. The majority, however, were directives concerned with abolishing the remaining safety and technical barriers to the free movement of goods. As we have seen in Chapter 14, they were intended to provide common standards, so that the free movement of goods envisaged by Art 30 could be achieved without encountering differing national rules and reliance on the exceptions contained in the 'mandatory requirements' in relation to indistinctly applicable measures, as laid down by the Court of Justice in *Cassis*, and the exceptions in Art 36. The new approach to the drafting of directives created only broad 'essential requirements', which could be met at national level in a number of different ways. It is impossible to examine the whole United Kingdom response to these directives which are intended to remove barriers to the free movement of a great many different products, but two different products will serve to show how the process has worked in the United Kingdom.

FOOD PRODUCTS

The directive and implementing national legislation

Food products comprise a very important part of inter-state trade in the Community. The food industry represents the largest sector of European manufacturing and trade, and the case law of the Court in relation to both Arts 30 and 36 has been dominated by food products. Much of the discussion about the nature of the controls that remain necessary in the interest of health turns on the extent to which effective protection of consumers can be reconciled with a genuine free market in goods (Burrows, N. and Hiram, H., 'The Official Control of Foodstuffs' in Daintith, T., *Implementing EC Law in the United Kingdom: Structures for Indirect Rule* (1995)). It has been said by Micklitz and Weatherill that the Court's decisions involve 'a preference for the consumer advantages of free trade over the advantages for the consumer of national regulation which impedes trade' Micklitz and Weatherill, S. *Consumer Policy in the European Community: Before and After Maastricht* (1993) 16 J Consumer Pol 285–322.

Directive 89/397 on the Official Control of Foodstuffs lays down general rules to be followed by national enforcement authorities in relation to the inspection of production and distribution of foodstuffs. It is a new approach directive, in the sense that it does not lay down specific requirements as to how the objectives of safe and hygienic food processing are to be achieved, but sets out only general objectives. The directive reflects both the second *Cassis* principle and the principle of proportionality as interpreted in Art 36 (*see*, for example, *Commission* v *UK (UHT Milk)* (Case 124/81)), in that importing member states are expected to accept the validity of tests carried out by the exporting state. This requirement is not without difficulty in the UK as there is a level of mistrust about the extent to which health and safety regulation is carried out in other member states. There is, however, little hard evidence of inadequate enforcement in other member states. The DTI Single Market Compliance Unit was set up to deal with complaints about non-compliance with single market measures in other member states and to date, most of its work has been concerned with potential breaches of Arts 30, 52 and 59, and the few complaints about breaches in the regulatory process have been anecdotal, without supporting evidence (para 2.24, Department of Trade and Industry Review of the Implementation and Enforcement of EC Law in the UK (1993)).

The directive was implemented by both primary legislation, the Food Safety Act 1990, which set out the broad principles, and delegated legislation made by the Minister of Agriculture, Fisheries and Food under s 17 of the Act. The British regulations deal with the more detailed aspects of food regulation, for which a broad discretion is given to member states. The Food Safety (Exports) Regulations (SI 1991/1476), for example, apply the directive to exports, and the Food Safety (Sampling and Qualifications) Regulations (SI 1990/2463) defines the qualification of food inspectors involved in the inspection and sampling processes.

Enforcement

Breaches of food safety are dealt with by Environmental Health Inspectors. The Food Safety Act 1990, ss 7, 8, 14, and 15 creates four criminal offences:

1 rendering food injurious to health;
2 selling food which does not comply with food safety requirements;
3 selling food, to the purchasers' prejudice, which is not of the nature, substance or quality demanded by the purchase; and

4 falsely describing or presenting food. There are maximum fines of £2000 or six months imprisonment. As the authors of a recent study have observed:

> The introduction of new offences, more serious criminal sanctions, wider administrative powers and a commitment to training in relation to food safety would appear to indicate the rigour with which the government is determined to enforce its own, and EC policy. On closer examination, however, the reality appears very different since each of the tough enforcement tactics with which this aim is backed up are mitigated (or, indeed, offset) by other, less demanding features. (Burrows and Hiram op. cit., p. 153)

As with product liability generally, the Food Safety Act 1990 provides a defence of 'due diligence' which is also to be found in the Consumer Protection Act 1987 in relation to manufactured products (*see* above). Again, there is no such defence referred to in the directive, and it would seem that British law goes further than is provided for in the directive. The lack of adequate resources and problems of proof where breaches have been discovered have led the Institute of Environmental Health Officers to declare that 'the ultimate aim of the directive is the facilitation of free trade within the EC, and not the protection of the consumer'. (Burrows and Hiram op. cit., p. 163).

THE PERSONAL PROTECTIVE EQUIPMENT DIRECTIVE

The directive and national implementation

The Personal Protective Equipment (PPE) Directive 89/686 provides a framework of safety standards for a wide variety of safety equipment intended to protect the wearers against a number of hazards likely to cause ill-health or even death. These include motor cycle helmets, safety boots and shoes, eye protection devices, industrial safety belts, mountaineering equipment, gardening gloves and sunglasses. It is a new approach directive, specifying essential safety requirements. The directive classifies PPE products into three categories:

1 *Simple PPE* (Category I) is defined in the text of the directive and includes equipment that protects against hazards which are essentially low-risk, such as gardening gloves or sunglasses.
2 *Complex PPE* (Category III) protects the user against immediately life threatening hazards. Equipment in this category includes respirators, breathing apparatus and motor cycle helmets.
3 Equipment in Category II is classified as *intermediate*.

Equipment which meets the minimum safety requirement is entitled to carry a 'CE' mark. This is only possible after the product has been satisfactorily tested. Products which bear the CE mark can expect to be admitted readily to markets in other member states (*see*, above, Chapter 14)

Implementation into British law was achieved by a statutory instrument made under the Consumer Protection Act 1987. Unusually, instead of the adaptation of the content of the directive to conform to the wording and structure of a statutory instrument (often called 'the elaborative approach'; *see*, for example, the Toy Safety Directive 88/378 implemented by the Toys (Safety) Regulations SI 1989 No. 1275), the PPE Directive was implemented on a 'copy-out' basis. That is, the UK Regulation simply reproduced the wording of the directive. This has the advantage that Community law is precisely implemented, in the sense that there is no tendency, if it is 'added on' to other UK obligations, that the end result is 'over-implementation'.

Enforcement

The disadvantage is that Community directives rarely have the precision of English legislation. Although the directive is to be enforced with the penalties created by the Consumer Protection Act 1987, prosecutions are likely to be infrequent. Enforcers have complained that because of the absence in clarity in the directive, the consequences of non-compliance are not clear to those at whom the provisions in the directive are aimed. The transitional period for compliance, in which manufacturers are enabled to change their production methods to comply with the objectives of the directive, only expired in June 1995, so that it is not yet clear how far the defects in transposition are likely to affect the enforcement. The lack of clarity of what determines culpability, coupled with the limited resources of trading standards authorities who will have to test products prior to any prosecution, suggests that prosecution, which although not always necessary must always be available as an ultimate sanction, will be rare indeed (*see*, Department of Trade and Industry Review of the Implementation and Enforcement of EC Law in the UK (1993) Annex D, pp 145, 146).

Further reading

Burrows, N., and Hiriam, H., The Official Control of Foodstuffs in Daintith, T., (ed) (1995) *Implementing EC Law in the United Kingdom: Structures for Indirect Rule.*

Bieber *et al* (1992) *One European Market*

Department of Trade and Industry Review of the Implementation of EC Law in the UK (1993).

D'Sa, R., *European Community Law and Civil Remedies in England and Wales*, Sweet and Maxwell.

Micklitz, J., and Weatherill, S., 'Consumer Policy in the European Community: Before and After Maastricht' (1993) 16 J Consumer Pol 285.

Weatherill, S., 'Playing Safe: The United Kingdom's Implementation of the Toy Safety Directive' in Daintith, T., (ed) *Implementing EC Law in the United Kingdom.*

Weatherill, S., 'Consumer Safety Legislation in the United Kingdom and Article 30 EEC' (1988) 13 EL Rev 87.

Part IV
COMPETITION LAW

17 Competition law: state monopolies and state aid

When the Community was formed, state ownership of major utilities played an important part in the economic and social policies of the founding states. It continues to do so, although state ownership is now less favoured, and subsidies and direct or indirect regulation of private undertakings providing important services have become more common. State intervention will continue to provide a safety net to industries in decline or facing sudden crises, and to support undertakings providing important public services. Although these activities by the state may well breach the Community's commitment to a single market, in which goods and services compete on an equal basis, the Community's own support for agriculture and agricultural products and its regional and social funds demonstrate an equal commitment to social, educational, health and cultural objectives supported by Community intervention. This support has been continued and expanded by the Treaty on European Union (Arts 123–129 (as amended by TEU)). The Treaty seeks to strike a balance between state intervention and the operation of the market. In member states, the position of public ownership is, like private ownership, protected by Art 222. The balance between public and private ownership is a matter for national policy, but state ownership is subject to similar constraints as private ownership. The title to that ownership is a matter of state policy, but the exercise of ownership rights, if it affects trade between member states, is governed by the law of the Community.

STATE MONOPOLIES

The position with regard to state monopolies is dealt with by Art 37:

> Member states shall progressively adjust any state monopolies of a commercial character so as to ensure that when the transitional period is ended no discrimination regarding the conditions under which goods are procured and marketed exists between nationals of member states.

The provisions of this Article shall apply to any body through which a member state, in law or in fact, either directly or indirectly supervises, determines or appreciably influences imports or exports between member states. These provisions shall likewise apply to monopolies delegated by the state to others.

Art 37 must be read in conjunction with Art 90. Article 37 is concerned with the procurement and marketing of goods while Art 90 is concerned with services. Art 90 provides:

1. In the case of public undertakings and undertakings to which member states grant special or exclusive rights, member states shall neither enact nor maintain in force any measure contrary to the rules contained in this Treaty, in particular to those rules provided for in Art 6 and Art 85 to 94.
2. Undertakings entrusted with the operation of services of general economic interest or having the character of a revenue-producing monopoly shall be subject to the rules contained in this Treaty, in particular to the rules on competition, in so far as the application of such rules does not obstruct the performance, in law or in fact, of the particular tasks assigned to them.

Art 90(3) requires the Commission to enforce this Article by addressing, where necessary, appropriate directives or decisions to member states.

The nature of 'state monopolies of a commercial character' referred to in Art 37 was considered by the Court of Justice in *Costa* v *ENEL* (Case 6/64). The case concerned the compatability with Community law of the nationalisation of the Italian electricity industry.

> ... One must consider ... carefully paragraph (1) of Art 37. This prevents the creation not indeed of all national monopolies but only of those that present 'a commercial character' and even of these, insofar as they tend to introduce the discrimination aforesaid. It follows, therefore, that *to come within the terms of the prohibition of this Article, national monopolies and bodies must on the one hand have as objects transactions in commercial products capable of competition and exchanges betweeen member states; and on the other hand play a leading part in such exchanges.* (emphasis added)

Whether or not a state monopoly exists is a matter of law and fact. A plaintiff who proves the existence of a breach of Art 37 and loss caused by that breach may obtain an award in damages, since the provision is directly effective (*Hansen* v *Hauptzollamt Flensburg* (Case 91/78)).

The operation of a body enjoying a state monopoly may involve potential restrictions on the importation of goods into a member state, breaching Art 30, discrimination by such a body in the relation of the provision of such goods and services and the abuse of a monopoly position. An example of the interplay of these provisions was considered recently by the Court of Justice in *Société Civile Agricole de la Crespelle* v *Coopérative d'Elevage de la Mayenne* (Case C-323/93). In this case, under French law certain approved bovine insemination centres were granted exclusive rights within a defined area. Breeders established in those areas were, effectively, obliged to use their services. Such licensed centres enjoyed what the Court described as 'a contiguous series of monopolies territorially limited but together covering the entire territory of a member state.'

The Court held, firstly, that the mere creation of such a dominant position by the granting of an exclusive right within the meaning of Art 90(1) was not as such incompatible with Art 86 of the Treaty. A member state contravened the prohibitions contained in those two provisions only if, in merely exercising the exclusive right granted to it, the undertaking in question could not avoid abusing its dominant position. An undertaking abused its dominant position where it had an administrative monopoly and charged for its services fees which were disproportionate to the economic value of the services provided. Secondly, the Court held that national rules which required importers of bovine semen from a member state to deliver it only to an approved insemination or production centre were in breach of Art 30, but were, in the circumstances saved by Art 36 as necessary for the protection of animal health. Although the point was not specifically dealt with in this case, the Court has held that an exclusive right, inter alia, to import particular goods falls within the scope of Art 37 (*Manghera* (Case 59/75)).

In *Hansen* v *Hauptzollamt Flensburg* the Court had to consider the extent to which the German state alcohol monopoly was compatible with Art 37. It held, firstly, that after the end of the transitional period, Art 37 remained applicable wherever the exercise by a state monopoly of its exclusive rights entailed a discrimination or restriction prohibited by that Article. Secondly, that Art 37 prohibited a monopoly's right to purchase and resell national alcohol from being exercised so as to undercut imported products with publicly subsidised domestic products.

STATE UNDERTAKINGS AND THE NEED FOR TRANSPARENCY

Where an undertaking is state-owned, or directly or or indirectly controlled by the state, it is subject to the provisions of Directive 80/723. This directive (the 'transparency Directive') was made under Art 90(3) EC Treaty and requires that financial relations between public authorities and public undertakings are transparent. 'Transparency' in this context means transparency to the Commission: Art 5, Directive 80/723. The particular matters requiring disclosure are the amount of public funds made available directly by public authorities to the public undertakings concerned, or through intermediaries, and the uses to which such public funds are put (Art 1, Directive 80/723). The extent and nature of such support may well be of concern to the Commission in determining whether or not unlawful state aids have been provided.

State aids

There is no absolute prohibition of state aids in the Treaty. Rather, the prohibitions are directed against the use of state aids in ways that are not 'compatible with the common market'.

Article 92(1) provides:

> Save as otherwise provided in this Treaty, any aid granted by a member state or through state resources in any form whatsover which distorts or threatens to distort competition by favouring certain undertakings or the production of certain goods shall, in so far as it affects trade between member states, be incompatible with the common market.

Article 92(1) is not concerned with how state aid is given. It is rather directed at aid given by the state or derived from state resources which either distorts competition by favouring undertakings and affects trade between member states. 'Aid' is a wide concept, including but not confined to, state subsidies.

> The concept of an aid is ... wider than that of a subsidy because it embraces not only positive benefits, such as subsidies themselves, but also interventions which, in various forms, mitigate the charges which are normally included in the budget of an undertaking and which would without, therefore, being subsidies in the strict sense of the word, be similar in character and have the same effect.
> (*Steenkolenmijnen* v *HA* (Case 30/59))

Aid may come in a large number of different guises and has been held to include: exemption from duties and taxes; exemption from parafiscal charges; preferential interest rates; guarantees of loans on especially favourable terms; making land or buildings available either for nothing or on especially favourable terms; provision of goods or services on preferential terms; indemnities against operating losses and the purchase of shares of a company in financial difficulties (*Intermills* v *Commission* (Case 323/82); *Spain* v *Commission* (joined cases C- 278, 279, 280/92)).

Despite the wide definition of aid favoured by the Commission, the Court has tended to insist that if it is to be regarded as 'aid' it must constitute a government measure 'involving a charge on the public account' of the state concerned (*Sloman Neptun* (Case C72/91); *Kirsammer Hack* (Case C-189/91)). This was not, however, the view of the Advocates-General in both cases. Both decisions have been the subject of criticism for allowing too much scope for states to give unfair competitive advantages to undertakings in their territories by such devices as relaxing environmental and planning controls, or by making various beneficial administrative concessions (Slotboom, M., 'State Aid in Community Law: A Broad and Narrow Definition (1995) 20 *EL Rev* 289).

Some types of aid are, *per se*, deemed to be compatible under Art 92(2):

The following shall be compatible with the common market:
1   aid having a social character, granted to individual consumers, provided that such aid is granted without discrimination related to the origin of the products concerned;

2   aid to make good the damage caused by natural disasters or exceptional occurrences;

3   aid granted to the economy of certain areas of the Federal Republic of Germany affected by the division of Germany, in so far as such aid is required in order to compensate for the economic disadvantges caused by that division.

An example of aid of the kind referred to in (1) would be sales of basic food products such as bread, pasta and butter at a low, fixed price. In these cases the wholesaler might be compensated by the state for the loss of his profit. The proviso would, however, require that such support would be equally available to imported and home-produced products. The aid referred to in (2) is self-explanatory and the aid to which Germany was entitled under (3) is now seen by the Commission as no longer necessary. However, it could be argued that the very considerable difficulties suffered by the Eastern territories of the Federal Republic on re-unification were consequent upon the original division, and justified state subsidies to the Eastern industries to bring them up to Western standards, provided that the aid given is no more than is necessary to achieve that purpose.

Other types of aid are seen as potentially justifiable. Under Art 92(3), there are five categories of aid. Before a member state commences or alters any of the aid projects falling within categories (1) to (5) below, it must notify the Commission in sufficient time to enable the Commission to comment. The Commission has the power to block the project or require its amendment (Art 93(2), (3)).

The categories are:

1   aid to promote the economic development of areas where the standard of living is abnormally low or where there is serious underemployment;

2   aid to promote the execution of an important project of common European interest or to remedy a serious disturbance in the economy of a member state;

3   aid to facilitate the development of certain economic activities or of certain economic areas, where such aid does not adversely affect trading conditions to an extent contrary to the common interest;

4   aid to promote culture and heritage conservation where such aid does not affect trading conditions and competition in the Community to an extent that is contrary to the common interest;

5   such other categories of aid as may be specified by decisions of the Council acting by a qualified majority on a proposal from the Commission.

(1) The promotion of economic development of areas of low income and high underemployment

In *Philip Morris* v *Commission* (Case 730/79) the Commission's criteria to determine whether or not an aid scheme should be approved received the support of the Court of Justice. Firstly, the aid must promote or further a project that is in the Community interest as a whole. Aid which, therefore, promotes a national interest is unacceptable. Secondly, the aid must be necessary for promoting the first objective and thirdly, the way in which the aid is provided must be proportional to the legitimate object, and must not be likely to affect trade between member states and distort competition.

In the *Morris* case, the Netherlands government proposed to grant the applicant capital assistance to enable it to increase cigarette production so that it would account for nearly 50 per cent of cigarette production in the Netherlands. Eighty per cent of that production would be exported to other member states. There was here the possibility that aid could have an effect, therefore, on trade between member states. Philip Morris argued that Art 92(3) only required that the investment plan only had to be compatible with the objectives set out in paragraphs (a), (b) and (c). It did not have to be shown that the aid would contribute to the attainment of one of those legitimate objectives. The development of cigarette manufacture was to take place in Bergen-op-Zoom, where underemployment was high and the per capita income was lower than the national average in the rest of the Netherlands. The company maintained that the Commission had been wrong to compare unemployment and income not with that prevailing elsewhere in the Netherlands but with that elsewhere in the Community.

The Court rejected the argument that trade with other member states was not likely to be distorted:

> When state financial aid strengthens the position of an undertaking compared with other undertakings competing in intra-Community trade, the latter must be regarded as affected by that aid. In this case the aid which the Netherlands government proposed to grant was for an undertaking organised for international trade and this is proved by the high percentage of its production which it intends to export to other member states. The aid in question was to help enlarge its production capacity and consequently to increase its capacity to maintain the flow of trade including that between member states. On the other hand the aid is said to have reduced the cost of converting the production facilities and has thereby given the applicant a competitive advantage over manufacturers who have completed or intend to complete at their own expense a similar increase in the productive capacity of their plant.

The Court also refused to accept the company's argument that it was legitimate to look at unemployment and income levels only in the Netherlands, and that the Commission had been wrong to take a broader view of all the circumstances:

> These arguments put forward by the applicant cannot be upheld. It should be borne in mind that the Commission has a discretion the exercise of which involves economic and social assessments which must be made in a Community context. That is the context in which the Commission has with good reason assessed the standard of living and serious underemployment in the Bergen-op-Zoom area, not with reference to the national average in the Netherlands but in relation to the Community level ... The Commission could very well take the view, as it did, that the investment to be effected in this case was not 'an important project of Common European interest' ... since the proposed aid would have permitted the transfer to the Netherlands of an investment which could be effected in other member states in a less favourable economic situation

than that of the Netherlands, where the national level of unemployment is one of the lowest in the Community.

Although the Court has held that decisions of this kind involve the making of complicated economic assessments with which the Court will not readily interfere, when the Commission purports to be acting according to a stated economic policy, its decisions must be compatible with that policy (*Spain* v *Commission* (above)).

(2) The promotion of the execution of a project of common European interest or to remedy a serious economic disturbance

The sort of projects which have been approved by the Commission under this head are mostly ones in which there is cross-Community co-operation in some technological or environmental project. In this connection the Court stated in *Exécutif Régional Wallon and Glaverbel* v *Commission* (Case 62/87) that there will be no common European interest in a scheme 'unless it forms part of a transnational European programme supported jointly by a number of governments of the member states, or arises from concerted action by a number of member states to combat a common threat such as environmental pollution'. As a result, the Court found that a scheme under which modernisation aid was granted to Glaverbel, who were manufacturers of glass in Belgium, was not an important project of European interest, since it was not part of a transnational programme.

(3) Aid to facilitate the development of certain economic activities or certain economic areas

In its *First Report on State Aids* in the European Community published in 1989 the Commission reported a vary large increase in the preceding ten years of cases notified and investigated under Art 92. A survey in the report indicated that over 108 billion Ecus were given in aid each year over that period, the majority of which went to manufacturing companies under Art 92(3)(c). In its *18th Report on Competition Policy,* published the same year, the Commission described its approach to applications made by member states for approval of state aids in relation to the regional aspect of Art 92(3)(c):

> Regions falling under Art 92(3) are those with more general development problems in relation to the national as well as the Community situation. Often they suffer from the decline of traditional industries and are frequently located in the more central prosperous parts of the Community. In its Art 92(3)(c) method, the Commission has established a system which takes account of national regional problems and places them into a Community context.

The Commission has, in the context of Art 92(3)(c), operated on the basis of two primary indicators. The first is income (as measured by gross domestic product or gross value added) and the second is structural unemployment. In this context (unlike that with regard to the criteria applicable to Art 92(3)(a), above), the assessment of conditions is made in the national and the Community context. The better the position of the member state in which the region is located in relation to the Community as a whole, the wider must the disparity be between the region concerned and the state as a whole, to justify the aid. Broadly, regions wanting to receive aid must, in relative terms, be worse off than regions in poorer member states before aid is approved by the Commission. In addition, for approval of the Commission to be secured, any aid proposal must be linked to a major re-structuring of the sector of the industry concerned. It should not be used either simply to 'prop up' an ailing concern or allow an undertaking to gain an unfair competitive advantage (*Spain* v *Commission* (Case C-42/93)).

(4) The promotion of heritage conservation

This new provision, added by the TEU, must be read in the light of Art 128(2) EC. This provides that:

> Action by the Community shall be aimed at encouraging co-operation between member states and, if necessary, supporting and supplementing their action in the following areas: – conservation and safeguarding of cultural heritage of European significance.

Heritage conservation is closely linked to the promotion of tourism, the right of access to which is a primary service under Art 59 (*Luisi and Carbone* (Case 286/83)).

(5) Specific state aids approved by the Council

A number of directives have been made under Art 92(3)(d) (which corresponds to what is now Art 92(3)(e) in the amended Treaty), including Directive 90/684 on state aid to shipbuilding. Under the directive, state aid could be deemed to be compatible with the common market if it related to shipbuilding and ship conversion granted as development assistance to a developing country. The Commission had to verify the development content of the proposal in accordance with criteria laid down by an OECD Working Party. In October 1991 the German government notified the Commission of its intention to grant aid to mainland China in the form of aid credit for three container vessels to be operated by a state-owned Chinese trading company, Cosco. The Commission informed the Federal Republic that the proposed aid could not be regarded as 'genuine development aid … and is therefore incompatible with the common market'. It declared that it was not satisfied that the aid was any more than 'an operating aid to the German shipyards … rather than a genuine aid to a developing country'. This decision was challenged by the German government in an action to annul the decision under Art 173 EC.

The Court of Justice upheld the Commission's decision. The directive conferred a discretion on the Commission which was required to satisfy itself that the aid complied with the OECD criteria. It also had to verify the particular development content of the project. It decided that Cosco was not a company that needed development aid in order to contribute to the general development of China. It was entitled to come to that decision and was well within its discretion to do so.

THE COMMISSION'S ROLE OF MONITORING THE GRANT OF STATE AID

The Commission has a general obligation to keep all systems of state aid under review, both those which are, prima facie, lawful under Art 92(2) and those which have been approved under the Commission's discretionary powers under Art 92(3), to ensure that both continue to be operated in a way that is compatible with the single market. It is the Commission which has to decide whether any kind of state aid is compatible with Community law, except for those types of aid which have been given specific clearance by the Council under Art 92(3)(e).

To enable it to assess whether or not any new aid scheme is permitted under Art 92, there is a clearance procedure which must be followed by member states. Under Art 93(3):

> The Commission shall be informed, in sufficient time to enable it to submit its comments, of any plans to grant or alter aid. If it considers that any such plan is not compatible with the common market having regard to Art 92, it shall without delay initiate the procedure provided for paragraph 2. The member state concerned shall not put its proposed measures into effect until this procedure has resulted in a final decision.

The Commission is required to decide quite quickly if a proposed measure is justified under Art 92. In *Germany* v *Commission* (Case 84/82), the Court declared that two months should suffice for this purpose. If at the end of that time the Commission had not defined its attitude towards the proposal, the member state that had made it could go ahead with it, but should notify the Commission of its intention to do so.

If the Commission decides that the proposed state aid is incompatible with the Treaty, or if aid which has previously been approved by it is being misused, it can inform the state concerned that the aid scheme should be abolished or altered within a timescale fixed by the Commission, and that the aid, together with interest, should be recovered by the state (*Commission* v *Italy* (Case C-348/93)). Failure to comply can result in that state being brought before the Court of Justice (Art 93(2)). Although it is not specifically provided for in Art 93, the Court has accepted that any aid which has been unlawfully paid may also be recovered by the Commission (*Commission* v *Germany* (Case 70/72)). Even though the aid may have been accepted by an undertaking in good faith, without any reason to believe that it had been paid in breach of Community law, that innocent receipt cannot found a legitimate expectation that the aid may be retained. The effect of doing so could be fatal to the effective operation of Arts 92 and 93:

> ... A member state whose authorities have granted aid contrary to the procedural rules laid down in Art 93 may not rely on the legitimate expectations of recipients in order to justify a failure to comply with the obligation to take the steps necessary to implement a Commission decision instructing it to recover the aid. If it could do so, Arts 92 and 93 of the Treaty would be set at naught, since national authorities would thus be able to rely on their own unlawful conduct in order to deprive decisions taken by the Commission under provisions of the Treaty of their effectiveness.
> (*Commission* v *Germany* (Case C-5/89))

It is not only the Commission which will have an interest in the payment of state aids. Rival companies may also feel threatened by the actual or proposed distribution of state support and may wish to challenge a decision of the Commission approving it. In *ASPEC and AAC* v *Commission* (Case T-435/93) aid had been approved by the Commission under Arts 92 and 93 in relation to the production of starch in the Mezzogiorno region of Italy which would have had the consequence of increasing production by some seven per cent at Community level and of establishing a production level in Italy alone which would have exceeded the previous total production capacity of that country. The challengers would have been seriously affected by the decision and the Court recognised that they had a sufficient interest to mount a challenge under Art 173 (*see* Chapter 23). Although the Court has held that the Commission enjoys a wide discretion in granting approval, its reasoning must be consistent with its declared policy, and it must adopt proper procedures in adopting its decision (*see Spain* v *Commission* (above)). In this case, the decision had never actually been taken by the full Commission but, in breach of its own procedures, had been delegated to Ray MacSharry, the then Agriculture Commissioner, on the eve of the Commission's annual holiday. The decision to approve the aid was, accordingly, annulled by the Court.

Finally, it should be noted that damages can be awarded against the government of a member state that has granted competition distorting state aids without having notified these to the Commission for review (*Fédération National du Commerce* v *France* (Case 354/90)).

Further reading

Evans, A. and Martin, M., 'Socially Acceptable Distortions of Competition: Community Policy on State Aid' (1991) 16 EL Rev 79.

Frazer, T., 'The New Structural Funds, State Aids and Interventions in the Single European Market' (1995) 32 CML Rev 3.

Green, N., Hartley, T.C. and Usher, J.A., (1991) *The Legal Foundations of the Single European Market*, OUP, Chapter 21.

Hancher, L., Ottervanger, T. and Slot P.J., (1993) *EC State Aids*.

Quigley, C., 'The Notion of State Aid in the EEC' (1988) 13 EL Rev 242.

Ross, M., 'Challenging state aids – the effect of recent developments' (1986) 23 CML Rev 867.

Schütte, M., and Hix, J.P., 'The application of the EC state aid rule to privatisations: the East German example' (1995) 32 CML Rev 215.

Slotboom, M., 'State Aids in Community Law : A Broad or a Narrow Definition?' (1995) 20 EL Rev 289.

Steiner, J., (1994) *Textbook on EC Law*, (4th edn) Blackstone Press, Chapters 10 and 11.

Wyatt, D. and Dashwood, A., (1993) *European Community Law* (3rd edn), Sweet & Maxwell, Chapter 18.

18 Competition law: cartels and restrictive agreements (Article 85)

COMPETITION LAW AND POLICY

In its *First Report on Competition Policy* the Commission emphasised the value of effective competition in the Community. Competition is the best stimulant of economic activity, since it guarantees the widest possible freedom of action to all. An active competition policy, pursued in accordance with the provisions of the Treaties establishing the Communities, makes it easier for the supply and demand structures to continually adjust to technological development. Through the interplay of de-centralised decision-making machinery, competition enables enterprises continuously to improve their efficiency, which is essential for the steady improvement of living standards and employment prospects within the countries of the Community. From this point of view, competition policy is an essential means for satisfying to a great extent the individual and collective needs of our society.

Competition is not, however, regarded as an end in itself. It is one of the most important means by which a genuinely integrated market is achieved. Arts 85 and 86 match Arts 30 and 34, in the sense that the latter are aimed at measures taken by member state governments which have the effect of restricting the free movement of goods, while the former are concerned with restrictive and abusive practices by undertakings which have the effect of excluding or restricting goods or services from member states. The distinction between state and private undertaking in this context is not, of course, absolute. States may run commercial monopolies and private undertakings and may secure an unfair competitive advantage by injections of state capital and other state aids. Both practices are subject to restriction under the Treaty and have been examined in Chapter 17. Major sectors of the West European economy are dominated by large private business corporations, some of which have a bigger annual turnover than the gross domestic product of many small states. Abusive practices by such businesses may have more impact on cross-border trade than the actions of smaller member state governments. Paradoxically, to create a genuinely free and competitive market, some restrictions are essential to ensure that the largest actors in the market place do not distort the working of the market to their own advantage and to the disadvantage of competitors and consumers. The primary objective, therefore, of European competition policy has been market integration. A secondary one has been a form of equity or equality of competition, an aspect of 'the level playing field' to which many businesses aspire in the Community. The third aspect of competition policy is that espoused by the Commission in its first report, the promotion of efficiency. Increasingly, this is seen in the context of the wider trading context of North and South America and the Pacific rim.

Competition law, more than any other area of Community law, is informed by economic factors. Conduct which may be lawful in one context, may be unlawful in another. The behaviour of business actors will have to be assessed in the light of prevailing economic circumstances, and the way in which particular markets may react. The pricing policy of a company which has a monopoly will be a subject of acute interest to consumers, whereas overpricing by a company in a highly competitive market will rapidly be corrected by the effect on that company of consumers taking their custom elsewhere. The behaviour of business undertakings in relation to competition law and policy must always, therefore, be viewed in the context of such matters as degrees of concentration and the relevance of market power, the importance of entry barriers and actual and potential competition.

Community competition policy, taking the objectives discussed above into account, is directed towards three kinds of anti-competitive activity:

1 Restricting trading agreements between otherwise independent business undertakings which may affect trade between member states and which distort competition within the common market (Art 85).
2 Abusive, anti-competitive practices of large undertakings which dominate markets for goods or services which affects trade between member states (Art 86).
3 Major mergers of undertakings resulting in positions of market dominance in the Community are subject to control under Regulation 4064/89.

Each of these kinds of anti-competitive practice is subject to regulation and control by the Commission. Its powers and the way in which they are interpreted and applied will be examined in Chapter 20. First, however, it is necessary to understand the primary law on which the regulation of anti-competitive practices is based.

ARTICLE 85

Article 85 is directed against co-operation between companies that operate in an anti-competitive way. Article 85(1) prohibits all agreements between undertakings, decisions by associations of undertakings and concerted practices which may affect trade between member states and which have as their object or effect the prevention, restriction or distortion of competition within the common market.

A number of examples of the type of agreements covered by Art 85(1) are provided in Arts 85(1)(a) to (e):

1   directly or indirectly fix purchase or selling prices or any other trading conditions (Art 85(1)(a));
2   limit or control production, markets, technical development, or investment (Art 85(1)(b));
3   share markets or sources of supply (Art 85(1)(c));
4   apply dissimilar conditions to equivalent transactions with other trading parties, thereby placing them at a competitive disadvantage (Art 85(1)(d));
5   make the conclusion of contracts subject to acceptance by the other parties of supplementary obligations which, by their nature or according to commercial use, have no connection with the subject of such contracts (Art 85 (1)(e)).

Article 85(2) provides that any agreement or decision prohibited pursuant to Art 85(1) shall be automatically void. Although the list in Art 85(1) does not comprise an exhaustive one it is indicative of the kind of practices which will breach the prohibition. It is primarily aimed at 'horizontal' co-operation between nominally competing companies, the classic cartel, but it is also designed to deal with restrictive agreements between manufacturers, wholesalers and retailers, i.e., 'vertical agreements', which also affect the availability of goods and services and the terms on which they are supplied. The Commission remains free to identify other agreements or practices which are operated in an anti-competitive way. There are, in addition, a number of agreements, decisions and practices which may be declared not to breach the prohibition in Art 85(1). These are listed in Art 85(3):

The provisions of paragraph 1 may, however, be declared inapplicable in the case of:

- any agreement or category of agreements between undertakings;
- any decision or category of decisions by associations of undertakings;
- any concerted practice or category of concerted practices

which contributes to improving the production or distribution of goods or to promoting technical or economic progress, while allowing consumers a fair share of the resulting benefit, and which does not:

(a)   impose on the undertakings concerned restrictions which are not indispensable to the attainment of these objectives;
(c)   afford such undertakings the possibility of eliminating competition in respect of a substantial part of the products in question.

Undertakings

The term 'undertaking' includes every kind of natural or legal person engaged in economic or commercial activity. They must be established in order to make a profit. The Court has recently had to consider the nature of 'undertakings' to which Arts 85 and 86 are applicable. In *Poucet v Assurances Générales de France*, (Case C-159/91) the Court decided that regional social security organisations were not 'undertakings'. Complaints had been made alleging anti-competitive restrictions on market access for 'consumers' of social insurance 'services'. The Court distinguished between bodies pursuing economic activities as such and those activities which are based upon a principle of solidarity and which are pursued entirely without intention to make a profit. In *SAT v Eurocontrol* (Case C-364/92) the Court concluded that Eurocontrol, a body set up by treaty to recover fees payable by airlines for traffic control services, was not an 'undertaking'. It undertook the tasks assigned to it in the public interest with a view to assuring the maintenance and improvement of air transport. There was not a sufficient economic element in the work of Eurocontrol, which could not be held responsible for the amounts which it collected. The fees payable had been established by the states which were parties to the treaty by which it was established.

Agreement

Article 85 is only applicable if there is an 'agreement', 'decision by an association of undertakings' or 'concerted practice'. Agreements are not confined to binding contracts of whatever kind, but include understandings and 'gentlemen's agreements' (*ACF Chemiefarma v Commission* (Case 41/69)). The type of loose arrangement that may fall foul of Art 85(1) is demonstrated by the facts of *BMW Belgium v Commission* (Case 32/78). In this case an attempt was made by BMW's subsidiary in Belgium to discourage car dealers there from selling the cars to other member states. BMW dealers in Belgium had received a circular from BMW Belgium urging them not to engage in such sales. They were asked to indicate assent to this policy by signing and returning a copy of the circular. It was made clear that this was not a contractual document, but the Court nonetheless held that it was an 'agreement' under Art 85(1). In *Tréfilenrope Sales SARL v Commission*, (Case T-141/89) the Court of First Instance declared that:

> For there to be an agreement within the meaning of Art 85(1) of the Treaty, it is sufficient for the undertakings in question to have expressed their joint intention to conduct themselves in the market in a particular way.

A decision by an association of undertakings

The commonest kind of decision at which Art 85(1) is aimed is that of a trade association which lays down standards for the activities of its members. Standardisation of pricing or the way in which a service may be supplied may well fall foul of the provisions of Art 85. Even an agreement to supply information about sales by competitors, although it is concerned neither prices nor any anti-competitive arrangement has been held to fall within Art 85, since it could enable the dominant suppliers to adopt strategies to resist market penetration by those competitors (*Fiatagri UK Ltd* v *Commission* (Case T-34/92)). The body concerned does not, however, have to be engaged in commercial activity itself. In *NV IAZ International Belgium and Others* v *Commission* (Case 96/82) two Belgian Royal Decrees provided that washing machines and dishwashers could be connected to the main water supply only if they satisfied Belgian standards. For the purpose of monitoring the conformity of washing machines or dishwashers with those Belgian standards, the manufacturers and sole importers of electrical appliances affiliated to certain trade organisations made an agreement with the national association of water suppliers (the 'ANSEAU-NAVEWA' agreement). Under this agreement, all appliances put into commercial distribution had to bear a label issued by a designated trade organisation. The Commission made a decision that certain provisions of the agreement infringed Art 85(1). In its view, the offending provisions excluded the possibility for importers other than the sole importers to obtain a conformity check for the washing machines and dishwashers which they imported into Belgium under conditions which did not discriminate against them. ANSEAU attempted to argue that the agreement did not fall within Art 85(1) as its member undertakings were not legally bound by the agreement and since ANSEAU did not itself carry on any kind of economic activity. The Court rejected both arguments:

> Article 85(1) of the Treaty also applies to associations of undertakings in so far as their own activities or those of the undertakings affiliated to them are calculated to produce the results which it aims to suppress ... A recommendation, even if it has no binding effect, cannot escape Art 85(1) where compliance with the recommendation by the undertakings to which it is addressed has an appreciable influence in the market in question.

However, the Court recognised a limit to the application of Art 85 where the nominees of trade organisations concerned with the fixing of prices were genuinely independent of their parent bodies. In *Germany* v *Delta Schiffahrts und Speditionsgesellschaft mbH* (Case C-153/93) representatives of shippers and inland waterway ship operators were both represented on freight commissions which fixed inland waterway freight charges. The decisions of these commissions on relevant charges were approved by the Federal Minister of Transport and were then compulsory. These charges were challenged by a shipper as contrary to Art 85 and the question was referred to the Court under Art 177. The Court held that Art 85 did not preclude rules of a member state from providing that tariffs for commercial inland waterways traffic might be fixed by the freight commissions comprised of individuals recommended by the businesses concerned, provided that they were genuinely independent of those businesses and provided that the public authority retained a power to override their decisions.

Concerted practice

This term means some kind of co-ordinated action which, although it may fall short of an agreement, knowingly substitutes practical co-operation for competition (*ICI* v *Commission* (Case 48/69)). In the *ICI* case ICI was among a number of businesses producing aniline dyestuffs in Italy. It was the first to impose a price increase, but it was shortly followed by other producers of similar products, accounting for more than 80 per cent of the market. A similar pattern of price increases had taken place among the ten major producers of aniline dyestuffs who dominated the dyestuffs market in the Community. The Commission concluded from the circumstances that there had been a 'concerted practice' between the undertakings, and imposed fines on them. The undertakings challenged the Commission's decision, arguing that the price increases merely reflected parallel behaviour in an oligopolostic market where each producer followed the price leader. An oligopoly is a market in which a small number of suppliers supply the preponderant portion of demand (for a discussion on oligopolies, *see* Green, N., Hartley, T. C. and Usher, J. A., *The Legal Foundations of the Single Market* (1991) Chapter 15). The Court considered the circumstances and the nature of a concerted practice in the context of Art 85:

> Article 85 draws a distinction between the concept of 'concerted practices' and that of 'agreements between undertakings' or of 'decisions of associations'; the object is to bring within the prohibition of that Art a form of co-ordination between undertakings which, without having reached the stage where an agreement properly so called has been concluded, knowingly substitutes practical co-operation between them for the risks of competition.
>
> By its very nature, then, a concerted practice does not have all the elements of a contract but may inter alia arise out of co-ordination which becomes apparent from the behaviour of the participants. Although parallel behaviour may not by itself be identified with a concerted practice, it may, however, amount to strong evidence of such a practice if it leads to conditions of competition which do not correspond to the normal conditions of the market, having regard to the nature of the products, the size and number of the undertakings and the volume of the said market.
> (paras [64], [65] and [66])

In the event, the Court decided that there was evidence of a concerted practice that breached Art 85. Concertation is difficult to prove and the mere fact of parallel price increases is not conclusive. There must be 'a firm precise and consistent body of evidence' on concertation to justify such a finding (*Åhlström Oy* v *Commission* (joined cases C-89, 104, 114, 116, 117, 125-129/85)).

An agreement between undertakings

As we have seen above, the concept of an 'undertaking' is wide, and it includes all legal and natural persons involved in economic or commercial activity, such as companies, sole traders and state-owned public utilities. Undertakings may be engaged in the manufacture, sale or distribution of products or the provision of services and may comprise several companies which are owned or controlled by another one. There must be an agreement or concerted practice by two or more of such undertakings. There will be no agreement between 'undertakings' where it is within

> one economic unit within which subsidiaries do not enjoy real autonomy in determining their course of action in the market. Where, as in this case, the subsidiary, although having a separate legal personality, does not freely determine its conduct on the market but carries out instructions given to it directly or indirectly by the parent company by which it is wholly controlled, Art 85(1) does not apply to the relationship between the subsidiary and the parent company with which it forms an economic unit. (*Viho Europe BV* v *Commission* (Case T-102/92)).

The substantive requirements of Article 85

Having established the kind of agreement or arrangement which, potentially, may breach Art 85, what is the content of such a deal which will infringe Art 85? Not all agreements which affect trading relations between undertakings will breach Art 85. Clearly, the conferring of the power on the Commission in Art 85(3) to grant exemptions recognises that the potentially restrictive effect of some agreements may be outweighed by their beneficial effect. Before an assessment can be made of the grounds for exemption, however, it is necessary to isolate the constituent elements in Art 85 which will enable one to identify an offending agreement.

An agreement which may affect trade between member states

Art 85(1)(a) – (e) provides a non-exhaustive list of the sort of agreements which will, prima facie, breach Art 85, but they must be seen in a Community context. The kind of conduct at which Art 85 is primarily aimed is the conclusion of agreements or concerted practices between apparently competing producers or distributors who agree to give each other a 'free run' in specific national territories. Such horizontal agreements clearly continue to partition what should be a single market on a national basis, and attempt to defeat one of the primary aims of the Community. In *Suiker Unie* v *Commission* (Case 40/73), for example, sugar producers agreed to keep out of one another's territories, and in *ACF Chemiefarma* v *Commission* (Case 41/69) the undertakings concerned agreed (in a 'gentleman's agreement') to share out domestic markets and to fix common prices of synthetic quinidine. Clearly, in these cases trade is affected, and the effect of these horizontal agreements is to deny consumers the benefit of competitive products from other member states. The possible effect on trade between member states received careful examination by the Court in relation to a vertical agreement, that is, an agreement between a manufacturer and a distributor, in the landmark case of *Consten and Grundig* v *Commission* (Case 56/64).

In the *Consten* case, as part of its international distribution network, the German manufacturer of electrical equipment, Grundig, came to an agreement with the French distributer, Consten, by which Consten, was appointed as Grundig's sole representative in France, Corsica and the Saarland. Under that agreement Consten was authorised to use Grundig's name and trademark, and Consten duly registered the Grundig trademark 'GINT' in France. Consten then brought proceedings for infringement of a trademark against a French company, UNEF, which had attempted to sell Grundig products in France which it had bought in Germany. The Commission, after an investigation, decided that the Consten/Grundig agreement breached Art 85 and Grundig and Consten applied to the Court of Justice for annulment of that decision under Art 173(2). The applicants argued that the Commission had relied on a mistaken interpretation of the concept of an agreement which may affect trade between member states, and had not shown that such trade would have been greater without the disputed agreement. The Court rejected the argument:

> The concept of an agreement 'which may affect trade between member states' is intended to define, in the law governing cartels, the boundary between the areas respectively covered by Community law and national law. It is only to the extent to which the agreement may affect trade between member states that the deterioration in competition caused by the agreement falls under the prohibition of Community law contained in Art 85; otherwise it escapes the prohibition. In this connection, what is particularly important is whether the agreement is capable of constituting a threat, either direct or indirect, actual or potential, to freedom of trade between member states in a manner which might harm the attainment of the objectives of a single market between states. Thus the fact that an agreement encourages an increase, even a large one, in the volume of trade between states is not sufficient to exclude the possibility that the agreement may 'affect' such trade in the above mentioned manner. In the present case, the contract between Grundig and Consten, on the one hand by preventing undertakings other than Consten from importing Grundig products into France, and on the other hand by prohibiting Consten from re-exporting those products to other countries of the common market, indisputably affects trade between member states.

It was not necessary, moreover, to wait to see if trade was, in fact affected by the way in which the agreement was intended to operate. The Court said that 'there is no need to take into account the concrete effects of an agreement *once it appears that it has as its object the prevention, restriction or distortion of competition*' (emphasis added).

The effect of the *Consten and Grundig* decision is that Art 85 applies not only to competing undertakings on a horizontal level, but also to vertical agreements between companies which are not themselves competing with each other, but which aim to exclude competitors from the market, provided that the agreement is one that affects trade between member states. Such vertical supply agreements can be caught by Art 85, as affecting trade between member states even if they are not in any way concerned to affect trade outside one member state. Trade may, however, in fact be affected if the agreement, taken in the context of trading conditions in that state, is likely to affect trade into that state. This situation is most likely to occur in relation to 'sole supply' agreements between producers and retailers. In *Brasserie de Haecht SA* v *Wilkin (No. 1)* (Case 23/67) the proprietor of a café in Belgium obtained a loan from a Belgian brewery on the basis that he would obtain supplies of beverages exclusively from the brewery. The legality of the agreement in the context of Art 85(1) was raised in subsequent proceedings and referred by the Belgian court to the Court of Justice under Art 177. The Court held that the validity of the agreement under Art 85 had to take into account not only the scope and affect of the agreement itself, but the trading conditions in the state in which it was made. The agreement, when viewed in isolation did not, as Advocate-General Roemer observed in the case, 'seem to be prejudicial to the common market in any way ... On the other hand it is possible for such an effect to occur as the result of the combined operation of all the beer distribution agreements in a member state.' The Court agreed, and said:

> Article 85(1) implies that regard must be had to such effects in the context in which they occur, that is to say in the economic and legal context of such agreements, decisions and practices and where they might combine with others to have a cumulative effect on competition. In fact, it would be pointless to consider an agreement, decision or practice by reason of its effects if those effects were to be taken distinct from the market in which they are seen to operate and could only be examined apart from the body of effects, whether convergent or not surrounding their implementation.

The context within member states may also have to take account the actions of undertakings outside the Community, where those actions have an effect within member states. In *Ahlstrom Osakeyhito* v *Commission* (*Re Wood Pulp*) (joined Cases C-89, 104, 116, 117 & 125-129/85) concerted action by forestry undertakings in Finland, Sweden (then both outside the Community) and Canada was said to have had an effect on wood pulp prices in the Community. The undertakings submitted that Art 85 did not extend to regulate conduct restricting competition outside the Community merely because it had economic repercussions within it. The Court disagreed, holding that where wood pulp producers established outside the Community sell directly to purchasers established in the Community and engage in price competition in order to win orders from those customers, that constitutes competition within the common market. Where those producers concert on the prices to be charged to their customers in the Community and put that concertation into effect by selling at prices which are actually coordinated, they are taking part in concertation which has the object and effect of restricting competition within the common market within the meaning of Art 85 of the Treaty.

There is a *de minimis* presumption by the Commission, contained in a Notice of 3 September 1986 on Agreements of Minor Importance (OJ C231 00.00.86, p 2), under which the Commission declares that it holds the view that agreements between undertakings engaged in the production or distribution of goods or in the provision of services generally do not fall within the prohibition of Art 85 if the goods and services which are subject to the agreement, together with other related goods and services of the participants, do not, all together represent more than five per cent of the total market for such goods or services in the area of the common market affected by the agreement. The notice only raises a presumption. It does not alter the law, so that it can be rebutted by evidence to the contrary. In *Distillers Company Ltd* v *Commission* (Case 30/78) the presumption in the notice was held to have been displaced by evidence of a distribution agreement of a product the entire production of which was in the hands of a large undertaking.

The object or effect of distorting competition

Article 85 prohibits both conduct which is intended to affect trade between member states, and conduct which, although not based upon any such intention, in fact has, or is likely to have such an effect. As we have seen, in *Consten and Grundig* (above) there will be a breach of Art 85 even if an agreement is likely to increase trade between member states. Article 85 is, unlike Art 30, aimed not at restrictions on trade between member states as such, but at the use of restrictive agreements to partition markets and to distort the flow of trade which would normally take place in a genuine open market. The Court stated the underlying principle of Art 85 in *Züchner* v *Bayerische Vereinsbank AG* (Case 172/80):

> A basic principle of the EEC competition rules is that each trader must determine independently the policy which he intends to adopt on the common market and the conditions which he intends to offer to his customers. This does not prevent the traders adapting themselves intelligently to the existing or anticipated conduct of their competitors; it does, however, strictly preclude any direct or indirect contact between such traders the object or effect of which is to create conditions of competition which do not correspond to the normal conditions of the relevant market, in the light of the nature of the products or services offered, the size and number of the undertakings and the size of the market.

In cases where there is an attempt to rig the market by price-fixing and market-sharing agreements there is no problem in concluding that the object of any agreement or concerted action is the prevention, restriction or distortion of competition. Difficulties arise in identifying situations where, although there is no such attempt at market-distortion, the effect of an agreement may have the same, probably unintended, outcome. The intention of a sole-supply agreement may, for example, be that the supplier is repaid money that he may have lent the retailer and, at the same time, is guaranteed an outlet for his goods. A network of such sole-supply agreements across a member state, even if concluded between a large number of different suppliers and retailers, may have the effect of denying penetration of that market to producers in other member states of the goods which are subject to the agreements. This was the basis of the Court's reasoning in the *Brasserie de Haecht* case, (above), in relation to 'tied-houses' supplied by breweries in Belgium. In analysing the object and effect of an agreement the Court will look first to its content and then to its effect. Even if its terms do not indicate an intention to restrict or distort competition, its operation may have that effect. Factors such as the percentage of the market affected, the duration and terms of the agreements will all have to be assessed. In *Langnese-Iglo GmbH* v *Commission* (Case T-7/93) the Court of First Instance found that the applicant held more than 30 per cent of the market share of ice-cream sold through shops. These outlets were protected by a series of exclusive purchasing agreements under which the retailers bound themselves to sell only the applicant's ice-cream for two-and-a-half years and to use the freezer cabinets lent by the applicant only for the applicant's products. The Court concluded that, in view of the strong position occupied by the applicant in the relevant market and, in particular, its market share, the agreements contributed significantly to the closing-off of the market. A network of sole-supply agreements across a member state will, however, not automatically be regarded as providing an insurmountable barrier to market penetration from other member states. In *Sergios Delimitis* v *Henninger Bräu* (Case C 234/89) the Court emphasised that it was important to look at the state of the market in question to determine 'whether there are real concrete possibilities for a new competitor to penetrate the bundle of contracts'. (para [21]). An exclusive supply agreement may even, in some circumstances, assist in opening up competition.

In *Société Techniques Miniere* v *Maschinenbau Ulm GmbH* (Case 56/65) Maschinenbau Ulm (MU) agreed to give Société Technique Minière (STM) the exclusive right to sell its earth-moving equipment in France, on condition that STM should not sell competing machinery. The validity of the agreement was disputed in a French court, which referred the issue to the Court of Justice for a preliminary ruling. The Commission argued in the proceedings that the agreement in question breached Art 85. The Court did not agree. It described the two stages through which it was necessary to go to determine whether or not Art 85 was infringed. 'Object or effect' in this context are alternative not cumulative. It was first necessary to look at the precise purpose of the agreement, in the economic context in which it is to be applied. An intention to interfere with competition in the way prohibited by Art 85 was to be deduced, if at all, from the clauses of the agreement itself. If those clauses indicated an *intention* to restrict competition, the fact that the involvement of one of the participants had a negligible effect on competition, is irrelevant (*Usines Gustave Boël SA* v *Commission* (Case T-142/89)). If the agreement disclosed no such intention, or an effect on competition that was not 'sufficiently deleterious', the consequences of the agreement would then have to be considered. A consideration of those consequences would include, in the case of an exclusive sale agreement, the nature and quantity, limited or otherwise, of the products covered by the agreement, the position and importance of the grantor and the concessionaire on the market for the product concerned, the isolated nature of the disputed agreement or alternatively, its position in a series of agreements, the severity of the clauses intended to protect the exclusive dealership or alternatively, the opportunities allowed for other commercial competitors in the same products by way of parallel re-exportation and importation. In this case the Court also took into account the fact that there was here an attempt at market penetration in another member state and it doubted whether there was an interference with competition if the agreement 'was really necessary for the penetration of a new area by an undertaking'.

The *Société Technique Minière* case thus not only defined the relationship between the intention and the consequences of an agreement, but also introduced the concept of *de minimis* in the context of promoting the desirable objective of market penetration. In other words, a distributor of a new product in another member state may need some protection in order to get that product launched in the state. Essentially, the Court recognised that a balance needs to be struck in the legal control of agreements which appear, on their face, to be restrictive of competition, but which may, in fact, assist in promoting market integration and product distribution. Thus the limited restrictive effect of an agreement may be outweighed by its more beneficial long-term consequences. This has been described as a 'rule of reason'. As long as an agreement does not have as its object the restriction of competition, its anti-competitive effect may be outweighed by its ultimate competitive advantages. The apparently conflicting priorities contained within this rule of reason were considered by the Court in *Nungesser* v *Commission* (Case 258/78). In this case, there was an attempt to protect, in an agreement, techniques of cultivating new types of maize. An agreement conferring exclusive rights to the technique on Nungesser was challenged by the Commission, which concluded that its terms must, inevitably, breach Art 85. The Court disagreed with the Commission's approach. It decided that some protection for the licensee of the new technique for hybrid maize seeds was a necessary precondition for penetration by INRA, the developers of the technique, of the German market:

> The exclusive licence which forms the subject-matter of the contested decision concerns the cultivation and marketing of hybrid maize seeds which were developed by INRA after years of research and experimentation and were unknown to German farmers at the time when the co-operation between INRA and the applicants was taking shape ...
> In the case of a licence of breeders rights over hybrid maize seeds newly developed in one member state, an undertaking established in another member state which was not certain that it would encounter competition from other licensees for the territory granted to it, or from the owner of the right himself, might be deterred from accepting the risk of cultivating and marketing that product; such a result would be damaging to the dissemination of new technology and would prejudice competition in the Community between the new product and similar existing products. (paras [55] and [56] of judgment)

Given that the launching of the new seed and cultivation technique called for some protection for the licensee, did that mean that total protection of the production and distribution of the seed was justified? The Court would not go so far, citing its view in *Consten and Grundig* that absolute territorial protection granted to a licensee in order to enable parallel imports to be controlled and prevented, results in the artificial maintenance of separate national markets, in breach of the Treaty. It would, however, countenance the grant of an open exclusive licence, under which the grantor would not himself compete with the licensee in Germany and would not license anyone else there to do so. Such a license should not, however, contain an assurance by the grantor that he would protect the licensee from parallel imports, by preventing licensees in other member states from exporting to Germany. A limited approval by the Court has also been given to apparently restrictive franchise agreements, provided that the restrictions are no more than strictly necessary to ensure that the know-how and assistance provided by the franchisee do not benefit competitors, or which establish the control necessary for maintaining the identity and reputation of the network identified by the common name or symbol. However, provisions which share markets between the franchisor and the franchisee or between franchisees do breach Art 85 (*Pronuptia de Paris GmbH* v *Pronuptia de Paris Irmgaard Schillgalis* (Case 161/84)).

The list of agreements likely to breach Art 85(1)

Art 85(1) contains a list, in paragraphs (a) – (e) of the kind of agreements which will be prohibited. The cases examined so far range far beyond those described in that list, and it provides no more than a guide to the sort of agreements which will fall foul of the prohibition. However, with the help of the list and the case law of the Court of Justice, it is possible to come to some conclusions as to the type of agreement which may breach Art 85. A list indicative of the types of offending agreements could include:

- exclusive distribution agreements
- exclusive purchasing agreements
- exclusive licences of intellectual property rights (such as patents, copyright and trade marks)
- selective distribution agreements
- franchise agreements
- research and development agreements
- joint ventures on development
- joint sale and buying agencies
- information-sharing agreements

All of these types of agreement have been held at some time or other to be actually or potentially in breach of Art 85. If they are found to breach Art 85(1), they are, by Art 85(2) automatically void. The effect of this finding is that they cannot, for example, form the basis of a claim or a defence in contract in national courts. Art 85 was used in this way in both the *Brasserie de Haecht* and the *Société Technique Minière* cases (above). The Court is obliged, in many of the cases, to give an indication, on the basis of the facts (as found by the Commission) in the relevant market, and after weighing up all the relevant circumstances, of whether the agreement actually breached the prohibition. If it does breach Art 85(1) there always remains the possibility that it may, nonetheless be granted exemption by the Commission under Art 85(3).

The grant of exemptions under Article 85(3)

The object of Art 85(3), set out at the beginning of this chapter, is to provide criteria for the grant of exemption by the Commission. Essentially, exemption may be granted in cases where the anti-competitive effects of an agreement or concerted practice are outweighed by the economic benefit to consumers or the public at large. Exemption may either result from an individual decision of the Commission or as a consequence of an agreement falling within a type to which a block or group exemption has been granted. In order to obtain an exemption, undertakings which have entered into restrictive agreements must either make a formal application to the Commission or must draft their agreements to comply with the regulations which have been specifically drawn up by the Commission in such a way that an agreement in compliance with the regulation automatically obtains exemption without the necessity for a formal application. The grant of exemption will depend on the applicants satisfying four conditions:

1 The agreement must contribute to the improvement of the production or distribution of goods or the promotion of technical or economic progress.
2 The agreement must allow consumers a fair share of the resulting benefit.
3 The agreement must not impose upon the undertakings concerned restrictions which are not indispensable to the attainment of the above objects.
4 The agreement should not provide the undertakings with the possibility of eliminating competition in respect of a substantial part of the product in question.

These are all linked conditions which must, in each case, be satisfied (Commission Decision 73/323 *Prym-Werke* [1973] CMLR D250). Each agreement must be notified to the Commission and exemption obtained under the procedure established for the purpose under Arts 4, 19 and 21 of Regulation 17/62. Exemptions may only be granted for specific periods, conditions may be attached and the exemption may be renewed or revoked. Because of the delays of two or three years that may ensue following an application, and the practical problems attending the requirement that a fully reasoned decision must be given in each case, the Commission has tended to try to avoid formal decisions which are normally reserved for what are seen as important cases. In other cases a *comfort letter* will be issued after informal meetings with the parties concerned stating that, in the Commission's view, the agreement that has been notified does not infringe Art 85(1) at all or is of a type which falls within an exempt category. The file is then closed, although it may be re-opened if the legal, material or factual circumstances change. The parties are then entitled to rely upon the letter and enjoy a legitimate expectation that the Commission will take no further action. Comfort letters have only a limited legal status and since they are not 'Decisions' cannot be challenged in Art 173 proceedings in the Court of Justice (*SA Lancombe* v *ETOS BV* ('*Perfumes*') (Case 99/79)). Nor are opinions expressed in such letters 'binding on the national courts but constitute a factor which the latter may take into account in examining whether or not the agreements are in accordance with the provisions of Art 85'. The reliance which the parties can put on a comfort letter depends very much on the circumstances in which the letter was issued remaining the same. Any change in those circumstances, or any misrepresentation, will result in the re-opening of the file (*Langnese-Iglo* v *Commission* (Case T-73/93)

Besides meeting the formal requirements set out in (1) to (4) above, applications for exemption will also be examined in the light of the Commission's broader policy objectives in relation to agreements between undertakings. The Commission's aim is to encourage those agreements which favour the introduction of new technology resulting in better production methods, economies of scale, the faster or more effective development of new products or the process of change in older industries. Agreements which are highly unlikely to secure exemption are price-fixing agreements, agreements limiting production or controlling markets or which are aimed at retaining dominance in a national market. An example of an application that met both the specific and general criteria can be seen in *Prym-Werke* [1973] CMLR D250, [1981] 2 CMLR 217 (*see* also the *ACEC/Berliet* (Decision) [1968] CMLR D35; *Re Vacuum Interrupters (No. 2)* [1981] 2 CMLR 217). In *Prym-Werke*, Prym agreed to give up making needles and instead buy them from Beka, who agreed to supply Prym. Beka could than specialise in needle production. The Commission explained the approach it had adopted in its decision:

> … The concentration of manufacturing agreed on by Prym and Beka has, from the point of view of the improvement of production, favourable effects analagous to those of specialisation; it causes an increase of at least 50 per cent in the quantity of needles to be manufactured at the European factory, which makes it possible to make more intensive use of the existing plant and to introduce production-line manufacture.

The sort of application that will not attract approval from the Commission was considered by the Court of First Instance in *SPO* v *Commission* (Case T-29/92). In this case the applicants were a group of associations of building contractors in the Netherlands. Since 1952 they had had a body of rules with a view to organising competition. The rules were intended to 'promote and administer orderly competition, to prevent improper conduct in price tendering and to promote the formation of economically justified prices'. From 1980, these rules became binding on all contractors belonging to the member associations of the SPO. In 1988 the SPO notified its amended rules with a view, inter alia, to obtain an exemption under Art 85(3). The Commission rejected the application for exemption and found the SPO rules in breach of Art 85(1). The Court upheld this decision. It had no hesitation in finding that the provision of information to SPO by contractors submitting tenders for contracts which enabled other contractors to adjust their commercial behaviour and their prices amounted to unlawful concertation in the Netherlands building market affecting not just Dutch contractors but contractors wishing to tender from other member states. It therefore breached Art 85(1). The Court, applying the four criteria for exemption, also found the rules wanting. The applicants had argued that an open tendering system would necessarily lead to ruinous competition which would ultimately have adverse repercussions on contract awarders. The Court observed drily that it was impossible to distinguish between normal competition and ruinous competition as potentially, any competition is ruinous for the least efficient undertakings. That is why, by taking action to counteract what they regard as ruinous competition, the applicants necessarily restrict competition and therefore deprive consumers of its benefits.

Block exemptions

The four criteria for exemption are reflected in the Block Exemption Regulations. Block exemptions have come about as a result of the huge burden placed on the Commission by the requirement in Regulation 17/62 to investigate each application before delivering a decision. The delays caused great uncertainty for business and as a result the Commission has increasingly relied on its power to grant block exemptions by means of regulations.

The value of block exemptions is that undertakings can make their own assessment as to whether or not the agreement to which they are a party falls within the terms of an apparently relevant block exemption regulation. If the agreement is clearly within it, they do not need to notify it to the Commission and may treat it as *prima facie* valid and enforceable. If it falls outside any existing exemption they will have to apply to the Commission for individual exemption. The Commission does, however, remain free to decide that agreements which purport to fall within an existing block exemption do, in fact, fall outside it and to take the necessary action against the participants.

Eight major Block Exemption Regulations have been issued since 1983. They relate to exclusive distribution agreements (Regulation 1983/83), exclusive purchasing agreements (with special provisions relating to the supply of beer and petrol) (Regulation 1984/83), patent licensing agreements (Regulation 2349/84), selective distribution in the motor vehicle sector (Regulation 123/85), specialisation agreements (Regulation 417/85), research and development agreements (Regulation 418/85), franchise agreements (Regulation 4078/88) and know-how licensing agreements (Regulation 556/89), agreements in the insurance sector (Regulation 3932/92) and commercial air transport agreements (Regulation 1617/93). The pattern of Block Exemption Regulations is similar. They reflect both the content of Art 85(3) and the decisions of the Court of Justice in relation to individual applications concerning the activities covered by the regulation.

In the exclusive distribution agreement Regulation 1983/83, for example, the preamble emphasises the benefit to the consumer of continuity of supply and high-quality after-sales service and the value of such agreements to facilitate market-penetration in another member state by a new product (para (6)). At the same time, the regulation attempts to strike a balance between the restriction on competition that is necessary for these legitimate aims and those restrictions which are seen as anti-competitive. It makes clear that customers will only be assured of a fair share of the benefits resulting from exclusive distribution if parallel imports remain possible (recitals (11) and (12), Art 3). This reflects a persistent theme in the decisions of the Court of Justice *Consten SA and Grundig GmbH* v *Commission* (Cases 56 & 58/64);

Nungesser v *Commission* (Case 258/78)). The fact, however, that a distribution agreement falls within the terms of a Block Exemption Regulation, does not confer immunity under Art 85(1) on everything purported to be done under that agreement. If, for example, the operation of the agreement in practice excludes parallel imports, the effect of the agreement will still be to restrict competition (*P Automobiles Peugeot SA* v *Commission* (Case C- 322/93)).

Further reading

Bellamy, C. and Child, G., (1987) *Common Market Law of Competition*, Sweet & Maxwell, Chapters 1–6

Ehlermann, C. D., 'The Contribution of EC Competition Policy to the Single Market' (1992) 29 CML Rev 257.

Frazer, T., 'Competition Policy after 1992: the next step' (1990) 53 MLR 609.

Green, N., Article 85 in Perspective (1988) 9 ECLR 190.

Green, N., Hartley, T. C., and Usher, J.A., (1991) *The Legal Foundations of the Single Market, Pt III* OUP.

Steiner, J., (1994) *Textbook on EC Law*, (4th edn) Blackstone Press, Chapter 13.

Tillotson, J., (1993) *European Community Law; Text, Cases and Materials*, Cavendish Publishing Ltd, Chapter 14.

Weatherill, S., (1994) *Cases and Materials on EC Law*, (2nd edn) Blackstone Press, Chapter 11.

Weatherill, S., and Beaumont, P., (1995) *EC Law* (2nd edn) Penguin Books, Chapter 22.

Whish, R., (1993) *Competition Law*, Butterworths, Chapter 1.

Wyatt, D., and Dashwood, A., (1993) *European Community Law*, (3rd edn), Sweet & Maxwell, Chapter 14.

19 Competition law: abuse of a dominant position (Article 86)

Article 86 provides that:

Any abuse by one or more undertakings of a dominant position within the common market or in a substantial part of it shall be prohibited as incompatible with the common market in so far as it may affect trade between member states. Such abuse may, in particular, consist in:

(a) directly or indirectly imposing unfair purchase or selling prices or other unfair trading conditions;

(b) limiting production, markets or technical development to the prejudice of consumers;

(c) applying dissimilar conditions to equivalent transactions with other trading parties, thereby placing them at a competitive disadvantage;

(d) making the conclusion of contracts subject to acceptance by the other parties of supplementary obligations which, by their nature or according to commercial usage, have no connection with the subject of such contracts.

There are three key elements in Article 86. There must be:

1 a dominant position;
2 an abuse of that position and
3 the abuse must affect trade between member states.

Whereas Art 85 is directed at co-operation between nominally competing businesses, which has the effect of diminishing or distorting competition, Art 86 is aimed at the position and conduct of one undertaking. Essentially, Art 86 is not concerned with the *fact* of monopoly power in the Community, but *abuse* of that monopoly or dominant position. To determine whether or not that has occurred each of the key elements mentioned will have to be analysed and applied to the relevant circumstances.

A DOMINANT POSITION

The concept of dominance must be viewed in the context of the relevant market for the goods or services produced or distributed by the undertaking the conduct of which is in question. The Court of Justice in *United Brands* v *Commission* (Case 27/76), at para 65, defined a dominant position as:

> A position of economic strength enjoyed by an undertaking which enables it to hinder the maintenance of effective competition on the relevant market by allowing it to behave to an appreciable extent independently of its competitors and customers and ultimately of consumers.

To determine whether or not an undertaking is 'dominant' one has, therefore, to look at the relevant product market. A useful example for this exercise is the case of *United Brands Co.* v *Commission* (Case 27/76). United Brands Co. (UBC), at the time of the Commission's investigation, was a conglomerate which handled 40 per cent of the EC banana trade. In some member states – the Benelux countries, Germany, Denmark and Ireland – its share of the banana market was much greater. The Commission accordingly concluded that it enjoyed a dominant position in the banana market which, on the facts, it was abusing. UBC challenged the decision on a number of grounds, inter alia, that it did not enjoy a dominant position in the fruit market, which was the proper context for the examination of its position. Bananas compete with other fresh fruit in the same shops, on the same shelves, at prices which can be compared, satisfying the same needs: consumption as a desert or between meals. On the other hand, the Commission contended that there is a demand for bananas which is distinct from the demand for other fresh fruit, especially as the banana is a very important part of the diet of certain sections of the Community, especially the very young and the very old. The specific qualities of the banana influence customer preference and induce him not to readily accept other fruits as a substitute. The Court accepted the Commission's argument that the relevant market was in bananas, and not in fruit generally:

> For the banana to be regarded as forming a market which is sufficiently differentiated from other fruit markets, it must be possible for it to be singled out by such special features distinguishing it from other fruits that it is only to a limited extent exchangeable with them and is only exposed to their competition in a way that is hardly perceptible.
>
> The ripening of bananas takes place the whole year round without any season having to be taken into account. Throughout the year production exceeds demand and can satisfy it at any time. Owing to this particular feature the banana is a privileged fruit and its production and marketing can be adapted to the seasonal fluctuations of other fresh fruit which are known and can be computed. There is no unavoidable seasonal substitution since the consumer can obtain this fruit all the year round...It

follows from these considerations that a very large number of consumers having a constant need for bananas are not noticeably or even appreciably enticed away from the consumption of this product by the arrival of other fresh fruit on the market and that even the personal peak periods only affect it for a limited period of time and to a very limited extent from the point of view of substitutability.

Consequently the banana market is a market which is sufficiently distinct from the other fresh fruit markets. (paras [22], [23], [24], [25], [26], [34] and [35] of the judgment)

The most noticeable feature of this part of the judgment is the way in which the Court focuses on *product-substitution* as a primary determinant in isolating bananas as a separate market. There are two kinds of substitutability: (1) demand-side substitutabilty and (2) supply-side substitutability.

Demand-side substitutability determines which products compete with each other from the perspective of the consumer. The Commission normally refers to the criteria of price, quality and intended use as the determining factors. In the *UBC* case the relatively constant price and lack of seasonal variation, and the suitability and intended use for children and the elderly meant that other fruits could not be readily substituted for bananas. This test can result in a very narrow market definition in appropriate cases. In *Hugin Kassaregister AB* v *Commission* (Case 22/78), the Commission held Hugin in breach of Art 86 for its refusal to supply spare parts for Hugin cash registers to Liptons. It defined the relevant product market as consisting of spare parts for Hugin machines required by independent repairers. This finding was rejected by Hugin as too narrow. It insisted that the relevant market was the very competitive cash register market. The Court, however, accepted the Commission's market definition in relation to the independent repairers of Hugin machines:

> The role of those undertakings [the repairers] on the market is that of businesses which require spare parts for their various activities. They need such parts in order to provide services for cash register users in the form of maintenance and repairs and for the reconditioning of used machines intended for re-sale or renting out....It is, moreover, established that there is a specific demand for Hugin spare parts, since those spare parts are not interchangeable with spare parts for cash registers of other makes. (para [7])

The Court recently accepted that there was dominance in an equally narrow market of information on the content of BBC and RTE television programmes in *RTE and ITP* v *Commission* (Cases C-241/91 & C-242/91P).

Supply-side substitutability is concerned with the ability of a manufacturer to switch his production system from product A to product B, and therefore constitutes a test of whether the manufacturer of product A is a rival to the manufacturer of product B. In *Tetra-Pak International SA* v *Commission* (Case T-83/91), the Court rejected Tetra-Pak's argument that there were separate markets for aseptic cartons and the related packing machinery and non-aseptic cartons and packaging machinery because of the relative ease with which the manufacturer could switch from one to the other. Also, in *Europemballage and Continental Can* v

Commission (Case 6/72), the issue involved packaging containers and the scope of the market. The Court held that, in order to be regarded as constituting a distinct market, the products must be individualised, not only by the mere fact that that they are used in packing certain products, but by the peculiar characteristics of production which make them specifically suitable for this purpose:

> Consequently, a dominant position on the market for light metal containers for fish and meat cannot be decisive, as long as it has not been proved that competitors from other sectors of the market for light metal containers are not in a position to enter this market, by a simple adaptation, with sufficient strength to create a serious counterweight.

Whether or not supply-side substitutability exists is a matter of fact to be investigated by the Commission. In *Instituto Chemicoterapico Italiano SpA and Commercial Solvents Corporation* v *Commission* (Cases 6 and 7/73), an American company, CSC, and its Italian subsidiary cut off supplies of aminobutanol to another Italian company, Zoja. Aminobutanol is an effective and cheap raw material used in the production of ethambutol, a drug used for treating tuberculosis. The Commission alleged that CSC had an almost worldwide monopoly in amino-butanol, and was considering manufacturing ethambutol in Italy, through its subsidiary there. There were other drugs for the treatment of tuberculosis, but they were based on different but less effective raw materials. The Court of Justice decided that the relevant product market was the supply of aminobutanol, and not the production of ethambutol. It could not accept that Zoja could readily adapt its production faciles to other raw materials for the manufacture of ethambutol. Only if other materials could be substituted without difficulty could they be regarded as acceptable substitutes.

The geographical market

In order to decide whether or not the dominant position is held in a substantial part of the common market, it is necessary to look not only at the geographical extent of the market in question but also at the economic importance of the area as defined, the pattern and volume of the production and consumption of the relevant product and the habits of producers and consumers in that area. An area can be defined by factors which promote its geographical isolation. Factors tending to emphasise that isolation might be lack of transport facilities, or the cost of transportation relative to the value of a product, giving an unchallengeable advantage to local producers. The transport cost factor was held in *Suiker Unie* v *Commission* (Case 40-48) to be very significant in defining the geographical market. Conversely, in *Tetra-Pak International SA* v *Commission* (Case T-83/91) the Court of First Instance supported the Commission's finding that the geographical market consisted of the whole of the Community, because, inter alia, the very low cost of transport for cartons and machines meant that they could be easily and readily transported between states. Sometimes the geographical market can be readily identified as lying within the borders of a member state. In *NV Nederlandsche Banden-Industrie Michelin* v

Commission. (Case 322/81) the Court found that tyre companies operated in the Dutch market through local subsidiaries, to which local dealers looked for their supplies. It therefore upheld the decision of the Commission to regard the Netherlands as the area in which the competition facing NBIM was located.

Another factor identifying a separate geographical market is its homogeneity. Article 9 of Merger Regulation 4064/89 recognises this factor:

> The geographical reference market shall consist of the areas in which the undertakings concerned are involved in the supply and demand of products and services, in which the conditions of competition are sufficiently homogenous and which can be distinguished from neighbouring areas because, in particular, conditions of competition are appreciably different.

These features were significant in the *United Brands* case (*see* above) when the Court considered the geographical market. Looking at the banana market throughout the Community, the Commission had identified three states which had distinctive rules for the import and sale of bananas. Italy, which operated a national sytem of quota restrictions, the United Kingdom, which had a system of Common-wealth preference and France, which had a similar preferential system favouring the African francophone states. Only the then remaining six member states had a completely free market in bananas. France, Italy and the United Kingdom were therefore excluded from the analysis by the Commission and the other six states were identified as the relevant geographical market. The Court supported this finding on the basis that ' … although the applicable tariff provisions and transport costs are of necessity different but not discriminatory … and … the conditions of competition are the same for all … (T)hese six states form an area which is sufficiently homogenous to be considered in its entirety'. (paras [52] and [53]).

Dominance in fact

Besides the ability to operate independently of its rivals, another indicator of dominance is the extent of market share. The larger this is, the more likely, and well-founded, will be an acceptance of dominance. In *Hoffmann-La Roche* v *Commission* (Case 85/76), the company's market shares over a three-year period of 75 per cent to 87 per cent were held to be so large that they were, in themselves, evidence of a dominant position. Whereas, in *United Brands*, a market share of between 40 and 45 per cent did not 'permit the conclusion that UBC automatically controls the market'. However, in *Tetra-Pak* (above), the company's 90 per cent share of the market in aseptic cartons and the relevant packaging machines made it 'an inevitable partner for packers and guaranteed it the freedom of conduct characteristic of a dominant position'.

Besides market share, there are a number of other factors indicative of actual dominance of the market. These will include ownership of, or ready access to, massive financial resources. In addition a firm's ability to establish and maintain a lead in product development or technical services may well contribute to the maintenance of a dominant position. The process of using financial resources or a technical advantage to maintain a dominant position could well, however, also constitute an abuse of that position.

ABUSE OF A DOMINANT POSITION

Art 86 (a) – (d) provides a non-exhaustive list of the sort of conduct which will constitute an abuse of a dominant position. It is primarily concerned with unfair trading practices, such as imposing unfair purchase or selling prices, restricting production to create an artificial shortage and discriminating unfairly between different trading partners. It was originally thought that Art 86 applied exclusively to practices which constituted an abuse of market power, rather than with activities intended to gain or maintain dominance. However, in *Continental Can* (above), the Court rejected such a narrow interpretation of Art 86 and declared that '...the provision is not only aimed at practices which may cause damage to consumers directly, but also at those which are detrimental to them through their impact on an effective competitive structure, such as is mentioned in Art 3 (f) of the Treaty'. Article 3 (f) (now 3 (g)) speaks of 'the institution of a system ensuring that competition in the internal market is not distorted'.

> Abuse may therefore occur if an undertaking in a dominant position *strengthens such position in such a way that the degree of dominance reached substantially fetters competition* i.e., that only undertakings remain in the market whose behaviour depends on the dominant one. (emphasis added)

In *Continental Can* the conduct complained of was an agreement by Continental Can to buy a competitor in the food packaging market that would, in the Commission's view, have enabled it to achieve absolute dominance in its sector of the market. The Court accepted, in principle, that this sort of conduct could breach Art 86, but decided, on the facts of the case, that the Commission had chosen the wrong relevant product market.

It should, however, be noted that gaining or maintaining dominance is not, *per se*, in breach of Art 86. In *Gottrub Klim Grovvareforening* v *Dansk Landbrugs Grovvaresel* (Case C-250/92) the Court held that the conduct of a co-operative of growers that dominated the market of purchasers for certain agricultural supplies was not in breach of Art 86. The co-operative had strengthened its own statutes to reduce competition from members who had left the cooperative. The Court held that 'neither the creation nor the strengthening of a dominant position is in itself contrary to Art 86 EC Treaty'. 'The activities of co-operative purchasing organisations may actually encourage more effective competition on some markets, provided that the rules binding members do no more than is necessary to ensure that the cooperative functions properly and maintains its contractual power in relation to producers.'

What is important is the effect of achieving or maintaining dominance. The Court explored the concept further in *Hoffmann–La Roche* v *Commission* (Case 85/76), where it stated:

> The concept of abuse is an objective concept relating to the behaviour of an undertaking in a dominant position where, as a result of the very presence of the undertaking in question, the degree of competition is weakened and which, through recourse to methods different from those which condition normal competition in products and services on the basis of the transactions of commercial operators, has the effect of hindering the maintenance of the degree of competition still existing in the market or the growth of that competition.

Specific abuses

Art 86 contains a number of examples of the type of conduct by an undertaking in a dominant position which constitutes an abuse. The list is exemplary and not exhaustive, but it provides a useful starting point for an examination of abusive practices.

(1) The imposition of unfair purchase or selling prices

The most obvious abuse by a supplier in a monopoly position is the imposition of extortionate prices on consumers. There is an element of subjectivity in any assessment of what is a fair price, but in *United Brands*, the Court declared that a price is excessive where 'it has no reasonable relation to the economic value of the product supplied'. In determining the economic value, one had to take into account the difference between the costs actually incurred and the price charged. A price may also be excessive if it is not attributable to ordinary market conditions. In *Tetra-Pak*, the Court of First Instance found that the very great disparity in charges between the prices paid by Italian purchasers and those paid elsewhere in the Community could not be explained by additional market or transport costs in Italy, but were derived simply from Tetra-Pak's dominance in that country. The prices charged in Italy were, essentially, discriminatory.

In relation to prices for services, an undertaking would be abusing its dominant position if it charged fees which were disproportionate to the economic value of the service provided. In *Société Civile Agricole de la Crespelle* v *Coopérative d'Elevage de la Mayenne* (Case C-323/93), artificial insemination centres providing bovine semen which enjoyed a virtuual monopoly under national legislation in each region of France were held by the Court to be abusing their position if they were to charge additional costs over and above those actually incurred in obtaining and conserving semen imported from other member states.

Unnaturally low prices may also amount to an abuse, where they are intended to drive an actual or potential competitor from the market. This practice is normally called 'predatory pricing'. A good example of this is the case of AKZO *Chemie BV* v *Commission* (Case C-62/86). Here, the Commission found that AKZO occupied a dominant position in the market for flour additives and for organic peroxides used in the making of plastics. Another company, ECS, which was already in the flour additives market, wished to enter the peroxide for plastics market in the United Kingdom. The Commission found that AKZO had made direct threats to ECS, and systematically offered and supplied flour additives to ECS's customers at abnormally low prices and had also offered them products which it did not normally supply at below cost price. The Court repeated its previously stated position that Art 86 prohibits a dominant undertaking from eliminating a competitor and thus reinforcing its position by means other than competition on merit. In that sense, not all price competition can be regarded as legitimate.

> Prices lower than the average total costs by which a dominant undertaking seeks to eliminate a competitor must be regarded as an abuse. A dominant undertaking has no interest in offering such prices except to eliminate its competitors in order then to raise its prices again on the basis of its monopolistic position, since every sale involves it in a loss, namely all the fixed costs and at least a part of the variable costs relating to the unit produced.

(2) Exclusive supply

It is not uncommon for suppliers to give discounts to customers who place large orders with them and indeed there is nothing wrong, in principle, with such arrangements. But if the discount is tied to a requirement that the purchaser has to purchase all or a very large part of his supplies from the dominant undertaking, then the arrangement may very well fall foul of Art 86. In *Hoffman-La Roche* (Case 85/76) the investigation by the Commission revealed that the company, which was the largest producer of pharmaceuticals in the world, occupied a dominant position in markets for a number of vitamin products. It sold these products on the basis that customers were bound by an exclusive or preferential purchasing commitment in favour of the company for all or a large proportion of their requirements. This was achieved either by an express exclusive purchase agreement, or as a result of 'fidelity rebates'. The Court rejected these arrangements, since the discounts did not reflect any real cost saving as a result of a bulk purchase (i.e. transport, storage etc) but were a direct attempt to 'buy' the exclusive custom of the purchaser.

Similarly, in *Michelin* v *Commission* (Case 322/82), the company gave target bonuses to its dealers according to their marketing efforts. Dealers were not given a clear indication of the basis on which such bonuses were calculated. The Commission found that the system had the effect of ensuring that the dealers remained attached to Michelin in the hope of receiving the often unknown, but hoped-for bonuses. The Court accepted the Commission's finding and ruled that discounts had to be justified by a benefit conferred on the supplier which reduced the supplier's costs and enabled the supplier to pass on the benefit in terms of reduced prices. Across-the-board discounts on a range of products are also an abuse, because they make it more difficult for other suppliers who may not have a similar range of products to compete for an opportunity to supply.

(3) Tied sales

These are specifically prohibited by Art 86 (d), which forbids 'making the conclusion of contracts subject to acceptance by the other parties of supplementary obligations which by their nature or according to commercial usage, have no connection with the subject of such contracts'. Typically, this applies to an arrangement under which the supplier requires the purchaser to purchase its requirements of a second product (the 'tied' product) as a condition of being able to buy a first product (the 'tying' product). In *Tetra-Pak* (Case T-83/91), the Commission had found that Tetra-Pak held approximately 90 per cent of, inter alia, the market of machines for making aseptic cartons for liquids. Purchasers of such machines were required to obtain their supplies of cartons exclusively from Tetra-Pak or from a supplier designated by it. The Court declared:

> ... It is clear that the tied-sale clauses [in the agreements with purchasers] ... went beyond their ostensible purpose and are intended to strengthen Tetra-Pak's dominant position by reinforcing its customers' economic dependence on it. Those clauses are therefore wholly unreasonable in the context of protecting public health and also go beyond the recognised right of an undertaking in a dominant position to protect its commercial interests. Whether considered in isolation or together, they were unfair.'

(4) Refusal to supply

Whether or not a dominant undertaking's refusal to supply another undertaking is an abuse or not will be very much a matter of fact, depending on the circumstances of the refusal and the previous dealings of the parties. In *Commercial Solvents Corporation* v *Commission* (Cases 6 and 7/73), the Corporation had decided to discontinue sales of aminobutanol to another manufacturer, Zoja, because it has decided to manufacture its derivative, ethambutol, itself. The Court held that the decision to manufacture ethambutanol itself did not justify a refusal to supply the raw material to a potential rival. To do so would effectively eliminate one of the principal manufacturers of ethambutanol in the Community. There may, however, be objectively justifiable reasons for not supplying a commodity.

In *BP* v *Commission* (Case 77/77), BP refused to sell oil to an intermittent purchaser during the oil crisis in the early 1970s. There was, effectively, an oil embargo of Western Europe and BP had drawn up a list of regular customers whom it would continue to supply, and others whom it would not, or would only supply as and when it was able. The Court of Justice held that, in such a supply crisis, a refusal to supply was justified. There must, however, be an objective justification for a refusal. In *United Brands* v *Commission* (Case 27/76), the issue, it will be remembered, was the nature of the banana market (*see* above) and a number of alleged abuses by UBC. One of these was refusal to supply certain, hitherto, regular customers. One of these, Olesen, had participated in an advertising campaign run by one of UBC's rivals and it was this participation that UBC wished to 'punish'. The Court rejected this attempted justification of a refusal to supply:

> Although it is true, as the applicant points out, that the fact that an undertaking is in a dominant position cannot disentitle it from protecting its own commercial interests if they are attacked, and that such an undertaking must be conceded the right to take such reasonable steps as it deems appropiate to protect its said interests, such behaviour cannot be countenanced if its actual purpose is to strengthen this dominant position and abuse it.
>
> Even if the possibility of a counter-attack is acceptable, that attack must still be proportionate to the threat taking into account the economic strength of the undertakings confronting each other.
>
> The sanction consisting of a refusal to supply by an undertaking in a dominant position was in excess of what might, if such a situation were to arise, reasonably be contemplated as a sanction for conduct similar to that for which UBC blamed Olesen.

Another example of a refusal to supply being used to retain dominance in a market occurred in a decision which did not go to the Court of Justice *British Brass Band Instruments* v *Boosey and Hawkes* [1988] 4 CMLR 67. In this decision, the Commission found that Boosey and Hawkes produced and sold 90 per cent of the market in British brass band instruments (BBBI). The BBBI wished to import and distribute brass band instruments originating in other parts of the Community. Boosey and Hawkes refused to continue to supply the BBBI with British instruments until it desisted in its importation and sale of Continental brass band instruments. The Commission found the discontinuance of supply abusive. Where an undertaking has a monopoly of information, a refusal to supply that information to a potential publisher of television programmes can constitute a refusal to supply under Art 86(b) (RTE & *ITP* v *Commission* (Cases C-241/91P and C-242/91P)).

(5) Other abusive practices

The ingenuity of undertakings seeking to extend their dominance and to exclude competitors makes it impossible to provide more than some examples of common abusive practices. In *Tetra-Pak International SA* v *Commission* (Case T-83/91), for example, besides the tying agreements and excessive and predatory pricing which have already been considered, Tetra-Pak was found by the Commission to have engaged also in the following abusive practices: buying back competitors' machines with a view to withdrawing them from the market; obtaining an undertaking from one of the dairies with which it did business not to use two machines it had acquired from competitors of Tetra-Pak; eliminating in Italy all Resolvo aseptic packaging machines developed by a rival comapany; and finally, appropriating advertising media by obtaining an exclusive rights agreement with an Italian milk industry journal under which Tetra-Pak's rivals would not be allowed to advertise in the journal.

AFFECTING TRADE BETWEEN MEMBER STATES

As with Art 85, there must be some effect on trade between member states for Art 86 to apply. To satisfy this condition, it is not necessary that the effect on trade should be of a particular kind. Typically, it would meet the requirement if the effect of the conduct would be to partition markets in the Community. In *Greenwich Film Production* v *SACEM* (Case 22/79), SACEM was an association formed to collect royalties arising out of the performance of artistic and other works in France and elsewhere. SACEM demanded payment of royalties arising out of the performance of music in films distributed in France. Greenwich argued that SACEM effectively had a monopoly of such rights in France and was abusing its position. SACEM contended, inter alia that even if this was so, it did not affect trade between member states. The Court, however, accepted that there might be some effect. It recognised that in certain member states organisations such as SACEM were entrusted by composers to supervise performances of their work and to collect royalties. It held that it is possible in those circumstances that 'the activities of such associations may be conducted in such a way that their effect is to partition the common market and thereby restrict the freedom to provide services which constitutes one of the objectives of the Treaty'.

This will not be the case where the activites are exclusively directed at part of a member state. In *Hugin* v *Commission* (Case 22/78), the Commission had found that Hugin, the Swedish manufacturers of cash registers, had refused to supply spare parts of their machines to a London based firm, Liptons. Liptons serviced, repaired and re-conditioned such machines. Their business was essentially local, and they did no work outside the United Kingdom. The Court concluded that the abuse did not have the effect of preventing Liptons from carrying out their servicing in other member states or affect the trade in parts between member states, because those requiring the parts would normally obtain them direct from the manufacturers in Sweden (which was not, then, of course, either in the Community or the European Economic Area).

Relationship between Articles 85 (1) and 86

It is clear that many undertakings in a dominant position will endeavour to reinforce that position by various kinds of loyalty, tying and other agreements. Such agreements in themselves may infringe Article 85(1) or they may also constitute forms of abusive behaviour which breaches Art 86. On the other hand, agreements between undertakings and subsidiaries may not breach Art 85 simply because they are subsidiaries, and their action is seen as the action of one and the same entity: *Viho Europe BV* v *Commission.* In such circumstances, the agreement between a parent company and subsidiaries, may, however, where it is intended to drive or exclude a competitor from the market, constitute an abuse of a dominant position. In *Instituto Chemioterapico Italiano and Commercial Solvents Corporation* v *Commission* (Cases 6 and 7/73), it was CSC, the controlling company, which had instructed its subsidiary ICI not to supply aminobutanol to Zoja.

An agreement between several undertakings, each of which has a powerful position in a particular market, may come close to creating dominance which may then be subject to abuse by them. Article 86, indeed, refers to abuse by 'one or more undertakings'. However, the undertakings involved are more likely to be penalised for a breach of Art 85 (1) than a breach of Art 86 (Commission decision on *Italian Flat Glass* [1990] 4 CMLR 535). The nearest the Court has come to accepting a breach of Art 86 where there is a linkage of several undertakings is in the case of an actual or proposed merger of those undertakings (*see,* for example, *Continental Can* (Case 6/72)). Tacit collusion between major undertakings comprising, in effect, a tight oligopoly, may be difficult for the Commission to deal with. In *Hoffman-La Roche* (Case 85/76) the Court declared (in response to Advocate-General Lenz's observation that there was a problem in knowing where a collective monopoly ends and an oligopoly begins):

> A dominant position must also be distinguished from parallel courses of conduct which are peculiar to oligopolies in that in an oligopoly the courses of conduct interact, while in the case of an undertaking occupying a dominant position the conduct of the undertaking which derives profits from that position is to a great extent determined unilaterally.

In the absence of clear evidence, a concerted practice breaching Art 85 (1) may not be demonstrable. If that is the case, then, *a fortiori,* an abuse by connected undertakings cannot be shown to breach Art 86.

Mergers

A merger takes place when two or more undertakings which were formerly independent are brought under common control. As a result of the decision of the Court of Justice in *Continental Can* (above), it was clear that a merger between undertakings could, in the appropriate circumstances, breach Art 86. What those circumstances were became the subject, after prolonged discussions, of a new Council regulation on mergers (Council Regulation 4064/89, on the control of concentrations between undertakings). Under the regulation, the Commission is given sole competence to take decisions with regard to 'concentrations with a Community dimension'.

Such concentrations may be viewed from two perspectives. On the one hand, the combined economic strengths of fully merged undertakings, or the co-operation between undertakings which have partly merged, may produce a degree of market control and distortion of competition that is detrimental to the effective operation of the market. On the other hand, the merger may produce economies of scale, and result in the creation of an undertaking whose size and strength may enable it to compete effectively on world markets. In considering the effect of a merger under the regulation the Commission has to strike a balance between competing objectives.

Art 2 (1) of the regulation requires the Commission to make an appraisal of the proposed merger, taking into account:

(a)   the need to maintain and develop effective competition within the common market in view of, amongst other things, the structure of all the markets concerned and the actual or potential competition from undertakings located either within or outwith the Community;

(b)   the market position of the undertakings concerned and their economic and financial power, the alternatives available to suppliers and users, their access to suppliers or markets, any legal and other barriers to entry, supply and demand trends for the relevant goods and services, the interests of the intermediate and ultimate consumers, and the development of technical and economic progress provided that it is to consumers' advantage and does not form an obstacle to competition.

Concentrations which do, or do not, create or strengthen a dominant position impeding or limiting competition are to be declared by the Commission to be compatible with the common market, or incompatible, according to the facts as found by the Commission (Art 2 (2), (3)).

The Community dimension of a merger is achieved when the aggregate world-wide turnover of all the undertakings concerned is more than 5,000 million ECU and the aggregate Community-wide turnover of at least two of the undertakings involved is more than 250 million ECU, unless each of the undertakings concerned achieves more than two-thirds of its aggregate Community-wide turnover in one and the same member state.

The regulations have not, to date, constituted much of a barrier to mergers and the vast majority of the mergers notified to the Commission have obtained clearance. The Commission seems to see the mergers as a way of reducing national control of undertakings and promoting the strength of large Community under-takings on the world market. Less attention appears now to be paid to the possible adverse effects on consumers in the Community. One of the few cases where the Commission denied clearance, *Aerospatiale-Alenia-de Haviland* [1992] 4 CMLR M2, on the grounds that the merger would have had an unacceptable impact on customers' freedom of choice and the balance of competition in the Community, was widely criticised by governments, many with clear political interests in a different outcome than that resulting from the decision.

Further reading

Baden Fuller, C.W., 'Article 86 EEC: Economic Analysis of the Existence of a Dominant Position' (1979) 4 EL Rev 423.

Brittan, Sir Leon., 'The Law and Policy of Merger Control in the EEC' (1990) 15 EL Rev 351.

Downes, T.A. and Ellison, J. (1991), *The Legal Control of Mergers in the European Communities* Blackstone Press.

Goyder, D.G. (1993), *EEC Competition Law*, (2nd edn), OUP.

Gyselen, L. and Kyriazis, N., Article 86 EEC: 'The Monopoly Power Measurement Issue Revisited' (1986) 11 EL Rev 134.

Plender, R. and Usher, J. (1993), *Cases and Materials on the Law of the European Communities*, Butterworths, Chapter 11.

Sharpe, T., 'Refusal to Supply' (1983) 99 LQR 36.

Siragusa, M., 'The Application of Article 86 to the Pricing Policy of Dominant Companies' (1979) 16 CML Rev 179.

Tillotson, J. (1993), *European Community Law: text, cases and materials*, Cavendish Publishing Ltd, Chapters 15 and 16.

Weatherill, S. (1994), *Cases and Materials on EC Law*, Blackstone Press, Chapter 12.

Weatherill, S. and Beaumont, P. (1993), *EC Law* (2nd edn), Penguin Books, Chapter 23.

Whish, R. (1993), *Competition Law*, Butterworths, Chapter 8.

Wyatt, D. and Dashwood, A. (1993), *European Community Law*, (3rd edn), Sweet & Maxwell, Chapter 15.

20 Enforcement of competition law by the European Commission

The European Commission has a general duty, imposed on it by Art 89(1) 'to ensure the application of the principles laid down in Arts 85 and 86'.

Art 89(1) requires that:

> On application by a member state or on its own initiative, and in co-operation with the competent authorities in the member states, who shall give it their assistance, the Commission shall investigate cases of suspected infringement of these principles. If it finds that there has been an infringement, it shall propose appropriate measures to bring it to an end.

Under Art 89(2), if the infringement is not brought to an end, the Commission is required to record details of the infringement in a reasoned decision and to authorise member states to take the necessary measures to remedy the situation.

Article 89 enables the Commission to make the appropriate decision, but it does not confer specific investigative powers, define the investigative process or prescribe any means of enforcement by the Commission. These powers and duties are conferred on the Commission by Regulation 17/62, and, with the exception of transport (subject to a special process under Regulation 141/62) they apply to all investigations by the Commission.

INITIATING ACTION BY THE COMMISSION

Where an apparent breach of Arts 85 or 86 has come to the notice of the Commission through, for example, a question by a member of the European Parliament, or a report in the press, the Commission can, under the general power conferred on it by Art 89, commence an investigation. Article 3 of Regulation 17/62 provides that member states and 'natural and legal persons who claim a legitimate interest' may apply to the Commission to decide whether or not there has been an infringement. Since, however, the Commission has its own residual power to commence such an investigation, even a person who does not have a claim to a legitimate interest can bring details of a possible breach of Arts 85 or 86 to the attention of the Commission with an expectation that it will be investigated (*see* Hunnings, N.M., 'The Stanley Adams Affair or the Biter Bit' (1987) 24 CML Rev 65 (Adams' complaint ultimately resulted in a decision against his former employers); *Hoffmann-La Roche* (Case 85/76), and a claim against the Commission itself (*Adams* v *Commission* (Case 145/83) (*see* Chapter 23)).

Although the Commission is not obliged to investigate every complaint it receives, it must, when it does decide to open an inquiry, do so 'with the required care, seriousness and diligence in order to evaluate, in full knowledge, the elements of fact and law submitted for its assessment'. (*Asia Motor France* v *Commission (No. 2)* (Case T-7/92)). The element of care involves showing proper regard for the interests of both the complainant and the respondent in the proceedings. A growing number of decisions made by the Commission have, in recent years, been struck down by the Court and the Court of First Instance because proper procedural requirements have not been met. This has occurred partly because Regulation 17/62 is not at all specific as to how the rights of the parties should be respected during consideration of a complaint and the subsequent investigation. The regulation has, therefore, been 'fleshed' out by the Court, drawing on a variety of sources, including the European Convention on Human Rights, the International Covenant of Civil and Political Rights and the domestic constitutional systems of member states (*National Panasonic* v *Commission* (Case 136/79); *Orkem* v *Commission* (Case 374/87)). The Commission has had to learn by a process of trial and error whether its procedures met the evolving standards of the Court. The other reason for the failure of the Commission to meet the Court's procedural requirements has been the chronic shortage of resources which has, on occasion, compelled it to take short cuts in the process, and to rely increasingly on national anti-trust agencies and national courts to deal with infringements of competition law where there is both a national and Community dimension (*see* Shaw, J., 'A Review of Recent Cases on Arts 85 and 86: Procedural Issues' [1995] EL Rev 83, 84).

If the Commission decides to reject a complaint, it is required by Art 190 to give reasons for that decision. In *Tremblay and Others* v *Syndicat des Exploitants de Lieux de Loisirs (SELL)* (Case T-5/93) the Commission had received a number of complaints against the Société des Auteurs, Compositeurs et Editeurs de Musique (SACEM). The complainants, who ran discotheques throughout France, alleged that SACEM, which manages copyright in musical works in France, had infringed Arts 85 and 86. In response to the complaints, the Commission undertook an investigation and subsequently informed the complainants that its investigation provided no basis 'for concluding that the conditions for the application of Art 86 are fulfilled with regard to the level of tariffs at present applied by SACEM'. In relation to Art 85, the Commission told the complainants that the practices of which they complained were essentially national, there was no Community interest involved and the issues involved were, in any event, already before a number of French courts. The Court found that the decision did not give the applicants grounds for rejecting their complaint as to the alleged partitioning of national markets by reciprocal representation contracts made between various copyright management societies in different member states. It rejected the challenge to the Commission's finding of a lack of a sufficient Community interest and held that the fact that a national court or national competition authority is already dealing with a case concerning the compatability of an agreement or practice with Art 85 or 86 is a factor which the Commission may take into account in evaluating the extent to which a case displays a Community interest (*see Automec Srl v Commission (Automec No. 2)* (Case T-24/90); Shaw, J., 'Competition complaints: a comprehensive system of remedies?' (1993) 18 EL Rev 427; Friend 'Rights of Complainants in EC Competition Proceedings' (1994) 110 LQR 209.

A complainant has no right to insist that the Commission adopt a final decision as to the existence or otherwise of an alleged infringement. Where the Commission does not propose to initiate infringement proceedings, it is required by Art 6 of Regulation 99/63 to inform any complainants of its reasons and to fix a time limit within which they may submit further comments in writing. In such a case, if the Commission then decides that further investigation is unwarranted or unnecessary, it should provide a sufficiently reasoned decision to the complainant to enable its legality to be challenged in judicial review proceedings under Art 173 EC Treaty (*Ladbroke Racing (Deutschland) GmbH v Commission* (Case T-74/92)).

APPLICATIONS BY PARTIES TO A POSSIBLE INFRINGEMENT

Article 2 enables undertakings concerned with agreements which may breach Art 85 (1) or Art 86 to apply to the Commission for negative clearance. This may be followed by a formal grant of clearance. This consists of a decision by the Commission certifying that, on the basis of the facts in its possession, there are no grounds for action to be taken in respect of the agreement or conduct in question. The chief advantage of obtaining clearance is that activity can continue under an agreement or practice until the Commission makes a decision (Art 15(5), Regulation 17/62). If clearance is obtained, it provides a bar to action by the Commission while it is extant. The full facts must, however, be disclosed to the Commission. Failure to disclose them could result in revocation of the clearance and the imposition of a fine on the defaulting undertaking (Art 15(1)(a), Regulation 17/62).

Art 4 provides for the notification to the Commission of agreements, decisions and concerted practices defined by Art 85(1) EC Treaty and for which the parties seek a declaration under Art 85(3) that the agreement or practice is not subject to Art 85(1). A decision of this kind will be for a fixed period, but it may be renewed if the requirements of Art 85(3) continue to be satisfied (*see* above, Chapter 17). The Commission can revoke or amend its decision, or prohibit certain acts by the parties where there has been any change in the facts which formed the basis of the decision, where the parties have breached a condition attached to the decision, where the decision was based on incorrect information or was induced by deceit or where the parties abuse the exemption conferred on them by the decision (Art 8(3), Regulation 17/62).

The effect of application for negative clearance or for exemption under Art 85(3) may result in refusal of clearance or the granting of an exemption by the Commission or precipitate a demand for more information or even a full investigation.

The provision of information to the Commission

Article 11 of Regulation 17/62 is intended to assist the Commission in obtaining the information necessary to investigate a suspected infringement. Under it the Commission can obtain all necessary information from the governments of the member states and from undertakings and associated undertakings (Art 11(1)). The Commission is required, when making a request for information, to state the legal basis and the purpose of the request and also the penalties under Art 15(1)(b) for supplying incorrect information. The undertakings are under a legal obligation to supply the full information required, with a penalty for failure to do so (Art 11(4) and (5), Arts 15(1)(b) and 16(1)(c)). Non-co-operation in the supply of information can take the form of unhelpful replies to questions as well as an outright refusal to answer them. In *Scottish Football Association* v *Commission* (Case T-46/92), the Court of First Instance held that the Commission was under no obligation either to pursue lengthy informal correspondence or to engage in oral discussions with the applicant, who had provided only half the information requested. It could simply, as it had done in this case, demand the information on the basis of Art 11(5), on pain of a penalty of ECU 500 per day for non-disclosure.

The request for information must specify the kind of anti-competitive practice to which it relates and details of the request must be sent to the government of the member state in which the principal office of the undertaking is based (Art 11(2) and (3)).

In *Société General* v *Commission* (Case T-34/93), the Commission was making inquiries into the operation of the so-called Helsinki Agreement which fixed a differential system of charges made to payees of Eurocheques. This followed an investigation which had already resulted in the imposition by the Commission of heavy fines on other parties to the agreement and the abandonment of the agreement by French banks: Commission Decision 92/212 [1992] OJ 195/50 (*Groupement Bancaire and Europay* v *Commission* ('*Eurocheques*'); *see* Shaw, J., op. cit. p 68). It sent a letter to Société General requesting information about an apparently discriminatory charge imposed on a private payee and about the operation of another inter-bank agreement called the Package Deal Agreement. Société General refused to supply the information, even after the Commission had explained how it related to its investigation, and argued that a reply on the application of the Package Deal would infringe its rights as a defendant. The Court rejected both arguments, accepting that the Commission had adequately explained its purpose in requiring the information on charging practices. It held that the answers requested were purely factual and could not be regarded as capable of requiring the Société General to admit an infringement of the rules on competition.

The obligation to co-operate with the Commission in its inquiries extends to the provision of all relevant information, even that which might support a finding of an infringement. However, informants are not obliged to incriminate themselves. The issue of possible self-incrimination was raised in *Solvay* v *Commission* (Case 27/88) and *Orkem* v *Commission* (Case 374/87). The applicants in these cases argued that the Commission decisions requiring them to provide information under Art 11 sought to force them to incriminate themselves. The Court noted that Regulation 17/62 recognises no such right of non self-incrimination, but, instead, calls for active co-operation from the party investigated. The Court did, however, look at the issue in the context of the fundamental rights to which all Community law is subject. It decided that there was no such right in relation to legal persons (companies) where infringements of economic law are in issue. This distinction was criticised by the European Court of Human Rights in *Funke* v *France* (Case A/256-A) (in relation to the application of Art 6(1) ECHR) and it is doubtful if the *Orkem* decision is still good law (*see* also, *Société Stenuit* v *France* (1992) 14 EHRR 509 (a decision of the Human Rights Commission that fines imposed by the European Commission for breaches of competition law were of a criminal nature).

Whatever the extent of the application of the right against self-incrimination, the rules on the right of the defence do have the effect of not requiring those being investigated to make any admissions of infringement:

> While ... the Commission is entitled to oblige the company to furnish all necessary information relating to facts of which it is aware and, if necessary, to communicate to it the relevant documents in its possession even if these may be used to prove anti-competitive behaviour by it or another company, *it may not, by a request for information, compromise the rights of defence of a company. Thus, the Commission may not oblige a company to furnish replies by which it would be induced to admit the existence of the infringement which it is for the Commission to prove.* (*Solvay*, paras [31] and [32]), (emphasis added)

In *Société General* (above) the Court accepted that those under investigation were not obliged to accept the existence of an infringment of the rules of competition. However, there may well be a very fine line between admission of the facts which constitute the infringement and admission of the infringement itself.

The Commission's powers of investigation

The Commission can take a more pro-active role in the conduct of its inquiries by carrying out investigations in the territory of member states. Under Art 14 of Regulation 17/62 the Commission is authorised to undertake all necessary investigations of undertakings and associations of undertakings. To this end the officials authorised by the Commission are empowered:

1   to examine the books and other business records;
2   to take copies of or extracts from the books and business records;
3   to ask for oral explanations on the spot;
4   to enter any premises, land, and means of transport of undertakings. (Art 14(1))

Officials who are authorised by the Commission to act in relation to these powers are entitled to exercise them on production of an authorisation in writing, specifying the subject matter and purpose of the investigation and the penalties for not supplying or for supplying incomplete books and other business records. Undertakings are obliged to submit to investigations ordered by a decision of the Commission. In good time before the investigation the Commission has to inform the relevant authority in the host state and identify the officials concerned (Art 14(2) and (3)). Before the decision to conduct an investigation of this kind is made, the Commission must consult the relevent authority in the host state. That authority is bound to give every assistance to the Commission officials, especially where the undertaking concerned is opposing the investigation (Art 14(4), (5) and (6)).

In *Hoechst* v *Commission* (Case 46/87), two Commission investigators conducted a 'dawn raid' (during office hours!) on Hoechst in Germany on 15 January 1987, armed with the necessary decision under Art 14(3), for the purpose of investigating various suspected infringements relating to price fixing and market sharing in the market for PVC and polyethylene. Hoechst refused to submit to the investigation, on the grounds that it was a search which was illegal in the absence of a judicial warrant. On 17 January the investigators tried again, accompanied by two officials of the Federal Cartel Office and two policemen. Hoechst again refused to submit, for the same reason. A third attempt also failed. The Commission eventually obtained access following the issue of a search warrant to the Commission by the German Court. A year later the Commission imposed a fine of 55,000 ECUs on Hoechst for its refusal to submit to the investigation. Hoechst appealed to the European Court of Justice.

The Court re-affirmed its earlier rulings that fundamental rights, and the European Convention on Human Rights in particular, are part of the general principles of law. In interpreting Article 14 of Regulation 17/62, particular regard had to be had to the rights of the defence. It held that some rights of the defence, especially those relating to legal representation and the privileged nature of correspondence between solicitor and client had to be recognised from the preliminary inquiry stage of an investigation. Having said that, the Commission emphasised the importance of the Commission's investigative powers, and the need to secure access where their inquiries were thwarted:

> That right of access would serve no useful purpose if the Commission's officials could do no more than ask for documents or files which they could identify precisely in advance. On the contrary, such a right implies the power to search for various items of information which are not already known or fully identified. Without such a power, it would be impossible for the Commission to obtain the information necessary to carry out the investigation if the undertakings concerned refused to co-operate or adopted an obstructive attitude.

The Court made it clear that, where the Commission's entry is opposed, Commission officials cannot force an entry without first seeking the assistance of national courts. Those courts must, however, ensure that the Commission's actions are effective, and cannot substitute their own assessment of whether or not the investigation ordered by the Commission is necessary, since that function is the exclusive prerogative of the Commission, subject only to review by the Court of Justice itself. In these circumstances, therefore, the Commission requires a national warrant but the national courts are more or less obliged to grant it! The decision is, in many ways, an uncomfortable compromise between fundamental principles of national law and the need for effective Commission powers. In such cases there is an inevitable conflict between the need to give adequate notice to the person or body concerned of the purpose of the search (under Art 14(3)) on the one hand and, on the other, the difficulty of knowing precisely what is in the hands of the suspected undertaking and ensuring that it remains there when the officials arrive (for comment, *see* Forrester, I. and Norall, C., 'Competition Law' (1988) 9 YEL 271, 300; Shaw, J., (1990) 15 EL Rev 326; for parallel problems in English law, *see IRC v Rossminster* [1980] AC 952 (Lord Wilberforce)).

Information obtained in the course of an investigation must only be used for the purpose of the relevant request or investigation. The Commission is bound to publish its decisions, but it must make sure that it takes into account the legitimate interest of undertakings in the protection of their business secrets (Arts 20 and 21, Regulation 17/62). Although the Commission has a general obligation to send copies of the most important documents to member states, where an undertaking has expressly raised the confidentiality of a particular document containing business secrets with the Commission, the Commission may have to decide not to send a particular document or set of documents to the relevant member state (*Samenwerkende Elektriciteits-produktiebedrijven NV v Commission* (Case C-36/92P)). The obligation of secrecy is owed not only to undertakings under investigation, but also to informants and complainants (*Adams v Commission* (Case 145/83)).

THE RIGHT TO A HEARING

Before it adopts a decision applying Art 85 or 86, the Commission must, under Art 19 of Regulation 17/62, give the undertakings concerned the opportunity of being heard on the matters to which Commission has taken objection. If the Commission or the relevant authorities in the member states consider it necessary, they can also hear representations from other legal or natural persons, provided they can show a sufficient interest. Under Regulation 99/63 such representations will normally be in writing, although under Art 7 of Regulation 99/63 undertakings may, if they have requested it in their written submissions, or if the Commission proposes to impose a fine on them or a periodic penalty, put forward their arguments orally.

To enable undertakings to exercise their right to make representations effectively, they must be informed of the facts and considerations on the basis of which the Commission is minded to act (Art 2(1), Regulation 99/63; *NTN Toyo Bearing Company and other* v *Council and Commission (Ballbearings)* (Case 113/77) (A G Warner)).

In *Hoffmann-La Roche* v *Commission* (Case 85/76), the Court ruled that undertakings must be afforded 'the opportunity during the administrative procedure to make known their views on the truth and relevance of the facts and circumstances alleged and on the documents used by the Commission to support its claim that there has been an infringement'.

The duty of disclosure is not, however, absolute. There is a *class* of documents, including correspondence with member states and purely internal Commission documents which are regarded as confidential and which do not have to be disclosed. Other documents, such as correspondence with third-party undertakings, might legitimately be witheld where disclosure might lead to retaliation against them by the undertaking involved in the proceedings (*BPB Industries plc and British Gypsum Ltd* v *Commission* (Case C-310/93P)).

THE DECISION

There is a general principle of Community law contained in Art 190 that '... decisions ... shall state the reasons on which they are based'. They should also be made by the Commission according to the proper procedure and according to the proper form. Failure to observe these principles may render the decision a nullity from the start. In *Commission* v *BASF AG and Others* (Case C-137/92 P), the Court of First Instance had declared non-existent a Commission decision under which the applicants and others had infringed Art 85 in relation to the production of PVC

(Commission Decision 89/190/EEC of 21 December 1988). The Court of First Instance had found that the original decision had been altered after it had been adopted by the Commissioners 'by persons who were clearly not Commissioners'. The CFI also found that the contested decision had adopted the decision only in its English, German and French versions, leaving it to the Commissioner then responsible for competition, Mr Sutherland, to adopt the text of the decision in the other official langauges of the Community. The CFI noted that Mr Sutherland had no competence to do this and held that the measure was 'vitiated by particularly serious and manifest defects rendering it non-existent in law'.

The Commission appealed against this decision, and the appeal was allowed by the Court of Justice. The Court pointed out that, as a general rule, acts of the Community institutions are presumed to be lawful and productive of legal effects even if affected by irregularities, until such time as they are annulled or withdrawn. There was, however, an exception to that rule in relation to acts

> ... tainted by an irregularity whose gravity is so obvious that it cannot be tolerated by the Community legal order. [Such acts] ... must be treated as having no legal effect, even provisional, that is to say that they must be regarded as legally non-existent. The purpose of this exception is to maintain a balance between two fundamental, but sometimes conflicting, requirements with which a legal order must comply, namely stability of legal relations and respect for legality.

The Court emphasised the collegiate nature of the Commission's decision making process. It rejected the Commission's argument that in the decision making process the college of Commissioners can confine itself to making clear its intention without having to become involved in the drafting and finalisation of the act giving effect to its intention. After the final form of the decision had been approved by the Commissioners as a body, only simple corrections of spelling and grammar could be made to the text. In the event, however, the Court of Justice thought that the CFI had gone too far in holding the decision to be non-existent. It was, however, anulled on the same procedural grounds on which the CFI decision had been based.

If the Commission decides that there has been an infringement of Arts 85 or 86, the Commission may, under Art 3(1), Regulation 17/62, adopt a decision ordering the infringement to be brought to an end. Under Article 16 it can impose a periodic penalty payment of 50 to 1,000 units of account per day, from the date of the decision, until the infringement is brought to an end. It can also impose fines on the undertakings concerned.

FINES

The Commission has the power, by decision, to impose fines for intentionally or negligently supplying incorrect or misleading information, or for refusing to submit to an investigation (Art 15(1), Regulation 17/62). In cases where the Commission has found a breach of Arts 85 or 86, it may, by decision, impose on an undertaking or association of undertakings fines from 1,000 to 1,000,000 units of account, or a sum in excess of that figure, provided that this is no more than ten per cent of the turnover in the preceding year of each of the undertakings participating in the infringement. Fines can only be imposed where the undertakings have acted intentionally or negligently. The criteria for the appropriate level of fine should, the Court has stated, take into account in particular the nature of the restrictions on competition, the number and size of the undertakings concerned, the relative proportions of the market controlled by them and the situation in the market where the infringement was committed. (*ACF Chemiefarma* v *Commission* (Case 41/69)).

The Commission's policy on fines can be seen in *Welded Steel Mesh* (OJ 1989 L 260 p 1). In this case 14 companies in France, the Benelux, Germany and Italy shared markets between themselves, fixed prices and volumes and took action to enforce their cartel. The activities of the participants amounted to 'a sustained effort, carried on for a long period covering at least five years ... to frustrate ... one of the main aims of the Treaty, namely the creation of a common market, by interference in the price mechanism, restrictions on import penetration of one another's domestic markets, quantity restrictions and market sharing'. Mitigating factors were taken into account namely, the parties sometimes did not respect the price and quota regime they had established; the welded mesh sector had not been profitable; welded mesh was subject to competition from reinforced bars, which exercised price-restraint on the cartel; some companies had financial problems; one company gave the Commission some assistance in its investigations. All in all, the Commission decided not to impose 'very large' fines, and to set the fines 'considerably below the level which would normally be justified'. The fines imposed ranged from 1,375,000 ECUs to 13,000 ECUs (*see* Forrester, I. S., and Norall, C., 'Competition Law' (1989) 9 YEL 271, 286). One of the companies in the *Welded Steel Mesh* cartel was, however, successful in obtaining a reduction of the fine imposed on it, on the basis that the Commission had, by its conduct given the appellant cause to believe that the agreement was not unlawful (*Baustahlgewebe GmbH* v *Commission* (Case T-145/89)).

JUDICIAL REVIEW OF COMMISSION DECISIONS

Like any other legal act of the institutions, decisions made by the Commission in relation to alleged infringements, including findings of infringements and the imposition of fines and periodic penalties, are subject to judicial review. The Court of First Instance may review such acts under Art 173 EC Treaty. There is an appeal on a point of law to the Court of Justice itself in relation to decisions of the CFI. The

Court of First Instance, in reviewing the legality of the decision of the Commission, has the power not only to quash any decision, but to reduce or increase any fine imposed by the Commission (Art 172 EC, Art 17, Regulation 17/62 (*see* Chapter 23)).

Further reading

Forrester, I., and Norall, C., 'Competition Law' (1988) 9 YEL 271.

Friend, 'Rights of Complainants in EC Competition Proceedings' (1994) 110 LQR 209.

Harris, B., 'Problems of Procedure in EEC Competition Law' (1989) NLJ 1452.

Hunnings, N. M., 'The Stanley Adams Affair or the Biter Bit' (1987) 24 CML Rev 65.

Shaw, J., 'A Review of Recent Cases on Articles 85 and 86 EC: Procedural Issues' [1995] EL Rev 83.

Shaw, J., 'Competition Complaints: a Comprehensive System of Remedies?' (1993) 18 EL Rev 427.

Steiner, J., (1994) *Textbook on EC Law* (4th edn) Blackstone Press, Chapter 15.

Tillotson, J., (1993) *European Community Law: text, cases and materials*, Cavendish Publishing Ltd, Chapter 17.

Waelbroeck, D., 'New Forms of Settlement of Anti-Trust Cases and Procedural Safeguards: Is Regulation 17 Falling into Abeyance?' (1986) 11 EL Rev 268.

Weatherill, S., (1994) *Cases and Materials on EC Law* (2nd edn), Blackstone Press, Chapter 13.

Weatherill, S. and Beaumont, P., (1993) *EC Law* (2nd edn), Penguin Books, Chapter 24.

Wyatt, D. and Dashwood, A., (1993) *European Community Law* (3rd edn), Sweet & Maxwell, Chapter 16.

21 Co-operation between the European Commission and member states in the enforcement of competition law

THE ROLE OF THE COMMISSION IN RELATION TO NATIONAL COURTS

As we have seen in the previous chapter, the Commission is obliged, under Art 10, Regulation 17/62 to transmit to the authorities responsible for competition policy in the member states copies of any applications made to the Commission about the conduct of undertakings or, for example, for exemption under Art 85(3) EC in relation to agreements or concerted practices. The Commission is assisted by an Advisory Committee on Restrictive Practices and Monopolies composed of officials, drawn from a number of member states, competent in restrictive practices and monopolies. The Commission is under an obligation to carry out its procedures in close co-operation with the competent authorities in member states. These authorities have the right to express an opinion about the procedures adopted by the Commission during the course of an investigation (Art 10, Regulation 17/62).

The competition authorities in member states may also be asked by the Commission to assist in the carrying out of investigations initiated by the Commission. Under Art 13 of Regulation 17/62, national officials may be called upon to gather information on behalf of the Commission under Art 14, and may be assisted by Commission officials while doing so, if the Commission so requests. There is a general assumption that national authorities will co-operate with the Commission in the enforcement of competition law. National courts are also expected to co-operate with the Commission, as the Court explained in *Stergios Delimitis* v *Henninger Brau* (Case C-234/89):

> It should be noted in this context that it is always open to a national court, within the limits of the applicable national procedural rules and subject to Art 214 of the Treaty [prohibiting the disclosure of confidential business information], to seek information

from the Commission on the state of any procedure which the Commission may have set in motion and as to the likelihood of its giving an official ruling on the agreement in issue pursuant to Regulation 17. Under the same conditions, the national court may contact the Commission where the concrete application of Art 85 (1) or Art 86 raises particular difficulties, in order to obtain the economic and legal information which the institution can supply to it. Under Art 5 of the Treaty, the Commission is bound by a duty of sincere co-operation with the judicial authorities of the member state, who are responsible for ensuring that Community law is applied and respected in the national legal system. (para [53] of judgment)

In an important notice issued in 1993 on co-operation between national courts and the Commission in applying Arts 85 and 86 of the EC Treaty (OJ 1993 C 39 p 5) the Commission has expressed the view that, by encouraging more effective participation by national courts in the day-to-day application of Community competition law, it will free up the Commission to 'perform its administrative task, namely to steer competition policy in the Community' (para 34). Although the Commission accepts that national courts cannot grant exemptions under Art 85(3), it envisages that where an agreement or concerted practice is apparently in breach of Article 85(1), but may, nonetheless attract exemption under Art 85(3), or fall within some existing block exemption regulation, the Court can stay the proceedings to enable the Commission to reach a decision. The division of competence between national courts and the Commission and the criteria to be applied in deciding whether or not a national court should refer a case to the Commission were considered by the Court of Justice in *Fonderies Roubaix-Wattrelos* (Case 63/75):

The direct applicability of those provisions [Arts 85 and 86 EC Treaty] may not, however, lead the national courts to modify the scope of the exemption regulations by extending their sphere of application to agreements not covered by them. Any such extension, whatever its scope, would affect the manner in which the Commission exercises its legislative competence.
[47] It now falls to examine the consequences of that division of competence as regards the specific application of the Community competition rules by national courts. Account should here be taken of the risk of national courts taking decisions which conflict with those taken or envisaged by the Commission in the implementation of Arts 85(1) and 86, and also of Art 85(3). Such conflicting decisions would be contrary to the general principles of legal certainty and must, therefore, be avoided when national courts give decisions on agreements or practices which may subsequently be the subject of a decision by the Commission.
… The national court may have regard to the following considerations in applying Art 85. [50] If the conditions for the application of Art 85(1) are clearly not satisfied and there is, consequently, scarcely any risk of the Commission taking a different decision, the national court may continue the proceedings and rule on the agreement in issue. It may do the same if the agreement's incompatability with Art 85(1) is beyond doubt and, regard being had to the exemption regulations and the Commission's previous decisions, the agreement may on no account be the subject of an exemption decision under Art 85(3).

The question of whether or not to stay proceedings in an English court where an application has been made to the Commission for an exemption under Art 85(3) may raise difficulties for the court. In *MTV Europe* v *BMG Records (UK) Ltd* the plaintiff brought an action in damages for breach of Art 85. Although the agreement in issue had been notified to the Commission, no decision had yet been delivered on whether it attracted exemption under Art 85(3), and one was not likely for some time. The Commission's decision would be retrospective to the extent that the agreement could be validated from the date of notification, that validation could not be effective *prior* to notification. There was still a prospect that the plaintiff could recover damages in relation to that time. The Court (Evans-Lombe J), in inter-locutory proceedings, decided to continue with the case, despite the involvement of the Commission. It decided that the proceedings should continue until they reached the point of setting down for trial. If that point were to be reached before the Commission's decision, proceedings should at that point be stayed, and the stay should remain in effect until one month after the Commission's decision.

The Commission foresees that, although it will retain its overall function in competition law, and will co-operate with national courts and national authorities in supplying both factual and advisory information, individual claims alleging breaches of Community law by those who have suffered loss will increasingly be dealt with by national courts, and will, in its view, be better served by them. The reasons for preferring national courts (besides the lessening of the Commission's investigative burden) are:

1   The Commission cannot award compensation for loss suffered as a result of an infringement of Art 85 or 86. Such claims may be brought only before national courts. Companies are more likely to avoid infringements of the Community competition rules if they risk having to pay damages or interest in such an event.
2   National courts can usually issue interim orders to stop the infringment more quickly than the Commission.
3   Claims for breaches of Community law in national courts can usually be coupled with claims for breaches of national law. This cannot be done in procedures before the Commission.
4   In those member states where the successful party is awarded costs, these can be awarded in a claim for breach of Community law. A succesful complainant in administrative procedures before the Commission has no such right, although if the proceedings are taken to the Court of First Instance, costs may be awarded in relation to that Court.

The argument in favour of national courts as the primary fora for individual complaints is not, however, as clear cut as the Commission has maintained. As Riley has argued:

A complaint to the Commission can be very cheap. A complaint can be anonymous. Anonymity is of great importance when the complainant is one of a number of small businesses who are threatened by the practice of much larger competitors. In addition, the Commission has considerable fact-finding powers culminating in its power to carry out on-the-spot inspections under Art 14 of Regulation 17. (Riley (1993))

Whether the national courts are to have such an increasing role will depend, in the absence of Community legislation, on complainants' willingness to use them and on the degree to which the Court of Justice supports the Commission's approach. This may be seen in the Court's case law on the application of Arts 85 and 86 in those courts and in the allocation of functions between the Commission and national courts.

THE ROLE OF NATIONAL COURTS IN THE ENFORCEMENT OF COMMUNITY COMPETITION LAW

The Court has recently demonstrated some sympathy for the Commission's attempt to leave individual complaints which have a largely national dimension, although potentially affecting trade between member states, to the courts of the state most affected. In *Automec and Asia Motor France* v *Commission* (Cases T-24 & 28/90), the Court of First Instance held that the Commission was not under an obligation to commence proceedings to determine whether or not a violation of Community law has occurred. Where the national court would be able to rule on the compatability of a national distribution agreement for cars under Art 85(1) and provide the appropriate remedies if there was a breach, there was no need for Commission intervention. In *Tremblay* v *Commission* (Case T-5/93), the Commission had declined to investigate further an alleged abuse of a monopoly position enjoyed by the *Société des Auteurs, Compositeurs et Editeurs de Musique* (SACEM) in relation to musical copyrights on the grounds, *inter alia*, that the effects of the alleged infringements outside France were limited and that several cases raising the same issues were pending before the French courts. The Court supported this approach:

> The fact that a national court or national competition authority is already dealing with a case concerning the compatability of an agreement or practice with Art 85 and 86 of the Treaty is a factor which the Commission may take into account in evaluating the extent to which a case displays a Community interest. ... The Court considers that where the effects of the infringement alleged in a complaint are essentially confined to the territory of one member state and where proceedings have been brought before the courts and competent administrative authorities of that member state by the complainant against the body against which the complaint was made, the Commission is entitled to reject the complaint through lack of any sufficient Community interest, provided however that the rights of the complainant or its members can be adequately safeguarded, in particular by the national courts.

Article 85(1) and Art 86 are both directly effective in national courts and may be used both offensively and defensively. The availability remedies for private parties in national courts on the basis of Community competition rules arises from the decision of the Court of Justice in *BRT* v *SABAM* (Case 127/73). In this case, the Court held that Arts 85 and 86 are both horizontally and vertically effective. As a result of this decision, a party may claim that an agreement is void under Art 85(2), that an injunction should be granted to enforce the competition rules and that damages are payable for breach of Arts 85 or 86.

The Court noted in *Tremblay* (above) that the national court was a satisfactory forum provided the rights of complainants can be adequately safeguarded. This may not always be the case. In this context, Community law may have to eschew subsidiarity, and provide, for example, that national courts should operate on the basis of legal presumptions against defendants or deeming certain conduct to be an infringement of the competition rules, subject to rebuttal by the defendant, if they are to be as effective as the Commission under the powers conferred by Regulation 17/62.

RELATIONSHIP BETWEEN COMMUNITY AND NATIONAL COMPETITION LAW

The potential for conflict between national competition rules and those of the Community was addressed by the Court in *Walt Wilhelm* v *Bundeskartellamt* (Case 14/68). The case related to a dyestuffs cartel. The Court held that, since their objectives are different, national competition rules may be applied in parallel with those of the Community, but not so as to prejudice the uniform application of Community rules throughout the common market. In practice, this means that there must be a set-off between any fines which are imposed by the national courts and the Commission, so that the later sanctions take account of earlier ones:

> ... The case-law of the Court of Justice has accepted the possibility of concurrent sanctions resulting from two parallel procedures pursuing different ends, the acceptability thereof deriving from the special system of sharing jurisdiction between the Community and the member states with regard to cartels. However, the Court of Justice has established that, by virtue of a general requirement of natural justice, the Commission must take account of penalties which have already been borne by the same undertaking for the same conduct, where they have been imposed for the infringement of the cartel law of a member state and, consequently, have been committed on the Community territory. (*Sotralenz SA* v *Commission* (Case T-149/89))

Conduct which infringes Arts 85 or 86, but which does not infringe national law, cannot be held to be lawful in that state. However, there may be situations where an agreement or prohibited conduct does not infringe Arts 85 or 86 because it does not affect trade between states, but it may still breach national competition law, and an agreement or concerted practice which has been exempted by the Commission under Art 85(3) may be lawful, even if it breaches national competition rules (Competition Report 1974, p.29).

IMPLEMENTING COMMUNITY COMPETITION LAW IN THE ENGLISH COURTS

Article 85, since it is directly effective, may be used in English courts both as a defence to a claim for breach of contract and, for example, as the basis for a claim that an unlawful agreement between competitors has damaged an undertaking that is not a party to that agreement (*MTV Europe* v *BMG Records (UK) Ltd* (above); *Society of Lloyds* v *Clementson* [1995] 1 CMLR 693). In *Cutsworth* v *Mansfield Inns* [1986] 1 CMLR 1, for example, the plaintiffs had for many years, under an agreement with the tenants, supplied coin-operated amusement machines to more than 50 public houses in the Humberside area. The public houses were taken over by Mansfield Inns in 1985, and, not long after this, the defendants gave to their tenants a list of suppliers of amusement machines from whom tenants were permitted to purchase. The plaintiffs who were not on that list applied for an injunction to restrain the defendants from restricting their tenants from buying from them. They claimed that there was a seriously arguable case that the covenant in the licensees' tenancy agreement had the object or effect of distorting competition and potentially affected trade between member states, contrary to Art 85(1) EC Treaty. This argument was accepted by the Court and the injunction was granted (*see* also *Holleran and Evans* v *Daniel Thwaites plc* [1989] 2 CMLR 917). It now seems clear that a declaration that an agreement breached Art 85(1) would not be sufficient. Under Community law, the national court would have to make an award of damages (*H. J. Banks and Co. Ltd* v *British Coal Corporation* (Case C-128/92)). Article 85 can also be used defensively. In *Société Technique Minière* v *Maschinenbau Ulm* (Case 56/65), the defendant distributors were held able to plead the invalidity of the distribution agreement in the national courts as a defence to breach of contract (*see* also *Brasserie de Haecht* v *Wilkin (No. 1)* (Case 23/67).

Article 86 can also provide the basis for a claim for damages in the English courts.The leading case is *Garden Cottage Foods Ltd* v *Milk Marketing Board* [1984] AC 130. In this case an application was made for an interlocutory injunction to restrain the defendants from refusing to supply milk to the plaintiffs. The refusal to supply was alleged by the plaintiffs to be an abuse of a dominant position by the board and much of the case is concerned with whether or not it was appropriate, in the circumstances, to grant an interlocutory injunction. In determining this point, the House had to consider whether or not an award of damages would be available if the plaintiff was successful in the substantive proceedings. Lord Diplock, who delivered the principal speech thought that damages could be awarded under English law for a breach of Art 86:

> This article of the Treaty of Rome (the EEC Treaty) was held by the European Court of Justice in *Belgische Radio en Televisie* v *SV SABAM* (Case 127/73) to produce direct effects in relations between individuals and to create direct rights in respect of the individuals concerned which the national courts must protect. This decision of the European Court of Justice as to the effect that Art 86 is one which s 3(1) of the European Communities Act 1972 requires your lordships to follow. The rights which the article confers upon citizens in the United Kingdom accordingly fall within s 2(1) of the Act. They are without further enactment to be given legal effect in the United Kingdom and enforced accordingly. A breach of the duty imposed by Art 86 not to abuse a dominant position in the common market or in a substantial part of it, can thus be categorised in English law as a breach of statutory duty that is imposed not only for the purpose of promoting the general economic prosperity of the common market but also for the benefit of private individuals to whom loss or damage is caused by breach of that duty.

There is little case law on successful claims for damages for breach of Art 86 as a breach of statutory duty, but the principle has been accepted in the only other common law jurisdiction in the Community, the Republic of Ireland. In *An Bord Bainne Co-operative Limited (The Irish Dairy Board)* v *The Milk Marketing Board*, Neill J declared that the speeches of their lordships in the *Garden Cottage* case provided 'compelling support for the proposition that contraventions of EEC regulations which have "direct effects" create rights in private law which national courts must protect.' Article 86 could also provide a defence to an action that, for example, an exclusive supply agreement was entered into by one party while being subject to abuse of a dominant position by another undertaking. Thus, the United Kingdom purchasers of Tetra Pak drinks packaging machines who were required to buy only Tetra Pak cartons for use in those machines would be free to buy other cartons and could use the breaches of Arts 85 and 86 found by the Court of First Instance as a defence to any action for breach of contract in the courts of England and Wales (*Tetra Pak International SA* v *Commission* (Case T-83/91).

Further reading

Davidson, J., 'Action for Damages in the English Courts for Breach of EEC Competition Law' (1985) 34 ICLQ 178.

D'Sa, R., (1994) *European Community Law and Civil Remedies in England and Wales*, Sweet & Maxwell, Chapter 10.

Jacobs, F., 'Damages for Breach of Article 86' (1983) EL Rev 353.

Riley, A. J., 'More Radicalism, Please. The Notice on Cooperation between National Courts and the Commission: Applying Articles 85 and 86 of the EEC Treaty' (1993) 3 ECLR 91.

Steiner, J., 'How to make the Action Fit the Case; Domestic Remedies for Breach of EEC law' (1987) 12 El Rev 102.

Tillotson, J., (1993) *European Community Law: Text, Cases and Materials*, Cavendish Publishing Ltd, Chapter 17.

Weatherill, S., (1994) *Cases and Materials on EC Law* (2nd edn), Blackstone Press, Chapter 13.

Weatherill, S. and Beaumont, P., (1995) *EC Law*, (2nd edn), Penguin Books.

Part V
REMEDIES AT COMMUNITY AND NATIONAL LEVEL

$7 \times 100 = 700$

$10 - 4 = 6$

$75 - 6 = 69$

789

75

1000 24

300 300

700

28

$728.$

$4, 1, 7$

4

22 Enforcement of Community law against member states

THE OBLIGATION OF MEMBER STATES UNDER THE EC TREATY

Member states have a general duty, under Art 5, to 'take all appropriate measures, whether general or particular, to ensure fulfilment of the obligations arising out of [the Treaty] or resulting from action taken by the institutions of the Community. They shall facilitate the achievement of the Community's tasks.' The obligation to observe Community law extends beyond the Treaties, secondary legislation and decisions of the institutions to agreements made by the Community with other states under Art 228(1) EC Treaty (*Sevince* (Case 192/89) (para 13] of the judgment); First EEA Case Opinion 1/94. This positive duty to do both what is required of them under the Treaty and under legislation enacted by the institutions is underpinned by a negative obligation in the second limb of Art 5 to 'abstain from any measure which could jeopardise the attainment of the objectives of [the] Treaty'. The Commission is empowered 'to ensure the proper functioning and development of the common market…[that] the provisions of the Treaty and the measures taken by the institutions pursuant thereto are applied' (Art 155 EC Treaty).

The obligation to observe Community law binds, as we have seen in the discussion on the vertical effect of directives, not only the state but organs and emanations of the state (*see* Chapter 5). Those organs include government departments, state-funded and regulated agencies providing public services, local authorities and state governments (the Länder, for example, in Germany) in federal systems and local authorities (*Constanzo* (Case 103/88) *Johnstone* v *RUC* (Case 222/84) and the courts. All are, potentially, indirectly, the subject of enforcement proceedings, although the actual defendant in each case will be the state itself. There have, as yet, been no proceedings where courts have refused to follow or apply principles of Community law, although these have occasionally been called for (*see Minister of the Interior* v *Cohn-Bendit (Conseil d'Etat)* [1980] 1 CMLR 543, where the Conseil refused to follow the decision of the European Court of Justice in *Van Duyn* v *Home Office* (Case 41/74) and give vertical effect to Directive 64/221). In these cases the Court has preferred to rely on establishing a co-operative relationship with national courts and achieving the necessary change in the approach of the national court by persuasion rather than by litigation.

In some cases where action is required, lack of Commission resources may limit or delay its response to unlawful action or inaction in member states. A more appropriate response than a Commission initative may be reliance by individuals on the direct effect of Treaty and other Community provisions in the courts of the offending member state (*see* Chapter 5). Despite the liberal interpretation of the Treaties and the secondary legislation by the Court of Justice, not every Community provision is sufficiently clear, precise and unconditional to be directly effective. In addition, individuals may not have the means to start proceedings or to obtain the evidence to prove a breach. Action by individuals in the courts of the state alleged to have breached Community law does not preclude action by the Commission in the Court of Justice. In 1977 the United Kingdom government banned the importation of main crop potatoes. A Dutch potato exporter challenged this by applying for a declaration in the English High Court that the ban breached Art 30. A reference was made to the Court of Justice under Art 177 which confirmed that the ban was indeed unlawful. A parallel case was also brought by the Commission in the Court of Justice under Art 169 (*Meijer* v *Department of Trade* (Case 118/78); *Commission* v *United Kingdom* (Case 231/78)).

If an individual is unable or unwilling to commence proceedings in relation to the alleged breach, there may be no practical alternative to action by the Commission. The Commission has the power to commence proceedings. Where member states fail to implement Community law, or fail to eliminate obstacles to its implementation, it can take the necessary action under Art 169:

> If the Commission considers that a member state has failed to fulfil an obligation under this Treaty, it shall deliver a reasoned opinion on the matter after giving the state concerned the opportunity to submit its observations.
>
> If the state concerned does not comply with the opinion within the period laid down by the Commission the latter may bring the matter before the Court of Justice.

As an alternative to Art 169, action can be commenced by other member states under Art 170:

> A member state which considers that another member state has failed to fulfil an obligation under this Treaty may bring the matter before the Court of Justice.
>
> Before a member state brings an action against another member state for an alleged infringement of an obligation under this Treaty, it shall bring the matter before the Commission.
>
> The Commission shall deliver a reasoned opinion after each of the states concerned has been given the opportunity to submit its own case and its observations on that of the other party both orally and in writing.
>
> If the Commission has not delivered an opinion within three months of the date on which the matter was brought before it, the absence of such opinion shall not prevent the matter from being brought before the Court of Justice.

Member states have shown a marked reluctance to use Art 170 and although states have quite frequently brought breaches of Community law to the attention of the Commission it could, politically, be damaging for a complainant to take action all the way to the Court of Justice. The increased use of majority voting has made the governments of member states more aware of the need to retain the goodwill of fellow states. A very public confrontation in the Court of Justice is not likely to be regarded as helpful. In fact, only one case has come to judgment in the life of the Community *France* v *United Kingdom* (Case 141/78). For that reason, any action in the Court of Justice that results from a complaint to the Commission about the failure of a member state to meet its obligations is likely to brought under Art 169.

THE STAGES OF ART 169 PROCEEDINGS

The Administrative Stage

Suspected breaches of Community law generally come to the notice of the Commission as a result of the complaints of individuals or undertakings affected by the breach. The first stage is usually an informal inquiry by letter to the government of the member state concerned to ascertain the relevant facts. Member states have a legal duty to co-operate with Commission investigations into alleged breaches by them (*Commission* v *Spain* (Case C-375/92)). As with complaints of alleged breaches of competition law, the Commission does not have to carry out a formal investigation, but it does at least have to 'consider' whether or not there may have been a breach. Where the Commission does consider that there has been a breach, it must, after giving the member state an opportunity to submit observations on the suspected breach, deliver a reasoned opinion to the government of the state concerned. The reasoned opinion will often follow prolonged correspondence between the member state and the Commission. The Commission will have to decide, at some stage in its discussions with (or, in some cases, non-cooperation by) member states, whether or not to proceed to delivery of a formal opinion which will stipulate a date by which time the necessary remedial action should have taken place. The Commission may decide to take no further action if it considers the breach may not be serious and that its resources may be better applied to other infractions.

It would seem the Commission does have a discretion, but it also has a duty under Art 169. It must consider the possibility of whether or not there has been a breach and it must take the most appropriate action. This may be to decide not to commence proceedings. Advocate-General Roemer gave some indication of the appropriate considerations which the Commission should have in mind in *Commission* v *France* (Case 7/71). He said that it might be justifiable not to start formal proceedings where there is a possibility that an amicable settlement may be achieved if formal proceedings are delayed, where the effects of the violation are only minor, where there is a major political crisis which could be aggravated if proceedings are commenced in relation to relatively minor matters and where there is a possibility that the Community provision in issue might be altered in the near future. As the Advocate-General noted in this case, member states resent proceedings being brought against them and the Commission is not always anxious, on this account alone, to take action. Many breaches go for years without being remedied. For example, the British government failed to implement Directive 64/221 for more than 20 years after it had been held to have been in default in *Van Duyn* (*see* now, the Immigration (European Economic Area) Order 1994) SI 1994 No. 1895, Chapter 12, above), while the French Government was, in 1994, again before the Court of Justice for failing to amend its Code du Travail Maritime, 20 years after the Court in *Commission* v *France (Re French Merchant Seamen)* (Case 167/73) had held that it breached Arts 6 and 48 of the EC Treaty (*Commission* v *France* (Case C-355/94), and see, *Commission* v *Belgium* (Case C-37/93) (similar restrictions on Belgian ships)). Some of the cases on which action has not been taken involve immigration and social issues which tend to be more politically sensitive.

Despite the embarrassment which Art 169 proceedings may occasionally cause to member states, the Commission has shown an increasing willingness to use them and has employed Art 169 as part of the process of achieving the single market. In its *Tenth Annual Report on the Application of Community Law for 1992* (COM (93) 320), the Commission noted that it had sent 1,210 letters to member states as a preliminary to Art 169 proceedings, compared to 853 in 1991. There continues to be an increase. In 1994 the Commission initiated 89 separate proceedings under Art 169 which was double the figure for 1993 (*The European*, 7 July 1995).

The Reasoned Opinion

If the Commission decides that a violation of Community law has occurred it must record the infringement in a reasoned opinion or decision served on the offending member state. In arriving at that opinion the Commission must take into account the replies to its enquiries with the state and any defences which may have been advanced. The Court has said that an opportunity to submit such observations before a reasoned opinion is served is an essential procedural requirement. A failure to observe it may invalidate the whole process (*Commission* v *Italy* (Case 31/69) (para 13 of the judgment)).

A large number of infringements concern either the failure to implement directives or a failure to implement them properly, or to observe their terms when implemented. Other infringements may involve direct breaches of Treaty provisions. Whether or not there is an infringement will often depend on the nature and effect of national legal provisions and of the administrative steps taken to give effect to the Community provision, and it is on these legal and factual issues that many disputes with the Commission over implementation occur. A few recent examples will serve to indicate the diversity of the actions brought by the

Commission under Art 169 and the issues involved. In *Commission* v *United Kingdom* (Case C-337/89) proceedings were brought by the Commission against the UK for failing to legislate to implement Directive 80/778/EC to ensure that water used for food production met the maximum nitrate levels in the directive. The UK government argued that most food production was carried out with water from the domestic supply and that legislation was not necessary. The Court upheld the Commission's view that, in the absence of a specific derogation in the directive, all water used for food production should be made to comply. However, in *Commission* v *Belgium* (Case C-376/90), the Court rejected the Commission's interpretation of Directive 80/836/Euratom which required the adoption of national laws protecting the general public and workers against specified levels of ionising radiation. The Commission considered that member states were not allowed to fix different dose limits to those laid down in the directive, even if they were stricter than those specified. The Court disagreed, holding that the directive only laid down maximum exposure levels and Belgium was not, therefore, in breach for enacting lower permitted exposure levels.

It will also be a breach by the member state if, while implementing the directive, it does not provide an effective remedy or uses means which cannot be relied upon by individuals in the national courts. Directive 77/187 protects employees who are employed by undertakings which are transferred to new owners. The Directive had been implemented in the United Kingdom by the Transfer of Undertakings (Protection of Employment) Regulations 1981 (SI 1981 No. 1794) and inter alia provided for consultation with employee's representatives. The Regulations, however, provided no means for recognising such representatives. Effectively, in the United Kingdom, therefore, the duty to consult could be negated by a refusal of the employer to recognise employee representatives and there was no effective remedy for this failure to consult. The Court held that where a Community Directive does not specifically provide any penalty for an infringement, Art 5 of the Treaty requires the member states to guarantee the application and effectiveness of Community law. For that purpose, while the choice of penalties remains within the discretion of the member state, they must ensure in particular that infringements of Community law are penalised under conditions, both procedural and substantive, which are analogous to those applicable to infringements of national law of a similar nature and importance and which, in any event, make the penalty effective, proportionate and dissuasive (*Commission* v *United Kingdom* (Case C-382/92) (para [55] of judgment)).

The opinion must spell out the Community provision and specific details of the breach, together with a response to the member states arguments that there has been compliance or attempting to justify delay in compliance and it must detail the steps to be taken by the member state to correct its infringement. The opinion has to be more fully reasoned than a legislative act under Art 190 (*Commission* v *Germany (Re Brennwein)* (Case 24/62)). The Commission must also set a time limit within which the member state must end its violation. This gives the member state a period of grace within which it is protected from the threat of sanctions or legal proceedings.

If the Commission does subsequently bring proceedings, it has the obligation of proving that the violation was not ended before the expiry of the time limit (*Commission* v *Belgium* (Case 298/86)). It cannot rely in those proceedings on matters which have not been included in the reasoned opinion (*Commission* v *Belgium* (Case 186/85) (para [13] of judgment)).

The judicial stage

The Commission does not have to commence proceedings immediately on the expiry of the period specified in its opinion. In one case it waited six years before commencing proceedings (*Commission* v *Germany* (Case C-422/92)). It is envisaged that it may wish to give the offending state more time to take the necessary remedial action (*Commission* v *France* (Case 7/71), para [5] of judgment).

Member states have attempted a number of defences to breaches of Community law, but the Court has not, generally, been receptive. In relation to non-transposition of directives, it is frequently argued either that there has been a shortage of parliamentary time or, alternatively, that transposition is not necessary because the terms of the directive are, in fact, observed and conflicting national legislative provisions are not adhered to. The first defence was resolutely disposed of by the Court in *Commission* v *Belgium* (Case 77/69). Belgium had imposed a discriminatory tax on wood which violated Art 95 EC Treaty (*see* Chapter 13). A draft law to amend the tax scheme had been laid before the Belgian Parliament, but had fallen with the dissolution of Parliament. The Belgian government argued that these were matters out of its control and it had been prevented from legislating by force majeure. The Court was curt in its dismissal of the argument:

> The obligations arising from Art 95 of the Treaty devolve upon states as such and the liability of a member state under Art 169 arises whatever the agency of the state whose action or inaction is the cause of the failure to fulfil its obligations, even in the case of a constitutionally independent institution. The objection raised by the defendant cannot therefore be sustained. (paras [15] and [16] of judgment) (*see also, Commission* v *Belgium* (Case 1/86))

Nor is the fact that the requirements imposed by a directive are difficult to meet accepted as a defence. In *Commission* v *United Kingdom* (Case C-56/90), the United Kingdom attempted to justify its failure to take all necessary measures to ensure that bathing beaches in Blackpool and Southport met the environmental and health standards set by Directive 76/160/EEC by arguing that implementation was made more difficult by local circumstances. The Court said that, even assuming that absolute physical impossibility to carry out the obligations imposed by the Directive might justify failure to fulfil them, the UK had not established such impossibility in this case. Nor can member states qualify their obligations imposed by directives in response to the demands of 'special' local circumstances or particular economic or social interest groups. In *Commission* v *Hellenic Republic* (Case C-45/91), the Greek government attempted to justify its failure to implement a directive on the safe disposal of toxic waste because of 'opposition by the local population'. The Court commented that it had consistently held that a member state cannot rely on an internal situation to justify disregard of its obligations. Similar defences relating to local conditions have been advanced, and rejected, in two Art 169 proceedings following the failure of member states to implement Directive 79/409/EEC on the protection of wild birds (*Commission* v *Netherlands* (*Re Protection of Wild Birds*) (Case 339/87); *Commission* v *Spain* (Case C-355/90)).

In *Commission* v *Greece* (Case C-105/91), the Greek government defended its admittedly unlawful and discriminatory tax on foreign vehicles by arguing that the Greek vehicles concerned constituted no more than 10 per cent of the internal demand and that there was no manifest discrimination. The Court rejected the defence on the ground that it had consistently held that a member state was guilty of a failure to fulfil its obligations under the Treaty regardless of the frequency or the scale of the infringement. The defence that a directive or regulation is observed in practice or 'administratively' where there are conflicting national provisions has also been rejected by the Court on a number of occasions (*Commission* v *Italy* (Case 166/82); *Commission* v *Germany* (*Re Nursing Directives*) (Case 29/84); *Commission* v *UK* (*Re Tachographs*) (Case 128/78)). However, the use of existing, legally binding provisions of national law may be used, if they provide an effective means of implementing the directive. Such legislation may, therefore, provide a defence to non-implementation (*Commission* v *Netherlands* (Case C-190/90)). Individuals must, nonetheless, be able to rely on a text of national law that accurately reflects their rights and on which they can rely in the event of a judicial challenge (*Commission* v *France* (Case 167/73)). For this reason, a Community obligation cannot be implemented by the government of a member state by simply accepting assurances from the bodies affected that they will meet the terms of the Community provision. It is suggested, therefore, that *R* v *Secretary of State for the Environment, ex parte Friends of the Earth* [1994] 2 CMLR 760, in which Schiemann J. held that an undertaking from water authorities given to the Secretary of State that they would meet Community requirements on water quality was an acceptable way of meeting the United Kingdom's Community obligations, is probably wrongly decided.

Once judgment has been given against a member state, failure to observe the terms of that judgment will constitute a further breach of Art 171 EC Treaty. A number of judgments have not been implemented for as long as five years after the hearing (Audretsch, H.A.H., *Supervision in European Community Law* (1986). The Treaty on European Union significantly strengthened the hand of the Court of Justice in those cases (the vast majority) in which member states are found to have breached Community law. Article 171 (as amended by TEU) provides:

1   If the Court of Justice finds that a member state has failed to fulfil an obligation under this Treaty, the state shall be required to take the necessary measures to comply with the judgment of the Court of Justice.

2   If the Commission considers that the member state concerned has not taken such measures it shall, after giving that state the opportunity to submit its observations,

issue a reasoned opinion specifying the points on which the member state concerned has not complied with the judgment of the Court of Justice.

If the member state concerned fails to take the necessary measures to comply with the Court's judgment within the time limit laid down by the Commission, the latter may bring the case before the Court of Justice. In so doing it shall specify the amount of the lump sum or penalty to be paid by the member state concerned which it considers appropriate in the circumstances.

If the Court of Justice finds that the member state concerned has not complied with its judgement it may impose a lump sum or penalty payment on it.

This procedure shall be without prejudice to Art 170.

The effect of this provision is to enable the Commission to bring a member state, against whom the Court has made a declaration of a breach in Art 169 proceedings, before the Court again for failing to comply with that judgment. The Treaty does not specify any limit to the amount of the fines and doubt has been expressed, as to how payment of the fines will be enforced. A possibility would be for the Commission to deduct the sum from payments it makes to member states. However, a consequence of this action by the Commission may be retaliation by the state concerned by deducting an equal amount from sums owed to the Commission (*see*, Hartley, op. cit. pp. 334, 335). Decisions of the Court of Justice and the practice of the Commission will, in due course, indicate how these issues can, if at all, be resolved. There is no doubt, however, that the possibility of a fine under Art 171, together with the possibility of claims for damages brought by individuals under *Francovich* (Cases 6/90 and 9/90) now constitute a much more real deterrent to breaches of Community law by member states. The Court has, however, not as yet been called upon to impose a fine under the amended Art 171 EC (Report of the Court of Justice on Certain Aspects of the Application of the Treaty on European Union (May 1995), para 9), but the Commission has expressed its willingness to make full use of the fines procedure (Twelfth Report of the European Commission on the Monitoring and Application of Community Law. OJ 1995 C-254)

Interim measures

Breaches of Community law may occur inadvertently or intentionally. In the former case, member states will normally take remedial action when the breach is brought to their attention by the Commission. In the latter, member states may, consciously, risk action by the Commission when they are confronted by internal political pressures which they cannot, or will not, resist. They will often do so in the hope that, by the time the Commission commences proceedings, a solution can be found and the illegal action can be terminated. Such considerations appear to have motivated the French government in the ban it imposed on the import of lamb and mutton from other member states, principally Britain (*Commission* v *France (Re Sheepmeat)* (Case 232/78)). Similar action seems, at least, to have been contemplated by the German government recently in response to pressure from German public opinion about British beef affected by Bovine Spongiform Encephalitis (BSE) or 'Mad cow disease'. Given that several years may elapse between the initial complaint to the Commission and the hearing before the Court of Justice, the Commission, in circumstances where continuing damage is being caused while the case is processed, may apply to the Court for interim relief.

Interim relief may be granted by the Court under Art 186, which simply states:

> The Court of Justice may in any cases before it prescribe any necessary interim measures.

The speed of the relief available is demonstrated by *Commission* v *Ireland* (Case 61/77R). In this case, Ireland had introduced fisheries conservation measures which the Commission regarded as contrary to the Treaty. It commenced Art 169 proceedings, and, at the same time, made an application for an interim order requiring Ireland to suspend the operation of the legislation. Only nine days later the Court gave judgment ; it doubted the validity of the Irish legislation on grounds of discrimination and, after several adjournments to promote a settlement, ordered the Irish government to suspend the measures within five days. The case of *Commission* v *United Kingdom* (Case C-246/89R), also arose out of pressure to conserve diminishing fishing stocks. The British government, concerned about fishing vessels from other member states operating in British waters under British 'flags of convenience' to gain access to British fishing quotas, enacted the Merchant Shipping Act 1988. The Act confined the issue of fishing licences to companies registered in the United Kingdom and whose owners or shareholders were British or were ordinarily resident in the United Kingdom. The Act was clearly discriminatory under Art 7 (now Art 6) EC Treaty, and it was an obstacle to establishment under Art 52 EC Treaty. The British government argued that the measures were necessary to protect the British fishing quota. Pending the hearing of the case, could the Spanish shipowners who had challenged the licensing system continue to fish? The Court noted that the owners of the vessels were suffering heavy losses while their ships remained idle, and would soon have to sell them under very adverse conditions. Prima facie, the companies had a right to continue in business and given the urgency of the situation, the Court ordered the United Kingdom to suspend the relevant provisions of the Merchant Shipping Act 1986. The substantive hearing subsequently found that there was unlawful discrimination (*Factortame* (Case C-221/89)).

In another case, *Commission* v *Germany* (Case C-195/90R), the Federal Republic had imposed a new tax on heavy goods vehicles with a view to encouraging greater use of water transport on the country's inland waterways. The tax, which was to be imposed largely for environmental reasons, was to take effect on 1 July 1990. The Commission applied for what was, in effect, an *ex parte* interim order from the President of the Court, which was ordered on 28 June, pending the full hearing of the interim application. Under Art 83(2) of the Rules of Procedure of the Court, applicants need to state grounds indicating, firstly, a prima facie case establishing the breach of the law alleged and, secondly, urgency and the need for the interim measures.

On the law allegedly infringed, the Commission argued that the new German tax breached the 'stand-still' provisions of Art 76, which were intended to protect the present position until a common Community transport policy was adopted under Art 74. It also breached Art 95 (the prohibition against discriminatory taxation, *see* Chapter 13), since the charge, although payable by all vehicles of the appropriate weight, was offset in relation to German vehicles by a reduction in German vehicle tax. The Court accepted that these arguments constituted a sufficiently strong case to meet the first requirement of the Rules of Procedure. But were the circumstances sufficiently urgent for interim relief? The Court has laid down that the urgency of an application for an interim measure was to be assessed in the light of the extent to which an interim order was necessary to avoid serious and irreparable damage (Case C-170/94R *Commission* v *Greece* (compare the criteria for the grant of interim relief in English courts under the rules laid down s 37, Rules of the Supreme Court Act 1981 and in *American Cynamid* v *Ethicon* [1975] AC 396 of 'the balance of convenience'). The Commission argued that the new German tax would disrupt its attempts to create a common transport policy and would drive a number of carriers out of business before the full proceedings could be heard. The German government insisted that if the tax was suspended it would suffer irreparable damage in the loss of tax, which could not be recovered subsequently if the tax was found to be lawful in the main proceedings. The Court accepted the Commission's argument of the need to protect the status quo and the need to avoid irreparable damage to transport undertakings. The German government could hardly be said to be suffering a loss to its exchequer, since the tax had never existed before. The interim order to suspend the operation of the new tax was, therefore, confirmed.

A more recent application for interim relief arose out of the award of contracts to replace old buses in Belgium and the alleged breach of the procedures laid down in Directive 90/531/EEC by the Société Regionale Walloon du Transport (SRWT). The contract had been awarded (wrongly, the Commission maintained) and the delivery of the first buses was due to take place before the full hearing could take place. The Commission argued that there was a risk of serious and irreparable damage, in that the award of the contract and the first deliveries would confront the Commission, guardian of the treaties responsible for the application of Community law, with a *fait accompli*, and would create the conditions for a serious and immediate threat to the Community legal order. The Court agreed that the failure to comply with a directive applicable to a public contract constituted a serious threat to Community legality, and that a declaration at the conclusion of Art 169 proceedings could not cancel the damage suffered. However, the Court felt that an applicant for interim relief should act with due diligence. The Commission took more than two months to apply for relief after one of the unsuccessful tenderers had informed it of the situation. The formal contract was, in the meantime, concluded. Relief was, accordingly, refused by the Commission (*Commission* v *Belgium* (Case C-87/94)).

Other actions against member states

The power of the Commission to take cases directly to the Court of Justice where a member state has granted state aid to an undertaking in breach of Art 92, has already been considered in Chapter 17. Failure to abolish the offending aid within the time specified will entitle the Commission to proceed without giving a reasoned opinion, as required under Arts 169 and 170.

There are also special powers given to the Commission under Art 100a(4) to enable it to bring member states before the Court of Justice without going through the Art 169 procedure in cases where a member state has used its power to derogate from a harmonising directive on grounds of major needs or protection of the environment or the working environment. This can be done where the Commission believes that the member state is using its power of derogation improperly.

Further reading

Audretsch, H. A. H., (1986) *Supervision in European Community Law*, (2nd edn), North Holland.

Barav, A., 'Failure of Member States to Fulfil their Obligations under Community Law' (1975) 12 CML Rev 369.

Dashwood, A., and White, R., 'Enforcement Actions and Articles 169 & 170' (1989) 14 EL Rev 388.

Evans, A., 'The Enforcement Procedure of Article 169 EEC: Commission Discretion' (1970) 4 EL Rev 442.

Gray, C., 'Interim Measures of Protection in the European Court' (1979) 4 EL Rev 80.

Hartley, T. C., (1994) *The Foundations of European Community Law*, (3rd edn), Clarendon Press, Chapter 10.

Snyder, F., 'The Effectiveness of European Community Law: Institutions, Processes, Tools and Techniques' (1993) 56 MLR 19.

Steiner, J., (1994) *Textbook on EC Law*, (4th edn), Blackstone Press, Chapter 25.

Weatherill, S., (1994) *Cases and Materials on EC Law*, (2nd edn), Blackstone Press, Chapter 17.

Weatherill, S., and Beaumont, P., (1995) *EC Law*, (2nd edn), Penguin Books, Chapter 7.

23 Judicial review of acts of Community institutions

Although the Community does not have a formal constitution, the EC Treaty confers specific powers and duties on each of the institutions and establishes what the Court of Justice has, on a number of occasions referred to as 'a new legal order' (Opinion 1/91 [1991] ECR I-6079). Each of the institutions has a limited competence and must carry out its functions in the way specified in the Treaty and according to general principles of Community law (Art 4(1) EC Treaty). If an institution exceeds its powers or uses them unlawfully, its acts may be subject to review by the Court of Justice under Art 173:

> The Court of Justice shall review the legality of acts adopted jointly by the European Parliament and the Council, of acts of the Council, of the Commission and of the European Central Bank, other than recommendations and opinions, and of acts of the European Parliament intended to produce legal effects *vis-à-vis* third parties.
>
> It shall for this purpose have jurisdiction in actions brought by a member state, the Council or the Commission on grounds of lack of competence, infringement of an essential procedural requirement, infringement of this Treaty or of any rule of law relating to its application, or misuse of powers.
>
> The Court shall have jurisdiction under the same conditions in actions brought by the European Parliament and by the ECB for the purpose of protecting their prerogatives.
>
> Any natural or legal person may, under the same conditions, institute proceedings against a decision addressed to that person or against a decision which, although in the form of a regulation or a decision addressed to another person, is of direct and individual concern to the former. The proceedings provided for in this Art shall be instituted within two months of the publication of the measure, or of its notification to the plaintiff, or, in the absence thereof, of the day on which it came to the knowledge of the latter, as the case may be.

The terms of Art 173 raise *five* questions which need to be answered:

1 What acts may be reviewed?
2 Who may challenge them i.e. who has, in the language of English administrative law, the *locus standi* to mount a challenge ?

3   When is an action barred by lapse of time ?
4   What are the grounds for challenge ?
5   What are the consequences of an annulment ?

REVIEWABLE ACTS

Not every act of an institution may be reviewed. Prima facie, it is only those acts which Art 189 defines as legally binding, namely regulations, directives and decisions, which are subject to review. Opinions and recommendations are not reviewable. Other acts, however, not specified in Art 189, have been treated by the Court of Justice as subject to review. In *Commission* v *Council* (Case 22/70), the Court held that a resolution passed by the Council to participate in a European Transport Agreement was reviewable under Art 173. It refused to interpret Art 189 restrictively, and declared that 'an action for annulment must ... be available in the case of all measures adopted by the institutions, whatever their nature and form, which are intended to have legal effects'. The Court of Justice has frequently emphasised that the determining factor is whether or not an act has legal consequences, however it may have been arrived at:

> In order to ascertain whether the measures in question are acts within the meaning of Article 173 it is necessary ... to look to their substance. According to the consistent case law of the Court any measure the legal effects of which are binding on, and capable of affecting the interests of, the applicant by bringing about a distinct change in his legal position is an act or decision which may be the subject of an action under Art 173 for a declaration that it is void. However, the form in which such acts or decisions are cast is, in principle, immaterial as regards the question whether they are open to challenge under that article. (*IBM* v *Commission* (Case 60/81)).

It is, however, often difficult to distinguish between form and substance. An act may not have any legal consequence precisely because it has not been adopted in the form required. In *Air France* v *Commission* (Case T-3/93) the Commissioner responsible for competition policy, Sir Leon Brittan, had issued a press statement about the merger between Dan Air and British Airways, declaring that it would result in a sufficient concentration of air transport to have a Community dimension. Air France's attempt to challenge the statement failed at the first hurdle, because the statement had not been adopted by the whole Commission and did not have the *form* of a legal act. It could, therefore, have no legal consequences (*see* also *Nefarma* v *Commission* (Case T-113/89).

As it was originally drawn, Art 173 made no mention of measures adopted by the European Parliament. Despite this, the Court held, in *Parti Ecologiste ('Les Verts')* v *European Parliament* (Case 294/83) that measures adopted by the parliament intended to have legal effects *vis-à-vis* third parties were subject to annulment under

Art 173 (*see* also, *Luxembourg* v *European Parliament* (Case C-213/88)). The Court has also held that a declaration made by the President of Parliament at the conclusion of the debate by parliament on the Community's budget has the character of a legal act and is also subject to annulment (*Council* v *Parliament* (Case 34/86); *Council* v *European Parliament* (Case C-284/90)). Measures taken by the parliament affecting third parties are now specifically subject to review as a result of amendments made to Art 173 by the TEU. A measure adopted by the Court of Auditors has also been held to be reviewable under Art 173 (*Maurissen and others* v *Court of Auditors* (Cases 193 & 194/87)). A decision by the Commission to close the file on a complaint alleging breach of Art 86 has also been held to be a 'decision' reviewable under Art 173 (*SFEI and others* v *Commission* (Case C-39/93P)).

Although the acts of the Council are reviewable, the representatives of the member states must be acting *as* the Council for Art 173 to apply. In *Parliament* v *Council* (C-181/91 & C-248/91), the Parliament attempted to challenge a decision made at a Council meeting granting special aid to Bangladesh. The Court held that acts adopted by representatives of the member states acting not as members of the Council but as representatives of their governments, amounted to the collective exercise of the competences of the member states. They were not, therefore, acts of the Council and were not, consequently, subject to review by the Court of Justice.

WHO MAY APPLY FOR REVIEW?

Article 173 confers specific and unlimited rights of challenge on member states, the Council of Ministers and the Commission. The European Parliament and the European Central Bank have more limited rights of challenge to enable them to protect their prerogatives. Their powers to do so reflect decisions of the Court of Justice made on the basis of Art 173 in relation to the Parliament as it was originally framed, before amendment by the Treaty on European Union. Member states may apply for review, even though they have no direct or indirect interest in the subject matter of the case but, for example, are concerned that the appropriate procedure should be used (*Italy* v *Commission* (Case 41/83)).

The fourth paragraph of Art 173 confers a right of challenge on 'any natural or legal person' although this right is much more limited compared with member states and Community institutions. A 'natural or legal person' is entitled only to challenge:

1   a decision addressed to himself, or
2   a decision, in the form of decision or regulation addressed to another person, which is of direct and individual concern to himself.

Community law has had as much difficulty as has English law in defining who has a sufficient interest to be recognised by the Court as being a proper person to be recognised for judicial review purposes (*compare,* s 31(3), Supreme Court Act 1981 and Order 53, RSC). Many decisions which are subject to challenge are made by the Commission in relation to competition law, and are challenged by those against whom they are made. Individuals who have, for example, complained that the conduct of an undertaking infringes Art 86, where the Commission refuses to investigate the complaint, will have standing to challenge that refusal (*Demo-Studio Schmidt* v *Commission* (Case 210/81); *compare, Lord Bethell* v *Commission* (Case 246/81)). The concept of 'direct and individual concern' has been narrowly construed by the Court of First Instance in relation to the *locus standi* of employees' representatives to challenge Commission decisions approving mergers which are likely to result in redundancies. In both *Comité Central d'Enterprise de la Société Generale des Grandes Sources and Others* v *Commission* and *Comité Centrale d'Enterprise de la Sociéte Anonyme Vittel and Others* v *Commission* (Case T-96/92), the Court held that the employee representatives only had standing to challenge the decisions of the Commission in so far as the mergers that would result following the Commission's approval affected rights of representation of the employee organisations concerned. The Court was not satisfied that redundancies were an inevitable consequence of the mergers. Even if they were, the effect on the representatives of the redundancies would 'only be of an indirect nature' and they did not, therefore, have standing to challenge the decisions.

A regulation adopted may have an adverse effect upon a small group of individuals or commercial undertakings. Will they have the standing to challenge it under Art 173? If the regulation is of a general kind, the answer will be in the negative. However, in the case of anti-dumping regulations, the Court recently accepted the standing of a company to challenge a regulation of a general character (*Codorniu* (Case C-309/89)). If, however, the regulation is intended to affect a specific group of undertakings, it may be 'a conglomeration of individual decisions . . . under the guise of a regulation', then those affected may have the status to challenge it (*International Fruit Co.* v *Commission* (Case 41/70). If, however, a regulation is a genuine one, the fact that it affects a small group of undertakings positively, and the complainant negatively, does not give the complainant the right to bring Art 173 proceedings (*Campo Ebro SA* v *Council* (Case T-472/93)).

The fact that a decision, although addressed to a member state, will have a direct effect on a specific undertaking, and where the decision is made with that undertaking in mind, for example, in relation to a proposed state aid, will clearly give that undertaking standing to mount a challenge to that decision (*Philip Morris Holland* v *Commission* (Case 730/79); *Intermills* (Case 332/82)). This will be the case even if the complainant may not benefit from the state aid if the state concerned decides otherwise, provided that the possibility of non-payment by the state is 'purely theoretical' (*ASPEC* v *Commission* (Case T-435/93)). If, however, a decision is not of 'individual concern' to an undertaking, although it may be adversely affected by it, that undertaking will not be regarded as having sufficient standing (*Plaumann* v *Commission* (Case 25/62)). Many of the cases show a nervousness on the part of the Court to 'opening the flood-gates' to a multiplicity of claims by bodies adversely affected by Community legislation, and they are not wholly consistent. Perhaps the most striking example of the limited scope given to the concept of 'direct and individual concern' was the recent failure of the Court of First Instance to concede *locus standi* to Pacific islanders to enable them to challenge a Commission decision on French nuclear tests, despite the fact that the Court accepted that they might be affected physically as a result (*Danielson and Others* v *Commission* (Case T-219/95)) It should, however, be noted that, in its Report to the 1996 Intergovernmental Conference (May 1995), the Court has declared:

> It may be asked … whether the right to bring an action for annulment under Art 173 of the EC Treaty (and the corresponding provisions of the other Treaties), which individuals enjoy only in regard to acts of direct and individual concern is sufficient to guarantee for them effective judicial protection against possible infringements of their fundamental rights arising from the legislative activity of the institutions.
> (p.12 of the Report)

TIME LIMITS

Article 173(3) provides that proceedings should be instituted within two months of:

1   the publication of the measure; or
2   its notification to the plaintiff, or, in the absence thereof;
3   the day in which it came to the knowledge of the latter, as the case may be.

The two month period expires at the end of the day in the last month which bears the same number as the day of the occurrence of the event which caused time to start running (*Misset* v *Council* (Case 152/85)). The Court of First Instance has recently held that where an applicant lets the time limit for bringing an action against a decision unequivocally affecting his interests expire, he cannot start time running again by asking the institution to reconsider its decision and then start proceedings against the confirmation of the decision (*Cobrecaf SA* v *Commission* (Case T- 514/93)). The expiry of the period of time allowed for bringing proceedings will not be fatal if the applicant can rely on the second paragraph of the Statute of the Court which provides:

> No right shall be prejudiced in consequence of the expiry of the time limit if the party concerned proves the existence of unforeseeable circumstances or of force majeure.

The Court of Justice has, however, shown reluctance in allowing applications outside the statutory time limits. Time limits do not apply where the issue of the legality of a Community measure is raised in Art 177 proceedings. However, a national court cannot refer a case under Art 177 to the European Court of Justice where the plaintiff could have challenged the Community measure within the time limit under Art 173, but failed to do so *TWD Deggendorf* (Case C-188/92) (*see* Chapter 24).

THE LEGAL BASIS FOR A CHALLENGE

Article 173 provides four possible bases for a challenge. These are:

1 Lack of competence.
2 Infringement of an essential procedural requirement.
3 Infringement of the Treaty or any rule of law relating to its application.
4 Misuse of powers.

These are not mutually exclusive and two or even three may be cited together in an application for judicial review.

Lack of competence

This corresponds in English law to substantive *ultra vires*; a body can only do that which it authorised to do by law. As we have seen, a number of challenges have been mounted on the grounds that the Commission has chosen the wrong legal base for a legislative proposal (*see* Chapter 3; *Commission* v *Council (Re Titanium Dioxide Waste)* (Case C-300/89)) or a decision. In *Germany, France, Netherlands, Denmark and the United Kingdom* v *Commission* (Cases 281, 283–285, 287/85) the Commission had adopted a decision under Art 118 EC Treaty under which member states were required to consult with the Commission on measures relating to the integration of workers from states outside the Community. The Court of Justice held that the social policy objects of Art 118 were confined to measures that affected migrants from other member states, and did not extend, as this decision purported to do, to measures affecting only migrants from states outside the Community.

There are not a great many challenges which are successful on this basis, but a recent example is *France* v *Commission* (Case C-327/91), where the Commission had concluded an agreement with the United States to promote co-operation and co-ordination and to lessen the possibility of conflict between the parties in their application of their competition laws. The case concerned the competence of the Commission to conclude the agreement. In a challenge by the French government, the Court held that the Commission did not have the competence to do so. Under Art 228 (before amendment by TEU) the Commission had power to negotiate agreements with states outside the Community or with international organisations, but they had to be concluded by the Council.

Infringement of an essential procedural requirement

This is probably the most oft-cited basis of challenge and is equivalent to procedural *ultra vires*. It comprises both breaches of formal procedural requirements laid down in the EC Treaty and in secondary legislation and the more informed rules of fairness required by general principles of Community law. The most important general procedural requirement in the EC Treaty is that laid down in Art 190, under which secondary legislation must state the reasons on which it is based. The Court has recently emphasised the importance of this provision:

> According to a consistent line of case law, the purpose of the obligation to state the reasons on which an individual decision is based is to enable the Community judicature to review the legality of the decision and to provide the person concerned with sufficient information to make it possible to ascertain whether the decision is well founded or whether it is vitiated by a defect which may permit its legality to be contested. The extent of that obligation depends on the nature of the measure in question and on the context in which it was adopted. (*Eugenio Branco Ld* v *Commission* (Case T-85/94))

In this case, and two similar previous cases, the Court annulled Commission decisions withdrawing approval or partial support of projects financed by the European Social Fund. Besides the obligation imposed by Art 190 EC Treaty, there was also a breach of the requirement imposed by Art 6(1) of Regulation 2950/83, under which the Commission, before deciding to suspend, reduce or withdraw Fund aid, had to give the relevant member state the opportunity to comment (*Consorgan Lda* v *Commission* (Case C-181/90); *Socurte Ld and Others* v *Commission* (Cases T432-34/93)).

Breach of a procedural requirement may be so fundamental that the decision or other measure may be void *ab initio*. No decision will, in effect, have come into existence. In *Commission* v *BASF AG and Others* (Case C-137/92P), the Court of First Instance had dismissed as inadmissible actions for annulment of a measure which purported to have been taken by the Commission under Art 85 of the EC Treaty, on the ground that the measure was 'non-existent'. The full Court of Justice allowed an appeal, noting that, while acts of the Community institutions are, in principle, presumed to be lawful and accordingly produce legal effects, even if they are tainted by irregularities, until such time as they are annulled or withdrawn, there are some acts which are so tainted by irregularity whose gravity is so obvious that they cannot be tolerated by the Community legal order. They must be treated as having no legal effect, even provisional. However, the Court said that such a conclusion, with all its potentally serious consequences, should only be reached in 'quite extreme circumstances'. In this case, both the operative part of the decision and the reasons for it had been adopted by a single Commissioner and three of the texts of the decision in the relevant languages had never been seen by the full Commission, contrary to the Commision's Rules of Procedure. It amounted to breach of an essential procedural requirement and was consequently annulled by the Court under Art 173. The decision of the Commission had not, however, been 'non-existent'.

Infringement of the Treaty or any rule relating to its application

There is an obvious overlap here between Art 190 and the need to give reasons, procedural requirements and the general principles of fairness and natural justice which are fundamental principles of Community law (*see* Chapter 6). There are also the principles of the European Convention on Human Rights, principles of non-discrimination, proportionality, legitimate expectation, respect for property rights and equal treatment. These latter rights are not absolute and may, in appropriate circumstances, have to give way to restrictions imposed in the interest of the common organisation of the market, 'provided that those restrictions in fact correspond to objectives of general interest pursued by the Community, and do not constitute a disproportionate and intolerable interference, impairing the very substance of the rights guaranteed'. (*Germany* v *Commission (Re Banana Market)*.)

Misuse of power

This ground for challenge stems from the French *détournement de pouvoir*. This is the equivalent, in English administrative law, of using a power conferred for an improper or illegitimate purpose. Since the power is itself lawful, a challenger must prove a subjective matter, the purpose for which it has been used (*Netherlands* v *High Authority* (Case 6/54)). Since outsiders are not privy to the reasons for institutional decisions unless they are made public, most of the few successful cases have relied on published documents, or the reasons given under Art 190, which indicate that the institution has misunderstood the purpose for which a power has been conferred on it (*Giuffrida* v *Council* (Case 105/75)).

CONSEQUENCES OF ANNULMENT

Under Article 174:

> If the action is well founded, the Court of Justice shall declare the act concerned to be void. In the case of a regulation, however, the Court of Justice shall, if it considers this necessary, state which of the effects of the regulation which it has declared void shall be considered as definitive.

Under Art 176:

> The institution or institutions whose act has been declared void or whose failure to act has been declared contrary to the Treaty shall be required to take the necessary measures to comply with the judgment of the Court of Justice.
>
> The obligation shall not affect any obligation which may result from the application of the second paragraph of Art 215.

Since decisions and other acts having legal consequences will effect only single undertakings or individuals or groups of undertakings, the Court, if it finds the decision or other act to be void, will declare it to be void from the moment of the delivery of the judgment. It can, of course, declare an act, non-existent, but, as we have seen in the *BASF Case* (Case C-137/92, above, Chapter 20), it is, reluctant to do this because of the disruption which this may cause to actions which may have been based on the assumption that the act was valid. The second paragraph of Art 173 enables the Court to declare part of a decision void. In the case of Community legislation, it will frequently declare that, for example, the provisions of an annulled directive or regulation will remain effective until a new regulation is adopted. (*See*, for example, the Court's declaration on annulling Directive 90/366 on students' rights in *European Parliament* v *Council* (Case C-295/90), and on Council Regulation 2454/92 on transport undertakings operating in other member states in *European Parliament* v *Council* (Case C-388/92).)

Article 176 requires the institution concerned to take the necessary remedial action to correct the failure which has been established by the judgment of the Court. There is no time limit for this, but the Court has held that such steps should be taken within a reasonable period from the date of the judgment (*European Parliament* v *Council* (Case 13/83)).

INDIRECT CHALLENGE TO A COMMUNITY ACT UNDER ART 184

The legality of a Community act may become an issue in proceedings in which the object is not the Community act itself, but some action of an institution which purports to be based upon it. The issue can only be raised if it is relevant to the proceedings (*Italy* v *Commission* (Case 32/65)). Attacks on the legality of Community acts in this way are normally called indirect challenges and they may result in the judicial review of the legality of Community acts long after the time has passed for an application for review under Art 173. The issue of legality may arise in both the Court of Justice and the Court of First Instance at Community level or in national courts. Where it arises at Community level it is subject to the rules laid down in Art 184 which provides:

> Notwithstanding the expiry of the period laid down in the third paragraph of Art 173, any party may, in proceedings in which a regulation of the Council or of the Commission is in issue, plead the grounds specified in the first paragraph of Art 173 in order to invoke before the Court of Justice the inapplicability of that regulation.

The first point to note is that an indirect challenge in this way is only available in relation to regulations and cannot, therefore, be used in relation to other Community acts having legal effect. Secondly, the effect of Art 184 is limited to proceedings brought before the Court of Justice (*Wöhrmann* v *Commission* (Case 31/62)). Although Art 184 excludes an indirect challenge to other acts having legal effect, this rule may, in some cases, be circumvented where the issue arises in a national court. The question of the legality of the Community measure may then be raised, as we have already noted in connection with time limits under Art 173, in the national court and referred to the Court of Justice under Art 177. The operation of Art 177 is examined in Chapter 24, but the relevant part of that Art enables national courts to ask for a preliminary ruling, inter alia, in relation to 'the validity and interpretation of acts of the institutions of the Community…'.

If a national body purports to act on the basis of, say, a decision or a directive which is, arguably, invalid, a party to the proceedings may ask the Court to refer the question of the validity of that measure to the Court of Justice. Such a reference will be necessary if the issue arises, because national courts have no power themselves to rule on the validity of a Community measure (*Fotofrost* v *HZA Lubeck Ost* (Case 314/85)). An important restriction on that principle is, however, the rule laid down by the Court in *TWD Deggendorf* (Case C-188/92). In that case the Court held that no indirect challenge to a Commission decision could be made under Art 177 where the party had been informed of the Commission decision and could 'without doubt' have challenged it directly before the Court of Justice under Art 173, but had not done so.

CHALLENGING A FAILURE TO ACT

Institutions may act unlawfully not only by exceeding or abusing their powers, but by failing to carry out a duty imposed on them by the Treaty or some other provision having legal effect. This form of inaction may result in proceedings brought under Art 175:

> Should the European Parliament, the Council or the Commission, in infringement of this Treaty, fail to act, the member states and the other institutions of the Community may bring an action before the Court of Justice to have the infringement established.
>
> The action shall be admissible only if the institution concerned has first been called upon to act. If, within two months of being called upon, the institution concerned has not defined its position, the action may be brought within a further period of two months.
>
> Any natural or legal person may, under the conditions laid down in the preceding paragraphs, complain to the Court of Justice that an institution of the Community has failed to address to that person any act other than a recommendation or an opinion.
>
> The Court of Justice shall have jurisdiction, under the same conditions, in actions or proceedings brought by the European Central Bank in the areas falling within the latter's field of competence and in actions and proceedings brought against the latter.

Standing to challenge a failure to act

The position of 'privileged' applicants (i.e. member states and institutions) who can bring proceedings under Art 175 irrespective of any particular interest, and legal and natural persons who need to establish a special interest, is the same under Art 175 as in relation to challenges under Art 173. The Court has, in fact, stated that 'in the system of legal remedies provided for by the Treaty, there is a close relationship given between the right of action given in Art 173 ... and that based on Art 175 (*European Parliament* v *Council (Re Transport Policy)* (Case 13/83)).

Scope for challenge

There have not been many successful actions brought on this basis. Many of the duties which are conferred on the institutions involve both a duty and a discretion of whether, and how to exercise that duty. To satisfy Art 175, the institution needs, generally, only to have addressed the issue and defined its position and in the case of natural or legal persons, if the only outcome of its deliberations will be an opinion or a recommendation, a failure to produce either is not a failure which can be dealt with by Art 175. Where there is a clear duty to act, as there is imposed on the Commission by Art 89 (1) in relation to breaches of Arts 85 and 86 under Art 89, a statement by the Commission that it is not going to respond to a complaint might give grounds for an action under Art 173, after the appropriate warning has been given. For example, in *Ladbroke Racing (Deutschland) GmbH* v *Commission* (Case T-74/92), Ladbroke had complained to the Commission about a denial of access for the televising of horse racing, alleging a breach of Arts 85 and 86 by German and French companies in the horse racing and communications businesses. After deciding to investigate the complaint in December 1990, the Commission had still not defined its position on the alleged breach of Art 86 by June 1992, when it was formally requested to do so. The Court of First Instance found that there was a breach of Art 175. The Commission could have either initiated the procedure for establishing a breach of Art 86, dismissed the complaint in a formal letter to the complainant or made a reasoned decision not to pursue the complaint on the ground of a lack of Community interest. It had, however, done none of these things. If there is a refusal to pursue an investigation, it may in itself constitute a decision which is best attacked under Art 173 (*SFEI and Others* v *Commission* (Case C-39/93P)).

The difficulty of launching a successful action under Art 175 is illustrated by the *Transport Policy* case (above) concerning Arts 74 and 75 of the Treaty that require the Council to adopt a common transport policy for the Community. More than 20 years after the Treaty had come into force no such policy had been adopted, and the Parliament brought proceedings against the Council for failure to act under Art 175, after a number of requests had been made to the Council for progress in this area. The Court agreed that the Council had been 'called upon to act, by the Parliament, as required by Art 175(2), and had produced equivocal replies as to what, if any, action it proposed to take'. The requirement in Arts 74 and 75 of the EC Treaty was not sufficiently precise, however, to amount to an enforceable obligation. Other cases have failed because the Court decided that all that was required was an opinion (*Chevally* v *Commission* (Case 15/70)), or because the decision which the applicant required was not to be addressed to him (*Lord Bethell* v *Commission* (Case 246/81)).

RELATIONSHIP BETWEEN JUDICIAL REVIEW AND REFERENCES MADE BY NATIONAL COURTS TO THE COURT OF JUSTICE UNDER ARTICLE 177 EC TREATY

The validity of a Community act may be raised as an issue in proceedings in national courts and the question that must be addressed is can a national court rule on the validity of that act? In *Foto-Frost* (Case 314/85) the Court ruled, decisively that it could not stating that while national courts could declare a Community act valid, they have no power to declare it invalid. The proper course for a national court to adopt when confronted by an argument based on the alleged invalidity of a Community measure is to refer the matter to the Court of Justice under Art 177. This course is not, however, available where the party alleging invalidity had the standing to challenge the measure when it was issued, but failed to do so within the time limit laid down in Art 173 (*TWD Deggendorf* (Case C-188/92)).

The circumstances in which an Art 177 reference can be made are examined in more detail in Chapter 24.

CLAIMS FOR DAMAGES AGAINST COMMUNITY INSTITUTIONS FOR UNLAWFUL ACTS

Article 176 specifically preserves the question of non-contractual liability as a separate issue from the legality or otherwise of institutional acts. As in English law, the fact that a public body has acted unlawfully does not, *per se*, mean that the body concerned is under a duty to compensate those adversely affected by its action, although a court does have the power to order the payment of compensation at the conclusion of an application for judicial review (s 31(4), Supreme Court Act 1981). Whether or not damages are payable under Community law depends on the way in which the Court, which, under Art 178 has exclusive jurisdiction over damages claims against the institutions, has interpreted the provisions of Art 215 of the EC Treaty. The liability of Community institutions in contract will generally be governed by the law of the member state where the institution is situated. Liability in non-contractual matters (tort, in English law) is governed by Art 215(2) which provides that:

> In the case of non-contractual liability, the Community shall, in accordance with the general principles common to the laws of the member states, make good any damage caused by its institutions or by its servants in the performance of their duties.

The Court laid down some basic rules for liability in *Lütticke v Commission* (Case 4/69). There must be actual damage to the plaintiff and a causal link between the damage and the alleged unlawful conduct of the institution. Fault is not an essential element in liability, in the sense that the institution does not have to be conscious of any wrong doing. The only type of fault that need be established is an unlawful act by the relevant institution. Where there is a positive duty to do something, there must be an omission to do it and where there is a discretion, it must have been exercised in an unlawful way. The wrongdoing is likely to have been the result of carelessness, failure to make appropriate inquiries or the giving of misleading information. The conduct giving rise to a claim under Art 215 will usually amount to no more than *faute de service* or poor administrative practice causing loss to the plaintiff. The scope for liability is much wider than under English law, however and institutions can be liable for wrongful legislative acts. This liability is however, limited by the so-called *Schöppenstedt formula* (*Zückerfabrik Schöppenstedt v Council* (Case 5/71)). Under the formula the Court holds that 'the Community does not incur liability on account of a legislative measure which involves choices of economic policy unless a sufficiently serious breach of a superior rule of law for the protection of the individual has occurred' (*HNL v Council and Commission* (Case 83/77), para [4] of judgment; *Unifruit Hellas v Commission* (Case T-489/93)).

Adams v Commission (Case 145/83), illustrates the circumstances in which an institution may be liable. Stanley Adams was employed by Hoffmann-La Roche, one of the largest pharmaceutical companies in Europe. Although the company was based in Switzerland, its products were widely sold throughout the Community, and it came to the attention of Adams that the company, which dominated parts of the pharmaceutical market, appeared to be engaged in a number of abuses. He passed various documents to the Commission, requesting that it did not identify him and the documents subsequently enabled the Commission to establish the existence of the abuses and to fine the company (*Hoffmann-La Roche v Commission* (Case 85/76)). During the course of exchanges with the company in its investigation, the Commission sent it copies of various documents supplied by Adams. Some of these documents contained marks and other indications which identified Adams as the informant. As a consequence, he was arrested and charged under Swiss law for the criminal offence of breach of employee confidentiality and economic espionage. He was prevented from communicating with his wife during his detention and she committed suicide. His conviction susbsequently led to the collapse of a business he had established in Italy (*see*, Hunnings, N. M., 'The Stanley Adams Affair or the Biter Bit' (1987) 24 CML Rev 65).

Adams later brought proceedings against the Commission for breach of its duty of confidentiality under Art 214 EC Treaty and Art 20 of Regulation 17/62. The Court found that the Commission had breached that duty of confidentiality by handing over the documents to Hoffmann-La Roche, and had compounded the damage to Adams by failing to warn him of the company's intention to institute criminal proceedings against him which it learned of some months before his arrest by the Swiss police. The Commision was held liable for non-contractual damage under Art 215, but the damages payable to Adams were reduced by half, because he had failed to inform the Commission of the possibility that he might be identified from the documents and had returned to Switzerland without enquiring of the Commission whether he might be at risk from doing so.

The Court has not developed a comprehensive set of principles concerning the type and extent of damages which may be recovered, but certain rules have emerged in the case-law. Actual financial loss that results from the unlawful action by the Commission may be recovered, but it must be established that this results directly from the unlawful conduct (*Dumortier Frérès* v *Council* (Case 64/76)). The Court has also awarded damages for shock, disturbance and uneasiness in Community staff cases (*Algera* v *Commission* (Case 7/56)).

Difficulties may arise where a national authority has acted on what subsequently transpires to have been an unlawful act by a Community institution. Who is liable? Should the injured party sue the institution which promulgated the unlawful act, or the national institution which implemented it, or both? Where the plaintiff's loss has occurred as a result of being obliged to pay money under an unlawful act, and he is claiming restitution, he will be expected to claim in the national courts against the national institution (*Vreugdenhil* v *Commission* (Case C-282/90)). Where there is no remedy in the national courts, claims can be brought against the relevant institution in the Court of Justice (*Krohn* v *Commission* (Case 175/84) paras [24]–[29] of judgment).

Further reading

Arnull, A., 'Private applicants and the action for annulment under Art 173 of the EC Treaty (1995) 32 *CML, Rev* 7.

Brealey, M. and Hoskins, M., (1994) *Remedies in EC Law*, Longman.

Dinnage, J., 'Locus Standi and Article 173 EEC' (1974) 4 *EL Rev* 15.

Greaves, R.M., 'Locus Standi under Article 173 when Seeking Annulment of a Regulation' (1986) 11 *EL Rev* 119.

Harding, C., 'The Private Interest in Challenging Community Action' (1980) 5 *EL Rev* 345.

Harlow, C., 'Towards a Theory of Access for the European Court of Justice' (1992) 12 YEL 213.

Hartley, T.C., (1994) *The Foundations of European Community Law*, P IV (3rd edn) Clarendon Press.

Lewis, A.D.E., 'Joint and Several Liability of the European Communities and National Authorities' (1980) *Current Legal Problems*, 99.

Schermers, H.G., Mead, P. and Heukels, T., (eds) (1988) *Non-Contractual Liability of the European Communities*, Nijhoff Publications.

Schwarze, J., (1992) *European Administrative Law*, Sweet & Maxwell.

Steiner, J., (1995) *Enforcing EC Law*, Blackstone Press.

Steiner, J., (1994) *Textbook on EC Law* (4th edn) Blackstone Press, Chs 27 and 30.

Weatherill, A., (1994) *Cases and Materials on EC Law*, (2nd edn) Blackstone Press, Ch 16.

Weatherill, A. and Beaumont, P., (1993) *EC Law*, (2nd edn), Penguin Books, Ch 8.

Wils, W., 'Concurrent Liability of the Community and a Member State (1992) 17 *EL Rev* 191.

Wyatt, D. and Dashwood, A., (1993) *European Community Law* (3rd edn), Sweet & Maxwell, pp. 109–166.

24 The role of national courts in the application of Community law

National courts perform a crucial role in administering and applying Community law. The Court of Justice has developed an important body of case law on the application of directly effective Community provisions in the courts of member states, as we have seen in Chapter 5, but it depends on the national courts to co-operate with it to make those provisions effective. As the Court said in *Simmenthal* (Case 196/77):

> A national court which is called upon, within the limits of its jurisdiction, to apply provisions of Community law is under a duty to give full effect to those provisions, if necessary refusing of its own motion to apply any conflicting provisions of national legislation, even if adopted subsequently, and it is not necessary for the court to request or await the prior setting aside of such provisions by legislative or other constitutional means.

There is a clear danger that, given the disparate national legal traditions of the member states, Community law will develop differently in the national courts. If this were to happen, individuals and businesses would be operating under different rules and many of the benefits of an open Community and a genuine common market would be lost. The Community has, therefore, a fundamental interest in ensuring that its law has the same meaning and effect in all the member states. The only effective way of doing this is to provide that ultimate authority for deciding the meaning of Community law should reside in one court. That court is, of course, the Court of Justice. The best way to ensure the harmonious development of Community law would have been to have established the Court of Justice as a final Court of Appeal on matters of Community law. That course seemed to constitute too direct a challenge to the supremacy of national legal systems, and was rejected by the founding fathers of the Community. They opted, instead, for a system of references by national courts. Art 177, which establishes the reference procedure, is the only provision of the Treaty which expressly acknowledges the enforcement role of the courts of the member states.

The Court of Justice has recently recognised that there is some concern about the time which such references take in its Report to the 1996 Intergovernmental Conference (May 1995) but it has unequivocally rejected suggestions that the scope for references be limited:

> To limit access to the Court would have the effect of jeopardising the uniform application and interpretation of Community law. But that is not all. The preliminary ruling system is the veritable cornerstone of the operation of the internal market, since it plays a fundamental role in ensuring that the law established by the Treaties retains its Community character with a view to guaranteeing that the law has the same effect in all circumstances in all the member states of the European Union. Any weakening, even if only potential, of the uniform application and interpretation of Community law throughout the Union would be liable to give rise to distortions of competition and discrimination between economic operators, thus jeopardising equality of opportunity between those operators and consequently the proper functioning of the internal market.

REFERENCES FROM NATIONAL COURTS UNDER ARTICLE 177

Art 177 envisages a partnership role between the Court of Justice and the national court, with jurisdiction divided between the Court of Justice, which interprets the law, and the national courts, which apply it. It must be emphasised that Art 177 references have a different function to an appeal. In an appeal, the initiative lies with the parties and if the appeal is successful, the appellate court can substitute its own decision for that of the lower court. In a reference, however, it is the lower court itself which takes the decision to refer the case. The Court of Justice rules on the issues which have been raised, but it is then for the lower court to apply the ruling of the Court of Justice to the facts of the case before it. At the end of the day, the decision in that case will be that of the national court. The whole object of the reference procedure is to retain the independence of the national courts, while at the same time preventing 'a body of national case law not in accord with the rules of Community law from coming into existence in any member state' (*Hoffmann-La Roche* v *Centrafarm* (Case 107/76)).

Article 177 provides:

The Court of Justice shall have jurisdiction to give preliminary rulings concerning:

(a) the interpretation of this Treaty;
(b) the validity and interpretation of acts of the institutions of the Community and of the ECB;
(c) the interpretation of the statutes of bodies established by an act of the Council, where those statutes so provide.

Where such a question is raised before any court or tribunal of a member state, that court or tribunal may, if it considers that a decision on the question is necessary to enable it to give judgment, request the Court of Justice to give a ruling thereon.

Where any such question is raised in a case pending before a court or tribunal of a member state against whose decision there is no judicial remedy under national law, that court or tribunal shall bring the matter before the Court of Justice.

What matters can be the subject of a reference under Article 177 ?

Article 177 refers to three kinds of provisions which can be the subjects of a reference to the Court for a preliminary ruling on interpretation and validity. 'Interpretation of the Treaty' covers any part of the Treaty of Rome, the amending Treaties and the Treaties of Accession, the latter being normally made expressly subject to Art 177. In the case of the entry to the Community of the UK, this was achieved by Art 1(3) of the Treaty of Accession of 1972 (*Department of Health and Social Security* v *Barr and Montrose Holdings Ltd* (Case C-355/89)). Only the parts of the Treaty on European Union relating to Common Defence and Security Policy and Justice and Home Affairs, which are not intended to be subject to legally binding decisions, will be excluded from the referral procedure (Art. L EC Treaty) (Case C-167/94). 'Community acts' will include not only legally binding acts, such a directives, regulations and decisions, but also opinions and recommendations where these are relevant to the interpretation of Community law by the courts of member states: *Frecassetti* (Case 113/75); *Grimaldi* v *Fonds des Maladies Professionelles* (Case C-322/88)). In *Deutsche Shell AG* v *Hauptzollamt Hamburg* (Case C-188/91), the Court held that 'arrangements' made by a joint committee responsible for implementing a convention on a common transit policy between EEC and EFTA formed 'part of the Community legal order'. The Court noted that the fact that a Community legal measure lacked compulsory effect did not exclude the Court from giving a legal ruling on them, because national courts were obliged to take them into account when interpreting the convention.

In the *Deutsche Shell* case the Court emphasised that it did not have jurisdiction under Art 177 to give a ruling on the compatability of a national measure with Community law. However, it does in fact come very close to doing so. Characteristically, it will describe the national measure in hypothetical terms and state that, if there were such a measure, it would not be compatible with Community law!

Which courts or tribunals are able to refer ?

Depending on the status of the court or tribunal, some *may*, while others *must* refer questions of European Community law to the Court of Justice. Before the question is answered of when such a reference must and when it may be made, it is necessary to ask which courts or tribunals should consider the possibility of a reference under Art 177. The Art refers to 'any court or tribunal of a member state' so that, at first glance, it would appear that references can only be made by courts and tribunals within the state's judicial structure. However, the essential elements to determine the status of the body in relation to Art 177 is its power to make legally binding decisions, its independence from the parties and the recognition of its decision-making function by the state. To be able to make references under Art 177 it will have to satisy all these criteria. An arbitrator, although conferred with a power by contract to make legally binding decisions on the parties, and also being independent of the parties, lacks the official recognition to make his decisions 'judicial' in character, and he cannot, therefore, make a reference under Art 177 (*Nordsee* v *Reederei Mond* (Case 102/81)). However, an arbitration board or a disciplinary body which is recognised by the state as having a function in making legally binding decisions in relation to an industry or a professional body may well be a 'court or tribunal' for the purposes of Art 177 (*Broekmeulen* v *Huisarts Registratie Commissie* (Case 246/80)). Even a national court determining an appeal against an arbitration award, not according to law but according to what is 'fair and reasonable' may be regarded as a 'court' for the purposes of Art 177 (*Municip Almelo and Others* v *Energie-bedvijf NV* (case C-393/92)). In the United Kingdom, besides references from magistrates' courts, crown courts and county courts, there have also been references from VAT tribunals, the Employment Appeal Tribunal and the Social Security Commissioners.

What is the appropriate stage in the proceedings for a reference ?

A reference to the Court of Justice may be made at any stage in the proceedings, even before a full hearing, either during the interlocutory stage or where the case is being dealt with in the absence of one of the parties (*Simmenthal* v *Amministrazione delle Finanze dello Stato* (Case 70/77); *Balocchi* v *Ministero delle Finanze dello Stato* (Case C-10/92)). The Court does, however, think it desirable that an *inter partes* hearing takes place before the reference, if that is possible (*Eurico Italia Srl* v *Ente Nazionale Risi* (Case C-332/92)).

Although the Court will not hear arguments that the national court or tribunal should not, under national law, have made the reference *Reina* v *Landeskreditbank Baden Wurttemberg* (Case 65/81), it does expect the case to have reached a stage at which the relevant facts have been established and the issues identified on which the assistance of the Court of Justice is required:

> It might be convenient, in certain circumstances, for the facts in the case to be established and for questions of purely national law to be settled at the time the reference is made to the Court of Justice so as to enable the latter to take cognisance of all the features of fact and of law which may be relevant. (*Irish Creamery Milk Suppliers Association* v *Ireland* (Case 36/80))

In *Telemarsicabruzzo SpA* (joined cases C-320 322/90), the Court refused to give a ruling, stating that the need to give a practical interpretation of Community law requires the national court to define the factual and legal framework in which the questions it puts arise, or that at least it explains the factual assumptions on which those questions are based. Neither had been done in this case. In *Vaneetveld* (Case

C-316/93), however, although all the relevant facts were not included, the Court held that there was sufficient information in the case file and in the pleadings to give a preliminary ruling.

How should the discretion to refer be exercised ?

The penultimate paragraph of Art 177 contemplates a situation in which the national court or tribunal considers that it is 'necessary' to refer a question raised in the proceedings before it to the Court of Justice to enable to give judgment in the case. In such a case, it may refer the question to the Court. The decision on whether or not to make a reference is essentially a matter for the national courts. The Court has said:

> ... In the context of the division of judicial functions between national courts and the Court of Justice, provided for by Art 177, the Court of Justice gives preliminary rulings without, in principle, needing to enquire as to the circumstances which led to the national court submitting questions to it ... The only exception to that principle would be in cases in which it appeared that the procedure provided for in Art 177 had been abused and where the question submitted sought, in reality, to lead the Court of Justice to make a ruling on the basis of an artificial dispute, or where it is obvious that the provision of Community law submitted to the Court of Justice could not be applied.
> (*Dzodzi* v *Belgium* (joined Cases C-297/88 and C-197/89))

In *Dzodzi* the Court allowed a reference where the national court needed a ruling to determine a question of national law in an area of law that was outside the competence of the Community, but which had been based on Community law.

Although the national court has the discretion to assess the need for a reference, it should explain how it has come to the conclusion that a reference is necessary, so that the Court of Justice can be satisfied that it has the jurisdiction to deal with the matter (*Foglia* v *Novello (No. 2)* (Case 244/80)). Once it is satisfied that it has the jurisdiction to deal with a reference, the Court is, in principle, bound to give a ruling. It cannot refuse to do so on the basis that, if its ruling were to have the effect of annulling a Community or national provision, this would create a 'legal vacuum' in a member state. It would be then for the national court to interpret national law in such a way as to fill any gap (*Gmurzynska* (Case C-231/89)) and *Helmig and Others* (joined cases C-399/92, C-409/92, C-425/92, C-34/93, C-50/93 and C-78/93). However, the national court does have, the Court of Justice said in *Rheinmuhlen* (Case 166/73), paras [3] and [4], 'the widest discretion'. The power to make a reference arises 'as soon as the judge perceives either of his own motion or at the request of the parties that the litigation depends on a point referred to in the first paragraph of Art 177.'

If one of the parties to the national proceedings withdraws from them, the Court of Justice cannot, however, continue to deliver a judgment on the reference, because such a judgment would then be no longer 'necessary' for the outcome of the case (*Teres Zabala Erasun and Others* v *Instituto Nacional de Empleo* (joined cases C-422/93, C-423/93 and C-424/93). Even if a superior national court had decided the issue, the lower court was not precluded from making a reference by the national rules. Although the national court has a discretion to refer, or not, where it is a lower court and where its decisions are subject to appeal (see below), it has little real discretion in cases where its decision depends on the disputed validity of a Community measure. It has itself no power to declare the Community measure invalid, so it has no choice but to refer the matter to the Court of Justice for a ruling on its validity (*Foto-Frost* (Case 314/85)).

When must a reference to the Court of Justice be made?

The final paragraph of Art 177 requires a national court to make a reference to the Court of Justice where that court or tribunal is one 'against whose decision there is no judicial remedy under national law'.

The concept of 'no judicial remedy under national law' clearly includes situations where there is no further appeal. That situation may arise where the court is, like the House of Lords, the highest in the hierarchy of courts. It may also arise in specific cases where an appeal is denied from a court which is very low in the hierarchy. In some jurisdictions, for example, there may be no appeal where the amount claimed or the value of the goods concerned is below a certain figure. In the landmark case of *Costa* v *ENEL* (Case 6/64), the amount claimed was less than £2. There was no appeal from the magistrate's decision because of the smallness of the sum. The magistrate was, therefore, under Art 177 obliged to refer the question before it to the Court of Justice.

In English courts, a reference may have to be made where the Court concerned, although not the final court of appeal, refuses leave to appeal, and where the upper court also refuses it. The avenue for an appeal would then be totally blocked. In the English courts the term 'judicial remedy' is wide enough to include applications for judicial review. Even when, therefore, there is no appeal from, say the Immigration Appeal Tribunal, its decisions are subject to judicial review and may, subsequently be referred to the Court of Justice in the course of those judicial review proceedings (*see*, for example, *R* v *Immigration Appeal Tribunal, ex parte Antonissen* (Case C-292/89)). In such a case, it would appear that there is no obligation on the tribunal to refer and an English tribunal has, in fact, refused to refer a case because it has held that it is not obliged to do so because of the availability of judicial review of its decisions (*Re a Holiday in Italy* [1975] 1 CMLR 184 (National Insurance Commissioner)). This point has still to be decided by the Court of Justice.

Not every question concerning the interpretation of Community law that is relevant to the outcome of a case requires a reference under the mandatory provisions in the last paragraph of Art 177. In *CILFIT* (Case 283/81), the Court of Justice held that even a court bound by the mandatory reference provisions is not obliged to refer a case where the answer to a question of interpretation of Community law is 'so obvious as to leave no scope for any reasonable doubt'. (para [16] of the judgment). This situation of an apparently transparent interpretative point is normally referred to in Community law as *acte clair*. The Court described the position in *CILFIT* (paras [10] [13] and [16] of the judgment) on the circumstances in which a reference should be made:

> ... It follows from the relationship between the second and third paragraphs of Art 177 that the courts and tribunals referred to in the third paragrph have the same discretion as any other national court or tribunal to ascertain whether a decision or question of Community law is necessary to enable them to give judgment. Accordingly, those courts or tribunals are not obliged to refer to the Court of Justice a question concerning the interpretation of Community law raised before them if that question is not relevant, that is to say, if the answer to that question, regardless of what it may be, can in no way, affect the outcome of the case.
>
> It must [also] be remembered that ... the authority of an interpretation under Art 177 already given by the Court may deprive the obligation of its purpose and thus empty it of its substance. Such is the case when the question raised is materially identical with a question which has already been the subject of a preliminary ruling in a similar case.
>
> Finally, the correct application of Community law may be so obvious as to leave no scope for reasonable doubt as to the manner in which the question raised is to be resolved. Before it comes to the conclusion that such is the case, the national court or tribunal must be convinced that the matter is equally obvious to the Courts of the other member states and to the Court of Justice. Only if those conditions are satisfied, may the national court or tribunal refrain from submitting the question to the Court of Justice and take upon itself the responsibility for resolving it.

The responsibility imposed on a court in declining to refer a question which, by virtue of the lack of possibility for further appeal or review of its decisions, it, prima facie, ought to refer, is thus an onerous one. An English judge has recognised the

> ... advantages enjoyed by the Court of Justice. It has a panoramic view of the Community and its instiutions, a detailed knowledge of the treaties and of much subordinate legislation made under them, and an intimate familiarity with the functioning of the Community market which no national judge denied the collective experience of the Court of Justice could hope to achieve. (Bingham J. in *Customs and Excise Commissioners* v *Samex* [1983] 3 CMLR 194)

Other English courts have not been so mindful of their limitations. In *R* v *London Boroughs Transport Committee, ex parte Freight Transport Association* [1991] 3 All ER 915, the case involved the interpretation of directives on vehicle brake construction and the powers of national authorities to impose further restrictions on vehicles. The House of Lords refused to make a reference although the issues were complex. Lord Templeman noted that 'no plausible grounds had been advanced for a reference to the European Court'. The refusal to refer has been criticised, and one of the parties has made a complaint to the Commission about the refusal (*see*, Weatherill, S., 'Regulating the Internal Market: Result Orientation in the House of Lords' (1992) 17 EL Rev 299, 318). The case is not, however, indicative of a general unwillingness to refer cases by the House of Lords, as the *Factortame* and the equal treatment cases demonstrate (*R* v *Secretary of State for Transport, ex parte Factortame (No. 1)* (Case C-221/89); *R* v *Secretary of State for Transport, ex parte Factortame (No. 2)* (Case

C-213/89); *Webb* v *EMO Cargo* [1993] 1 WLR 49, *R* v *Secretary of State for Employment, ex parte EOC* [1995] 1 CMLR 345. There is, however, continuing evidence of a reluctance to refer by English courts and tribunals, not least because of the time which such references take (*see*, for example: *Johnson* v *Chief Adjudication Officer* (CA) [1994] 1 CMLR 829; *Gould and Cullen* v *Commissioners of Customs and Excise* (VAT Tribunal) [1994] 1 CMLR 347; *R* v *Ministry of Agriculture, Fisheries and Food ex parte Portman Agrochemicals Ltd* (QBD) [1994] 1 CMLR 18).

The outcome of the reference

It may be as long as two years before a decision on a reference under Art 177 is available from the Court of Justice. The Court of Justice has jurisdiction under Art 186 to 'prescribe any interim measures' and will sometimes do so where the legality of a Community measure is being challenged under Art 173 (*see* Chapter 23). Under Art 177, the validity of any act of the institutions may be raised in a reference. The following questions need to be addressed: Can the allegedly invalid Community measure be supended by the national court pending the outcome of the reference? Will the Court of Justice suspend it? Should national courts suspend national legislation which is alleged to conflict with Community law or which implements a Community measure whose validity is disputed?

The Court of Justice may use its power under Art 186 to order a member state to cease to pursue a course of conduct which, prima facie breaches Community law, and which is requested by a party to the proceedings (*Commission* v *United Kingdom (Re Nationality of Fishermen)* (Case 246/89R); *Commission* v *Germany* (Case C-195/90)). This will normally be an interim measure in the course of Art 169 proceedings against a member state (*see* Chapter 22). Alternatively, national courts may be required to suspend a provision of national law which, arguably, conflicts with EC Law (*Factortame*, above). Although the criteria for granting interim relief are national (in the United Kingdom, according to the American Cynamid formula (*American Cynamid* v *Ethicon* [1975] AC 397), presumptions about the validity of primary national law should not act as a bar to its interim suspension.

The position with regard to the suspension of national measures implementing a provision of Community law the validity of which is challenged was discussed by the Court of Justice in *Zuckerfabrik Suderdithmarschen* v *HZA Itzehoe* (Case C-143/88). The Court declared that, to enable Art 177 references to work effectively, national courts must have the power to grant interim relief where a national measure was disputed on the grounds of the validity of the Community measure on which it was based on the same grounds as when the compatability of a national measure with Community law was contested. The national court had to be careful before doing so, however:

> It must first of all be noted that interim measures suspending enforcement of a contested measure may be adopted only if the factual and legal circumstances relied on by the applicants are such as to persuade the national court that serious doubts exist as

to the validity of the Community regulation on which the contested administrative measure is based. Only the possibility of a finding of invalidity, a matter which is reserved to the Court, can justify the granting of suspensory measures.

National courts can apply national criteria for weighing up, in the particular circumstances, whether or not to grant suspensory relief, but the national measures must be effective in providing the necessary remedies to protect rights conferred by Community law (*Factortame (No. 2)* (above) (Case C-213/89)) and to prevent 'irreparable damage' to the person seeking relief, pending the outcome of the reference (*Atlanta Fruchthandelsgesellschaft mbH* v *Bundesant für Ernährung und Fortwirtschaft* (C-465/93))

APPLYING COMMUNITY LAW IN THE ENGLISH COURTS: ADAPTING ENGLISH REMEDIES TO THE REQUIREMENTS OF COMMUNITY LAW

Some consideration was given in Chapter 5 to the approach of English courts towards the enforcement of unimplemented directives and that approach is complicated by the uniquely British concept of parliamentary sovereignty and the less distinctive, but equally difficult, separation of powers between legislature and judiciary. The same problems are apparent when the prospective litigant seeks an appropriate avenue for the enforcement of a right derived from Community law or the redress of a wrong resulting from its breach in the courts of England and Wales.

The effectiveness of remedies in national courts has become an increasing preoccupation of the European Court of Justice and the Court has moved from its original position on national remedies. In *Comet* v *Produkschap voor Siergewassen* (Case 45/76), it held that the remedy to deal with a breach of Community law should be 'no less effective' than that available to protect a right derived from national law and should not make it impossible in practice to obtain relief. This comparative standard with a very low irreducible minimum does not fully take into account the deficiencies of national legal remedies which may place all kinds of obstacles in the path of a litigant seeking to enforce a Community right. Although the way in which national courts operate is, in theory at least, outside the competence of Community law, the practical effects of deficiencies in national legal systems have led the Court to put an increasing emphasis on the duty of co-operation in Art 5 of the EC Treaty, and the extent to which it binds national courts. Consequently, the Court took a stronger line in *R* v *Secretary of State for Transport, ex parte Factortame (No. 2)* (Case 213/89). In this case, where the House of Lords had declared that national law did not allow an interim order against the Crown to suspend the operation of the Merchant Shipping Act 1988, the Court held that the national court must 'set aside' any national rule which precluded it from granting interim relief. In *Johnston* v *Chief Constable of the RUC* (Case 222/84), the

Court specifically adopted Art 13 of the European Convention on Human Rights as a fundamental principle of Community law. Article 13 provides that:

> Everyone whose rights and freedoms as set forth in this Convention are violated shall have an effective remedy before a national authority notwithstanding that the violation has been committed by persons acting in an official capacity.

The effect of the Court's judgment in the *Factortame* case is that there is now a necessary implication in Community law that 'an appropriate legal remedy must be created if one does not exist'. (Advocate-General Mischo in *Francovich* v *Italy* (Case C-6/90). Community legislation may also prescribe the type of remedy and the amount of damages that should be awarded (*see*, for example, Directives 93/37 and 93/38 on public procurement contracts). Some directives may specify the bodies or types of bodies which should have the standing to challenge decisions infringing the directive (Directive 93/12/EC (unfair consumer contract terms)). Directives have recently also tended to make specific requirements as to penalties, with a view to ensuring that national implementing legislation contains real deterrent sanctions (Directive 92/59 (Product Safety) or Directive 89/592 (Insider Dealing)). Where there is no penalty prescribed by Community law, the Court has held that national law should provide a penalty that is 'effective, proportionate and dissuasive'. (*Commission* v *United Kingdom*) (Case C-382/92)).

Public law remedies: judicial review

The obligation to implement Community law in the United Kingdom falls primarily on the government and the various agencies which it has chosen to carry out the functions of public administration. In English law, all bodies which exercise public powers, whether conferred by statute or common law, and whether public or private in origin, are subject to control and review by the courts (*Council of Civil Service Unions* v *Minister for the Civil Service* [1985] AC 374; *R* v *Panel on Takeovers and Mergers, ex parte Datafin plc* [1987] QB 815). In relation to Community law, that process of control and review extends to decisions made about the implementation of Community law. If the decision relates to the exercise of a power conferred on a subordinate body to legislate by way of delegated legislation, the court may intervene to prevent an abuse of those delegated legislative powers (*R* v *HM Treasury, ex parte Smedley* [1985] QB 657). If, on the other hand, the decision is by parliament itself on the scope and content of primary legislation by parliament then the decision on whether or not to legislate, and in what form, is not subject to any control or review by the courts (*Blackburn* v *Attorney-General* [1971] 1 WLR 137; *R* v *Secretary of State for Foreign and Commonwealth Affairs, ex parte Rees Mogg* [1993] 3 CMLR 101).

It is now accepted by the English courts that they are able to rule on the compatability of English law with Community law (*Factortame Ltd* v *Secretary of State for Transport* [1989] 2 All ER 692). The appropriate remedy in such a case is a declaration on the extent of incompatability (*R* v *Secretary of State for Employment, ex parte EOC* [1994] 2 WLR 409). Although, however, a court in judicial review proceedings has the power to award damages under s (4), Supreme Court Act 1981, damages may only be awarded where these would be available in an ordinary action. Although the European Court of Justice has decided that a member state could be required to compensate an individual in the national courts for its failure to implement Community law, there is, as yet, no reported decision where damages have been awarded against the government, either in an ordinary action, or in connection with an application for judicial review in the English courts . The House of Lords has, however, observed in an obiter dictum that the government could be liable in damages for failing to amend national legislation to bring it into line with Community law (*Kirklees MBC* v *Wickes Building Supplies Ltd* [1993] AC 227 at 282 (*per* Lord Goff of Chievely)). The Divisional court in *R* v *Coventry City Council and Others, ex parte Phoenix Aviation* [1995] 3 All ER 37, appeared to believe that local authorities which prevented the export of livestock, prima facie in breach of Art 34 EC Treaty would have no defence under Art 36 EC Treaty (*per* Simon Brown LJ p 68), but the issue of liability in damages remains to be decided in subsequent proceedings.

Claims in tort against the state

As we have seen in Chapter 5, the Court of Justice has held on many occasions that, subject to Treaty provisions being sufficiently clear, precise and unconditional, such provisions could create rights which were enforceable at the suit of individuals in the courts of member states (*Van Gend en Loos* (Case 26/62)). The application of this doctrine in relation to those Treaty provisions found to be directly effective has to be worked out in the national courts according to substantive and procedural national rules. In English law, where damages are claimed, this has meant that the breach of Community law has had either to be recognised as a new tort, or incorporated within the bounds of an old one.

In *Bourgoin* v *Ministry of Agriculture, Fisheries and Food (MAFF)* [1985] 3 All ER 385, the proceedings arose out of a ban imposed by the Ministry on the importation of turkeys from France in the run-up to Christmas 1981. The ban was imposed, ostensibly, on animal health grounds, but in *Commission* v *United Kingdom* (Case 40/82) the European Court of Justice held that the real reason behind the ban was a desire to protect the home market from foreign competition. It was not, therefore, justified under Art 36. Bourgoin was an importer who suffered considerable loss by the action of the British Government. He brought an action in damages, claiming infingement of Art 30 as a breach of statutory duty, breach of an innominate tort, or for misfeasance in public office. The Court of Appeal held, by a majority, that the only appropriate remedy was judicial review and that damages would not be available. Although the House of Lords had held in *Garden Cottage Foods Ltd* v *Milk Marketing Board* [1984] AC 130, that a breach of Art 86 of the Treaty gave rise to a claim for breach of statutory duty, a breach of Art 30 by a public authority was different. Article 30 did not confer private rights, simply a right to ensure that a public duty was performed. That duty could be enforced in judicial review proceedings and, in accordance with general principles of administrative law, damages would not normally be available. In *Bourgoin* the majority of the court (Oliver LJ dissenting) thought that only if the plaintiff could prove that the minister was guilty of misfeasance in office could damages be obtained.

Misfeasance in office is an ancient, but, until recently an inadequately defined tort. As late as 1982 it was described as 'not firmly anchored in the English case law' and 'not likely to become so'. (De Smith, S., *Judicial Review of Adminstrative Action* (1980), Harlow, C., *Compensation and Government Torts* (1982)). It requires, for a public person or body to be liable for acting in the performance of his duties, that that person or body must have been conscious of the fact that he was acting contrary to law (*Racz v Home Office* [1994] 1 All ER 97 (HL)). To be liable, the Court of Appeal held in *Bourgoin*, the minister would have to have known that he was acting in breach of Art 30 and that this would injure the plaintiff. *Bourgoin* has not been overruled, but it has been overtaken by the case law of both the European Court of Justice and the House of Lords. It is now clear from *Francovich* (Cases C-6 & 9/90), that state liability follows on from the breach of Community law, irrespective of any proof of fault by the state concerned. Some further light has been thrown on the possible extent of state liability in national courts for breach of Community law by the recent Opinion of Advocate-General Leger in *R v Ministry of Agriculture, Fisheries and Food, ex parte Hedley Lomas (Ireland) Ltd* (Case C-5/94) (*see*, Demetriou, M. 'Are Member States being led to the slaughter?' 145 *New Law Journal*, 1102 (21 July 1995). The opinion may not, of course, be followed by the Court of Justice.

The Advocate-General first of all dismissed any suggestion that the application of the decision of the Court of Justice in *Francovich* should be confined to breaches by member states of their obligation to implement directives. *Francovich* had established a general principle of state liability. Nor were member states in the same position as the Community institutions, whose liability was limited where they were acting in a legislative capacity in relation to measures of economic policy to situations where 'a sufficiently flagrant violation of a superior rule of law for the protection of the individual' had occurred. Member states should be liable whenever a state was guilty of 'serious' fault and the seriousness of the fault would differ according to the circumstances. Liability would, however, depend on some knowledege of wrongdoing but the standard suggested is much lower than that advocated by the majority of the Court of Appeal in *Bourgoin* (above). Advocate-General Leger gives some examples of the circumstances which might act as indicators of the seriousness of the fault. Thus, the breach of a clear provision of Community law or of a provision already interpreted by the Court of Justice would be serious. So, too, would be a repeated breach or one which had been repeated despite a judgment declaring there has been a failure to fulfil obligations. Also, a member state would be liable if it adopted legislation clearly at odds with the Treaty. These principles have recently been substantially adopted by the Court in three cases: *Brasserie du Pêcheur SA v Germany; R v Secretary of State for Transport, ex parte Factortame (No 4)* (Joined Cases C-46 and C-48/93) and *R v HM Treasury, ex parte British Telecommunications plc* (Case 392/93).

It is now clear, as a matter of English law, that a person who argues that he has suffered a loss as a result of a breach of a public law duty is not now compelled to proceed by way of judicial review, with its highly restrictive three month time limit for commencement of proceedings. Provided that he can show a particular loss, he does not need to prove a breach of a duty giving rise to a claim in tort, or the existence of a contract to bring a private action (*Roy v Kensington and Chelsea and Westminster FPC* [1992] 1 AC 624; *Administrative Law: Judicial Review and Statutory Appeals*, para. 3.15 The Law Commission, HC 669, 24 October 1994). There seems little doubt that a person who has suffered loss as a result of a breach by a public body of a Treaty provision or a legally binding act of the institutions of the Community, and who can satisfy the criteria laid down by the Court of Justice in *Francovich* should be able to succeed in the English courts. (See view expressed *obiter* by Lord Goff in *Kirklees MBC v Wickes* (above)).

It is not clear, however, whether the claim that Lord Goff contemplates is a breach of statutory duty under the European Communities Act 1972, a re-formulation of the principles of liability for misfeasance in office or a new tort, *sui generis*, of a breach of a Community obligation. It would have to be a tort, however, that imposed a higher duty than that required in negligence. English courts have, in any case, shown a marked reluctance even to impose a duty of care on bodies acting for the benefit of the community (*Hill v Chief Constable of West Yorkshire* [1989] AC 53 (HL); *Murphy v Brentwood DC* [1991] AC 398 (HL); *Marc Rich & Co v Bishop Rock Marine* [1995] 3 All ER 307 (HL)). There are a number of cases pending in the English courts which may, at last, give a definitive answer as to how liability for breach of Community law is to be approached.

Claims in tort between private individuals for breaches of Treaty provisions

There seems little doubt that individuals who have suffered loss as a result of breach of a directly effective provision of the Treaty can claim damages against another individual who has caused that loss. This is clearly the case in relation to Art 86 (*Garden Cottage Foods v Milk Marketing Board* [1984] AC 130). Damages may also be payable in English courts for breach of Art 85 (*H.J. Banks and Co Ltd v British Coal Corporation* (Case C-128/92); *MTV Europe v BMG Records (UK) Ltd* [1995] 1 CMLR 437). Individuals are also clearly entitled to damages for discriminatory treatment at work in breach of Art 119 or on grounds of Community nationality under Art 6 EC Treaty. An individual might, for example, not only wish to secure equal treatment, but to obtain damages where national law precluded them. As we have seen in *Defrenne v SABENA* (Case 43/75), an individual may make such a claim for compensation for loss of equal pay simply on the basis of the Treaty provision (*Macarthys Ltd v Smith* (Case 129/79)).

Any national limitations on the extent of compensation payable in cases of sex discrimination should not be observed, where they prevent the complainant from being adequately compensated for the damage suffered. Although the decision in

Marshall v *Southampton and South-West Hampshire Health Authority (No. 2)* (Case 271/91), was limited to the interpretation of Art 6 of Directive 76/207 in relation to the amount of damages payable, the principles laid down are wide enough to cover other claims against the state and emanations of the state (*see* Woolridge, F., and D'Sa, R., 'Damages for Breaches of Community Directives: The Decision in Marshall (No. 2)', *European Business Law Review*, Vol. 4, No. 11, November 1993). This view seems now to be supported by the Court's decision in *Commission* v *United Kingdom* (Case C-382/92), where the Court held that the United Kingdom's implementation of Directives 77/187 (Transfer of Undertakings) and 75/129 (Consultation on Redundancy) did not provide sufficient compensation for workers affected by a breach of the rules by the employer. The Court held that the compensation payable under the Employment Protection Act 1975, which purported to implement Directive 75/129, was potentially so little as to deprive the measure of its practical effect:

> ... Where a Community directive does not specifically provide any penalty for an infringment or refers for that purpose to national laws, regulations and administrative provisions, Art 5 of the Treaty requires the member states to take all measures necessary to guarantee the application and effectiveness of Community law. For that purpose, while the choice of penalties remains within their discretion, *they must ensure in particular that infringements of Community law are penalised under conditions, both procedural and substantive, which are analgous to those applicable of a similar nature and which, in any event, make the penalty effective, proportionate and dissuasive.*
> (emphasis added)

Although the Court was speaking of 'penalties', it is clear from the circumstances of the case that it had in mind both criminal sanctions and civil damages which could, in appropriate circumstances, be punitive in nature. It would seem from the words in italics that the Court has now moved on from merely requiring equivalent remedies. Where the national remedy is not effective, the remedy for the breach of Community law should be *effective, proportionate and dissuasive.* This principle will apply whether or not the defendant is the state, an emanation of the state or a private individual or undertaking.

COMMUNITY LAW AS THE BASIS FOR A CLAIM IN CONTRACT, A DEFENCE IN BREACH OF CONTRACT PROCEEDINGS AND FOR CLAIMS IN QUASI-CONTRACT

Community law may be used to found or assist in a claim for breach of contract in English courts. Under Art 119 EC Treaty, for example, discriminatory provisions in collective agreements are made unlawful and any contract, therefore, which incorporates the terms of such a discriminatory agreement will be void in so far as it offends Art 119 (*Defrenne* v *SABENA* (above)). Community law may also be used as a defence to a claim for breach of contract. If an individual is sued for breach of a contract which, for example, infringes the prohibition on restrictive agreements in Art 85(1), he may raise the issue of validity of the agreement under Community law as a defence (*Brasserie de Haecht* v *Wilkin* (Case 23/67); *Society of Lloyds* v *Clementson* [1995] 1 CMLR 693).

In *Amministrazione delle Finanze* v *San Giorgio* (Case 199/82), the European Court of Justice decided that an individual is entitled to recover charges that have been levied on him contrary to a directly effective provision of Community law. The right of recovery was a necessary adjunct to the right to equal treatment. National law should, therefore, enable individuals who have been wrongly taxed or charged in this way to recover the payments which they have made. It will be recalled that an EU citizen in receipt of educational services must not be charged a different fee to home students (*Gravier* v *City of Liège* (Case 293/83), nor may importers be levied for tax at a rate which exceeds that payable in respect of home-produced goods of the same kind, under Art 95. When this has happened, the individuals affected should be able to recover the sums overpaid.

The rule laid down by the Court of Justice in *San Giorgio* conflicted with an established rule of English law that a person who has paid money under a mistake of fact can generally recover it, but a person who has paid money under a mistake of law cannot, generally, do so (Goff and Jones, *The Law of Restitution* (1993) (4th edn) Chapter 3; Tettenborn, A., *Law of Restitution* (1993) pp 36–38; D'Sa, R., op. cit. pp 247, 248). However, mistake of law is narrowly construed so that, for example, a payment made on the basis of a misunderstanding about a rule of foreign law is regarded as a mistake of fact. Community law is not 'foreign law', of course, since it is incorporated into English law and must be treated as a question of law and not fact (*R* v *Goldstein* [1983] 1 CMLR 252). The House of Lords narrowed the rule further, so that money paid to a public body in response to an unlawful demand on the basis of a mistake of law is now recoverable (*Woolwich Equitable Building Society* v *IRC* [1992] 3 WLR 366). Referring to the right to recovery in relation to money wrongfully paid under Community law, Lord Goff of Chievely remarked:

> … At a time when Community law is becoming increasingly important, it would be strange if the right of the citizens to recover overpaid charges were to be more restricted under domestic law than it is under Community law.'

A similar extension of Community principles into the wider application of the Common law followed the decision of the Court of Justice in *Factortame* that interim orders should bind the Crown, when the House of Lords subsequently held that such orders were available even in cases not involving Community law (*Re M* [1994] 1 AC 377).

COMMUNITY LAW AS A DEFENCE IN CRIMINAL PROCEEDINGS

Many of the land-mark decisions of Community law have been made by the Court of Justice on references from national courts during the course of criminal proceedings. In *Procureur du Roi* v *Dassonville* (Case 8/74), it will be remembered that the defendant was prosecuted for selling Scotch whisky without supplying purchasers with a certificate of origin (*see* Chapter 14). The Court held that the legislation under which he was prosecuted was incompatible with Art 30 and as a consequence the national court would, therefore, have been obliged to have dismissed the charge against him. Similarly, the defendants in *R* v *Henn and Darby* (Case 34/79) were able to raise their prosecution and the seisure of the allegedly obscene material as, potentially, in breach of Art 30, although the Court held that, in the circumstance, the UK legislation was justifiable under Art 36.

In the English courts, so-called 'Euro-defences' have been successfully raised in criminal proceedings for 'overstaying', contrary to the Immigration Act 1971. In *R* v *Pieck* (Case 157/79) the charge against the defendant had to be dismissed because the requirement imposed on the defendant to obtain 'leave' for his continuing residence was held to be contrary to the rights of residence conferred on him by Art 48 EC Treaty (*see also, R* v *Kirk* (Case 63/83)). Also, where Community law provides a defence in an unimplemented directive, the defendant may rely upon it (*Pubblico Ministero* v *Ratti* (Case 148/78). On the other hand, prosecutors cannot rely on an unimplemented directive to interpret the criminal law in such a way as to secure a conviction. This offends the Community principle of legal certainty and non-retroactivity (*Officier van Justitie* v *Kolpinghuis Nijmegen BV* (Case 80/60)). On this principle of legal certainty, it would seem that, where English law incorporates a defence of, say, due diligence, in the legislation implementing a Community Directive on health and safety at work where the Directive appears to create strict liability, such a defence can be used, even though it conflicts with the Directive.

Euro-defences, using Art 30, have been widely attempted by businesses prosecuted under the Shops Act 1950, until this avenue was finally closed by the Court of Justice in *Stoke-on-Trent and Norwich City Councils* v *B & Q* (Case C-169/91) (Chapter 14). Prosecutions are, in any event, much less likely following the liberalising of Sunday trading in England and Wales by the Sunday Trading Act 1994. The scope for the use of Art 30 to defeat prosecutions under national laws aimed at consumer protection has also been considerably diminished by the decision of the Court of Justice to tighten its definition of measures which are likely to affect trade between states in *Keck and Mithouard* (Case C-267 & 268/91).

Further reading

Anderson, D., References to the European Court, Sweet and Maxwell, 1995.

Arnull, A., 'The Use and Abuse of Article 177 EEC' (1989) 52 *MLR* 622.

Arnull, A., 'References to the European Court' (1990) 15 *EL Rev* 375.

Arnull, A. and Dashwood A., 'English Courts and Article 177 of the EEC Treaty' (1984) 4 YEL 255.

Brown, L.N. and Jacobs, F., (1994) *The Court of Justice of the European Communities* (4th edn), Sweet & Maxwell, Ch 9.

Collins, L., (1990) *European Community Law in the United Kingdom* (4th edn), Butterworths, Chapter 3.

De Smith, S., (1980) *Judicial Review of Administrative Action.*

D'Sa, R., (1994) *European Community Law and Civil Remedies in England and Wales*, Sweet & Maxwell, Chapters 9 and 10, pp 46–58.

Harlow, C., (1982) *Compensation and Government Torts.*

Hartley, T.C., (1994) *The Foundations of European Community Law*, (3rd edn), Clarendon Press, Chapter 9.

Jacobs, F., 'The European Court of Justice: some Thoughts on its Past and its Future' *The European Advocate* (1994/1995) p 2.

Lasok, D. and Bridge, J.W., (1991) *Law and Instiutions of the European Communities*, Butterworths, Chapter 10.

Maher, I., (1995) 'A Question of Conflict: The Higher English Courts and the Implementation of European Community Law' in Daintith T., (ed.) *Implementing EC Law in the United Kingdom: Structures for Indirect Rule*, John Wiley and Sons.

Mancini, F. and Keeling, D., 'From CILFIT to ERT: The Constiutional Challenge Facing the European Court' (1991) 11 YEL 1.

Rasmussen, H., 'The European Court's Acte Clair Strategy in CILFIT' (1984) 9 CML Rev 242.

Report of the Court of Justice on Certain Aspects of the Application of the Treaty on European Union for the Purposes of the 1996 Intergovernmental Conference (May 1993).

Steiner, J. (1995) *Enforcing EC Law*, Blackstone Press, Chapters 6 and 7.

Tillotson, J., (1993) *European Communty Law: text, cases and materials,* Cavendish Publishing Ltd, Chapter 9.

Toth, A., 'The Authority of Judgments of the European Court of Justice: Binding Force and Legal Effects' (1984) 4 YEL 1.

Vincenzi, C., 'Private Initiative and Public Control in the Regulatory Process' in Daintith, T., (ed.) *Implementing EC Law in the United Kingdom: Structures for Indirect Rule* (1995).

Weatherill, S., (1994) *Cases and Materials on EC Law* (2nd edn) Blackstone Press, Chapter 4 and pp 542–51.

Weatherill, S., 'Regulating the Internal Market: Result Orientation in the House of Lords' (1992) 17 EL Rev 299.

Weatherill, S. and Beaumont P., (1993) *EC Law*, Penguin Books, Chapter 9.

Woolridge, F. and D'Sa, R., 'Damages for Breaches of Community Directives' European Business Law Review, Vol. 4, No. 11.

Index